The Lives of Extraction: Identities, Communities and the Politics of Place

International Development Policy

Editor-in-Chief

Ugo Panizza

Guest Editors

Filipe Calvão
Matthew Archer
Asanda Benya

VOLUME 15

The titles published in this series are listed at *brill.com/idp*

The Lives of Extraction: Identities, Communities and the Politics of Place

Edited by

Filipe Calvão, Matthew Archer and Asanda Benya

BRILL | NIJHOFF

LEIDEN | BOSTON

Cover illustration: Open pit mining of iron ore and magnetite ores. Located in Kryvyi Rih, eastern Ukraine, Europe. © Andriy Solovyov. Available on Shutterstock.

The Library of Congress Cataloging-in-Publication Data is available online at https://catalog.loc.gov
LC record available at https://lccn.loc.gov/2023038818

Typeface for the Latin, Greek, and Cyrillic scripts: "Brill". See and download: brill.com/brill-typeface.

ISSN 1663-9383
ISBN 978-90-04-53884-9 (paperback)
ISBN 978-90-04-68599-4 (e-book)
DOI 10.1163/9789004685994

This book is printed on acid-free paper and produced in a sustainable manner.

Contents

Visit *International Development Policy* online
http://www.devpol.org and *http://debate.devpol.org*

International Development Policy—**Previous Titles**

1 *Africa: 50 Years of Independence*, No. 1, Geneva: Graduate Institute Publications, 2010, ISSN print 1663-9383 | ISSN online 1663-9405 | ISBN: 9782940415274.
2 *Energy and Development*, No. 2, Basingstoke/Geneva: Palgrave Macmillan/ Graduate Institute Publications, 2011, ISBN: 9780230282483.
3 *Aid, Emerging Economies and Global Policies*, No. 3, Basingstoke/Geneva: Palgrave Macmillan/Graduate Institute Publications, 2012, ISBN: 9781137003409.
4 *Religion and Development*, No. 4, Basingstoke/Geneva: Palgrave Macmillan/ Graduate Institute Publications, 2013, ISBN: 9781137329370.
5 *Education, Learning, Training: Critical Issues for Development*, No. 5, Leiden|Boston/ Geneva: Brill Nijhoff/Graduate Institute Publications, 2014, ISBN: 9789004281141.
6 *Large-Scale Land Acquisitions: Focus on South-East Asia*, No. 6, Leiden|Boston/ Geneva: Brill Nijhoff/Graduate Institute Publications, 2015, ISBN: 9789004304741.
7 *Combining Economic and Political Development: The Experience of MENA*, No. 7, Leiden|Boston/Geneva: Brill Nijhoff/Graduate Institute Publications, 2017, ISBN: 9789004336452.
8 *Development as a Battlefield*, No. 8, Leiden|Boston/Geneva: Brill Nijhoff/ Graduate Institute Publications, 2017, ISBN: 9789004349520.
9 *Alternative Pathways to Sustainable Development: Lessons from Latin America*, No. 9, Leiden|Boston/Geneva: Brill Nijhoff/Graduate Institute Publications, 2017, ISBN: 9789004351660.
10 *African Cities and the Development Conundrum*, No. 10, Leiden|Boston/Geneva: Brill Nijhoff/Graduate Institute Publications, 2018, ISBN: 9789004387928.
11 *The ILO @ 100: Addressing the Past and Future of Work and Social Protection*, No. 11, Leiden|Boston/Geneva: Brill Nijhoff/Graduate Institute Publications, 2019, ISBN: 9789004399006.
12 *Drug Policies and Development: Conflict and Coexistence*, No. 12, Leiden|Boston/ Geneva: Brill Nijhoff/Graduate Institute Publications, 2020, ISBN: 9789004440487.
13 *Gender in Peacebuilding: Local Practices in Indonesia and Nigeria*, No. 13, Leiden|Boston/ Geneva: Brill Nijhoff/Graduate Institute Publications, 2021, ISBN: 9789004498464.
14 *Governing Migration for Development from the Global South*, No. 14, Leiden|Boston/ Geneva: Brill Nijhoff/Graduate Institute Publications, 2022, ISBN: 9789004522763.

Geneva Graduate Institute
Graduate Institute of International and Development Studies
Institut de hautes études internationales et du développement
Research Office
P.O. Box 1672
1211 Geneva 1
Switzerland
devpol@graduateinstitute.ch
http://www.devpol.org
http://debate.devpol.org
http://graduateinstitute.ch

Preface

International Development Policy is a critical source of analysis of development policy and international cooperation trends, aimed at an audience of scholars, policymakers and development professionals. It offers a diverse range of academic views from both industrialised countries and emerging economies.

International Development Policy is edited by the Graduate Institute of International and Development Studies, an institution of research and higher education dedicated to advancing world affairs. Located in Geneva, at the heart of an international centre of multilateral governance, the Graduate Institute benefits from a rich legacy linked to the founding of the international system and the League of Nations in the 1920s, and the emergence of the developing world in the 1960s.

http://www.devpol.org

http://graduateinstitute.ch/research

We extend our thanks to the Swiss Agency for Development and Cooperation (SDC) and the Republic and State of Geneva—Service for International Solidarity (SSI) for their financial support.

Schweizerische Eidgenossenschaft
Confédération suisse
Confederazione Svizzera
Confederaziun svizra

Swiss Confederation

REPUBLIC
AND STATE
OF GENEVA

POST TENEBRAS LUX

Figures

Abbreviations

AGA	AngloGold Ashanti
AIDS	acquired immune deficiency syndrome
ARA	Architecture. Restoration. Archaeology (Asociația Arhitectură. Restaurare. Arheologie—Romanian NGO)
ASM	artisanal small-scale mining
CA	capability approach (of Amartya Sen)
CAF	Centre d'Autonomisation des Femmes (Centre for Women's Empowerment), Guinea
CBG	Compagnie des Bauxites de Guinée
CBK	Compagnie des Bauxites de Kindia
CCP	Chinese Communist Party
CDA	community development agreement
CECI	Centre for International Studies and Cooperation
CNT	Conseil National de Transition, Burkina Faso
CNY	Chinese yuan renminbi
CSR	corporate social responsibility
CZSSCM	Confederation of Zimbabwe Small-Scale Chrome Miners
DFG	German Research Foundation
DI	Devonshire Initiative
DNPF	Direction Nationale de la Promotion Féminine (Women's Promotion National Directorate), Guinea
EITI	Extractive Industry's Transparency Initiative
ESG	environmental, social and governance
ESRC	Economic and Social Research Council, UK
EU	European Union
FIPA	foreign investment promotion and protection agreement, Canada
FMDL	Mining Fund for Local Development, Burkina Faso
FPIC	free, prior and informed consent
FTLRP	Fast Track Land Reform Programme, Zimbabwe
GAC	Guinea Alumina Corporation
HDI	human development index
HIV	human immunodeficiency virus
IBA	Impact and Benefit Agreement
ICMM	International Council on Mining and Metals
ICOMOS	International Council on Monuments and Sites

IFC	International Finance Corporation
IIED	International Institute for Environment and Development
ILO	International Labour Organization
ILUA	Indigenous land-use agreement
Im4dc	International Mining for Development Centre
Ingeominas	Colombian Geology and Mining Institute
IWGIA	International Work Group for Indigenous Affairs
MAC	Mining Association of Canada
MCA	Minerals Council of Australia
MDGS	Millennium Development Goals, UN
MMSD	*Mining, Minerals and Sustainable Development* (IIED review)
MNC	multinational corporation
NAIF	Northern Australia Infrastructure Facility
NATSISS	National Aboriginal and Torres Strait Islander Social Survey, Australian Bureau of Statistics
NGO	non-governmental organisation
NNTT	National Native Title Tribunal, Australia
NRCAN	National Resources Canada
OECD	Organisation for Economic Co-operation and Development
PCDS	municipal development plans, Burkina Faso
PDAC	Prospectors & Developers Association of Canada
PDG	Parti Démocratique de Guinée
PLA	People's Liberation Army, PRC
PPP	public–private partnership
PRC	People's Republic of China
RMGC	Roșia Montană Gold Corporation, Romania
RONPhos	Republic of Nauru Phosphate Corporation
RPCS	regional processing centres, Australia
RSD	refugee status determination (the legal or administrative process)
SAPS	structural adjustment programmes
SDGS	Sustainable Development Goals, UN
SFB	Collaborative Research Centre (of the German Research Foundation)
SLiCA	Survey of Living Conditions in the Arctic
SLO	Social Licence to Operate
SUNY	State University of New York
TNC	transnational corporation
TSX	Toronto Stock Exchange
TSXV	Toronto Stock Exchange Venture Exchange

state), to facilitate and simplify 'new' processes of primitive accumulation. By the same token, we see how corporations adopt the 'biopolitical control of the population' and 'quieter registers of power' that involve the manipulation of people by promising them jobs and 'development'. Aided by the state, corporations also generate and amplify narratives that are meant to legitimise extractive projects and to manufacture consent, even as they generate dissent and discord among the locals. To manage dissent and resistance to dispossession and expansion, violence is co-deployed, at times involving the police. In response, local actors, in some instances led by women, have adopted creative tactics and resistance strategies that have helped them cement victories while building solidarity globally.

Jesse Jonkman and Eva von Roekel complicate the linear assumptions in temporal conceptions of resource extraction and suggest a muddling of time to indicate temporal porousness, the coexistence of, and entanglements between, social and economic lives, and overlapping resource cycles and potentialities. Using two cases, respectively from Colombia and Venezuela, they show that linearity is not how people in mine sites conceive of time or their lives in relation to extractive industries. Seeking to highlight and perhaps negotiate their vulnerability, people work with a 'muddled temporality'. By thinking of the 'extractive present' as distinct from the past or the future, they emphasise connections, or an 'afterlife' or 'a thing of the past' tied to or parallel to future pursuits. The authors, therefore, suggest that we consider present booms, lives, and policies alongside their histories and futures. The present thus has within it residues of the past and seeds of the future, in that 'one frontier's life is another frontiers afterlife'. Jonkman and von Roekel conclude by advocating for multiple temporalities and circularity, and not the finality of mining cycles that 'afterlife' might suggest. This reading of time challenges the temporary logics undergirding some of the studies presented in this volume, including those imagining finality, 'closures', and ends.

Finally, 'Extractive Frontiers: Narratives and Discourses' takes on the narratives that shape and are shaped by broader political and economic forces. Each chapter unfolds space-making and border-defining perceptions and representations of extractivism, and how indigenous peoples, racialised economies and other marginalised communities creatively resist, are swept into, or assert their own narratives and visions of their future. As corporate narratives, imaginative practices, and discursive constructions are weaved in and around extractive industries, these chapters examine what such representations can tell us about extractive activities, their relationship to communities, and the mobilisation of opposition to them, from refugees and displaced peoples to rumours and other forms of gossip.

Anneloes Hoff looks at how corporate discourses, performative practices of storytelling, imaginings and myth-making unfold and render exploration and ultimately the expansion of mining possible. In other words, how narratives produce and maintain mining frontiers and engender professional subjectivities that reproduce and sustain myths and investor interest. Focusing on AngloGold Ashanti in Colombia, Hoff looks at the inward- and outward-oriented narratives that facilitated the entrance and expansion of (and resistance to) this 'new' mining frontier, also known as the 'last Andean frontier'. The outward-oriented narrative targeted and managed investor and shareholders imaginations regarding the benefits and risks involved in gold mining in Colombia. The inward-oriented storytelling and practices were able to produce professional subjectivities and corporate identities that could be mobilised to sustain the narratives that made 'exploration success tangible'. Hoff notes how this mythmaking process is gendered and centred around a male hero figure who valorises particular masculine traits, while women in turn downplay femininity.

Moving outwards to the international refugee regime, Julia Morris extends the logics of extractive capitalism to include the experience and economy of human (im)mobility. Based on research on the Pacific island of Nauru and in Jordan, the lens of extractivism is applied here to examine the refugee industry as a practice of 'frontiering'. Morris's chapter draws our attention to the extractive economies governing human mobility in the processing and resettling of refugees, and to the power imbalances that come with the extraction of value from humans as resources. This is a stark reminder of the forms of human objectification and commodification associated with extractivism, and of the inherent violence of the extractive practices present in the process of incorporating migrants and asylum applicants into migration governance regimes.

Finally, Sardana Nikolaeva looks at how the villagers of Djelinde in a far north-eastern region of the Russian Federation used rumours to negotiate their marginality and precariousness and to articulate resistance to an extraction project. Nikolaeva first unpacks how rumours are generated and how they circulate and help people make sense of, and respond to everyday experiences of anxiety and collective uncertainties in the context of extractivism. In this instance, Nikolaeva reads rumours as a covert psychological tactic that facilitates the rejection of the hegemonic ideologies of development that legitimate extractivism. While she underscores the political potentialities of rumours, she also points to the contradictory effects of rumours and rumouring, and argues that while rumours can be used to process experiences and resist, they can also be fuelled by those in power, and ultimately co-opted into registers of control and intimidation. In other words, rumour can be 'strategically instrumentalised by the government' to bolster its power.

As this volume demonstrates, the processes and impacts of extraction are multifaceted and complex, affecting communities, labour, social life and identities in various ways. The contributors provide a critical and nuanced understanding of the social, cultural and political dimensions of extraction as deeply social and shaped by practices of storytelling, imagination, social practices and relations. These dimensions are crucial in making extraction possible and for sustaining its expansion into new domains, but likewise for identifying opportunities for resistance and for paving the way for alternative future post-extractive communities and economies.

The accompanying volume, *The Afterlives of Extraction: Alternatives and Sustainable Futures* (Calvão, Archer and Benya, 2023), weaves futures narratives that emerge in the face of extractive industries, and how we might move beyond the extractive paradigm towards alternative conceptions of sustainability and justice. Together, these volumes offer a comprehensive analysis of the challenges and opportunities presented by extraction, and provide a foundation for thinking about the conditions of possibility for creating more equitable and sustainable relationships with the earth's resources.

Acknowledgements

The guest editors wish to thank all the contributors to this thematic volume. We are deeply indebted to the anonymous reviewers and the discussants that offered their time and generous feedback during the authors' workshop: Philippe Le Billon, Jerry Jacka, Marc Hufty, Kuntala Lahiri-Dutt and Muriel Côte. Our gratitude is extended particularly to the editorial board of *International Development Policy*, to Dave Brooks, and for the indefatigable work of Marie Thorndahl.

References

Acosta, A. (2016) 'Post-Growth and Post-Extractivism: Two Sides of the Same Cultural Transformation', *Alternautas*, 3(1), pp. 50–71.

Alfonzo, P. (1976) *Hundiéndonos en el excremento del diablo* (Editorial Lisbona, Caracas).

Alonso-Fradejas, A. (2021) '"Leaving no One Unscathed" in Sustainability Transitions: the Life Purging agro-extractivism of Corporate Renewables', *Journal of Rural Studies*, 81, pp. 127–138.

Appel, H. (2017) 'Toward an Ethnography of the National Economy', *Cultural Anthropology*, 32, pp. 294–322, DOI: 10.14506/ca32.2.09.

Apter, A. (2005) *The Pan-African Nation: Oil and the Spectacle of Culture in Nigeria* (Chicago: The University of Chicago Press).

Arboleda, M. (2020) *Planetary Mine: Territories of Extraction under Late Capitalism* (London: Verso).

Auty, R. (1993) *Sustaining Development in Mineral Economies: the Resource Curse Thesis* (Abingdon: Routledge).

Bebbington, A., A.-G. Abdulai, D. H. Bebbington, M. Hinfelaar and C. A. Sanborn (2018) *Governing Extractive Industries: Politics, Histories, Ideas* (Oxford: Oxford University Press).

Benya, A. (2015) 'The Invisible Hands: Women in Marikana', *Review of African Political Economy*, 42, pp. 545–560, DOI: 10.1080/03056244.2015.1087394.

Bolay, M. and F. Calvão (2022) 'Labour, Incorporated: Dependent Contracting and Wageless Work in Africa's "Responsible" Mines', *Cahiers d'études africaines*, 245–246, pp.123–151, DOI: 10.4000/etudesafricaines.36190.

Bond, P. (2017) 'Uneven development and resource extractivism in Africa', in *Routledge Handbook of Ecological Economics* (Abingdon: Routledge), pp. 404–413.

Breglia, L. (2013) *Living with Oil: Promises, Peaks, and Declines on Mexico's Gulf Coast* (Austin, TX: University of Texas Press).

Bridge, G. (2010) 'Resource Geographies I: Making Carbon Economies, Old and New', *Progress in Human Geography*, 35(6), pp. 820–834.

Burchardt, H. J., and K. Dietz (2014) '(Neo-) Extractivism–a New Challenge for Development theory from Latin America', *Third World Quarterly*, 35(3), pp. 468–486.

Buu-Sao, D. (2021) Extractive Governmentality at Work: Native Appropriations of Oil Labor in the Amazon, International Political Sociology, Volume 15, Issue 1, pp. 63–82, DOI: 10.1093/ips/olaa019.

Calvão, F., M. Archer and A. Benya (eds.) (2023) *The Afterlives of Extraction. Alternatives and Sustainable Futures*, International Development Policy | Revue internationale de politique de développement, 16 (Geneva, Boston: Graduate Institute Publications, Brill-Nijhoff).

Calvão, F. and M. Archer (2021). 'Digital Extraction: Blockchain Traceability in Mineral Supply Chains', *Political Geography*, 87, 102381, DOI: 10.1016/j.polgeo.2021.102381.

Calvão, F., M. Bolay and L. Bell (2021) 'Dis/connection Matters: Natural, Synthetic, and Digital: Introduction', *Tsantsa*, 26, pp.7–17, DOI: 10.36950/tsantsa.2021.26.7680.

Calvão, F., C. Mcdonald, and M. Bolay (2021) 'Cobalt Mining and the Corporate Outsourcing of Responsibility in the Democratic Republic of Congo', *The Extractive Industries and Society*, 8, DOI: 10.1016/j.exis.2021.02.004.

Calvão, F., C. Ankenbrand, M. Ros-Tonen, and M. Beevers. (2021) 'Extractive Industries and Human Security: an Overview', *The Extractive Industries and Society*, DOI: 10.1016/j.exis.2021.101007.

Carbonnier, G., F. Brugger and J. Krause (2011) 'Global and Local Policy Responses to the Resource Trap', *Global Governance*, 17, pp. 247–264, DOI: 10.1163/19426720-01702010.

Collier, P. and A. Hoeffler (2004) 'Greed and Grievance in Civil War', *Oxford Economic Papers*, 56(4), pp. 563–595, http://www.jstor.org/stable/3488799.

Coronil, F. (2011) 'The Future in Question: History and Utopia in Latin America (1989–2010)', in C. Calhoun and G. Derluguian (eds). *Business as Usual: the Roots of the Global Financial Meltdown* (New York: New York University Press), pp. 231–264.

Coronil, F. (1997) *The Magical State: Nature, Money, and Modernity in Venezuela* (Chicago: The University of Chicago Press).

D'Angelo, L. and R.J. Pijpers (eds.) (2022) *The Anthropology of Resource Extraction* (London and New York: Routledge).

Dunlap, A. and J. Jakobsen (2020) *The Violent Technologies of Extraction. Political ecology, critical agrarian studies and the capitalist worldeater* (Basingtoke: Palgrave).

Fearon, J. (2005) 'Primary Commodity Exports and Civil War', *Journal of Conflict Resolution*, 49, pp. 483–507, DOI: 10.1177/0022002705277544.

Ferguson, J. (1999) *Expectations of Modernity: Myths and Meanings of Urban Life on the Zambia Copperbelt* (Los Angeles: University of California Press).

Ferry, E., A. Vallard and A. Walsh (eds.) (2019) *The Anthropology of Precious Minerals* (Toronto: University of Toronto Press).

Ferry, E. and M. Limbert (eds.) (2008) *Timely Assets: the Politics of Resources and Their Temporalities* (Santa Fe: School for Advanced Research Press).

Fisher, E. (2007) 'Occupying the Margins: Labor Integration and Social Exclusion in Artisanal Mining in Tanzania', *Development and Change*, 38(4), pp. 735–760.

Fraser, N. (2022) *Cannibal Capitalism: How our System is Devouring Democracy, Care, and the Planet and What We Can Do About It* (London: Verso Books).

Frederiksen, T. and M. Himley (2019) 'Tactics of Dispossession: Access, Power, and Subjectivity at the Extractive Frontier', *Transactions of the Institute of British Geographers*, 45, DOI: 10.1111/tran.12329.

Frynas, J. G., G. Wood and T. Hinks (2017) 'The Resource Curse without Natural Resources: Expectations of Resource Booms and their Impact', *African Affairs*, 116(463), pp. 233–260, DOI: 10.1093/afraf/adx001.

Geenen, S. (2012) 'A Dangerous bet: The Challenges of Formalizing Artisanal Mining in the Democratic Republic of Congo', *Resources Policy*, 37(3), pp. 322–330.

Gelb, A.H. (1988) *Oil windfalls: Blessing or curse?* (Oxford: Oxford University Press).

Gilberthorpe, E. and D. Rajak (2017) 'The Anthropology of Extraction: Critical Perspectives on the Resource Curse', *The Journal of Development Studies*, 53(2), pp. 186–204.

Golub, A. (2014) *Leviathans at the Gold Mine: Creating Indigenous and Corporate Actors in Papua New Guinea* (Durham: Duke University Press).

Gudynas, E. (2009). Diez tesis urgentes sobre el nuevo extractivismo. Contextos y demandas bajo el progresismo sudamericano actual. In Centro Andino de Acción

Popular —CAAP— y Centro Latinoamericano de Ecología Social —CLAES— (Eds.), Extractivismo, política y sociedad, pp. 187–225 (Quito: CAAP and CLAES).

Hilson, G., A. Hilson, R. Maconachie, J. McQuilken and H. Goumandakoye (2017) 'Artisanal and Small-scale Mining (ASM) in Sub-Saharan Africa: Re-conceptualizing Formalization and 'Illegal' Activity', *Geoforum*, 83, pp. 80–90.

Hilson, G., T. Sauerwein and J. Owen (2020) 'Large and Artisanal Scale Mine Development: the Case for Autonomous Co-existence', *World Development*, 130, pp. 104919, DOI: 10.1016/j.worlddev.2020.104919.

Hirschman, A. (1958) *The Strategy of Economic Development* (New Haven, Conn.: Yale University Press).

Jacka, J. (2018) 'The Anthropology of Mining: the Social and Environmental Impacts of Resource Extraction in the Mineral Age', *Annual Review of Anthropology*, 47, pp. 61–77, DOI: 10.1146/annurev-anthro-102317-050156.

Karl, T. L. (1997) *The Paradox of Plenty: Oil Booms and Petro-States* (Berkeley: University of California Press).

Katz-Lavigne, S. (2019) 'Artisanal Copper Mining and Conflict at the Intersection of Property Rights and Corporate Strategies in the Democratic Republic of Congo', *The Extractive Industries and Society*, 6(2), pp. 399–406.

Keen, D. (2012) 'Greed and Grievance in Civil War', *International Affairs*, 88, DOI: 10.1111/j.1468-2346.2012.01100.x.

Kemp, D., and J.R. Owen (2019) 'Characterising the Interface between Large and Small-Scale Mining', *The Extractive Industries and Society*, 6(4), pp. 1091–1100.

Kirsch, S. (2014) *Mining Capitalism:tThe Relationship between Corporations and Their Critics* (Oakland: University of California Press).

Krause, T. (2020) 'Reducing Deforestation in Colombia while Building Peace and Pursuing Business as Usual Extractivism?', *Journal of Political Ecology*, 27(1), pp. 401–418.

Le Billon, P. (2001) 'The Political Ecology of War: Natural Resources and Armed Conflicts', *Political Geography*, 20, pp. 561–584.

Lorca, M., M. Andrade, M. Escosteguy, J. Köppel, M. Scoville-Simonds and M. Hufty (2022) 'Mining Indigenous Territories: Consensus, Tensions and Ambivalences in the Salar de Atacama', *The Extractive Industries and Society*, 9(101047), DOI: 10.1016/j.exis.2022.101047.

Maconachie, R., and G. Hilson (2011) 'Safeguarding Livelihoods or Exacerbating Poverty? Artisanal Mining and Formalization in West Africa', *Natural Resources Forum*, 35(4), pp. 293–303.

Menton, M. and Le Billon, P. (eds) (2021) *Environmental Defenders. Deadly Struggles for Life and Territory* (London: Routledge).

Mezzadra, S. and B. Neilson (2019) *The Politics of Operations: Excavating Contemporary Capitalism* (Durham: Duke U. Press).

Milanez, B., S. H. Ali and J. de Oliveira (2021) 'Mapping Industrial Disaster Recovery: Lessons from Mining dam Failures in Brazil', *The Extractive Industries and Society*, 8(2), DOI: 10.1016/j.exis.2021.100900.

Mintz, S. (1985) *Sweetness and Power: the Place of Sugar in Modern History* (London: Penguin Press).

Moore, J. W. (2015) *Capitalism in the Web of Life: Ecology and the Accumulation of Capital* (London and New York: Verso).

O'Brien, K, and L. Lianjiang (2006) *Rightful Resistance in Rural China* (New York: Cambridge University Press).

Ødegaard, C. V., and J. J. R. Andía (2019) *Indigenous life projects and extractivism: Ethnographies from South America* (Berlin: Springer Nature).

Ovadia, J. (2016) 'Local Content Policies and Petro-development in Sub-Saharan Africa: a Comparative Analysis', *Resources Policy*, 49, pp. 20–30, DOI: 10.1016/j.resourpol.2016.04.003.

Peluso, N. and M. Watts, (eds.) (2001) *Violent Environments* (Ithaca: Cornell University Press).

Pijpers, R. J. and T.H. Eriksen (eds.) (2019) *Mining Encounters: Extractive Industries in an Overheated World* (London: Pluto Press).

Raffles, H. (1999) '"Local Theory": Nature and the Making of an Amazonian Place', *Cultural Anthropology*, 14, pp. 323–360.

Richardson, T. and G. Weszkalnys (2014) 'Introduction: Resource Materialities' *Anthropological Quarterly*, 87, pp. 5–30, DOI: 10.1353/anq.2014.0007.

Rodriguez Castro, L. (2021) 'Extractivism and Territorial Dispossession in Rural Colombia: a Decolonial Commitment to Campesinas' Politics of Place', *Feminist Review*, 128(1), pp. 44–61, DOI:10.1177/01417789211015269.

Ross, M. (1999) 'The Political Economy of the Resource Curse', *World Politics*, 51, pp. 297–322.

Rubbers, B. (2019). Mining Boom, Labour Market Segmentation and Social Inequality in the Congolese Copperbelt. *Development and Change*. 51. 10.1111/dech.12531.

Sachs, J. D. and A. M. Warner (1999) 'The Big Rush, Natural Resource Booms and Growth', *Journal of Development Economics*, 59(1), pp. 43–76.

Sawyer, S. (2004) *Crude Chronicles. Indigenous Politics, Multinational Oil, and Neoliberalism in Ecuador* (Durham: Duke University Press).

Shapiro, J. and J.-A. McNeish (eds) (2021) *Our Extractive Age: Expressions of Violence and Resistance* (Abingdon: Routledge).

Smith, N. (2008) *Uneven Development: Nature, Capital, and the Production of Space* (Athens: University of Georgia Press).

Snyder, R. (2006) 'Does Lootable Wealth Breed Disorder?' *Comparative Political Studies*, 39, pp. 943–968, DOI: 10.1177/0010414006288724.

Svampa, M. (2019) *Neo-extractivism in Latin America: Socio-environmental Conflicts, the Territorial Turn, and New Political Narratives* (Cambridge: Cambridge University Press), DOI: 10.1017/9781108752589.

Szeman, I., and J. Wenzel (2021) 'What Do We Talk about When We Talk about Extractivism?', *Textual Practice*, 35(3), pp. 1–19, DOI: 10.1080/0950236X.2021.1889829.

Tordo, S., M. Warner, O Manzano and Y. Anouti (2013) *Local Content Policies in the Oil and Gas Sector* (Washington D.C.: World Bank), DOI: 10.1596/978-0-8213-9931-6.

Tsing, A. (2005) *Friction: an Ethnography of Global Connection* (Princeton: Princeton University Press).

Turner, T. (1995) 'An Indigenous Peoples Struggle for Socially Equitable and Ecologically Sustainable Production: the Kayapo Revolt against Extractivism', *Journal of Latin America Anthropology*, 1(1), pp. 98–121.

Veltmeyer, H. and J. Petras (2014) *The new extractivism: a post-neoliberal development model or imperialism of the twenty-first century?* (London: Zed Books).

Verbrugge, B. and S. Geenen (2020) *Global Gold Production Touching Ground. Expansion, Informalization, and Technological Innovation* (London: Palgrave Macmillan).

Watts, M. (2021) 'Hyper-Extractivism and the Global Oil Assemblage', in J. Shapiro and J.-A. McNeish (eds.) *Our Extractive Age: Expressions of Violence and Resistance* (Abingdon: Routledge), pp. 207–248.

Watts, M. (2004) 'Resource Curse? Governmentality, Oil, and Power in the Niger Delta, Nigeria', *Geopolitics*, 9(1), pp. 50–80.

Weszkalnys, G. (2015) 'Geology, Potentiality, Speculation: On the Indeterminacy of "First Oil"', *Cultural Anthropology*, 30(4), DOI: 10.14506/ca30.4.08.

World Bank, 2009, *Mining Together: Large-Scale Mining Meets Artisanal Mining: a Guide for Action* (Washington, DC: World Bank), https://openknowledge.worldbank.org/entities/publication/31d68060-a101-588c-bf29-f24070860oac (accessed on 16 May 2023).

Ye, J., J. D. van der Ploeg, S. Schneider and T. Shanin (2020) 'The Incursions of Extractivism: Moving From Dispersed Places to Global Capitalism', *The Journal of Peasant Studies*, 47(1), pp. 155–183.

Zimmerman, E. (1933) *World Resources and Industries* (New York: Harper & Brothers).

Zhouri, A. R. Oliveira, M. Zucarelli and M. Vasconcelos (2017) 'The Rio Doce Mining Disaster in Brazil: between Policies of Reparation and the Politics of Affectations', *Vibrant: Virtual Brazilian Anthropology*, 14, DOI: 10.1590/1809-43412017v14n2p081.

PART 1

Community, Labout and Social Life

CHAPTER 2

Migrants and the Politics of Presence on the South African Platinum Mining Belt

Melusi Nkomo

Abstract

The platinum mining regions of South Africa's North West province attract numerous individuals from far and wide in search of mining jobs and other opportunities directly or indirectly related to the mines. Since the late 1990s many newcomers to the region have established informal settlements close to mining operations and nearby urban areas. Significant numbers of IsiXhosa-speaking migrants, primarily from the south-east of the country, reside in these settlements. This chapter examines particular social and cultural practices to argue that such mine-periphery settlements are significant sites for consequential social and political organisation and action. The chapter proposes that such politics, which can be termed the 'politics of presence', permits visible and audible claim-making and demands by the residents vis-à-vis the state and mining capital. Ordinary strategies for constructing and organising life entrench and expand their political presence, actions, and solidarity in a region that is, generally speaking, hostile to their presence. Instead of confronting, pathologising and marginalising the sociopolitical organisation and practices of informal settlement residence, policy-makers would do well to view the political space and structures created in informal settlements as potentially fruitful for progressive political communication and deliberations aimed at improving the lives of poor people over the long term.

1 Introduction

During the first decade and a half of the twenty-first century, the global commodities boom fuelled an enormous expansion of platinum mining in South Africa's North West and Limpopo provinces. In these platinum-rich provinces, mining companies such as Anglo-American Platinum, Lonmin plc and Impala Platinum engaged in profitable ventures, resulting in increased commercial activity and urban expansion in the surrounding areas. Rustenburg, Brits, Phokeng, Marikana and other cities provided many people with opportunities and 'dreams' for development, employment, entrepreneurship and escape

 | DOI:10.1163/9789004685994_003

from poverty (Rajak, 2012). From across South Africa and beyond its borders, many thronged to the region in search of mine jobs and other livelihood opportunities that are directly or indirectly related to the mining economy.

However, in spite of the image of a booming industry, the mines were able neither to absorb the overwhelming numbers of job seekers nor to satisfy the deep desire for development among local communities. Those able to secure mine jobs survived on insufficient salaries, a situation that among other things provoked the Marikana strikes and violence of 2012–13 (of which more later). Many others remained unemployed, but some entered the informal economy—selling liquor in unlicensed establishments, running hair salons, peddling drugs and prostitution and pursuing other, undefined income-generating activities. Or, as described by Joseph Mujere, they engaged in 'practices of waiting' for the various kinds of life opportunities, such as jobs, public services, development, etc., which they hoped could come with mining (Mujere, 2020; Rajak, 2016; 2012). This chapter argues that significant everyday and mundane activities, social relations and practices build into the conditions of political life and struggles of the many who were drawn towards the mining boom's many promises, but instead survive mostly on its edges. They find themselves on the margins, predominantly in the sprawling informal settlements dotted across the so-called platinum belt. The image of informal settlements right on the doorsteps of large-scale mining operations may evoke the underbelly of extractive activities, primitive accumulation, land dispossession, displacement, disruption of social arrangements and inequalities among local communities, as described by Capps and Mnwana (2015a; 2015b). However, these informal settlements on the edges of the mines, occupied by migrants and other poor, also constitute significant sites for active social and political organisation and actions. People who find themselves building a social world at the edge engage in what anthropologist Anne-Marie Makhulu (2015, xv) calls a 'politics of presence', which allows for visible and audible claim-making vis-à-vis the state and mining capital (see also, Bayat, 2007 and 2013). With such a politics, people grapple with the complexities of lived life, as Makhulu (2015, xv) suggests, by engaging in ordinary strategies of building and organising life, everyday struggles to survive, illegal settlement, protest, etc. while being able to 'make their presence felt, exercise leverage and make demands' (Li, 2017, 1253). As this chapter emphasises, the vibrant public politics of poor people on the platinum belt cannot be fully understood without interrogating the mundane, intimate and personal dispositions and actions of the actors (Hanisch, 1970; Enloe, 2011). A derivative argument, which is important to mention but will not be expanded upon in the present contribution to this thematic volume, is that the margins of the mining economy represent conduits of social reproduction and social mobility that are not directly organised by capital, but from which capital benefits immensely. Marginality, therefore, does not entail political insignificance, or dejected apathy on a mining frontier.

The chapter's insights are based on my ethnographic study in Marikana town in South Africa's North West province. I stayed in the informal settlements of Big House and eNkanini (the latter is sometimes called Wonderkop) for 14 months that were interspersed between 2014 and 2016. A number of my interlocutors, on whom I will focus in this paper, were isiXhosa-speaking male migrants who came to the area mostly from the rural regions of Eastern Cape province. I undertook fieldwork in the aftermath of the Marikana miners' strikes and crisis, which lasted from 2012 to 2013.[1] I conversed and interacted with, but also observed the life of, the town's people, especially those residing in informal settlements and surrounding poor communities. While I focus on men in this paper, my fieldwork in general was not limited to the stories of full-time male employees of the mines, but included the perceptions of casual, informal and unemployed individuals who were both female and male. Many of those I spoke with had hopes of one day getting a full-time mining job.

This chapter adds to the academic and policy debates on local-level politics in mining regions—that is, the politics of people living in areas affected by large-scale resource extraction (Filer and Le Meur, 2017, 24). Mining sites such as the one I depict are those social spaces, we are told, where capitalism '"hits the ground" and [is shaped, or] shapes conditions of everyday life' (Mezzadra and Neilson, 2019, 22; also, Tsing, 2005). In this relation, the academic argument exposes 'zones of noncommodification', in this case the grey zones of the sociocultural and political, on which mining capitalism 'depends for its very existence' (Fraser, 2017, 152) by its extraction and exploitation of labour, and life itself, while contributing very little to its reproduction. Such zones, as Lahiri-Dutt (2016, 204–13) has described in the context of coal mining in India, may also exhibit the intermingling of the formal and informal, resulting in 'diverse worlds' that are flexibly organised by transactions, labour and enterprise. To a great extent, this chapter augments the growing body of social science analyses of post-apartheid/postcolonial (that is, post-1994) mining by putting the everyday and quotidian social and political practices on the fringes of a mining economy under an ethnographic microscope.

In the last two decades, much of the research on South Africa's mining explored the changing political economies, social structures and political

1 On 16 August 2012, a gathering of mine workers and other community members—who were vocalising wage-increase demands from Lonmin—ended in bloodshed, as 34 of them were killed by members of the South African police and the mine company's security.

sociologies of labour, especially on the platinum mining belt (Bowman, 2016; 2018; Benya, 2016; 2017; Capps, 2010; 2015; Mnwana and Bowman, 2022; Forrest, 2015; Sinwell and Mbatha, 2016). Emphasis has been on how platinum mining impacts the dynamics of community formation, contentious inter-intra-community politics, and relations between communities, corporations, local government and the state, as well as forms of mine labour organisation and struggles. It is often agreed that 'the new mining' has been accompanied by a 'complex pattern of [both] continuity and change in the dynamics and geographies of the old migrant labour system' (Capps, 2015, 501; Bezuidenhout and Buhlungu, 2015; Stewart, 2015). Scholars also consider how the different land ownership statuses and patterns of authority in mining-affected areas facilitate conflict over control of land and mineral benefits (Bowman, 2016; Capps and Mnwana, 2015a; 2015b; Mnwana and Bowman, 2022). These conflicts manifest themselves in local social struggles, and are usually 'fought through claims to exclusive group identities and conflicting notions of belonging', which leads Mnwana to conclude that '[t]he politics and meanings of belonging and citizenship have hence become central to attempts to determine who benefits from the fruits of platinum mining and who doesn't' (Mnwana, 2015, 159). In the present chapter, I acknowledge the extensiveness and significance of work that has been done on South Africa's platinum belt society and local-level politics; however, and taking some inspiration from studies done elsewhere (see Lahiri-Dutt, 2016; Filer and Le Meur, 2017), I aim at gnawing underneath the totality of social structural analysis, and the oft-presented image institutional by exposing the distinct forms of everyday cultural practices, social processes, and other engagements undertaken by migrants and their communities without the direct organisation of capital, but definitely not without its exploitation. The evidence I bring forth, first, compliments the analyses of overarching power and structural relations between communities, governance institutions (state, chieftaincies and municipalities), labour and capital, but also invites different political actors to move beyond pathologising life in informal settlements and take seriously the public space and channels of political communication, deliberations, relations and discourses that are created in such places, which are often based on heterogenous practices of daily life.

2 Background and Context: the Roots of Migrants' Marginalisation Around South Africa's Platinum Mines

In Marikana and across the mining regions of the North West province, the description, designation and categorisation of isiXhosa-speaking mine workers and other migrants as social actors and groups and the roles they adopt can best be addressed by juxtaposing them against other actors such as the local communities, institutions and mining companies with whom they interact on a daily basis. At an institutional level they frequently interact with mining corporations, state institutions such as the police, and local government structures such the Bojanala Platinum District Municipality. The local communities are mostly seTswana-speaking populations who are represented by the Bapo-Ba-Mogale traditional authority (sometimes referred to as a 'chieftaincy'), bodies and groups of families purporting to be independent from the traditional authority. Many other people may claim to be 'locals', and affiliated to the area by virtue of speaking the seTswana, identifying with the culture of the region, acting and adopting certain roles that adhere them to local politics, and coming from other areas within North West province itself. From various actors there is a general resentment towards and marginalisation of migrants and their communities, particularly those residing in informal settlements. Locals often forward claims to indigeneity, autochthony, property (land and housing claims) and mine jobs that they see as threatened by the presence of a huge number of predominantly male 'outsiders' from other cultures and areas of South Africa and beyond (see Mujere, 2015; and Mnwana, 2015). In Marikana, Asanda Benya (2015, 550) observed how this resentment manifests itself in sites of everyday public and social life such as community clinics, for example between migrant residents of eNkanini and the locals of Emzini formal settlement, where the majority of residents are seTswana-speaking; she writes:

> The community clinic, meant to service all community members, has been absorbed into tribal politics that have led to migrant women sometimes being refused service [....] migrant women narrated stories of nurses and administrators who refused, ignored or turned them away for failing to respond to instructions given in the local language. To be serviced they have had to learn the local language, seTswana, or, when they can afford a taxi fare, seek help from clinics in other communities.

I also observed seething discontent across the platinum belt, especially among unemployed and despondent local youth, who expressed their disaffection through protests, rioting and other kinds of demonstrations while demanding mine jobs and other perceived entitlements such as the prioritisation of locals in the allocation of those jobs (Capps and Mnwana, 2015b). Daily interactions with a huge number of male migrants provides further and ready fodder for tensions that may come out as 'ethnic' and a revival of an 'insurrectionary brand of identity politics' (Capps and Mnwana, 2015a, 617). This resentment, however, is not new to the post-apartheid period and already occurred during the apartheid-era 'Bantustan' government of Lucas Mangope from 1977 to 1993, when 'a particularly virulent notion of "foreigners"' was fanned against migrants in the North West's regions in an attempt to incorporate various seTswana-speaking communities with 'pan-Tswana nationalism' (Capps and Mnwana, 2015b, 34).[2] Non-Tswana mineworkers, especially isiXhosa-speaking men, were often arrested and deported if found loitering in villages (Manson and Benga, 2012; Capps and Mnwana, 2015b). The end of apartheid might have put a stop to the deportations, but social contacts with migrants on the edges of the mines took on new forms with the commencement of profitable platinum mining in the first decade of the 2000s.

Capps (2010, 16) writes that a new, 'increasingly assertive "tribal nationalism"' among the various local chieftaincies and communities is continuously propped up by knowledge of platinum wealth and the promise of its redistribution (Capps, 2010, 16; Manson and Benga, 2012, 116). The promise of mining-led development, wealth redistribution and 'empowerment' among seTswana-speaking 'ethno-communities' has meant that locals are constantly rebranding themselves as a way of repositioning themselves in order to benefit from mining operations (Comaroff and Comaroff, 2009, 15; see, also, Rajak, 2016). To a large extent, the situation also means that relations vis-à-vis non-Tswana and other marginal, poor and migrant communities engender a '"segmentation" of citizenship or the "narrowing" of definitions of belonging' around mining projects (Mnwana, 2015, 161). In Koczberski and Curry's (2004, 367) study of migrant workers on palm oil plantations in Papua New Guinea (cited in Bainton, 2009, 24), similar 'insider–outsider' discourses also tend to promote and legitimise the socioeconomic and political power of the local community while homogenising the outsiders. The circumstances of resentment, exclusion and marginalisation with regard to residents of informal settlements therefore result in blanket but multiple forms of deprivation for most migrants in such settlements, the most obvious being deteriorating subsistence, infrastructurally poor residence, and general uncertainty of life.

The preceding depiction of social relations on the platinum belt should not be taken as my denying interethnic instances of cooperation that happen at

2 Lucas Mangope was the president of a short-lived black 'homeland' government (1977–93) that was situated mainly in the present-day North West province of South Africa. 'Homelands', or '*Bantustans*' were polities created by the apartheid regime as racially segregated and nominally 'self-governing' for black Africans. They usually grouped people according to perceived ethnic and linguistic homogeneity. They all collapsed in 1994 and were incorporated into the new democratic South Africa.

many different levels between individuals and many other actors with various backgrounds, not only between isiXhosa and seTswana speakers. Also, the divisions are by no means seamless. Most migrants speak fluent seTswana and the opposite is true for locals, who may speak isiXhosa and other Nguni languages, such as isiZulu, on top of English and Afrikaans. During and just after the Marikana strikes and crisis of 2012 for instance, the interests of most people in communities around the platinum belt seemed to converge, transcending linguistic and ethnic divisions as all and sundry came out in solidarity with the striking mineworkers (Naicker, 2017). While it is true that migrants and others exist in social cooperation beyond ethnolinguistic boundaries (e.g. during labour protests, sport events, political gatherings, etc.), what is undeniable is that everyday social contacts remain an important point where people come together, or become divided, around the platinum mines. A question then arises regarding how migrants position themselves socially and politically in order to wade through the deprived conditions of life and struggles. How do they perform, inscribe and claim a social and political presence on the platinum belt? The following ethnographic evidence points to heterogenous practices, whereby migrants progressively enhance their political and social presence, which they enact through the everyday building of sociocultural relations, networks and institutions. This politics, as Bayat (2007) argues about the Islamic world, is slowly 'encroaching' and persistent upon the constraints imposed upon its protagonists by institutions and the authorities.

3 Enacting Political Presence on the Platinum Belt

In the morning of June 21, 2015 at Big House informal settlement in Marikana, I joined a group of migrant men who basked and feasted at a yard on the banks of Sterkstroom, a creek running along the edge of the settlement. The men were my neighbours and acquaintances, whose invitations to many occasions and events I readily accepted during my fieldwork. In the small yard was an open fire on top of which was a large pot which burped and coughed out froth, lid tumbling from boiling meat. Jeke,[3] an old-timer mine worker and neighbour explained to me that the reason for the occasion he planned was 'welcoming

3 I use pseudonyms for my interlocutors to protect their identities. I introduce Jeke, because (as will become clear in the chapter) he embodies and symbolises male migrants' attempts at the creation of a certain sociocultural order, patriarchal authority and social world that has meaning to male migrants in the face of uncertain life conditions on the edges of a platinum economy.

our young men' ('*ukwamkela abafana basekhaya*', or just '*ukwamkela*'), in his isiXhosa language. The welcome, he explained, was for some young men who had arrived the previous day from Eastern Cape. The young men were known to Jeke from his rural village of Cabane, some 20 kilometres south of the closest town, Mount Frere, also in the Eastern Cape. Not all the 'young men' looked so young to me, and neither were they all 'new' to the platinum belt in general. Jeke, regularly addressed as '*utata*' ('father', or 'old man') by fellow residents and workmates alike, had been around the mines for as long as he could remember, and often gathered people of his own accord for beer-drinking occasions and settling small disputes between residents.

On that day, Jeke was cooking at the yard of a close friend of his, a fellow mineworker I knew as Miya. The two met at the end of the 1990s when the latter arrived on the platinum belt as a young man to find work. Jeke himself came to the platinum mines earlier, at the end of the 1980s, after he left another mine that shut down on the gold reefs near the city of Johannesburg. Jeke decided to prepare the meat at Miya's yard because there, he decided, it could be looked after while he attended to some other chores. Besides, he also considered that the goat's loud bleating during slaughter might 'invite the whole Big House', many more hungry mouths than he had planned for. For that day, Miya's place, at the edge of the informal settlement, was secluded from the public eye, and just ideal for a small-scale social occasion.

A few other men joined the group later, and the gathering swelled to about 15 people. All of them, I later found out, were originally from various regions of the Eastern Cape. Two were known to Jeke from his rural village. Three joined because the two from the village invited them. It was the same for the other men who joined us later. A few knew the host from work, or like me from staying together at the Big House informal settlement. We were just '*makhelwanes*' ('neighbours/co-residents'). The informality of the occasion makes it difficult to generalise its structure to other social activities of a similar nature that may occur elsewhere. On this occasion, friends, acquaintances, neighbours, workmates, chosen by the host and others, spread the word among themselves.

With the preceding vignette, I reiterate a trope in the anthropological literature about the reconstruction of social and kinship networks among mine workers who found themselves far from home on the mines of apartheid and colonial southern Africa (see Van Onselen, 1976; Harries, 1994; Dunbar Moodie and Ndatshe, 1994). The trope is still recognisable in contemporary studies, albeit with several modifications as the analysis below will reveal. Migrant mineworkers and their communities are discernible as social collectives on the platinum belt. Their inter- and intraethnic contacts, and adoption of different situational roles, engender social networks that become significant for everyday social and political relations and actions. The networks could be built from common rural origins, as among workmates, beer-drinking companions, among kin, and in various other daily engagements.

In the informal settlements under consideration, there exists an elaborate affective community in which idioms of family, friendship and other terms of classificatory kinship are readily deployed to denote ethnic affinity and affiliation, sometimes genuine and consanguineal, but not uncommonly fictive (see also Harries 1990; 1994). Several other close social ties are built and social roles adopted on the platinum belt among co-workers, co-residents and other people with whom migrants interact regularly. Such ethnocultural affiliations, roles and connections sometimes obscure narrower loyalties to social and moral institutions at rural homes of origin, such as loyalties to a particular headman or chief (ibid., 1990). For many migrant men, being a '*ndoda yom'Xhosa*' ('*Xhosa* man') is a general label of shared camaraderie and honour they are generally comfortable with. A significant number of them did sometimes identify themselves as belonging to a subgroup from the specific districts they came from, yet these particularities were frequently undercut by a broader rubric of isiXhosa speakers across the platinum belt.[4] As an example, a man from the Gcaleka, an isiXhosa-speaking subgroup, would comfortably admit to being 'a *Xhosa*' ('*ndingu mXhosa*', they would say) and identify with the broader group of people coming from various Eastern Cape regions, even those who are not Gcaleka. Being a '*mXhosa*' is therefore understood as emanating from an ethnolinguistic convergence, a shared province of origin, but crucially a sense of familiarity with certain general cultural ways and similar life circumstances both on the platinum belt and in their rural homes of origin.

The above observations resonate with Mahoney's (2012, 139) study among 'Zulus' who migrated for work in the early twentieth century and found themselves concentrated in South Africa's urban settlements, where people from different regions, chiefdoms, and districts assembled in a manner they might never have done in the countryside; as migrants, they adopted a broad Zulu belonging. Harries (1994, 39) similarly claims that far from their home, late nineteenth and early twentieth century Mozambiquan migrants forged ties in migrant communities for 'assistance and comradeship', and such communities were often wider than those of the chiefdom and clan from whence they came. Additionally, concepts of kinship became extended to include, within the classification of 'brothers' and 'family parties', men who were seen to share

4 One fundamental particularity would be 'initiation' into manhood, which involves circumcision, which many isiXhosa-speaking groups carry out, although exceptions such as the amaMpondo people do not.

FIGURE 2.1 A poster at Marikana calling members of an '*umbutho*' from Bizana, Eastern Cape, to a Sunday morning meeting. Below the time and venue is written, 'we succeed in numbers, fellows'
SOURCE: AUTHOR

a common repertoire of values and traditions (ibid.). On the platinum belt today, people coming from vastly separated areas of the Eastern Cape, such as eNgcobo, Mount Fletcher, Flagstaff, Mthatha and so on, find themselves concentrating into social groups and residential patterns whose basis is wider than those at their rural homes. The basis for coming together can be language and culture, but goes further to include various mutual interests—job opportunities, political affiliation, religious affiliation and land occupation, for example. Male migrants may thus congregate in associations called '*umbutho*' and gather to discuss and forward matters of converging interest.[5] Although meetings of such congregations are sometimes publicised through posters (see Figure 2.1), at other times they occur as regular sittings around beer, or a game of cards on easy Sunday afternoons, or more commonly after work, casual gathering in the small yards of the informal settlements. I did not have an opportunity to

5 The term '*Umbutho*' is also used to denote 'trade union'.

attend formally publicised *umbutho* meetings because invitations specifically included close compatriots from the same rural district, but the information I present here comes from similar gatherings (discussed in sections below) where people performed everyday interactional and behavioural repertoires. While the kind of politics practiced in these male groups could be understood in terms of Thompson's (1971) moral politics, which involves circumscribing one's own boundaries for collective action and 'mutually "acceptable" elements within a system of political domination and economic appropriation' (Dunbar Moodie, 1986, 2), it can also be understood as a politics of assertively digging into a particular political space. And thus as a politics of presence, with the intention of becoming visible and audible vis-à-vis dominant actors such as the state, local authorities and mining companies. It is not unusual that this politics finds some symbolic expression—for example, after a gathering such as the ones described above the migrants form a procession of singing and dancing through the streets. Much of the lyrics of the songs they sing (or sometimes poetry by an '*imbongi*', or poet, among them) reveal the world of their political imagination and desires, and a readiness to act and achieve that world. '*Ngcono sigoduke sizothul'mthwalo thina! Ngeke simele into yokudlala manye madoda*' ('Better we turn back [to our rural homes] and lay down our burdens! We can't wait to be played by other men'), they would chant and march in public places, referring to what they see as not being rewarded fairly for their labour in the mines, or as being treated unfairly in the region to which they have come to work and build lives. In the following section I explore further examples of these political and cultural symbolisms.

4 '*Khawuzithuthe khe!*' ('Praise yourself!'): Knowing One another On the Platinum Belt

Upon meeting one another for the first time, and on top of regular niceties such as asking one another's names, migrant men typically ask one another about particular clan names they call '*iziduko*', their specific chief's name, and rural districts of origin ('*ekhaya*'). The pleasantries around a beer drink could be conspicuously long. One might begin by saying, '*Molweni, mna ndingu Ntobeko, ndingumzukulu ko Ngcwangule, esizwe samaMpondo, eNdindindi*' and go on praising themselves ('Greetings, I'm Ntobeko, the grandson of Ngcwangule, who comes from Mpondo country, in Ndindindi district').[6] It is possible just to

6 This was not an actual interview, but I got this structure from the many introductory greetings I observed during my fieldwork.

stop having mentioned one's given names and where one comes from, but it is not rare that others may request more detail in a manner that sounds like asking 'Why are you withholding other information?' It is prudent, anyway, to be reticent about one's identity and origin in a place like the platinum belt, where spies ('*impimpis*') are deeply despised and if caught are harshly dealt with.[7] Indeed, at times people go further, requesting that an individual recite his clan praises during the introductions. '*Khawuzithuthe sikuve mhlekazi, ungubani waphi? Ukuze sazane!*' ('Praise yourself now sir; who exactly are you and from where? We want to hear you then know you!') Sometimes an individual would confess their lack of knowledge of ritual and cultural decorum in the Xhosa clan praise tradition that other migrants, especially senior men, would proudly flaunt.

A satisfactory introduction regularly invites heartfelt welcomes and nods of affirmation: '*Aw! iza uzohlala apha mntase. Awusijoyine mfokaNgwcangule sisele, sincokole njengamaXhosa*' ('Aw! Join us blood relative, son of Ngcwangule; sit here, drink and let us chat together as Xhosas'). Sometimes the clan names and praises could end up being used in day-to-day interactions instead of one's given names. At Big House settlement, some of my neighbours referred to me as '*Khumalo, Mntungwa*', which I later learnt was a clan praise among the isiXhosa-speaking amaMfengu or amaHlubi subgroups from the Thembuland regions of Eastern Cape province, who also have the surname 'Nkomo'.[8] I gladly took up the honour. For an individual in a potentially alienating environment, Harries (1994, 6) once concluded, this naming honour provides a concept of 'self' and closely links them to the moral collective, thus locating them in multiple patterns of social relations and obligations.

One's deliberate furtiveness, as briefly hinted at above, could raise suspicion in the platinum belt environment, where people fear and despise spies. However, whatever way an individual is welcomed, being an isiXhosa speaker and opening up about one's Eastern Cape origins might become a quick open sesame to getting involved in material, sociopolitical and moral relations that are important for most of the platinum belt's migrant communities. Social interactions, therefore, do not end with merely occupying the same living space, or with the fact of coming from the same region of origin as others. The

7 During my fieldwork, spies supposedly emanated from the police, mining companies, local authorities, rival trade unions, and political parties, among other groups and institutions, who were perceived as harbouring nefarious intentions (real or imagined) with regard to migrants and their communities.

8 As far as I know, my Ndebele-speaking people from Zimbabwe are Ngunis like isiZulu, isiSwati and isiXhosa speakers, but I cannot trace any relation to amaMfengu.

banalities of everyday life in informal settlements—accessing food, money, sex, dealing with health and illness, among other issues—have the potential to create networks, which in turn further entwine people into local spheres of political and/or social action. Such circumstances, I argue, exemplify the remaking political actions, social dependencies, and social dynamics and social forms through which individuals and collectives aspire for advancement in their lives.

5 Inscribing and Reinforcing the Politics of Presence

Earlier in the morning of 21 June 2015 (the occasion that I introduced in earlier sections of this chapter), Jeke had knocked at my door to check on me (it had become a habit of his whenever I was around) and invited me to come along to his friend's yard, where the '*ukwamukela*' was taking place. We found the young men in hushed conversation that was abruptly broken by Jeke's greeting, which he offered in a dramatic and commandeering tone. He removed a pot full of meat from the fire. After briefly explaining why he had decided to slaughter one of his animals, he invited everyone to partake in the fellowship. It was meant for 'people from home', he explained, 'so that they won't think we don't have relatives in Marikana'. A plastic bowl was thus passed around first, for each to pick out a thin roasted strand. In the meanwhile, Jeke and Miya prepared the boiled meat, which was later spread on two wide wooden platters (they were, in fact, cleaned pieces of old doors). People sat around the platters of meat in two separate groups. Older men were around one and younger men around the other. The sitting arrangement was at the host's insistence, to respect and show deference to one another ('*ntlonipha*'), he explained. It was the same format at traditional ceremonies and other social gatherings I observed—such as the '*ukukhulula izila*' ('removing of mourning clothes/stop the mourning', also 'home cleansing ceremony')—when people ate together on big occasions at migrants' rural homesteads in the Eastern Cape. As part of respect and avoidance, called *ukuntlonipha*-custom, junior men and senior men may not eat from the same platter. The custom extends to the relations and contacts between men and women in the homestead; they too could not share food from the same dish.

Hickel (2015, 76–78) shows that among other Nguni peoples, such as isiZulu-speaking populations, this circumspect generational separateness of *ukutlonipha* is a crucial part of traditional custom through which senior men maintain patriarchal ideologies and authority over their homesteads and juniors. In general, however, and with respect to migrant miners, it has been long recorded that this 'principle of seniority' is the basis on which social life among Nguni people is organised (Dunbar Moodie and Ndatshe, 1994, 129). 'Without respect for elders the entire political and moral economy of traditional Bantu-speaking societies would unravel', argues Dunbar Moodie and Ndatshe (1994). On the platinum belt, *ukuntlonipha* and general deference to one's seniors is still one of a litany of important sociocultural practices that are constantly evoked in the remaking of a social reality and a world with meaning to its actors. Migrants acknowledge that their social world and its organisation is not entirely divorced from the reality of their rural homes from whence they came. As much as material realities of lived life on the platinum belt are invariably linked to those of the countryside, so too are the sociocultural and moral realities that complete that social world.

On the day described here, senior migrant mine workers like Jeke and Miya carried themselves with the hubris of those in authority. It seemed to me a rather consciously performative authority for the most part, repetitively carried out, as if to inscribe a sense of obeisance and solidary into the psyches and on the bodies of their junior compatriots. Jeke did not eat much. No sooner had the eating started than he was wiping the meat's fat off his hands onto grass tufts and his overalls, after a few seemingly light pecks at the meat. He had a few extra slivers for himself, which he casually chucked into his mouth before going back to the fire, where he was preparing the rest of the meat into *biltong*. Miya and the other senior men called out to the junior men, '*heyi madoda thathani nantsiya inyama nitye*' ('Hey gentlemen, there is meat, take and eat'), and they fell upon it with the lust of the truly hungry. All the while, the senior men ordered about the youngest of the guests with many unceasing small requests, for instance telling them to sharpen the cleaver and penknives on nearby rocks, or for someone to bring salt from Miya's room.

In one instance, when a restless young fellow kept pacing up and down in front of the group, foraging for a paper to roll his tobacco, Jeke gave him more than a mild reproof: '*Rha! hlala phantsi ndoda! Jonga mna nabanye abantu! Sibadala kuwe*', he barked, pausing in-between each phrase for emphasis ('*rha!* man sit down and take note of other older people and me; we're older than you'). Jeke was reacting to the slightest of infractions with regard to the kind of ideal social order and comportment that was being performed and remade during the small gathering. The young man's infraction was, I suppose, one that could have passed without much thought or consequence, yet for the older men noticing such small 'infractions' is usually a technique via which to assert their attempts at lecturing juniors on a normative moral order. Some took the heed; some, maybe not. This time the reproved junior promptly replied, '*ndiyaxolisa maxhego*' ('apologies elders') before recoiling, smarting from his bruised ego. For the most part, however, the gathering was good-humoured; we laughed and talked a lot. Jokes, for instance, could be aimed by the seniors at the juniors, teasing them about being '*Ben 10s*',[9] not out of disdain but to remind them how the temptation to behave with 'childish' perversity in certain situations should be restrained. Small feasts such as the one discussed here are ubiquitous on the platinum belt, and offer seemingly strenuous but also light moments that characterise much of migrants' commitment to collective morality and political presence.

Indeed, tensions within the informal settlements are always close to the surface in the environs of the platinum belt, between generations, between genders, and with other social groups. Yet achieving an equilibrium seems more important than total disconnection between the social groups.[10] The attempts to perform and (re)create a particular social order and reality, and navigate the uncertain existence of life on the platinum belt do not necessarily suggest an imaginary place of perfect and uncontaminated bliss and cooperation. Far from it. These, after all, are communities that have witnessed their fair share of immense violence of many dimensions, as exemplified by the Marikana crisis that started in 2012 and continued for most of 2013. So, given half a chance and without their seniors' insistence, women and younger men may eschew hierarchies and authority. There were instances when I heard women and youths reminding older men that 'Rustenburg [the platinum belt] is not in the rural homes', and that people were there to make money above all else. They challenged attempts to establish patriarchal order and hierarchies. Nevertheless, senior men do not easily give up exerting pressure for normatively significant social relations and framework collective actions. They argue, as Jeke did, that the 'rebellious young', the '*Ben 10s*' as they call them, and 'women of the mines'[11] need that 'guidance', or even reprimand in the form of being cut out of migrant social circles. People like Jeke were, therefore, reinforcing the same moral refrains that young people and women would probably hear back at home in rural Eastern Cape, from relatives, parents, and community.

9 A 'Ben 10' in South African slang refers to a young man who makes immature decisions when it comes to sexual matters. Sometimes it is used for young men who fall in love with older women. The original 'Ben 10' is a character from an American animated television series that is popular with children in South Africa.

10 'Equilibrium' is used here in the sense suggested by Max Gluckman (1940, 28), to mean 'the interdependent relations between different parts of the social structure of a community at a particular period'.

11 "Women of the mines" was often said derisively of female migrants, especially those who came of their own volition to look for jobs and opportunities on the platinum belt.

As a restatement, food and drink facilitate quasi-traditional and customary gatherings that for many migrants mean the beginning of long-term platinum belt 'friendships' ('*ubuhlobo*'). Later, elsewhere on the platinum belt, such companions would be greeted in the form of groups of 'drinking buddies', called '*amabandla*' (singular '*ibandla*') among men. In addition to drinking, these men engage in a variety of other activities, such as gambling, playing sports, attending labour union meetings, and eating. For these migrants from Eastern Cape, new social relationships in North West province are usually built with others from their home region. However, mere acquaintances can grow in importance and become so close that they eventually regard each other as 'kin', even when they come from vastly diverse regions and family backgrounds in their home province. While it is preferable to have people of the same ethnic and regional background and even same village of origin in one's social circle, the boundaries of relations are not always stringent if trust, mutuality, dependency and obligation are created with others. Such companions could be drawn from neighbours in the informal settlement, from workmates, fellow trade union comrades, or from elsewhere across the vastness of the platinum mining belt. While, ideally, social networks and relations have an ethnolinguistic and regional character that draws in people from the same region, the boundaries are never etched in stone, so that any other acceptable persons, including myself, can be accommodated.

Migrant mineworkers' social networks in southern Africa have long been considered important forms of moral relations and association and they often came in the form of 'homeboys' and 'homegirls' groups. A congregation formed by rural networks, neighbourly acquaintance, or ethnic camaraderie was always part of sociability among migrants in pre-1994 mining compounds (Gordon, 1977; Clegg, 1981; James, 1999; Dunbar Moodie and Ndatshe, 1994; Donham, 2011). Dunbar Moodie and Ndatshe (1994, 166) specifically observe among migrants of the past that male camaraderie and drinking were 'indispensable to compound social life' not least because of the informal networks and affinities they nurtured, but also because they extended into other realms of human sociality: dance parties, sex and its acquisition, moral exhortation, maintenance of order, and so on and so forth. On the platinum belt, while remaining crucial for interconnectedness social networks are constantly adjusted to suit the migrants' contexts, desired outcomes, and the rapidly changing but marginal lives on a mining frontier (Kirsch, 2001).

5.1 *"One Doesn't Just Wriggle Out Like a Snake": Bidding Farewell*

When a migrant is leaving the platinum belt to go to back to their '*emakhaya*' (the rural 'home') in the Eastern Cape for good or for an extended period, this is sometimes taken as an opportunity to gather friends, neighbours and workmates together. Such an occasion may be called '*ukuvalelisana*' ('bidding each other farewell'). Again, invited guests would be regaled with stories, food, drinks, music, and not uncommon, ample amounts of cigarettes, tobacco and marijuana. Unlike '*ukwamukela*' (the welcoming occasion described above), the '*ukuvalelisana*' occasion could turn out to be an event at which people carouse and gorge themselves on food, depending on the depth of the host's pockets. It turns into a festive shindig if an individual is leaving on a good note and for happy reasons, and with something to show for it—so, for example, retirement, or having received one of the voluntary severance packages that Lonmin was offering in 2013 and in early 2016. One is not, meanwhile, expected by one's compatriots, friends, neighbours and other acquaintances to 'sneak out' as though one had survived all the years on the platinum belt alone. An interlocutor described such socially despised actions as the stealthy 'wriggling away of a serpent': '*ukurhubuluza kwenyoka*', he said. The imagery of a wriggling serpent, held by many to be an untrustworthy, ungrateful, unpredictable, evil creature, is informative here. Migrants often resent behavioural traits that disturb shared moral commitments to their communities, which they feel they are building or struggling to maintain in the uncertain circumstances of the mines.

For one such farewell, I drove into Big House late at night, coming from Johannesburg. In the yard of Kambani, a herbalist I had known for months after settling in Marikana, men sat around an enormous crackling fire, the air humming with conversation. It was not usual to see such late-night fire gatherings at the yards, and quite late too, so I cautiously approached to investigate.[12] 'What has happened that you stand there?' Kambani bellowed. 'Why are you not coming to join, do you want to scare us?' he added 'It's Malusi; I saw him park his car' a male voice replied on my behalf from somewhere in the darkness; it was another neighbour who joined us later. When their faces shone with the tall flames, I noticed some I had known from my stay at Big House. They had gathered to bid farewell to Kambani, a long-time resident of the place. Originally from Mozambique, he had spent his whole working career in

12 I had learnt by then that at Big House and eNkanini, such late night, dark corner, hushed-tones men's gatherings could easily be related to the volatile trade union politics or independent worker committees' caucuses. I had in mind events of the past few years, especially the 2012 strike and its bloody aftermath. Therefore, I could not be too sure about late night gatherings, and I did not want to be too intrusive. Some of the leading strategists of the strike, as we now know from researchers, came out of such informal settlement caucuses (see Sinwell and Mbatha, 2016).

the various mines of South Africa. First he was employed in the gold mining city of Welkom, in Free State province, and then on the platinum belt, where he arrived in the late 1990s. It was in Welkom that he met his second wife, an isiXhosa speaker, with whom he had two children. For his herbal and healing expertise many Big House residents called Kambani an '*ugqirha*' ('doctor'/ 'herbalist'/'diviner'); for marrying an isiXhosa-speaking women they called him '*mkwenyana*' ('son-in-law'); but for some he was just a '*umShangana*' ('Shangaan').[13]

Kambani had never gone back to Mozambique to his first wife and family ever since he received South African citizenship in 2004. He was an extremely reticent man, at least to me, so I relied a lot on the informal settlements' efficient rumour mill to learn more about his story. Even after dozens of mornings when we walked out of our respective rooms and exchanged morning civilities, all that I had got from him was that he had a house in Welkom with his second wife, the South African. He now considered the city of Welkom his home, and was moving there to retire. He had stopped working after his last long-term employer, the Lonmin mining company, offered him a severance package in 2013. Hundreds of other migrant mineworkers received the same offer from the company as part of the mine's 'restructuring of operations' that followed the major strikes of 2012, 2013 and 2014. With his severance package, Kambani bought an old Toyota Corolla car, whose performance on the road he proudly described to me. He, however, stuck around the informal settlements of Marikana after receiving his money and continued to take on temporary contract jobs with several subcontracted companies that operated on the platinum belt. After almost two years, he eventually decided that he was using more money from his package than he was earning with these short-term jobs, and risked squandering his savings, which were dwindling fast. For a career spent in the mines, however, Kambani still had something to celebrate and appreciate—a townhouse in Welkom, a car, a new family, and wife. He had a reason to be grateful and hold an '*ukuvalelisana*'.

For the farewell, he bought the main drink (it was primarily cheap brandy from a nearby liquor store) so that co-residents and friends could help him do what they called '*ukurhabulisana nje*' ('just allowing each other to sip'). On this evening, his wife and two small children had gone to sleep over at her relative's place in eNkanini, the other large, migrant-filled informal settlement across town. He reported that she said she would rather be away than wait

13 The term shangaan was historically used in the mines to refer to most immigrants from Mozambique, without much consideration for their specific ethnic background back home (see Donham, 2011).

and get incensed by heavy-drinking men. She still 'understood', he said, that it was an '*umcimbi wamadoda*' ('men's event'), something 'to expect' in general 'Xhosa custom' and that she could do little, if anything at all, to stop. So she had decided to leave for a while. Women, especially the wives of migrant mineworkers, if they are in Marikana or elsewhere on the platinum belt, often oppose such men's drinking and eating gatherings because they view them as wasteful of resources that could otherwise be used for essential household and family expenses. As in other studies on migrant society in southern Africa, the household and social investment priorities of rural communities often differ on gender lines, but also on generational lines (see, Ferguson, 1990, 135–66). Because of such differences, I witnessed open domestic conflicts reminiscent of stories that one would expect from South African tabloids such as the *Daily Sun* or *Drum* magazine. On Marikana's streets, life may imitate, or rather, reflect the tabloids. Picture a woman, a crying baby on her back, approaching her beer-swigging husband at a tavern, or at a street-side drinking and barbecue spot. She grasps him by the belt of his trousers and screams at him, reminding him that he has mouths to feed at home, a homestead to build and take care of, instead of wasting money on male friends, prostitutes, alcohol and meat. The husband tries to hide, takes to his heels, or stands his ground to defend his wounded masculine ego. Men often defend 'men's affairs', arguing they should be allowed time with their friends, away from women, to drink alcohol or watch football, or importantly, and often unsaid, as a way of buttressing male collectives. Such sociality, the very means by which male camaraderie and solidarity are built and consolidated among migrant mineworkers, is sometimes seriously contested by women, especially if it involves prodigality in a manner that is viewed as 'too much' by wives and/or other female partners. But these protestations by women go beyond mere disapproval of male prodigality, representing the struggles and conflicts (sometimes taking the form of gender, sometimes of generation) within the 'politics of presence'. The very social order (of patriarchal authority) that the men attempt to build is often brought into question, given the many setbacks it encounters in the uncertainty of platinum belt life.

In Kambani's case, his wife's protests were not as apparent as the street scene of my imaginary depicted above. In her case, she simply voted with her feet. Kambani organised for those who were physically present 'to sip', but also continually extolled his ancestors. He could not stop praising his ancestors because, as he said, they had seen him through his career as a mineworker, and made him meet the right people at the right times, such as those who had gathered around him that evening. A job completed without an accident or death, and which led to the accumulation of some measure of wealth (a car, a South

African home, payment of bride wealth) was attributed to the goodwill of God and the ancestors. Kambani used words to extol his ancestors and without laying out ornate tapestries of ritual action—just simple words of thanks and a libation with some brandy on the ground. Sometimes it was the Christian Jesus who received Kambani's praises in the excitement of the moment.

I observed that the informal rules of organising collective actions do not always strictly apply to other more casual occasions of feasting and drinking that the same people might organise, such as during a relaxed afternoon of barbecuing or other convivial activities. Such occasions could also be interpreted as attempts by migrants to inscribe and pin down, even for a short period, those domains of sociability that were critical for coordinated collective existence and actions. Among migrants, beer gatherings go beyond mere enjoyment of the drink and are individually and morally valuable for people striving for control over the conditions and meaning of their lives. A migrant, therefore, strikes the right moral code, in my opinion, when he accomplishes something that leaves his compatriots short of words but incessantly nodding and saying '*enkosi siyabulela mfundini, siyabulela ndoda yomXhosa*' ('thank you, big man; thank you, Xhosa man').

6 Conclusions

Life on the platinum belt is potentially alienating (and migrants know that well), yet it would be erroneous to give the standard picture, offered by some researchers, of migrant communities as people who often arrive on the platinum belt and in other mining regions knowing no one and with no local support (see, for example, Amnesty International, 2016). Such academic and policy conclusions are reached with insufficient understanding of how migrants organise their social life and assert a politics of presence, especially in the informal settlements. Although the struggle to survive and the physical discomfort are real for most migrants, policymakers will do well to engage with the emancipatory desires that are expressed in people's quotidian world-making at the fringes of a mining economy. In concrete terms, structures of social and political organisation built through people's own sociocultural imagination and practices should be harnessed for progressive political communication, deliberations and actions, instead of being pathologised and sidelined. Much of the heterogenous practices I have described in this chapter connect to deeply held sociocultural practices, some extending to rural practices, which can be harnessed toward collective political actions. As was the case at Marikana in 2012, cultural hierarchies and groupings such as the *umbutho* facilitated rapid mobilisation for strike actions. Dunbar Moodie (2016, 851–52, 856) has similarly observed that migrant connections are 'embedded in rural networks' and always available as alternative sources of collective solidarity on the platinum belt. The interconnectedness of migrants through social networks and the various roles they adopt are constantly evaluated and adjusted depending on prevailing conditions, most importantly while these migrants anticipate and react to the uncertainties of life and political struggles at the edge of the capitalist mining economy.

Sociocultural and moral imaginaries and their enactment are modalities through which migrants carve out a social presence and a political presence, sometimes in juxtaposition to or in challenging other actors such as state institutions and the mining companies. In entrenching this political presence, isiXhosa-speaking migrants are able to visibly and audibly make both symbolic and material claims on the platinum mining belt. They makes claims and demands for public services, such as health services, decent housing and amenities, for jobs and better wages, on the fringes of the mines, but build solidarities among themselves.

References

Amnesty International (2016) *Smoke and Mirrors: Lonmin's Failure to Address Housing Conditions at Marikana, South Africa* (London: Amnesty International Ltd), https://www.amnesty.org/en/documents/afr53/4552/2016/en/ (accessed on 28 July 2022).

Bainton, N.A. (2009) 'Keeping the Network out of View: Mining, Distinctions and Exclusion in Melanesia', *Oceania*, 79(1), pp. 18–33, https://www.jstor.org/stable/40495599 (accessed on 28 July 2022).

Bayat, A. (2013) *Life as Politics: How Ordinary People Change the Middle East, Second Edition* (Stanford: Stanford University Press).

Bayat, A. (2007) *Making Islam Democratic: Social Movements and the Post-Islamist Turn* (Stanford: Stanford University Press).

Benya, A. (2017) 'Going Underground in South African Platinum Mines to Explore Women Miners' Experiences', *Gender and Development*, 25(3), pp. 509–522, DOI: 10.1080/13552074.2017.1379775.

Benya, A. (2016) *Women in Mining: Occupational Culture and Gendered Identities in the Making*, unpublished Doctoral Thesis (Johannesburg: University of the Witwatersrand), http://hdl.handle.net/10539/22425 (accessed on 28 July 2022).

Benya, A. (2015) 'The Invisible Hands: Women in Marikana', *Review of African Political Economy*, 42(146), pp. 545–560, DOI: 10.1080/03056244.2015.1087394.

Bezuidenhout, A. and S. Buhlungu (2015) 'Enclave Rustenburg: Platinum Mining and the Post-Apartheid Social Order', *Review of African Political Economy*, 42(146), pp. 526–444, DOI: 10.1080/03056244.2015.1087395.

Bowman, A. (2018) 'Financialization and the Extractive Industries: the Case of South African Platinum Mining', *Competition and Change*, 22(4), pp. 388–412, DOI: 10.1177/1024529418785611.

Bowman, A. (2016) *Dilemmas of Distribution: Financialisation, Boom and Bust in the Post-Apartheid Platinum Industry*, Society, Work and Development Institute (SWOP) Working Paper 6 (Johannesburg: University of the Witwatersrand), https://media.wix.com/ugd/4e496b_4fbb161f0278440a9bd91716ca27576b.pdf (accessed on 28 July 2022).

Capps, G.J. (2015) 'Labour in the Time of Platinum', *Review of African Political Economy*, 42(146), pp. 497–507, DOI: 10.1080/03056244.2015.1108747.

Capps, G.J. (2010) *Tribal-Landed Property: the Political Economy of the BaFokeng Chieftancy, South Africa, 1837–1994*, Unpublished Dissertation (London: London School of Economics and Political Science), https://ethos.bl.uk/OrderDetails.do?uin=uk.bl.ethos.528664 (accessed on 28 July 2022).

Capps, G.J. and S. Mnwana (2015a) 'Claims from below: Platinum and the Politics of Land in the Bakgatla-ba-Kgafela Traditional Authority Area', *Review of African Political Economy*, 42(146), pp. 606–624, DOI: 10.1080/03056244.2015.1108746.

Capps, G.J and S. Mnwana (2015b) *No chief ever bought a piece of land!' Struggles over property, community and mining in the Bakgatla-ba-Kgafela Traditional Authority Area, North West Province*, Society, Work and Development Institute (SWOP) Working Paper 3 (Johannesburg: University of the Witwatersrand), https://2b912727-9f2a-44dd-9a10-190714b850bf.filesusr.com/ugd/4e496b_a0cb6067c0f545c09d361066dd54f272.pdf (accessed on 13 August 2022).

Clegg, J. (1981) *Towards an Understanding of African Dance: the Zulu Isishameni Style*, Paper Presented at the Second Symposium on Ethnomusicology (Grahamstown: Rhodes University).

Comaroff, J.L. and J. Comaroff (2009) *Ethnicity, Inc.* (Chicago: The University of Chicago Press), http://www.press.uchicago.edu/ucp/books/book/chicago/E/bo6206909.html (accessed on 28 July 2022).

Donham, D.L. (2011) *Violence in a Time of Liberation: Murder and Ethnicity at a South African Gold Mine, 1994* (Durham, NC: Duke University Press).

Dunbar Moodie, T. (2016) 'Making Mincemeat out of Mutton-Eaters: Social Origins of the NUM Decline on Platinum', *Journal of Southern African Studies*, 42(5), pp. 841–856, DOI: 10.1080/03057070.2016.1209846.

Dunbar Moodie, T. (1986) 'The Moral Economy of the Black Miners' Strike of 1946', *Journal of Southern African Studies*, 13(1), pp. 1–35, http://www.jstor.org/stable/2636674 (accessed on 28 July 2022).

Dunbar Moodie, T. and V. Ndatshe (1994) *Going for Gold: Men, Mines, and Migration* (Berkeley: University of California Press).

Enloe, C. (2011) 'The Mundane Matters', *International Political Sociology*, 5(4), pp. 447–450, DOI: 10.1111/j.1749-5687.2011.00145_2.x.

Ferguson, J. (1990) *The Anti-Politics Machine: "Development," Depoliticization, and Bureaucratic Power in Lesotho* (Cambridge: Cambridge University Press).

Filer, C. and P.Y. Le Meur (eds.) (2017) *Large-Scale Mines and Local-Level Politics: between New Caledonia and Papua New Guinea* (Canberra: Australian National University Press).

Forrest, K. (2015) 'Rustenburg's Labour Recruitment Regime: Shifts and New Meanings', *Review of African Political Economy*, 42(146), pp. 508–525, DOI: 10.1080/03056244.2015.1085850.

Fraser, N. (2017) '7. Behind Marx's Hidden Abode: for an Expanded Conception of Capitalism', in P. Deutscher and C. Lafont (eds.) *Critical Theory in Critical Times: Transforming the Global Political and Economic Order* (New York: Columbia University Press), pp. 141–159, DOI: 10.7312/deut18150-009.

Gluckman, M. (1940) 'Analysis of a Social Situation in Modern Zululand', *Bantu Studies*, 14(1), pp. 1–30, DOI: 10.1080/02561751.1940.9676107.

Gordon, R.J. (1977) *Mines, Masters and Migrants: Life in a Namibian Mine Compound* (Johannesburg: Ravan Press).

Hanisch, C. (1970) 'The Personal Is Political', in S. Firestone and A. Koedt (eds.) *Notes from the Second Year: Women's Liberation* (New York: Women's Liberation Movement Print Culture), pp. 76–79.

Harries, P. (1994) *Work, Culture, and Identity: Migrant Laborers in Mozambique and South Africa, C.1860–1910* (New York: Pearson Education).

Harries, P. (1990) 'Symbols and Sexuality: Culture and Identity on the Early Witwatersrand Gold Mines[1]', *Gender and History*, 2(3), pp. 318–336, DOI: 10.1111/j.1468-0424.1990.tb00103.x.

Hickel, J. (2015) *Democracy as Death: the Moral Order of Anti-Liberal Politics in South Africa* (Oakland: University of California Press).

James, D. (1999) 'Bagagešu (Those of My Home): Women Migrants, Ethnicity, and Performance in South Africa', *American Ethnologist*, 26(1), pp. 69–89, DOI: 10.1525/ae.1999.26.1.69.

Kirsch, S. (2001) 'Property Effects. Social Networks and Compensation Claims in Melanesia', *Social Anthropology*, 9(2), pp. 147–163, DOI: 10.1111/j.1469-8676.2001.tb00143.x.

Koczberski, G. and G.N. Curry (2004) 'Divided Communities and Contested Landscapes: Mobility, Development and Shifting Identities in Migrant Destination Sites in Papua New Guinea', *Asia Pacific Viewpoint*, 45(3), pp. 357–371, DOI: 10.1111/j.1467-8373.2004.00252.x.

Lahiri-Dutt, K. (2016) 'The Diverse Worlds of Coal in India: Energising the Nation, Energising Livelihoods', *Energy Policy*, 99, pp. 203–213, DOI: 10.1016/j.enpol.2016.05.045.

Li, T.M. (2017) 'After Development: Surplus Population and the Politics of Entitlement', *Development and Change*, 48(6), pp. 1247–1261, DOI: 10.1111/dech.12344.

Mahoney, M.R. (2012) *The Other Zulus: the Spread of Zulu Ethnicity in Colonial South Africa* (Durham: Duke University Press).

Makhulu, A.M. (2015) *Making Freedom: Apartheid, Squatter Politics, and the Struggle for Home* (Durham: Duke University Press).

Manson, A. and B.K. Mbenga (2012) 'Bophuthatswana and the North-West Province: from Pan-Tswanaism to Mineral-Based Ethnic Assertiveness', *South African Historical Journal*, 64(1), pp. 96–116, DOI: 10.1080/02582473.2012.648767.

Mezzadra, S. and B. Neilson (2019) *The Politics of Operations: Excavating Contemporary Capitalism* (Durham: Duke University Press).

Mnwana, S. (2015) 'Between 'Locals' and 'Foreigners': Mining and Rural Politics of Belonging in North West Province, South Africa', *Labour, Capital and Society / Travail, Capital et Société*, 48(1&2), pp. 158–181, https://www.jstor.org/stable/26476422 (accessed on 7 August 2022).

Mnwana, S. and A. Bowman (2022) 'Land, Conflict and Radical Distributive Claims in South Africa's Rural Mining Frontier', *The Extractive Industries and Society*, 11, DOI: 10.1016/j.exis.2021.100972.

Mujere, J. (2020) 'Unemployment, Service Delivery and Practices of Waiting in South Africa's Informal Settlements', *Critical African Studies*, 12(1), pp. 65–78, DOI: 10.1080/21681392.2019.1697312.

Mujere, J. (2015) 'Insurgent Citizenship and Patterns of Authority in Mining Affected Areas: Understanding Community Protests in Rustenburg, South Africa', *Labour, Capital and Society / Travail, Capital et Société*, 48(1&2), pp. 240–266, https://www.jstor.org/stable/26476425 (accessed on 7 August 2022).

Naicker, C. (2017) 'The Missing Women of Marikana', https://aidc.org.za/missing-women-marikana/ (accessed on 7 August 2022).

Rajak, D. (2016) 'Hope and Betrayal on the Platinum Belt: Responsibility, Violence and Corporate Power in South Africa', *Journal of Southern African Studies*, 42(5), pp. 929–946, DOI: 10.1080/03057070.2016.1207876.

Rajak, D. (2012) 'Platinum City and the New South African Dream', *Africa*, 82(2), pp. 252–271, DOI: 10.1017/S0001972012000046.

Sinwell, L. and S. Mbatha (2016) *The Spirit of Marikana: the Rise of Insurgent Trade Unionism in South Africa* (London: Pluto Press).

Stewart, P. (2015) 'Accelerated Mechanisation and the Demise of a Mass-Based Labour Force? Platinum Mines in South Africa', *Review of African Political Economy*, 42(146), pp. 633–642, DOI: 10.1080/03056244.2015.1087397.

Thompson, E.P. (1971) 'The Moral Economy of the English Crowd in the Eighteenth Century', *Past and Present*, 50, pp. 76–136, http://www.jstor.org/stable/650244 (accessed on 28 July 2022).

Tsing, A.L. (2005) *Friction: an Ethnography of Global Connection* (Princeton: Princeton University Press).

Van Onselen, C. (1976) *Chibaro: African Mine Labour in Southern Rhodesia, 1900–1933* (London: Pluto Press).

CHAPTER 3

Chromite Mining Cooperatives, Tribute Mining Contracts, and Rural Livelihoods in Zimbabwe, 1985–2021

Joseph Mujere

Abstract

Transnational corporations dominated chromite mining in Zimbabwe for the entire colonial period. However, the postcolonial period witnessed a gradual but significant shift toward small-scale and artisanal mining as liberalisation led to the informalisation of the mining sector. This chapter examines the impulses in the transformation of the chromite mining sector in the postcolonial period and the rise and development of chromite mining cooperatives since the 1980s. In particular, it analyses the impact of tribute mining arrangements on the emergence and growth of chromite mining cooperatives in Zimbabwe. The chapter argues that while tribute mining arrangements engendered the development and growth of mining cooperatives, the contracts also created an asymmetrical and exploitative relationship between cooperatives and large-scale mining companies that owned mining claims that they sublet to cooperatives. The chapter also considers the effects of Zimbabwe's redistributive land reform programme and Chinese participation in artisanal and small-scale mining on mining cooperatives. Overall, the chapter analyses the effects of the liberalisation of the mining sector in Zimbabwe and the centrality of mining cooperatives in the interface between large- and small-scale chromite mining.

1 Introduction

In August 2017, the Confederation of Zimbabwe Small-Scale Chrome Miners (CZSSCM) submitted a position paper to the Ministry of Mines and Mining Development detailing the challenges its members were facing. These challenges included constant conflicts between small-scale chromite miners and large-scale mining companies over ore prices and the fact that about 90 per cent of small-scale chromite miners continue to operate under tribute mining contracts entered into with large-scale mining companies who own the claims (Mhaka, 2018). Such challenges, however, were not new. The sector had faced

 | DOI:10.1163/9789004685994_004

myriad challenges since 1985 when the Zimbabwean government forced the large-scale chromite mining companies to cede some of their mining claims to mining cooperatives under tribute mining arrangements. Tribute mining arrangements and similar contracts continued to dominate small-scale and artisanal chromite mining in Zimbabwe with mining cooperatives being the dominant tributors.

This chapter uses chromite mining cooperatives as a lens through which to examine the effects of the liberalisation of mineral resource extraction in postcolonial Africa and the resultant contentious relationship between large-scale mining companies, on one hand, and small-scale and artisanal miners on the other. The liberalisation of the chromite mining sector in Zimbabwe soon after the attainment of independence in 1980 was largely informed by the newly installed government's desire to use the cooperative movement in the mining sector to foster social and economic development. The chapter considers how the liberalisation of the chromite mining sector contributed to the broadening of rural livelihoods and the alleviation of poverty. In addition, it uses the case of mining cooperatives to examine the interface between large-scale operations, on one hand, and small-scale and artisanal mining on the other. In particular, the chapter focuses on the tribute mining contracts concluded between mining cooperatives and the large-scale chromite mining companies Zimalloys (formerly a subsidiary of Anglo American Corporation) and Zimasco (formerly a subsidiary of Union Carbide). Finally, the chapter discusses the effects of Zimbabwe's Fast Track Land Reform Programme on artisanal mining as well as how it opened space for the participation of Chinese companies in small-scale and artisanal chromite mining. The chapter argues that although the asymmetrical relations between large- and small-scale mining have continued to afflict the latter, the interface between the two and the development of mining cooperatives have contributed to this broadening of rural livelihoods and the alleviation of poverty.

The chapter places developments in Zimbabwe's artisanal and small-scale chromite mining sector within the broader context of debates about mining cooperatives, rural livelihoods and the liberalisation of resource extraction (Banda and Chanda, 2021; De Haan and Geenen, 2016; Francescone, 2015; Hilson, Hilson and Adu-Darko, 2014; Wanyama, Develtere and Pollet, 2009). It also engages with extant literature on the interface between large- and small-scale mining (Aubynn, 2009; Kemp and Owen, 2019; Verbrugge, 2017). It draws on Kemp and Owen's (2019) deployment of the term 'interface' to characterise the interactions between large- and small-scale mining. In some cases, scholars have distinguished this interaction as characterised by 'grievance and conflict' (Carstens and Hilson, 2009), 'coexistence' (Hilson, Sauerwein and Owen,

2020), or a 'marriage of convenience' (Aubynn, 2009). However, while Kemp and Owen (2019) approach this interface from the vantage point of large-scale mining companies, the present chapter makes use of insights and experiences of members of mining cooperatives and individual artisanal miners to understand how small-scale and artisanal miners have either benefited from or been negatively affected by this relationship. The chapter thus uses the case of chromite mining cooperatives to gain a nuanced understanding of the entanglement of large- and small-scale mining in postcolonial Africa and of the extent to which this has resulted in the broadening of rural livelihoods and the alleviation of poverty.

The chapter is based on ethnographic research conducted in Mapanzure communal areas between 2019 and 2021. Oral interviews were conducted with traditional authorities, members of mining cooperatives, groups of artisanal miners, and some individuals working for Chinese companies. The majority of informants were interviewed more than once. In addition, several informants provided documents such as tribute contracts, records of their ore deliveries, constitutions of their cooperatives, and receipts. These documents proved very useful to an understanding of the nature of relationships between the large-scale mining companies and the mining cooperatives and of the importance of small-scale and artisanal mining as not just a rural livelihood option but one of the key rural livelihoods. The chapter also makes use of Zimbabwe Mining Development Corporation (ZMDC) Annual Reports, Secretary of Mines Annual Reports, newspaper reports, parliamentary debates, and parliamentary portfolio committee reports as well as tribute mining agreements. Apart from providing general information on small-scale mining, the ZMDC Annual Reports were particularly useful in providing annual statistics on the number of chromite mining cooperatives and their contribution to annual chromite production.

2 Liberalisation, Informalisation, and the Rise of Chromite Mining Cooperatives

There is extant literature on mining cooperatives in the global South, especially on their potential to foster social and economic development and alleviate poverty (Banda and Chanda, 2021; de Haan and Geenen, 2016; Francescone, 2015; Wanyama, Develtere and Pollet, 2009; de Haan and Geenen, 2015). According to Wanyama, Develtere and Pollet (2009, 362), 'cooperative development in Africa can generally be said to have traversed two main eras: the era of state control and that of liberalisation. The first era that lasted up to the early 1990s saw the origin and substantial growth of cooperatives on the continent under state direction'. This phase was followed by an era of liberalisation in which African governments adopted structural adjustment programmes on the advice of the International Monetary Fund (IMF) and World Bank. In these new, liberalised economic conditions, cooperatives 'were restructured and disentangled from the state so as to be run on business principles in line with the then evolving market economy' (Wanyama, Develtere and Pollet, 2009, 363). This was premised on the argument that state control stifled the development of the cooperatives.

It is important to highlight that scholarship on the interaction between large- and small-scale mining has largely focussed on the acrimonious relationship between the two. This has largely been a result of the framing of artisanal and small-scale miners as 'illegal' or as operating clandestinely (Bolay, 2014; Katz-Lavigne, 2020; Hilson and Potter, 2005). However, while the majority of artisanal and small-scale mining is informal and clandestine, mining cooperatives in several countries have tended to establish formal relationships with large-scale mining companies to gain access to mine claims and to the market (Banda and Chanda, 2021; de Haan and Geenen, 2016; Francescone, 2015). As will be demonstrated below, chromite mining cooperatives entered into mining contracts with transnational corporations (TNCs) that owned mining claims and had a monopoly in the market.

When Zimbabwe gained its independence from colonial rule in 1980, chromite mining was dominated by two large-scale mining companies: Anglo American Corporation (later Zimalloys) and Union Carbide (later Zimasco). However, as the companies struggled to deal with the slump in global base metals prices they were forced to scale down operations and retrench[1] surplus labour. Mining companies also argued that the low prices of chromite on the international market meant that they could not pay minimum wages without such retrenchment. This created an impasse between the government and TNCs as the government could not allow the companies to retrench workers without being seen as having abandoned its socialist experiment.

In addition to its reluctance to allow chromite mining companies to retrench workers, the newly installed Zimbabwean government outlawed the colonial contract labour system that was colloquially referred to as '*madobadoba*' in its bid to dismantle the colonial labour system. Under this contract mining labour system, 'workers would produce chrome ore individually, on a contract basis, and then sell the ore to the mining companies at largely the buyers' prices'

1 *Retrench* in the sense of make redundant.

(Chiwawa, 1990, 19). The government's move to reform labour relations by banning the contract labour system had, however, the unintended consequence of swelling the ranks of the unemployed.

In 1985, after a series of consultative meetings between the government, mining companies, workers' unions, the Chamber of Mines, and ZMDC, among other interested parties, it was finally resolved that mining companies could phase out the contract labour system and could retrench their workers under specific conditions agreed with the government. The most enduring legacy of this compromise between mining capital and the government was the condition that retrenched workers and former contract workers would be assisted by the government through ZMDC to establish and run mining cooperatives to mine on claims owned by the companies (Ministry of Information, 1985). Established through an Act of Parliament in 1982 (ZMDC Act No. 31 of 1982), ZMDC's mandate included fostering mining development projects, investing in mining on behalf of the government, and assisting in the establishment of mining cooperatives as well as providing them with technical assistance (Maponga, 1993, 16; Chiwawa, 1990, 21). Furthermore, ZMDC assisted mining cooperatives in acquiring mining equipment and training, and with regard to logistics and accessing loans (Chiwawa, 1990, 20). According to Ndakaripa (2017, 105), ZMDC was also supposed to ensure 'equitable distribution of wealth and increased local participation in the economy'.

Mining cooperatives, whose membership was supposed to be not fewer than ten individuals, were expected to work on a self-help basis, to pool their resources, and share the proceeds of their work. Writing about the organisation of artisanal gold miners and the importance of working as syndicates and cooperatives, Mkodzongi and Spiegel (2019, 2155) assert that 'working as a team enables the cooperative to tap and leverage on the varied skills and experiences of the miners to enhance their success. These skills range from administrative skills in organising and executing work and negotiating with "sponsors" and buyers to technical skills such as surveying and prospecting'. This also informed the organisation of chromite cooperatives, which usually require members with skills in geology, blasting, and accounting, as well as individuals with legal knowledge.

The majority of chromite mining cooperatives mined under contract from the two large-scale chromite mining companies, Zimasco and Zimalloys. Cooperatives would enter into tribute mining contracts under which they would be allocated claims to mine under contract. Tribute mining contracts have been at the core of small-scale and artisanal chromite mining in Zimbabwe since 1985 when Zimalloys and Zimasco agreed to lease some of their mine claims as well as loss-making mines to chromite mining cooperatives

(Chiwawa, 1990; Maponga and Ruzive, 2002). In tribute mining arrangements, 'tributors or cooperatives work on claims as though they were their own for a fee. Tributors also legally sublet claims to sub-tributors under similar arrangements'. (Maponga and Ruzive, 2002, 117). In addition, tributors were expected to pay a 5 per cent royalty and to sell their chromite to the grantor (claim holder) at prices determined by the latter, and also had the responsibility to rehabilitate he environment by filling the open pits and revegetating the environment (Maponga and Ruzive, 2002, 117). Furthermore, grantors determined the quality of the ore and the prices. It is also important to note that tributors were expected to work based on set monthly chromite production targets determined by the grantor. A consistent failure to meet the tonnage and ore quality targets could lead to the agreement being terminated. On their part, grantors sublet their claims, provide equipment and technical assistance, and purchase the ore.

Tribute mining contracts thus created an asymmetrical relationship between grantors (large-scale chromite mining companies that owned claims and bought the ore), on one side, and individual contractors and cooperatives mining under tribute arrangements, on the other. Despite this, however, in some instances tributors violated the terms of the tribute mining contracts by failing to meet set production targets, delivering poor quality ore, selling their ore to other merchants, or failing to rehabilitate he environment after mining, among other contractual breaches. The punishment for such violations is usually the termination of the contract.

Although large-scale mining companies ordinarily leased out some of their claims to individual tributors, it was not uncommon for a company to allow a cooperative to take over an entire loss-making mine. As has been observed by Chiwawa (1990, 21),

> Zimalloys let all of their Vanad Mine be taken over by five cooperatives, all of their Sutton Mine by another five cooperatives, all but Four Seam of their Caesar Mine by the cooperatives. This means that 13 of their total 15 tributing cooperatives (901 workers) took over existing (loss-making) mining operations.

Thus, alongside assisting their retrenched workers who were establishing mining cooperatives, large-scale mining companies were also using tribute mining arrangements to dispose of their loss-making mines. As Francescone (2015) observed in the case of mining cooperatives in Bolivia, once production becomes less profitable, large-scale mining companies lease out some of their claims to cooperatives whilst maintaining their control over marketing.

Consequently, cooperatives seldom have autonomy with regard to large-scale mining companies.

It is interesting to note that when ZMDC was established in 1982, Ingezi Chrome Mining Cooperative was the only registered cooperative in the country mining chromite. However, the number of registered chromite mining cooperatives rapidly increased after 1985. Among the factors that contributed to this rapid increase in and growth of chromite mining cooperatives are the tribute mining arrangements extended to cooperatives by large-scale chromite mining companies, abundant chromite deposits, and the availability of markets in the form of ferrochrome smelters operated by Zimalloys and Zimasco (ZMDC, 1985). ZMDC also contributed to this phenomenal growth in mining cooperatives by assisting several retrenched former mineworkers to establish and register cooperatives. In its 1986 Annual Report, ZMDC described how it had assisted 1,200 retrenched mineworkers and former contract workers to establish and run chromite mining cooperatives in the North Dyke (ZMDC, 1986, 15). The majority of members of chromite mining cooperatives in the 1980s were thus former mineworkers who had some mining experience.

In addition to helping former mineworkers to establish mining cooperatives, ZMDC also provided cooperatives with technical assistance in accessing mine claims, mining, and finding a market for their ore. ZMDC also deployed resident advisors to provide technical assistance for cooperatives seeking blasting licenses (ZMDC, 1990, 12). The government, meanwhile, provided mining cooperatives with loan facilities to help them set up their operations. In 1990, for instance, the Secretary of Mines reported that 'small-scale mines continued to receive financial assistance in terms of loans to develop mines, to establish beneficiation[2] plants, to connect power and water, and diamond-drilling services on a simple hire basis' (The Secretary of Mines 1990, 7).

Chromite mining cooperatives continued to dominate the mining cooperatives landscape in terms of their numbers and production throughout the 1980s and 1990s. In 1986 for example, out of the 38 registered mining cooperatives 23 were mining chromite, while in 1988 this number was 28 out of 44 (ZMDC, 1986; ZMDC, 1988; ZMDC, 1990). Apart from their sheer numbers, the annual chromite production of cooperatives bore testimony to their success and to how they were alleviating poverty among their members. Cooperatives continued to increase in number and contribution to the annual chromite production.

2 *Beneficiation*: the treatment of a raw material to improve its properties.

The upward trajectory in chromite production among cooperatives continued in the 1990s. For instance, between 1993 and 1999 chromite mining cooperatives and other tributors contributed an average of 55 per cent of the total production output per year (Maponga and Ruzive, 2002, 117). One of the drivers of this increase in the number of chromite cooperatives and of the upward trajectory of their contribution to annual production in the 1990s was the massive retrenchment associated with the structural adjustment programme. In several African countries that implemented such programmes, retrenched workers were forced to find new forms of livelihood, and sometimes this meant artisanal mining (Weng et al., 2015, 65). In Zimbabwe, for instance, retrenched workers filled the ranks of mining cooperatives with chromite cooperatives attracting the highest number of retrenched mine workers. As a result of this success, chromite mining cooperatives were seen as epitomising the cooperative movement's success story. And due to this success, by 1987 ZMDC had begun to encourage the establishment and registration of mining cooperatives 'to undertake the mining [of] minerals other than chrome' (ZMDC, 1987, 25).

Although small-scale chromite mining in Zimbabwe has been viewed as a success story, especially given the flourishing of chromite mining cooperatives, the sector also faced several challenges. Most stemmed from the tribute mining contracts that the cooperatives entered into with the large-scale mining companies Zimasco and Zimalloys. Chiwawa (1990, 4) identifies a 'lack of autonomy' and 'excessive technological dependency' as the key factors contributing to the vulnerability of chromite mining cooperatives.

Even though ZMDC was mandated to bargain for prices on behalf of cooperatives, prices were largely determined by the grantor (large-scale mining companies that owned the claims). In addition, penalties were imposed on tributors for subletting claims without the consent of the grantor, and for failure to meet the agreed monthly production targets, oversupply of ore, and failure to meet the specified quality of ore, among other conditions. An extract from one tribute agreement reveals a clause stating that 'the company also retains the right to terminate this contract if the supplier fails to supply the agreed tonnage and ore quality as set out in this agreement for a period of two or more consecutive months in any calendar year' (Kushanduka Mining Syndicate, 2011). Moreover, tributors were supposed to pay a 5 per cent royalty to the grantor, calculated based on the ore delivered. In some instances, the grantor would provide fuel, personal protective equipment, and machinery at set prices, and recover the costs of these from the amount due to the tributor after the delivery of the ore.

Despite the intermediary role played by ZMDC, tribute agreements between chromite mining cooperatives and grantors were largely skewed in favour of the latter and created an asymmetrical relationship. Tribute mining contracts invariably placed the tributor at the mercy of the grantor, who could reject ore supplied by the tributor or unilaterally terminate the agreement. In addition, a tributor could be punished for supplying *more* than the agreed tonnage, and could be compelled to remove the excess tonnage from the grantor's yard at the tributor's own cost. Most tributors consider the tribute agreements to be exploitative and the production targets they are set by the grantors difficult to meet. In 1990, ZMDC reported that cooperatives had failed to meet their production targets 'due to lack of appropriate mining equipment, transport for delivering mining consumables and spare parts' (ZMDC, 1990, 12). Cooperatives' lack of autonomy and their over-reliance on grantors and ZMDC financial and technical assistance thus affected their ability to meet targets.

Mining cooperatives were also greatly affected by the government's fluctuating chromite mining and export policies. In particular, the government intermittently banned the export of chromite to support local beneficiation. It was in this context that in 2007 the government banned raw chromite exports, citing the need to promote value addition through ferrochrome production. The ban was lifted in 2009, but another was imposed in 2011. The government resumed exports in 2015, only to impose another ban in 2017 (Makichi, 2017). While placing a moratorium on the export of unprocessed ore can potentially promote local beneficiation, export bans negatively affect artisanal and small-scale miners. The 2013 Parliamentary Portfolio Committee Report on Mines and Energy revealed that

> following the ban, small-scale producers were left with no option but to sell to the local smelters who were offering an average price of USD 60 compared to average international prices of between USD 110 and USD 235 prevailing at that time. In the process, this created a standoff between the small-scale producers and the local smelters.
>
> Parliament of Zimbabwe, 2013

3 Chromite Mining Cooperatives and Rural Livelihoods in Mapanzure Communal Areas

In the 1980s and 1990s the majority of chromite mining cooperatives in Zimbabwe operated in the North Dyke, stretching from Lalapanzi to Mutorashanga, very few cooperatives operating in the South Dyke, in areas such as Shurugwi, Zvishavane, and Mberengwa. This was a result of the fact that the North Dyke chromite claims had thin seams that were increasingly becoming less profitable for large-scale mining companies to exploit (Maponga, 1993, 21). However, in the 1990s Zimasco and Zimalloys began to lease out some of their marginal claims in the South Dyke—including in Mapanzure communal areas—to cooperatives and individuals, using the tribute system.

Initially, small-scale chromite mining in Mapanzure was dominated by cooperatives that had been established in the 1980s and had gained a lot of chromite mining experience in the North Dyke. Because of this prior experience, it was these cooperatives that initially entered into tribute agreements with Zimasco and Zimalloys to mine marginal claims in the area. Locals in Mapanzure communal areas remember the Ingezi Chrome Mining Cooperative, the oldest such cooperative, as having been the first to operate in the area. Other cooperatives that engaged in small-scale chromite mining in Mapanzure communal areas during this early period include the Makomborero Mining Cooperative and Tangawaedza Mining Cooperative, which had been established in Lalapanzi and had acquired tribute claims in Mapanzure communal areas.

When the Ingezi Chrome Mining Cooperative started its tribute mining operations in Mapanzure in 1988, the majority of locals showed little interest. Locals looked down on cooperative chromite mining, preferring to engage in artisanal gold mining and farming. This was further exacerbated by the fact that the first cooperatives to operate in the area were composed of non-locals. One research participant narrated that:

> The Ingezi cooperative started its mining activities in Mapanzure around 1988. During this period most of the local people were not interested in artisanal chromite mining. We were mostly farming as we considered chromite mining an activity done by outsiders. Ingezi cooperative started operating in Shauke Ward 3. The cooperative largely employed local labour and constructed compounds for the workers who could not work from home.
>
> Interview with Julia Chatira, Kudyakushanda Cooperative, Mapanzure, 15 December 2019

Gradually, however, locals began to appreciate small-scale chromite mining as they noticed how members of the cooperatives were making a living out of mining and also how they even managed to employ local labour. Local unemployed youths were also attracted by the flashy spending habits of contract workers working for mining contractors such as JR Goddard Contracting (Private) Limited and Madhatter (Private) Limited, which were contracted by Zimasco to mine some of its claims in the Torwood Block in Mapanzure communal areas. These elements encouraged locals to turn to artisanal chromite mining and to establish their own chromite mining cooperatives.

Mining cooperatives and syndicates established by local artisanal and small-scale miners in Mapanzure communal areas thus took inspiration from older chromite mining cooperatives operating in their area. The mining cooperatives and syndicates established in Mapanzure communal areas include the Kudyakushanda Mining Cooperative, Kushanduka Mining Syndicate and Upile Mining Syndicate. These cooperatives and syndicates also entered into tribute agreements with Zimalloys and Zimasco both in Mapanzure communal areas and in other areas such as Shurugwi, Mashava, and Mberengwa. In the following, I examine in some detail the establishment and operation of the Kudyakushanda Mining Collective Cooperative Society, one of the first local mining cooperatives to be established in Mapanzure.

The cooperative was established in 1993 by members of the local community. It began as an informal group of local artisanal chromite miners, who would illegally mine on Zimasco's claims and used registered tributors as middlemen to sell their chromite (group interview, Kudyakushanda Cooperative, 5 December 2019). The membership of the group rapidly grew to over 200, and members decided to formalise their operations by registering a mining cooperative, which they named the Kudyakushanda (meaning to be self-reliant) Mining Collective Cooperative Society. The name encapsulated the cooperative's desire to eke a living out of chromite mining through hard work and self-reliance. Zimasco encouraged the locals to establish cooperatives and enter into tribute arrangements to dissuade them from engaging in illegal artisanal chromite mining activities on its claims. The Kudyakushanda Mining Collective Cooperative Society grew, and became one of the biggest chromite mining cooperatives in Mapanzure communal areas. It also managed to enter into multiple and recurring tribute mining contracts with Zimasco.

The cooperative drafted a constitution, in which its objectives and structure were outlined. The constitution's preamble describes it as a 'grouping of artisanal miners with the common purpose of chrome mining to promote development, building individuals for a competitive, self-reliant and community development as well as alleviate poverty' (Kudyakushanda Mining Collective Cooperative Society Limited, n.d.). The cooperative was therefore set up following the basic principles of cooperative societies, especially the idea of self-reliance and community development.

Like other cooperatives, Kudyakushanda required new members to pay joining fees, and those who left and wished to rejoin were required to pay an agreed rejoining fee. The joining fee for new members was stipulated as the 'equivalent to the prevailing market value of ten tonnes of chrome ore on the date he/she joins the cooperative' (Kudyakushanda Mining Collective Cooperative Society Limited, n.d.). Old members who would have defaulted and applied to rejoin the cooperative were required to pay a joining fee equivalent to the value of five tonnes of ore. The constitution also provided those employed by the cooperative for at least five years with the opportunity to join as full members upon payment of a joining fee equivalent to the market value of five tonnes of chrome. Using the price of USD 50 per tonne, which was the average price of chromite in 2020, prospective members would be required to pay USD 500, which is quite a high figure, especially for people living in communal areas (formerly Tribal Trust Lands). Thus, members of chromite mining cooperatives were expected to be able to raise high joining fees. At the same time, a large proportion of villagers were excluded, as they could not afford such fees. Stories of people who sold livestock to raise money to join cooperatives or to apply for independent chromite claims reveal the potential financial returns from artisanal and small-scale chromite mining.

The members of the Kudyakushanda Mining Collective Cooperative Society had an arrangement that individuals mined portions of the claims leased to the cooperative using family or hired labour. They would combine their ore when transporting to Zimasco after taking note of each individual's tonnage. The cooperative would apportion the proceeds of the sale among the individuals according to individual tonnage. Thus, the cooperative arrangement was largely used to gain access to chromite claims and to enter into tribute arrangements; individuals' shares, meanwhile, were based on individual production.

The conditions of the cooperative's tribute contract with Zimasco include a monthly target of 5,000 tonnes of lumpy chromite and a 10 per cent deduction from chromite deliveries for the rehabilitation of the environment. The cooperative, however, struggled to meet this production target due to a lack of equipment such as excavators and haulage trucks. As the members of the cooperative narrated:

> We were supposed to produce 5,000 tonnes per month but because we were operating without machinery it was difficult for us to raise that amount of ore. [...] with picks and shovels, we were only able to produce slightly above 2,000 tonnes of chromite per month. This was because, during the early days of our cooperative, chromite belts (seams) were found closer to the [...] surface. We could mine from depths of 50 centimetres to around five meters without machinery. With time we began to face many challenges. One of the challenges we faced was delays in receiving our payments from Zimasco. In some cases, it took us more than two months before we received payments on our deliveries. In some cases, we were

> paid far less than we were expecting to receive. Because of this, there have been many conflicts between our cooperative and Zimsaco.
>
> Group Interview, Kudyakushanda Cooperative, 5 December 2019

As a result of constant pressure, Zimasco gradually ceded some of its claims to the government, which allowed sitting tenants to register them as independent claims.

Kudyakushanda was one of the cooperatives in Mapanzure communal areas that benefitted from this arrangement, managing to register several claims in its name. This meant that the cooperative could now operate independently of its former grantor and could sell its chromite to any licensed buyer. In addition, the cooperative was free to enter into mining or equipment rental agreements with Chinese investors without the encumbrance of tribute agreements.

From the narratives of members of cooperatives, it is evident that cooperatives in Mapanzure faced similar challenges to those faced by other mining cooperatives across the country. These include financial challenges, a lack of machinery, technical challenges, and exploitative tribute mining arrangements. Furthermore, cooperatives were also affected by internal squabbles, especially over financial mismanagement and the distribution of profits.

4 Land Reform, Chromite Mining Cooperatives, and Chinese Companies

Zimbabwe's Fast Track Land Reform Programme (FTLRP), which started in 2000, had a far-reaching impact on the rural populace's livelihoods and access to mineral resources. The interface between mining and farming, both rural livelihoods, is nothing new and peasants are known to oscillate between the two (Hilson, 2011; Hilson, 2016; Hilson, Hilson and Adu-Darko, 2014; Pijpers, 2014). The symbiotic relationship between the two means that developments in agriculture can easily affect artisanal mining, and vice versa. According to Pijpers (2014, 34), it is important to go beyond the perception of the relationship between farming and artisanal mining as being one purely based on competition, and to view the two livelihoods as cohabiting. The interconnectedness of the two can be observed in how peasants either seasonally shift between them or engage in both concurrently. The financial flows between the two livelihoods are a further demonstration of this symbiosis.

The FTLRP, with its focus on the redistribution of resources and on indigenisation, provided a new impetus for an upsurge in artisanal and small-scale mining, as villagers took the opportunity to 'invade' claims owned by large-scale mining companies and to illegally extract minerals. As Mkodzongi and Spiegel (2013, 2152) have observed, the land reform 'allowed peasants access to natural resources that were formerly enclosed under the previous agrarian structure'. The upsurge especially affected former white commercial farms that had been occupied by peasants. In addition, the land reform temporarily increased mobility and migration, as artisanal miners migrated to mineral-rich areas (see Mkodzongi and Spiegel, 2020).

As Mkodzongi and Spiegel (2020, 995) have observed, 'one of the major outcomes of FTLRP implemented in 2000 is the way it allowed resettled farmers to use the formerly inaccessible natural resources under a dualistic agrarian structure inherited at independence'. The aforementioned 'invasion' of mining claims owned by large-scale mining companies, encouraged by the land reform, took place without recourse to any legal document, and was referred to locally as *kubhomba* (literally, bombing). Further, it was part of the land invasion fervour led by Liberation War veterans and landless peasants and popularly referred to as *jambanja* (chaos), which gripped the country starting in 2000. *Kubhomba* was therefore the mining-claims-invasion equivalent of *jambanja* in land redistribution, land redistribution and mineral resource redistribution being interconnected processes with similar practices and discourses.

The leader would normally identify a claim and organise a team of artisanal miners to invade it (*kubhomba*), the leader's role being to provide team members with food, and the tools necessary to quickly mine and transport the ore to a safe place. Then the leader would contact a middleman, who would clandestinely buy the ore. These middlemen were usually local entrepreneurs who were already involved in chromite mining or were involved in tribute agreements. Thus, they could easily pass off illegally mined chromite as ore that they had mined at their own claims. Because this practice was illegal, artisanal miners involved in *kubhomba* usually sold their ore to middlemen at very low prices.

The post-2000 period saw the increased involvement of Chinese companies in buying chromite, engaging in contract mining, and hiring out mining equipment. A similar rise in the involvement of the Chinese in artisanal and small-scale mining has been observed in several countries in Africa (Hilson, Hilson, and Adu-Darko, 2014; Spiegel, 2015). The Chinese are introducing new types of mining contracts characterised by verbal agreements as well as introducing heavy mining machinery that contributes to rapid, mining-induced environmental degradation. The upsurge in the number of Chinese companies operating in Zimbabwe was largely a result of the government's response to sanctions imposed by the EU, the United Kingdom, and the United States following violent land redistributions. The government began to follow a new foreign policy, which was dubbed the 'Look East Policy', and under which Asian countries and companies received special treatment and had unfettered access to investment opportunities in the country. This was the context in which Chinese companies, and some Chinese nationals operating as individuals, invested in the chrome mining industry in Zimbabwe, and several of them engaged in equipment rental schemes and contract mining with local artisanal and small-scale miners with access to chromite claims.

The Chinese companies operating in Mapanzure include Bunday, Afrochine, Asia Ferry, and several smaller companies and individuals. Although Chinese investors are widely thought to be exploiting local artisanal miners, the latter—along with cooperatives—are forced to enter into mining and equipment hire agreements because of their own lack of equipment. The most common mining contract between Chinese investors and cooperatives is one in which the Chinese company would provide mining equipment and fuel and mine on behalf of a claim owner. The company would recoup its costs by claiming 80 per cent of the total tonnage, while paying the client 20 per cent of its total value. Generally, cooperatives and other artisanal miners find these agreements to be exploitative, and argue that the claim holder should get a much higher percentage.

The majority of the artisanal miners interviewed for this study reasoned that Chinese companies preferred verbal agreements to written agreements because they could be easily violated. For example, the company could make a verbal agreement with a cooperative that it would buy their ore at USD 50 per tonne before commencing the mining process, and then change the amount to USD 35 per tonne citing contentious reasons such as the poor quality of the ore or fluctuating global chromite prices (interview with Martha Moyo, 10 November 2020). One artisanal miner lamented:

> The Chinese companies are exploiting us. Can you imagine that we own these chromite claims, but in the end we only get 20 per cent of the proceeds from selling the ore while Chinese companies take 80 per cent for just mining? If you refuse to accept that arrangement, they demand five tonnes per hour for hiring their excavator. This is unfair. I wonder what the government is thinking about this exploitation of citizens by Chinese companies.
>
> Interview with John Phiri, 16 November 2020

It can be argued that although cooperatives and some individual chromite miners had been freed from the fetters of tribute mining contracts when they registered claims ceded to the government by both Zimalloys and Zimasco, they still had to deal with Chinese companies and with their equally exploitative verbal mining contracts.

Chinese companies are also accused of not initiating any meaningful corporate social responsibility programmes to help develop the communities in which they are doing business (Parliament of Zimbabwe, 2013). This has caused tensions between the companies and local communities. In 2018, a reporter for *The Standard* newspaper reported on how chromite mining operations damage the infrastructure and environment of Mapanzure communal areas, writing, 'The small-scale miners use heavy-duty equipment to extract chrome with little regard to infrastructures such as roads and schools. On the Zvishavane-Gweru highway, the miners are excavating land only a few metres from the road' (Mhlanga, 2018).

Despite the negative image Chinese companies have in chromite mining communities, some artisanal and small-scale miners see them as playing a positive role and plugging the gap left by TNCs. Cooperatives appreciated that while large-scale chromite mining companies such as Zimasco and Zimalloys only bought high-grade lumpy chromite, Chinese companies bought even low-grade ores and chromite 'fines'.[3] Furthermore, some miners argued that the 80 per cent to 20 per cent ratio chromite ore sharing arrangement with Chinese companies was justifiable based on the depth of the pits. One research participant highlighted that although previously Chinese companies had retained 70 per cent of the delivered chromite ore to cover their mining expenses when they mined on an individual or cooperative's claim, they increased the percentage to 80 per cent because near-surface chromite resources had been depleted and they were now mining at depths of up to 22 metres (interview with Shumirai Sibanda, 22 September 2020). It should also be highlighted that in the absence of government assistance with regard to mining equipment, cooperatives and artisanal miners depend on Chinese companies for that equipment, and for markets for their chrome ore (Chinembiri, 2020).

5 Conclusion

The relationship between large- and small-scale mining is a subject that has animated debates about mining in the global South. This interface has largely been engendered by the liberalisation of the mining sector and the increased informalisation that spawned widespread small-scale and artisanal mining.

3 *Fines* in the sense of small particulate matter.

Several scholars have examined the interaction between large- and small-scale mining, describing it as characterised by 'coexistence', an 'interface', a 'marriage of convenience', an 'asymmetrical relationship', or in some cases 'conflict' (Aubynn, 2009) or 'coexistence' (Hilson, Sauerwein and Owen, 2020). However, whilst the entanglement of large- and small-scale mining has often led to conflicts, especially given the hegemony of large-scale mining companies, it has also resulted in the broadening of rural livelihoods, and an alleviation of poverty brought about through artisanal and small-scale mining. This resonates with Verbrugge's (2017, 352) assertion that 'partnerships between mining companies and ASM-operators [artisanal and small-scale miners] may be a panacea to the conflicts between large- and small-scale mining'. Mining cooperatives, in particular, have demonstrated the potential of such partnerships to create opportunities for the alleviation of poverty in rural communities.

This chapter has demonstrated both how mining cooperatives encapsulate the relationship between large- and small-scale mining in Zimbabwe and such cooperatives' potential for creating rural livelihoods and alleviating poverty. Mining cooperatives have dominated artisanal and small-scale chromite mining in Zimbabwe since the early 1980s, when the government put pressure on the TNCs who controlled the chromite mining industry to lease out some of their claims to such cooperatives. Chromite mining cooperatives in particular were generally viewed as a success story because they were the most prevalent type in the mining sector and also because they contributed significantly to annual chromite production figures and offered a viable livelihood option to peasants. These cooperatives largely relied on tribute mining arrangements with Zimalloys and Zimasco, the two TNCs that dominated the chromite mining sector. The forgoing discussion has also revealed the interface between mining cooperatives, large-scale chromite mining companies, the Ministry of Mines and Energy, and various government departments.

The chapter has also examined how the Fast Track Land Reform Programme and its discourse and practice of redistribution have impacted artisanal and small-scale chromite mining by generating new discourses of resource redistribution and the dismantlement of the monopoly that large-scale mining companies (mostly TNCs) held over mineral resource extraction and marketing. Chromite mining cooperatives took advantage of the land reform to get access to chromite claims and to unshackle themselves from tribute mining arrangements. The period also witnessed the increased involvement of Chinese companies and middlemen in artisanal and small-scale chromite mining. The relationship between Chinese companies and chromite mining cooperatives is particularly interesting in that while it led to increased production and provided a large number of peasants with an opportunity to eke out a living through chromite mining, it also involved the exploitation of artisanal miners by Chinese mining companies and such companies' contribution to environmental degradation. This last point brings into focus the challenges that come with the participation of Chinese mining companies in artisanal and small-scale mining (see Hilson, Hilson and Adu-Darko, 2014). These include rapid environmental degradation caused by the increased use of heavy mining machinery, encroachment into farmlands, and exploitation of local artisanal miners and cooperatives by Chinese companies that buy ore and engage in contract mining.

References

Aubynn, A. (2009) 'Sustainable solution or marriage of inconvenience? the coexistence of large-scale mining and artisanal and small-scale mining on the Abosso Goldfields concession in Western Ghana', *Resources Policy*, 34(1–2), pp. 64–70, DOI: 10.1016/j.resourpol.2008.04.002.

Banda, W. and E.K. Chanda (2021) 'A proposed cooperatives strategy for artisanal and small-scale gold mining sector in Zambia', *Resources Policy*, 70, pp. 1–17, DOI: 10.1016/j.resourpol.2020.101909.

Bolay, M. (2014) 'When miners become "foreigners": Competing categorizations within gold mining spaces in Guinea', *Resources Policy*, 40(1), pp. 117–127, DOI: 10.1016/j.resourpol.2014.02.001.

Carstens, J. and G. Hilson (2009) 'Mining, grievance and conflict in rural Tanzania', *International Development Planning Review*, 31(3), pp. 301–326, DOI: 10.3828/idpr.31.3.5.

Chinembiri, V. (2020) 'Tensions flare between Zimbabwe miners and Chinese investors', *Global Press Journal*, 23 August, https://globalpressjournal.com/africa/zimbabwe/tensions-flare-zimbabwe-chrome-miners-chinese-investors/ (accessed on 22 June 2022).

Chiwawa, H. (1990) *Co-operatives and Contract Mining in the Zimbabwean Chrome Mining Industry: the Paradox of Industrial Democracy*, IDS Monograph Series no. 1 (Harare: Zimbabwe Institute of Development Studies), pp. 1–65.

Francescone, K. (2015) 'Cooperative miners and the politics of abandonment in Bolivia', *The Extractive Industries and Society*, 2(4), pp. 746–755, DOI: 10.1016/j.exis.2015.10.004.

de Haan, J. and S. Geenen (2015) *Mining Cooperatives in South Kivu: Saviour or Extortionist?* IOB Analyses and Policy Briefs, 14 (Antwerp: Universiteit Antwerpen, Institute of Development Policy).

de Haan, J. and S. Geenen (2016) 'Mining cooperatives in Eastern DRC: the interplay between historical power relations and formal institutions', *The Extractive Industries and Society*, 3(3), pp. 823–831, DOI: 10.1016/j.exis.2016.05.003.

Hilson, G. (2016) 'Farming, small-scale mining and rural livelihoods in Sub-Saharan Africa: a critical overview', *The Extractive Industries and Society*, 3(2), pp. 547–563, DOI: 10.1016/j.exis.2016.02.003.

Hilson, G. (2011) 'Artisanal mining, smallholder farming and livelihood diversification in rural Sub-Saharan Africa: an introduction', *Journal of International Development*, 23(8), pp. 1031–1041, DOI: 10.1002/jid.1829.

Hilson, G. and C. Potter (2005) 'Structural adjustment and subsistence industry: artisanal gold mining in Ghana', *Development and Change*, 36(1), pp. 103–131, DOI: 10.1111/j.0012-155X.2005.00404.x.

Hilson, G., A. Hilson and E. Adu-Darko (2014) 'Chinese participation in Ghana's informal gold mining economy: Drivers, implications and clarifications', *Journal of Rural Studies*, 34, pp. 292–303, DOI: 10.1016/J.JRURSTUD.2014.03.001.

Hilson, G., T. Sauerwein, and J. Owen (2020) 'Large and artisanal scale mine development: the case for autonomous co-existence', *World Development*, 130, pp. 1–19, DOI: 10.1016/j.worlddev.2020.104919.

Katz-Lavigne, S. (2020) 'Distributional impact of corporate extraction and (un)authorised clandestine mining at and around large-scale copper- and cobalt-mining sites in DR Congo', *Resources Policy*, 65, pp. 19, DOI: 10.1016/j.resourpol.2020.101584.

Kemp, D. and J.R. Owen (2019) 'Characterising the interface between large and small-scale mining', *The Extractive Industries and Society*, 6(4), pp. 1091–1100, DOI: 10.1016/j.exis.2019.07.002.

Kudyakushanda Mining Collective Cooperative Society Limited (n.d.) *Constitution* (Cooperative Secretary).

Kushanduka Mining Syndicate (2011) *Tribute Mining Agreement with Zimasco Private Limited* (Syndicate Secretary).

Makichi, T. (2017) *Ban on chrome ore exports welcome but*, The Herald, 14 February, https://www.herald.co.zw/ban-on-chrome-ore-exports-welcome-but/ (accessed on 20 June 2022).

Maponga, O. (1993) 'Small-Scale Mining Operations in Zimbabwe', *International Development Research Centre* (Zimbabwe: Institute of Mining Research, University of Zimbabwe).

Maponga, O. and B. Ruzive (2002) 'Tribute chromite mining and environmental management on the northern great dyke of Zimbabwe', *Natural Resources Forum*, 26(2), pp. 113–126, DOI: 10.1111/1477-8947.00012.

Mhaka, G (2018) *Government should address challenges bedeviling small-scale chrome miners*, Chronicle, 29 May, https://www.chronicle.co.zw/government-should-address-challenges-bedeviling-small-scale-chrome-miners/ (accessed on 14 November 2022).

Mhlanga, B. (2018) *The Midlands chrome curse: Miners leave trail of destruction*, The Standard, 18 November, https://thestandard.newsday.co.zw/2018/11/18/midlands-chrome-curse-miners-leave-trail-destruction/ (accessed on 22 June 2022).

Ministry of Information (1985) *Press Statement: Government to Sustain Mining viability says Sanyangare*, 21 May (Harare: Government of Zimbabwe).

Mkodzongi, G. and S. Spiegel (2019) 'Artisanal gold mining and farming: Livelihood linkages and labour dynamics after land reforms in Zimbabwe', *The Journal of Development Studies*, 55(10), pp. 2145–2161, DOI: 10.1080/00220388.2018.1516867.

Mkodzongi, G. and S.J. Spiegel (2020) 'Mobility, temporary migration and changing livelihoods in Zimbabwe's artisanal mining sector', *The Extractive Industries and Society*, 7(3), pp. 994–1001, DOI: 10.1016/j.exis.2020.05.001.

Ndakaripa, M. (2017) *Sate, Civil Society and the Politics of Economic Indigenisation in Zimbabwe, 1980–2016*, Unpublished PhD Thesis (South Africa: University of the Free State).

Parliament of Zimbabwe (2013) 'Portfolio committee on mines and energy report on chrome mining sector in Zimbabwe 2013', http://www.veritaszim.net/node/1634 (accessed on 12 December 2021).

Pijpers, R. (2014) 'Crops and carats: Exploring the interconnectedness of mining and agriculture in Sub-Saharan Africa', *Futures*, 62(A), pp. 32–39, DOI: 10.1016/j.futures.2014.01.012.

Secretary of Mines (1990) *Annual Report* (Harare: Zimbabwe).

Spiegel, S.J. (2015) 'Shifting formalization policies and recentralizing power: the case of zimbabwe's artisanal gold mining sector', *Society and Natural Resources*, 28(5), pp. 543–558, DOI: 10.1080/08941920.2015.1014606.

Verbrugge, B (2017) 'Towards a negotiated solution to conflicts between large-scale and small-scale miners? the Acupan contract mining project in the Philippines', *The Extractive Industries and Society*, 4(2), pp.352–360, DOI: 10.1016/j.exis.2016.10.011.

Wanyama, F.O., P. Develtere and I. Pollet (2009) 'Reinventing the wheel? African cooperatives in a liberalized economic environment', *Annals of Public and Cooperative Economics*, 80(3), pp. 361–392, DOI: 10.1111/j.1467-8292.2009.00390.x.

Weng, L., D. Endamana, A.K. Boedhihartono, P. Levang, C.R. Margules and J.A. Sayer (2015) 'Asian investment at artisanal and small-scale mines in rural Cameroon', *The Extractive Industries and Society*, 2(1), pp. 64–72, DOI: 10.1016/j.exis.2014.07.011.

ZMDC (Zimbabwe Mining Development Corporation) (1990) *Annual Report* (Harare: ZMDC).

ZMDC (1988) *Annual Report* (Harare: ZMDC).

ZMDC (1987) *Annual Report* (Harare: ZMDC).

ZMDC (1986) *Annual Report* (Harare: ZMDC).

ZMDC (1985) *Annual Report* (Harare: ZMDC).

CHAPTER 4

'Le fléau de la soude caustique': Bauxite Refining, Social Reproduction, and the Role of Women's Promotion Groups

Luisa Lupo

Abstract

This chapter examines the entanglements between two seemingly separate economies, women's promotion groups—grassroots arrangements bringing together self-employed women around shared activities to sustain their livelihoods—and bauxite refining. It starts by following the circulation of caustic soda, a chemical agent harmful to humans and used in soap making, fabric dyeing and aluminium production from bauxite, in and around the refinery of one of the leading aluminium companies in the world. The main argument is that diverse economies such as these women's groups are significantly shaped by and sustain the bauxite industry, with which they are in mutual constitution and tension. Drawing on original interviews with members of these groups, civil society, and government representatives in Guinea, the analysis demonstrates that the bauxite industry directly sustains women's promotion groups, both through the smuggling of caustic soda by factory guards and through corporate social responsibility initiatives. In turn, the groups subsidise extractive operations in times of crisis and factory closure, with many women becoming the sole income earners in their families and bearing the double burden of production and social reproduction. At the same time, women's groups elude extractivist logics; they represent a terrain where resilience, solidarity, and sociality can emerge. Attending more closely to how they are entangled with extractivism is important, not only to make them more visible as sites of enquiry and development policy, but also to advance alternatives to extractivism that are more just and sustainable.

1 Introduction

Caustic soda (sodium hydroxide) comes in various forms and is incredibly versatile. It can be a liquid, solid, or powder. It is odourless and tasteless, and transparent like water when liquid. In its different configurations it has numerous applications in our daily lives, from being a key ingredient of soap and

 | DOI:10.1163/9789004685994_005

detergents to manufacturing processes such as metal refining, textile production, and even food processing. In bauxite refineries, such as the Friguia complex in Fria, Guinea, caustic soda is used in an intermediate step of aluminium production, to separate alumina-bearing minerals from bauxite rocks. By contrast, when a caustic soda solution is mixed with oils, it induces saponification, while it can help fix dyes and expedite their absorption when it meets fabrics. Not handling and storing it properly can, however, have disastrous consequences. Its ingestion by humans causes burn injuries in the oral cavity and stomach, inability to swallow, gastrointestinal perforations, and lifelong respiratory complications, particularly among children (Botwe et al., 2015; Lupa et al., 2009). 'The curse of caustic soda' (*Le fléau de la soude caustique*), often used in reference to the injuries that it causes, is an important concern of women's promotion groups that depend heavily on its use for soap making and cloth dyeing activities. These groups, from the French *Groupements de Promotion Féminine*, are a popular arrangement across the country. They bring together self-employed women within the same community around shared activities to sustain their livelihoods and support one another.

In what follows, this (chemical) agent serves as an entry point to connect seemingly separate economies and explore activities and relations of social reproduction necessary for the maintenance of life (Katz, 2001), which have remained largely invisible in current debates on resource extractivism. How do women's promotion groups experience extractivism? What does it mean to use a social reproduction–centred approach to understand their experiences? To answer these questions, this paper examines the unique case of Fria in Guinea, a coastal country in West Africa, which hosts the refinery of one of the leading aluminium companies in the world, and the everyday experiences of women who are part of promotion groups around sites of extraction.

The analysis relies on 37 interviews with the members of groups of women soap makers and fabric dyers, soda vendors, health professionals, civil society representatives, civil servants, and government officials, carried out in August 2017 in Fria, Conakry and Mamou, as well as documentary evidence and follow-up research conducted remotely in 2021. The 2017 interviews were undertaken as a part of a larger study seeking to strengthen local capacity for the prevention and treatment of caustic injuries, including through the sensitisation activities of women's promotion groups.[1]

1 The interviews were conducted in French with some exceptions. In this latter case, they were conducted with the aid of simultaneous translation from Pulaar and Susu. All have been subsequently translated into English by the author for the purpose of this chapter. The names of the interviewees have been modified for confidentiality reasons.

Inspired by anthropology scholarship in the science and technology tradition (e.g., Laet and Mol, 2000), this chapter follows caustic soda to illuminate the realities of women's groups and the way they negotiate social reproduction vis-à-vis the extractivist logics of the bauxite industry. As argued by Appadurai, 'if from a theoretical point of view human actors encode things with significance, from a methodological point of view it is the things-in-motion that illuminate their human and social context' (Appadurai, 1986, 5). This approach entails drawing on a notion of agency that is not solely centred on humans, but also on relations between animate and inanimate actors, and how these affect and are affected (Fox and Alldred, 2015). It requires considering the research itself as an assemblage, in which material objects, people and ideas exist not in their integrity but in light of the relations that they engender (Deleuze and Guattari, 1987). Thus, assemblages allow bridging 'micro' and 'macro' levels of analysis, for example by highlighting the physical, emotional and social effects of integration in the global bauxite industry across different scales. Viewed in this light, the oesophageal burns caused by caustic soda among children in Fria or the smuggling of this chemical out of the refinery by underpaid factory guards are no longer 'micro' events, but rather coexist alongside 'macro' extractivist dynamics of the Guinean state and of the corporate social responsibility (CSR) practices of multinational bauxite corporations.

By bringing to light the gendered ways in which extractivism plays out across productive and reproductive realms, this chapter speaks to the recent literature in human geography on landscapes of extraction, intended as the material and social conditions by which 'life itself is produced' (Arboleda, 2020, 32). In particular, it seeks to challenge prevailing notions of extractivism narrowly defined in terms of the productive sphere, prompting the need for a renewed engagement with this term, centred around the notion of social reproduction, in order to make 'diverse economies', as Gibson-Graham puts it (2008), more credible as sites of enquiry and development policy.

The following section begins by reviewing key debates about extractivism and resource extraction from a gender perspective, building upon insights from recent feminist political economy and human geography scholarship that has recentred processes of capitalist development around social reproduction and diverse economies. Next, I present the study context by providing an overview of both bauxite mining in Guinea, and Fria more specifically, and women's promotion groups. In the analysis, I elaborate on the mutual constitution and tension between the economies of the bauxite industry and women's groups, connecting social reproductive and mining labour across the artificial dichotomies of household–market, production–social reproduction, and licit–illicit. Further, I interrogate the sustainability of corporate responsibility and state strategies seeking to practice social and environmental justice, discussing the extent to which these utilise women's groups to reproduce extractivist logics.

2 Extractivism: Bringing in Social Reproduction

Recently, scholars across different theoretical approaches and geographies have called for a broadening of the boundaries—both symbolic and territorial—of extractivism to include the sociotechnical apparatuses that sustain extractivism as a system (Arboleda, 2020). Especially across Latin America, there has been a proliferation of studies that have considerably expanded the concept of extractivism beyond the notion of exploitation of natural resources by corporate powers, to examine the role of financialisation, neo-liberal development strategies and dynamics of south–south cooperation in sustaining contemporary resource extraction (Farthing and Fabricant, 2018; Gago and Mezzadra, 2017).

As a term that relates to a history of colonial and neocolonial plunder and devastation, extractivism denotes a much broader and complex phenomenon than merely resource extraction. As Szeman and Wenzel suggest (2021, 12), it signifies 'a system or ideology, a representational and symbolic space linked to the use (and abuse) of nature-as-resource'. Alternatives for 'good coexistences' between people and environments have gained traction as ways of counteracting this system (Acosta, 2017, 3). This strand in the literature has argued for an expanded engagement with the extractive dimensions of capital across domains, such as technical and knowledge practices, and how these entail the construction of 'outsides that are already constructed as susceptible to appropriation by capital' (Mezzadra and Neilson, 2019, 190). The role of gender as a social construct that allows for the construction of such 'outsides' and how these, in turn, sustain extractivist dynamics have, however, been relatively under-theorised.

Increasingly, feminist studies of extractivism have illuminated the gendered nature of extractivist processes. Some scholars, for example, examine the history of women in mining (Gier and Mercier, 2006), and women's resistance to mining (Lahiri-Dutt, 2011), such as the opposition of indigenous women's movements (Sempértegui, 2021). Others, by contrast, document the gender inequalities inherent to extractivism, specifically the exclusion of women from formal employment in large-scale mining companies, as well as the negative environmental and health impacts that mining activities entail for local communities (Abrahamsson et al., 2014; Haile, 2020). As demonstrated by these studies, employment in this sector is precarious and highly dependent on ownership structures, shifts in governance arrangements, and commodity prices (Haile, 2020). These have important consequences for how workers, families and communities organise their lives, including from a gender perspective.

Nevertheless, there has been only limited engagement so far with feminist scholarship that has rearticulated processes of capitalist development around the concepts of social reproduction and diverse economies. The former is defined as the continuum of waged and unwaged activities and relations, such as domestic labour and childcare, as well as informal labour and subsistence production, that sustain life and communities, and the creation of economic value under capitalism (Prügl, 2021; Mezzadri, 2019; Gibson-Graham, 2008; Federici, 2004; Katz, 2001). One notable exception is Benya (2015), who adopts a social reproduction lens to examine individual and collective struggles in the aftermath of the Marikana massacre in South Africa. In her analysis, she demonstrates that domestic work largely performed by women is affected by the temporal and spatial patterns of mine work and that social reproduction is a key terrain for resistance against impunity.

The latter concept, that of diverse economies, pushes social reproduction debates forward by moving beyond gendered dichotomies that frame activities of social reproduction in binary opposition to capitalist production. Gibson-Graham defines them as 'the plethora of hidden and alternative economic activities that contribute to social well-being and environmental regeneration beyond market, waged and capitalist forms of enterprise', including cooperatives, housework, and self-provisioning (Gibson-Graham et al., 2013; Gibson-Graham, 2008, 6). The women's promotion groups examined in this chapter fit well within this frame, in that they are based on relations of interdependence and mutual support, while sustaining well-being, livelihoods and communities.

Rethinking what extractivism means and does from the perspective of social reproduction and diverse economies necessitates moving beyond narrow accounts of what counts as labour and value producing under resource-based capitalist development. This issue has been a longstanding concern of feminist and critical scholars of capitalism. In 1990, feminist scholar Cynthia Enloe asked a still pertinent question for international politics—'Where are the women?'—highlighting the role of the gendered division of labour in sustaining economic systems and the subordinate role ascribed to women relative to men. Along these lines, feminist scholars have brought to light the role that households play in both sustaining the functioning of global markets and devaluing women's contributions, specifically through home-based production (Mies, 1982; Prügl, 1999). Further, they have highlighted that this process of devaluation is closely linked to colonial penetration and its underlying mechanisms of violent appropriation, both economic and ideological, whereby women 'are treated as if they were means of production of "natural resources" such as water and land' (Mies, 1982, 5). Thus, recentring extractivism around issues of social reproduction provides an expanded horizon through which to examine the extractive dimensions of capital, and how these are organised along gender, racial, ethnic and class lines.

Arguably, both extractivism and the disenfranchisement of social reproductive activities and relations are inextricably linked to colonial and imperialist practices. Drawing from Maria Lugones's coloniality of gender and Ramón Grosfoguel's conceptualisation of extractivism, Rodriguez Castro (2021), for example, examines the varied forms of dispossession confronting *Campesinas* women in Colombia, and their struggles and resistance. In particular, she traces connections between territorial dispossession and 'epistemic dispossession through extraction of ideas and cultural practices', which rests upon the victimisation and objectification of *Campesinas* women, including in state development policy (Rodriguez Castro, 2021, 128). Indeed, this approach can be incorporated into social reproduction analyses of extractivism, to challenge the epistemic and ontological binaries that sustain extractivism as a system.

A social reproduction perspective contributes to deepening and expanding our understanding of extractivism. Firstly, it demonstrates that the systematic externalisation of costs of social reproduction to laborers, families and local communities is co-constitutive of extractivist processes (Mezzadri, 2021; Mezzadri, Newman and Stevano, 2021). Secondly, as an analytical lens it allows one to break the ontological binary that places such activities and relations in a separate and subordinate realm (Prügl, 2021). Thirdly, this approach brings attention to the role of the state in sustaining both extractivism and specific configurations of social reproduction. While feminist scholars have examined these dynamics particularly in relation to the retreat of

the neo-liberal welfare state in the global North (Arruzza, 2015; Bakker, 2007; Bakker and Gill, 2019), similar processes are at play in the global South as well, as demonstrated by the recent literature on extractivism as a state-led development strategy (Farthing and Fabricant, 2018). In fact, both states and corporations are deeply imbricated in social reproduction in and around sites of extraction, from the provision of electricity to water supplies and sewage systems, to the establishment of schools and hospitals in mining enclaves, as well as through the allocation of extractive revenues (Arellano-Yanguas and Acosta, 2014). By the same token, the social and ecological costs that extractivism creates for humans and environments pose significant challenges to the social reproduction of workers, families and communities around sites of extraction, though as Katz suggests (2001) these problems are seldom framed in these terms.

Lastly, focusing on diverse economies and their role in sustaining social reproduction around sites of extraction offers new opportunities to counter extractivist logics, bringing the sites where alternatives to capitalist modes of production can advance to the centre of the enquiry (Dalla Costa and Dalla Costa, 1999). This effort not only has the potential to help us understand people's everyday lives more fully, it also draws attention to the windows of opportunity for solidarity, resilience and resistance that can emerge in these spaces. The need to recognise the full range of economic activities undertaken in and around sites of extraction also resonates with attempts to move beyond narrow understandings of extractive industries, for example to include illicit and hidden economies (Calvão, 2017; Moodie, 1980), not in binary opposition to formal extractive economies but as constitutive of them.

3 Bauxite Mining and Women's Promotion Groups in Guinea

Extractive industries occupy a central role in the Guinean economy. In 2016, the country was the world's third largest exporter of bauxite—which accounted for over 80 per cent of Guinean revenues from mining, for a total of about USD 280 million—and a leading exporter of other mineral commodities such as gold, diamonds, iron and nickel (EITI, 2018). According to estimates, the country's bauxite reserves are the largest in the world (Knierzinger, 2014). Its extraction goes back to the late 1950s and has been a point of continuity from Guinea's colonial past to dictatorship and regime longevity in the post-independence period, to the strong foreign corporate influence that continues today (Diallo, 2019; Barry, 2004).

In the 1950s, the French colonial administration first introduced plans to produce aluminium through the extraction and refining of bauxite and the building of the city of Fria in the highlands of western Guinea. These plans only came to fruition when Guinea declared independence in 1958 under the Sekou Touré regime, leading to the establishment of the first alumina refinery on the African continent (Bolay and Knierzinger, 2021). Since then, Fria, also called the Paris of Guinea for its street lighting and state-of-the-art infrastructure, has served as a model for the establishment of other major mining enclaves. Though the capital intensity of bauxite extraction and refining processes only creates limited direct employment opportunities, for an estimated 2 per cent of the entire population of Fria (Diallo, 2017), the industrial complex itself owns the city's electricity, water, and sewage systems, and is involved to a significant degree in the financing (or lack thereof) of public services and infrastructure, such as medical care, schools, and roads (Knierzinger, 2014).

In 2001, the bauxite complex started to be administered by the private Russian company RUSAL, currently UC RUSAL, which also owns the Compagnie des Bauxites de Kindia (CBK) in Middle Guinea and another mining complex in Boké,[2] and is among the three largest aluminium companies in the world (Prokofeva et al., 2020). Fria's bauxite complex was fully privatised five years later and is currently the only one in the country to include a refinery for the processing of bauxite into alumina. It is the country's second-largest bauxite mine after the Compagnie des Bauxites de Guinée (CBG) in Boké, which is controlled by Alcoa, Rio Tinto-Alcan and the Guinean government.

The recent history of the RUSAL bauxite complex can be summarised in three time periods: 1) the period from 2001, when the complex was privatised, to 2012, when the Friguia refinery was closed abruptly by RUSAL; 2) the period of RUSAL's closure, from 2012 to 2017, which caused a profound crisis of social reproduction, including exclusion from basic services such as access to water and electricity; and 3) from when the company resumed operations in 2018 to date, a period characterised by exacerbated environmental damage and the unsustainability of extractive operations.

The first period, from 2001 to April 2012, as documented by scholars and activists, is marked by a gradual deterioration of living standards in Fria and a decline in factory conditions, as well as worsening relations between expatriates employed in the bauxite complex and Fria's population (Knierzinger, 2018 Diallo, 2017). In the words of the activist Ibrahima Talibé Diallo, the takeover by the Russian company fundamentally changed relations with the local population, further alienating the bauxite complex from the lives and livelihoods in its surroundings:

> They had heard that the French whites lived in the same habitat with the Guineans and shared their meals and that the Americans did almost the same. But they did not want to do that. Thus, they erected a cité right in city center that had privileged access to all the existing infrastructure and an extension of the initial cité. The principal characteristics of these two entities were the fact that they were closed (three meter walls with barbwire) and that they could only be entered by Russian personnel.
>
> Correspondence with Ibrahima Talibé Diallo in Knierzinger, 2018, 146

2 Boké is a region that has experienced a significant extractivist boom since 2016, fuelled by increasing foreign direct investment from China and the UAE (for an overview, see Widder, Pacioni, and Bocoum, 2019).

The second period covers the years from 2012 to 2017 and is marked by RUSAL's factory closure, which in turn engendered a profound humanitarian crisis in Fria (PROJEG, 2018). This not only caused adverse consequences for employees and subcontracted workers, it also jeopardised access to basic services such as electricity and water (Diallo, 2017).[3] During this period, the registration of women's promotion groups engaging in both artisanal business activities and agriculture intensified, while civil society organisations in Fria and abroad mobilised, calling for both immediate action and alternatives to reinvent the city (PROJEG, 2018).

In 2018, after long negotiations between RUSAL and the Guinean government, the refinery reopened. This more recent period, from the rehabilitation of Friguia to the present, marks another shift in Fria's extractivist landscape. Though alternatives to the refinery have lost salience according to civil society organisations (PROJEG, 2018), women's promotion groups have remained in the spotlight, becoming privileged beneficiaries of the CSR projects of mining corporations such as RUSAL, especially as demand for soap increased during the COVID-19 pandemic. In 2020, for example, the Guinea Alumina Corporation (GAC) released a video on YouTube illustrating how the company supported local communities' efforts to cope with the COVID-19 crisis by purchasing soap from women's promotion groups (GAC, 2020), while news outlets reported that RUSAL provided direct financial support, for the purchase of inputs and raw materials, to about 30 women's promotion groups in the city and nearby villages (Bha, 2020).

Before exploring the role of women's groups in sustaining extractivist processes in Fria and beyond, however, some clarification of the functioning and origin of these groups is warranted. Women's promotion groups aim at bringing together self-employed women from the same village or community around shared activities that can sustain their livelihoods and provide mutual support. An important feature of these groups is that they are formed at the grassroots level and are part of a broader structure of local and national federations, headed by the Women's Promotion National Directorate (Direction Nationale de la Promotion Féminine, DNPF). The groups are generally composed of about 20 members, including an elected president and a treasurer, and engage

3 Though official sources attribute the closure to conflictual relations with the local union, culminating in a large-scale strike and lockout, several activists contend that this merely served as a pretext for RUSAL to mitigate financial risks in a context of deteriorating aluminium prices and falling productivity due to declining technical conditions at the refinery (PROJEG, 2018; Knierzinger, 2018).

in training activities, the sharing of resources and knowledge among members, and in joint childcare, production and financial arrangements.

Although there are no estimates of the number of women's promotion groups currently active in Guinea, they have been an integral part of the economic and social fabric since independence. Throughout Guinea's history, women have engaged in nationalist struggles and politics, advocating for gender equality in both public and domestic spheres and against colonialism (Steady, 2011). Under the socialist regime of Sékou Touré, the ruling *Parti Démocratique de Guinée* (PDG) established an extensive network of committees and local councils, with women's bureaus at the district, sub-prefecture, and prefecture levels (Dessertine, 2019). These bureaus were crucial for the transmission of the party's messages to local communities, and for the mobilisation of political protests and the fostering of women's engagement in productive activities, especially in agriculture. While this system was abolished as the country embarked on the process of a gradual liberalisation and privatisation of the economy from the 1990s on, the organisation of women around groups engaging in business activities and agriculture continued to play an important role, and these groups were increasingly integrated into local development projects (Dessertine, 2019; Doumbouya, 2008; De Boodt and Cauberge, 1998). Nevertheless, the relations between these groups and extractive industries, specifically outside of formal wage relations with regard to mining, have been underexplored.

Taking the circulation of caustic soda as a heuristic tool, this chapter traces connections between the bauxite industry and the soap making and cloth dyeing activities of women's groups, making visible the mutually constitutive relations and tensions between these two seemingly separate economies. To do so, the remainder of the chapter explores the labour and negotiations that take place around sites of extraction, attending to how gender works to sustain extractivism as a system. The members of women's groups are primarily involved in social reproduction, yet they also perform 'productive' activities, sustaining the survival of their households and communities through their labour on a daily basis. As they use caustic soda within homes and workshops, oftentimes alongside domestic work, they contribute to creating diverse economies around sites of extraction, the logics of which transcend the extractivist dynamics of the bauxite industry.

4 'D'où vient la soude?'

The question 'Where does the soda come from?' (*D'où vient la soude?*) enables us to trace unpredictable connections, including among the caustic soda, the members of promotion groups, villagers and their children, and health personnel treating oesophageal injuries caused by accidental ingestions, as well as guards surveilling the bauxite complex, and government officials regulating trade in chemicals in Conakry, Guinea's capital. In tracing caustic soda's circulation, this section starts by exploring how families and communities confront extractivism through activities that cross boundaries of paid and unpaid labour, the licit and illicit, relations of production, and social reproduction. It then shows the mutual constitution and tension between the diverse economies that soap makers and cloth dyers are part of around sites of extraction and the operations of extractive industries themselves. While women's groups sustain extraction and are also affected by it, they are at the same time a terrain for alternatives, where resilience, solidarity, and sociality can emerge.

Firstly, caustic soda *works* in different ways and is entangled in a myriad of worlds that transgress its ordinary industrial usage. Oumar, a civil servant in Fria who has retired from the bauxite complex, recalls the thefts of caustic soda between Conakry's port and the mine as follows:

OUMAR: The soda arrives at the port. Then the soda is stored on the train and taken to Fria. The moment the train leaves Conakry, there are thefts.

LUISA: There are people who steal the caustic soda?

OUMAR: It's not official but that's how it is, from the port to the train, and even when the train is running, people steal it by putting it in cans.

Interview with civil servant in Fria, August 2017

Other interviewees in different locations describe similar dynamics. For example, when explaining the frequency of accidental caustic soda ingestions among children, a health professional in Conakry explains the prevalence of such accidents in relation to bauxite mining, arguing that extraction has contributed to making this chemical substance more available in markets across mining towns. In his words:

> Most of them [the victims of accidental ingestions] come from the interior, especially where there are factories that mine bauxite or manufacture aluminium;[4] this is the case for Fria and the surrounding villages,

4 Here and in similar instances, interviewees refer to aluminium as a shorthand for alumina (fr: alumine) or aluminium oxide, and not to pure aluminium. I retain the term as originally conveyed by my interlocutors.

> the case for Kamsa and the surrounding villages, and in Conakry as well, because the train takes the soda in liquid form here to the interior, and people take advantage of this to take the soda and sell it at the market.
>
> Interview with health professional in Conakry, August 2017

But the thefts do not stop once the caustic soda enters the factory gates, as Oumar explains:

> OUMAR: There are many entrances and exits. At the main entrance, there is a team that monitors. At the main exit, there is another team, and another in the warehouse where there is the aluminium. Everything is monitored by guards, who are paid to do this. They are underpaid; it is another company. There is a middleman who everyday recruits people to monitor … They are not paid like the employees.
>
> Before, in 1975, there was a military surveillance service, which guarded the factory, about a hundred people, back then we did not steal; it was less compared to today, when there are at least 400–500 guards.
>
> LUISA: 400–500 guards?
>
> OUMAR: Yes, more or less. Back then we were not even 100; there were thefts but not like the present.
>
> LUISA: So, as the number of guards increased, the thefts increased?
>
> OUMAR: Yes, of course. Before there was another system: when a worker is caught stealing, he is automatically fired, he loses all his social rights, if caught *in flagrante* he automatically loses all social rights, that's it; at that time it was like that. Now, when we catch the guards; it is not like before.
>
> Interview with civil servant in Fria, August 2017

This suggests that the smuggling of caustic soda cannot be examined in isolation, but rather in relation to the mining complex's shift from public to private ownership, and the subcontracting of surveillance services to private guards who are paid daily and lack the social rights of permanent employees, as pointed out by Oumar.

While the privatisation of the bauxite complex and its takeover by RUSAL caused a profound deterioration in living standards for workers and their families and escalating tensions between the company and worker representatives, as documented by Knierzinger (2018) the company increasingly sought strategies to minimise costs by lowering wages and cut social benefits through the establishment of subcontracting firms. One of these, Senta, is responsible for the hiring and payment of the majority of the local population working in the bauxite complex, which allows RUSAL to circumvent its obligations to ensure accommodation and access to staple foods for subcontracted workers, while continuing to hire foreign employees directly and providing them with access to these very same goods and services (AMINES, 2021).

In some instances, it is not only the caustic soda itself, but also the large, empty containers used to carry it to the refinery that serve to negotiate conflictual relations with workers and their representatives. As a government official in Conakry states,

> Often, it was the union that took care of the collection of these empty containers and for the industrialist, well, he is going to use this to distribute expenses a little, deal with social issues, etc. If these are containers of rice, that's alright, but chemical products? We said, 'be careful, you are not accommodating the union, but incriminating it, because there are penalties for that'. These are the failures. Sometimes there is also complicity between the industrialists and the traders, and that's how the soda in full form is in the markets.
>
> Interview with government official in Conakry, August 2017

According to this interviewee, the transfer of empty caustic soda containers to the union for discharge and reuse represents a strategy, albeit short-lived, for appeasing the union and the workers it represents, but it also exposes the union to incrimination, as the reuse of chemical containers is a violation of the existing regulations. This measure also causes caustic soda contaminations, with harmful ecological and health consequences since these containers are then used for domestic purposes, such as the storing food, or are disposed of along with regular waste.

This excerpt also refers to complicity between industrialists and traders engaging in illicit activities, which contributed to making caustic soda in full form—a more aggressive agent for industrial use compared to other caustic soda agents—available in local markets, with women increasingly supplying it for soap making and cloth dyeing activities. The official continued, referring to caustic soda, 'It ends [up] in the hands of users who don't really know its potential dangers, who are therefore exposed to those dangers. Two groups are most affected: local dyers and soap makers. The risk is there but we have not evaluated it; but it's there'. (Interview with government official in Conakry, August 2017.)

Bauxite mines are not the sole providers of caustic soda. It is also imported in bulk by retailers in Conakry, who in turn supply vendors in the interior of the country. Since the closing of the refinery, many vendors interviewed resorted to this strategy, as illustrated by the following interview with a caustic soda vendor, Halima, and a member of one of the promotion groups, Marie, at the market in Fria:

LUISA: So, where do you buy the soda?

HALIMA: At the Madina market in Conakry; I buy the bags there and retail it here, so I can earn a little, one kg, half [...] Sometimes I hire a driver and we go there, I buy ten bags and when it's finished, I go back. If I buy ten bags, it lasts for two weeks.

LUISA: How come you decided to sell the soda?

HALIMA: Before, when my husband was not dead, he did this job ... He worked at the factory, that's where he let the soda come out.

LUISA: He was taking the soda from the factory?

HALIMA: Yes.

MARIE: Hmm, this isn't right—tsk tsk.

HALIMA: It was the liquid, the liquid one. The powder comes from Conakry. When the factory was open, I used to sell that; now that the factory is closed, I go look for it in Conakry.

Interview with caustic soda vendor and group member in Fria, August 2017

This conversation brings to light the relationality of the public and private around sites of extraction. The struggles confronting Halima, such as her husband's death and the new strategies she devised to sustain her livelihood, cannot be examined in isolation but rather are entangled with the closure of the refinery. This interview also highlights the existing moral sanctions surrounding the smuggling of caustic soda, exemplified by Marie interrupting the conversation to express her disapproval. Through the circulations discussed in this section, caustic soda becomes visible as a boundary-crossing agent that bridges mutually constitutive licit and illicit, extractive and diverse economies. In the next section, I continue to unpack these relations of mutual constitution and tension, as the caustic soda moves into the hands of women soap makers and fabric dyers.

4.1 *Revaluating Women's Promotion Groups in Times of Crisis*

The experiences of women's promotion groups in Fria intertwine with the trajectory of the RUSAL bauxite complex. Understanding the struggles facing the women in these groups requires paying attention to RUSAL's operations and the abrupt closure of its refinery. At the same time, the operations of the bauxite complex cannot be fully grasped without first recognising the role of women's promotion groups in shouldering economic pressures times of crisis.

The women's promotion group in Fria was created only after the refinery was closed in 2012, though around half of the group's members already engaged in soap production and cloth dyeing activities prior to its formation, with one of the women there reporting to have started as early as 2001. Most of the members are married, have children, and recount that since the time when the group was formed their husbands have been unemployed due to the closure of the refinery, resulting in them being the sole or primary income earner in their household. In a context of widespread unemployment, frequent power cuts, and worsening economic conditions in Fria, joining a women's group provides an alternative for subsistence for many of the women. In the words of Fatou, 'In Guinea, especially in Fria, husbands do not work. We have children. What we make today is what we sell tomorrow, to earn money. Before, my husband worked in the factory' (interview with the member of a promotion group in Fria, August 2017). This excerpt demonstrates that women's activities within promotion groups have been indispensable for families around the bauxite complex, particularly when operations were halted.

In some instances, these activities created openings for recognition and support from husbands. As Kadiatou describes, 'It was a relief for my husband that I am part of this group, because when I became part of it he did not work'. Fatima, by contrast, explains that her husband was 'obliged' to accept her taking over a breadwinning role: 'He was obliged to accept this because he doesn't work. So, it's me who contributes to the household income'. Other women describe their husband's perceptions in more positive terms: 'My husband gives me advice; he is the one who motivates me not to leave the group. This group is really good', says Jeanne, while Hadia states, 'He's proud; he's happy' (interviews with members of the group in Fria, August 2017). Thus, group members' experiences are far from homogeneous; women do not talk about their position in terms of oppression, but rather highlight their own negotiations while confronting patriarchal structures and economic hardship.

Nevertheless, engagement in soap making and cloth dyeing activities did not translate into an equal redistribution of domestic and childcare responsibilities at home, but rather coexisted alongside this labour. As illustrated by the observation of an NGO interviewee, women's engagement in economic activities is often seen as an extension of, rather than a break with, women's role as mothers and carers within their families: 'The factory [in Fria] closed four years ago, so people turned to soap making and dyeing. In Guinea, in a couple that does not work, the woman is the most involved because of the children' (interview with NGO representative in Conakry, August 2017). This resonates with the gender dynamics documented by Evans (2016) for the case of Zambia's Copperbelt, where financial and economic displacements caused by extractive corporate practices led women to increasingly engage in breadwinning roles, while being accompanied by an asymmetric distribution of domestic and childcare work.

The coexistence of social reproductive work, especially childcare, with productive activities such as soap making and fabric dyeing is apparent when discussing accidental caustic soda ingestions by children with the women. As some of the groups' members describe, accidents involving children are frequent among women producers particularly when they engage in these activities on their own, as this often involves producing at home, storing chemicals in the kitchen, using kitchen utensils, and looking after children while working. Being part of a group, as is explained by some of the members, provides opportunities to move production activities to different and more secure places, such as a shed built for the purpose or a workshop at the Centre for Women's Empowerment (Centre d'Autonomisation des Femmes) (CAF). It also allows the women to share know-how on how to protect themselves and others from chemical burns and share childcare responsibilities, whereby one member looks after the children while the others process the soap and fabrics.

Notably, participation in the promotion groups creates a sense of solidarity among the women, as Binta explains:

> Before I used to work alone; now we are together. We help each other out. Before, if I had a problem, I was alone, but now, if I have a problem, all the women stand up. If one of us has a problem, the others stand up [...] My son has a heart disease, he is in Conakry; when I need, we all provide a contribution; there is a girl who got married, we did her dowry. The others, all stayed by my side.
>
> Interview with group member in Fria, August 2017

This is not confined to the group interviewed in Fria, but resonates with the experiences of women in different regions of Guinea. In the words of Salimatou, the member of a promotion group in Mamou: 'Before I worked alone. One alone is nothing!' (interview with a member of the group in Mamou, August 2017). In Fria, however, engagement in the promotion group intertwines with the refinery's closure and the economic hardship that unfolded as a result of this rupture. Fatoumata, for example, describes the social and economic benefits of joining the group and juxtaposes them to the experiences of others who were 'immobilised' by the crisis:

> There have been many positive changes in my social life since I joined this group. I am doing well; we hang out with each other. Also economically, the caustic soda is very expensive. [...] Since the factory closed, our means have changed, because the husbands don't work. There are some people who resorted to other income generating activities, but others had nothing to put on their plates; they spent all their money and were immobilised.
>
> Interview with group member in Fria, August 2017

Several members interviewed highlighted the benefits of working in a group relative to working alone, not only for themselves but also for their community. Aissata, for example, sees her participation in the group as an important contribution to the health of her neighbourhood:

> I benefited a lot from this [group] personally, because back then I did not know what precautions to take when a child swallows the soda, what are the first precautions to take before the child is treated at the hospital. So, we became aware of this. As soon as a child drinks it, we know what to do. Then my own protection. Also, what is important is that through me, all the neighbourhood receives the same information concerning the soda.
>
> Interview with group member in Fria, August 2017

In sum, following caustic soda from the port to the bauxite complex to promotion groups' workshops reveals the mutual constitution and tension between two seemingly separate economies, that of the refinery and that of the promotion groups within which women subsidise extractive practices, negotiate, and survive. Though breadwinning roles tend to be justified as an extension of family responsibilities and are accompanied by an unequal distribution of domestic and childcare work, engaging in these groups provides windows of opportunity for resilience, sociality, and solidarity in a time of crisis such as that caused by RUSAL's five-year closure.

5 'Notre ville est née de l'usine, et non l'inverse'

'Our city was born from the factory, and not the other way around' ('*Notre ville est née de l'usine, et non l'inverse*') is a quote from a resident of Fria cited in a report by PROJEG, a civil society consortium composed of 150 organisations including unions, women's associations and international NGOs (PROJEG,

2018, 4). It is telling with regard to the extent to which social reproduction in Fria is dependent on its mother mine on a daily and structural basis and at the same time is in tension with it. In the remainder of this chapter, I reflect on the sustainability of social reproduction in Fria and how this has been disenfranchised since the reopening of the refinery in 2018.

Firstly, as discussed in the previous section, women's promotion groups have increasingly become target beneficiaries of CSR projects initiated by RUSAL and other bauxite companies around sites of extraction. As stated in RUSAL's sustainability strategy, these measures are seen both as a way to take into account the 'interests of the local population' (RUSAL, 2021, 88) and as an investment in the 'creation of long-term business value' (RUSAL, 2021, 189). Nevertheless, by targeting these groups as beneficiaries, corporate discourses and practices inherently place women's groups in a subaltern position. This further marginalises women's activities, neglecting the crucial role that they have played in helping households survive the crisis since 2012.

While corporate responsibility provides a 'social license to operate' and represents the recognition of marginalised people and communities by corporate power (Syn, 2014), it ultimately legitimises extractive activities, providing an extension of extractive practices, whereby women are exploited as the 'last colony' of extractivism.

Furthermore, although bauxite corporations such as RUSAL increasingly target women's promotion groups as beneficiaries of CSR projects, several of these groups' members do not view these economies as a viable livelihood strategy for them in the longer term and would rather engage in a different activity. As Mariam states:

> We don't have the means […] what we earn with the soda is little. The bag [of caustic soda] outside there, that's 280,000 francs–300,000 francs; the oil there, that's 175,000 by the litre. When you sum this all up, there's little that's left […] if we had the means, we could start another activity that could help us earn more than the soap. That's it; if we can get the money, we will call everyone in the group, we will sit together and discuss what to do.
>
> Interview with group member in Fria, August 2017

This excerpt calls into question the sustainability of soap making and dyeing economies, suggesting that interventions by RUSAL to support the local community by fostering alternative economic activities are inadequate, but it also brings to light the importance of the collective ('sitting together') when it comes to making decisions for the future.

In addition, state regulation of the trade in chemicals risks complicating access to caustic soda, potentially displacing soap making and dyeing activities. In fact, since 2012 the Guinean state—particularly the Ministry of the Environment—has revamped its efforts to regulate chemical substances. The National Plan of Chemical Products 2012–2020, for example, classifies caustic soda as a chemical with a high priority and degree of concern on a national scale, though it also recognises the existing difficulties in tracking and reducing negative impacts (République de Guinée, 2011, 20). The view that such a chemical agent should be regulated despite potential repercussions for women's livelihoods was prevalent during interviews with government officials, as expressed by one: 'Allowing someone to start an activity that allows them to generate resources is good, but chemicals must be an exception' (interview with government official in Conakry, August 2017). This begs the question of whether diverse economies and more sustainable configurations of social reproduction can exist around sites of extraction and, if so, of what kind. In other words, can a city that was born out of the mine really be transformed? Some of the women interviewed demonstrate that it can, but not within the existing extractivist paradigm.

6 Conclusion

This chapter has examined the mutual constitution and tension between two seemingly separate economies, interrogating what it means to take a social reproduction–centred approach to extractivism. It has taken caustic soda as an entry point to illuminate the existing entanglements between bauxite mining and its extractivist logic, and women's groups, animated by a sense of community and solidarity. In so doing, it has traced connections between the activities of social reproduction performed by women's groups around sites of extraction and the extractive operations of the bauxite industry. In Fria, where social reproduction depends on extractivism on both a daily and a structural basis for access to basic services and livelihoods or lack thereof, material and social experiences of extractivism are particularly extreme and harmful, yet women's promotion groups are not an oppressed community. On the contrary, the relationship between women's activities and the bauxite industry as discussed in this chapter draws attention to the existing subsidy that women provide to extractive operations, as well as to the gendered contours of resilience and solidarity around sites of extraction.

The case of Fria is hardly generalisable as the city hosts the first and only currently operating bauxite refinery in the African continent, but this in itself is telling of the current mode of extraction in the continent and beyond. Crucially, in their specificity and locality, the struggles, negotiations, and openings for solidarity narrated in this chapter have important implications for how we study extractivism, as well as for development policy. The members of the women's group interviewed point to several avenues that have wider relevance. The first is to take social reproduction and diverse economies seriously, as sites where the 'immobility' caused by extractive industries can be actively and discursively resisted; the second is that as long as extractivism remains as a system, diverse economies that contribute to sustaining life and well-being will continue be marginalised; the third, that we need collective and participatory decision-making to move forward. They also prompt us to question whether different modes of extractivism are possible within the current structures of production and social reproduction, disenfranchisement, and devaluation, and, if not, to take urgent action.

Acknowledgements

I am extremely grateful to Elise Erickson and Kaila Clarke, whose sustained support and contribution has been invaluable for the development of this chapter and the research project on which it is based. My gratitude also goes to the editors of this thematic volume, the Gender Writing Group, Elisabeth Prügl, Boubacar Diallo, and colleagues in Guinea, for their constructive comments, encouragement, and valuable feedback. To the members of the women's promotion groups in Fria and Mamou, thank you for sharing your time and views with me, and for making this research possible. All errors and deficiencies are my own.

References

Abrahamsson, L., E. Segerstedt, M. Nygren, J. Johansson, B. Johansson, I. Edman and A. Åkerlund (2014) *Gender, Diversity and Work Conditions in Mining* (Luleå: Luleå University of Technology Press).

Acosta, A. (2017) 'Post-Extractivism: from Discourse to Practice—Reflections for Action', *International Development Policy | Revue Internationale de Politique de Développement*, 9, pp. 77–101, DOI: 10.4000/poldev.2356.

AMINES (Action Mines Guinée) (2021) *Rusal-Friguia: Les difficiles conditions de vie des habitants de Fria*, 1 October, https://actionminesguinee.org/rusal-friguia-les-difficiles-conditions-de-vie-des-habitants-de-fria/ (accessed on 28 March 2023).

Appadurai, A. (1986) *The Social Life of Things: Commodities in Cultural Perspective* (Cambridge: Cambridge University Press).

Arboleda, M. (2020) *Planetary Mine: Territories of Extraction under Late Capitalism* (London and New York City: Verso).

Arellano-Yanguas, J. and A.M. Acosta (2014) *Extractive Industries, Revenue Allocation and Local Politics*, UNRISD Working Paper 2014-4 (Geneva: UNRISD), https://opendocs.ids.ac.uk/opendocs/bitstream/handle/20.500.12413/4665/Extractive%20Industries%2c%20Revenue%20Allocation%20and%20Local%20Politics.pdf?sequence=1&isAllowed=y (accessed on 28 March 2023).

Arruzza, C. (2015) 'Functionalist, Determinist, Reductionist: Social Reproduction Feminism and its Critics', *Science and Society*, 80(1), pp. 9–30, DOI: 10.1521/siso.2016.80.1.9.

Bakker, I. and S. Gill (2019) 'Rethinking Power, Production, and Social Reproduction: Toward Variegated Social Reproduction', *Capital and Class*, 43(4), pp. 503–523, DOI: 10.1177/0309816819880783.

Bakker, I. (2007) 'Social Reproduction and the Constitution of a Gendered Political Economy', *New Political Economy*, 12(4), pp. 541–556, DOI: 10.1080/13563460701661561.

Barry, A. O. (2004) *Les racines du mal guinéen* (Paris: Karthala Editions).

Benya, A. (2015) 'The Invisible Hands: Women in Marikana', *Review of African Political Economy*, 42(146), pp. 545–560, DOI: 10.1080/03056244.2015.1087394.

Bha, A. (2020) 'FRIA: RUSAL en appui au groupement féminin de la préfecture', *JustinMorel.info*, 7 February.

Bolay, M. and J. Knierzinger (2021) 'Corporate Gift or Political Sacrifice? State-Sponsored CSR and Electricity Provision in Guinean Extractive Enclaves', *Political Geography*, 84, pp. 1–10, DOI: 10.1016/j.polgeo.2020.102300.

Botwe, B.O., S. Anim-Sampong, B. Dabo Sarkodie, W.K. Antwi, J. Obeng-Nkansah and G.G.N.A. Ashong (2015) 'Caustic Soda Ingestion in Children Under-5 Years Presenting for Fluoroscopic Examinations in an Academic Hospital in Ghana', *BMC Research Notes*, 8, pp. 1–7, DOI: 10.1186/s13104-015-1629-3.

Calvão, F. (2017) 'The Company Oracle: Corporate Security and Diviner-Detectives in Angola's Diamond Mines', *Comparative Studies in Society and History*, 59(3), pp. 574–599, DOI: 10.1017/S0010417517000172.

Dalla Costa, M. and G.F. Dalla Costa (1999) *Women, Development, and Labor of Reproduction: Struggles and Movements* (Trenton: Africa World Press).

De Boodt, K., and L. Cauberge (1998), *Femmes pionnières de Guinée: 10 ans d'appui aux groupements d'auto-promotion de Bangouya* (Paris: Karthala).

Deleuze, G. and F. Guattari (1987) *A thousand plateaus: Capitalism and schizophrenia* (Minnesota: University of Minnesota Press).

Dessertine, A. (2019) Women, Power, and the State in Guinea, *Oxford Research Encyclopedia of African History* (Oxford: Oxford University Press).

Diallo, P. (2019) *Regime Stability, Social Insecurity and Bauxite Mining in Guinea: Developments Since the Mid-Twentieth Century* (Milton Park: Routledge).

Diallo, P. (2017) 'The African Towns Falling into Decline and Poverty after Mining Companies use Resources then Exit', *The Conversation*, 16 January, https://theconversation.com/the-african-towns-falling-into-decline-and-poverty-after-mining-companies-use-resources-then-exit-69687 (accessed on 28 March 2023).

Doumbouya, O.S. (2008) *La situation sociale des femmes en Guinée: de la période précoloniale jusqu'à nos jours* (Paris: L'Harmattan).

EITI (Extractive Industries Transparency Initiative) (2018) *Guinea 2016 EITI Report* (Guinea: ITIE Guinée) https://eiti.org/document/guinea-2016-eiti-report (accessed on 28 March 2023).

Enloe, C. (1990) *Bananas, Beaches and Bases: Making Feminist Sense of International Politics*, First Edition (Berkeley: University of California Press).

Farthing, L. and N. Fabricant (2018) '*Open Veins* Revisited: the New Extractivism in Latin America, Part 2', *Latin American Perspectives*, 46(2), pp. 4–9, DOI: 10.1177/0094582X18822509.

Federici, S. (2004) *Caliban and the Witch: Women, the Body and Primitive Accumulation* (New York: Autonomedia).

Fox, N.J. and P. Alldred (2015) 'New Materialist Social Inquiry: Designs, Methods and the Research-Assemblage', *International Journal of Social Research Methodology*, 18(4), pp. 399–414, DOI: 10.1080/13645579.2014.921458.

GAC (Guinea Alumina Corporation) (2020) *COVID 19 Comment nous faisons face à la pandemie Communautés*, YouTube video, https://www.youtube.com/watch?v=UcnyzOU4k6U&ab_channel=GuineaAluminaCorporation (accessed on 28 March 2023).

Gago, V. and S. Mezzadra (2017) 'A Critique of the Extractive Operations of Capital: Toward an Expanded Concept of Extractivism', *Rethinking Marxism*, 29(4), pp. 574–591, DOI: 10.1080/08935696.2017.1417087.

Gibson-Graham, J.K., J. Cameron and S. Healy (2013) *Take Back the Economy: an Ethical Guide for Transforming Our Communities* (Minneapolis: University of Minnesota Press).

Gibson-Graham, J.K. (2008) 'Diverse Economies: Performative Practices for "Other Worlds"', *Progress in Human Geography*, 32(5), pp. 613–632.

Gier, J.J. and L. Mercier (eds.) (2006) *Mining Women: Gender in the Development of a Global Industry, 1670 to 2005* (New York: Palgrave Macmillan).

Haile, H. (2020) *The Gender Implications of Transformations in the Copper Value Chain: a Case Study of the Zambian Copperbelt*, UNRISD Research Paper (Geneva: UNRISD).

Katz, C. (2001) 'Vagabond Capitalism and the Necessity of Social Reproduction', *Antipode*, 33(4), pp. 709–728, DOI: 10.1111/1467-8330.00207.

Knierzinger, J. (2018) *Bauxite Mining in Africa* (Berlin: Springer).

Knierzinger, J. (2014) 'The Socio-Political Implications of Bauxite Mining in Guinea: a Commodity Chain Perspective', *The Extractive Industries and Society*, 1(1), pp. 20–27, DOI: 10.1016/j.exis.2014.01.005.

Laet, M. and A. Mol (2000) 'The Zimbabwe Bush Pump: Mechanics of a Fluid Technology', *Social Studies of Science*, 30(2), pp. 225–263, DOI: 10.1177/030631200030002002.

Lahiri-Dutt, K. (2011) *Gendering the Field: Towards Sustainable Livelihoods for Mining Communities* (Canberra: ANU E Press).

Lupa, M., J. Magne, J.L. Guarisco and R. Amedee (2009) 'Update on the Diagnosis and Treatment of Caustic Ingestion', *The Ochsner Journal*, 9(2), pp. 54–59.

Mezzadra, S. and B. Neilson (2019) *The Politics of Operations: Excavating Contemporary Capitalism* (Durham: Duke University Press).

Mezzadri, A. (2019) 'On the Value of Social Reproduction: Informal labour, the majority world and the need for inclusive theories and politics', *Radical Philosophy*, 204, pp. 33–41, https://www.radicalphilosophy.com/article/on-the-value-of-social-reproduction (accessed on 28 March 2023).

Mezzadri, A. (2021) 'A Value Theory of Inclusion: Informal Labour, the Homeworker, and the Social Reproduction of Value', *Antipode*, 53(4), pp. 1186–1205, DOI: 10.1111/anti.12701.

Mezzadri, A., S. Newman and S. Stevano (2021) 'Feminist Global Political Economies of Work and Social Reproduction', *Review of International Political Economy*, pp. 1–21, DOI: 10.1080/09692290.2021.1957977.

Mies, M. (1982) *The Lace Makers of Narsapur: Indian Housewives Produce for the World Market* (London: Zed Press).

Moodie, T.D. (1980) 'The Formal and Informal Social Structure of a South African Gold Mine', *Human Relations*, 33(8), pp.555–574, DOI: 10.1177/001872678003300803.

PROJEG (Programme concerté de Renforcement des capacités des Organisations de la société civile et de la Jeunesse Guinéennes) (2018) *Une ville et sa mine. Le combat de Fria pour se construire un nouveau destin*, Etude d'impact et de Prospective, https://www.coordinationsud.org/wp-content/uploads/04-PROJEG-FRIA_250x176-FINAL_WEB.pdf (accessed on 28 March 2023).

Prokofeva, E.N., A.V. Vostrikov, A.Y. Stebenev, D.M. Volchkov and B.L. Agasandyan (2020) 'Building of Effective Management Structures based on the Digital Technologies in the Mining Industry. a Case Study of UC RUSAL', *IOP Conference Series: Materials Science and Engineering*, 972(1), pp. 12–61, DOI: 10.1088/1757-899X/972/1/012061.

Prügl, E. (2021) 'Untenable Dichotomies: De-Gendering Political Economy', *Review of International Political Economy*, 28(2), pp. 295–306, DOI: 10.1080/09692290.2020.1830834.

Prügl, E. (1999) *The Global Construction of Gender: Home-Based Work in the Political Economy of the 20th Century* (New York: Columbia University Press).

République de Guinée (2011) *Profil National des Produits Chimiques* (Conakry: SAICM/UNITAR).

Rodriguez Castro, L. (2021) 'Extractivism and Territorial Dispossession in Rural Colombia: a Decolonial Commitment to Campesinas' Politics of Place', *Feminist Review*, 128(1), pp. 44–61, DOI: 10.1177/01417789211015269.

RUSAL (2021) *Transforming the Vision*, Sustainability Report 2020, https://rusal.ru/upload/iblock/e34/e3474184f80194b484cd848b7048b0f8.pdf (accessed on 28 March 2023).

Sempértegui, A. (2021) 'Indigenous Women's Activism, Ecofeminism, and Extractivism: Partial Connections in the Ecuadorian Amazon', *Politics and Gender*, 17(1), pp. 197–224, DOI: 10.1017/S1743923X19000023.

Steady, F.C. (2011) *Women and Leadership in West Africa: Mothering the Nation and Humanizing the State* (New York: Palgrave Macmillan).

Syn, J. (2014) 'The Social License: Empowering Communities and a better way Forward', *Social Epistemology*, 28(3–4), pp. 318–339, DOI: 10.1080/02691728.2014.922640.

Szeman, I. and J. Wenzel (2021) 'What do we talk about when we talk about Extractivism?', *Textual Practice*, 35(3), pp. 505–523, DOI: 10.1080/0950236X.2021.1889829.

Widder, L., T. Pacioni, and O. Bocoum (2019) 'Sustainably Growing Guinea's Bauxite-Aluminum Industry' in N. Edomah (ed.), *Regional Development in Africa*, pp. 47–68, DOI: 10.5772/intechopen.86471.

CHAPTER 5

Time for an Outcome Evaluation? The Experience of Indigenous Communities with Mining Benefit Sharing Agreements

Liz Wall and Fiona Haslam McKenzie

Abstract

Much has been written about the promise and potential of mining to deliver or catalyse development opportunities for host communities. Where mining projects affect Indigenous communities, leading practice often encapsulates these aspirations in benefit sharing agreements signed between mining companies and communities. In Australia and Canada these agreements often take the form of Indigenous Land Use Agreements and Impact Benefit Agreements, respectively. With more than 60 per cent of mining in Australia alone occurring in proximity to Indigenous communities, it is clear that the future of mining is dependent on effective delivery against the expectations and aspirations of Indigenous communities that form the basis of these agreements. In Australia and beyond, mining occurring on the lands of Indigenous peoples has become the source of increasing calls for a 'new development model'. However, in order to articulate a call for a new model, the success of the existing model needs to be adequately evaluated, and while this has been occurring during the operational period, it is also necessary when a mine (and an agreement) comes to an end. By reviewing the existing literature, and specifically that encapsulating practitioner experience, this chapter highlights the gap in research evaluating the effectiveness of the existing benefit sharing model for Indigenous communities, as judged by those communities, at the time of mine closure. To some extent this gap is due to the limited number of mines that have closed where benefit sharing agreements had been in place; opportunities for such research have, however, existed and now need to be pursued. Development projects and policies are typically subject to an outcome evaluation process, and given the criticality of the relationship between Indigenous peoples and the extractive sector the time is ripe to evaluate existing approaches in order to inform the benefit sharing models of the future.

 | DOI:10.1163/9789004685994_006

1 Introduction

While expectations of mineral development continue to evolve (Anaya, 2015), the components of the mineral development model that has informed benefit sharing agreements have remained largely unchanged for the past two decades (Sosa and Keenan, 2001). Arguably, the model has been premised on the assumption that the delivery of a combination of royalties, jobs, contracts and community investment to Indigenous communities would result in these communities being 'better off' for having hosted a mine on their land. Essentially this can be considered the hypothesis behind a multi-decade experiment, and only now, with the closure of some of the more progressive and iconic mines (with reputations for excellence in their delivery of the mineral development model) are the results able to be assessed.

The extent to which benefit sharing agreements are delivering on the expectations of Indigenous communities requires a consideration of several fields—mining's contribution to development, the application and purpose of benefit sharing agreements, and the social aspects of mine closure—and that we define what may constitute a successful outcome for an indigenous community. In reviewing the literature across each of these fields, this chapter reinforces existing calls (Bainton and Holcombe, 2018b; Cohen, 2017; O'Faircheallaigh, 1998; Rixen and Blangy, 2016) for more case study research on the experience of Indigenous communities and their perceptions of a successful outcome. This review addresses the need to conduct an outcome evaluation (United Nations Development Programme (UNDP), 2009; 2002) of existing benefit sharing approaches as judged at the time of mine closure. Reference sources selected for the chapter were drawn from three principal lines of evidence. Firstly, those references considered most influential from the experience of the lead author as a practitioner in the subject matter area over two decades of practical experience both from the mining industry perspective and that of a global funding agency. Secondly, from a literature search of peer-reviewed publications from mainstream scholarly publication houses. Thirdly, references from global institutions and active industry and government participants in the area of the paper's focus, including the World Bank, United Nations, mining companies, industry bodies, and applied academic research institutions. References were chosen primarily focusing on the period 2000–20, although references to prior seminal works in the field are also included to give due credit to past work on which the more contemporary contributions build.

2 Mining's Contested Contribution to Development

For many centuries, a large mineral endowment was considered beneficial to a country's development (McMahon and Moreira, 2014); however, this optimism was tempered during the twentieth century with global recognition that 'realising the potential for mining to contribute to development in all countries where it takes places is arguably one of the greatest priorities facing the mining and minerals sector' (International Institute for Environment and Development (IIED), 2002, 172). Questions related to mining's contribution to development arose in the 1950s, focusing on the weakness of linkages between primary production and the rest of the economy. These questions gained momentum with *The Economist*'s introduction of the concept of the Dutch Disease in 1977 (Mien and Goujon, 2021). This concept sought to explain the troubles experienced by the Dutch economy in the 1960s, in relation to the allocation of revenues from natural gas developments, and the consequence of these revenues on the strength of the currency and the competitiveness of the Netherlands' other exports (McMahon and Moreira, 2014). It was not until the late 1980s that Gelb (1988) analysed the growth rates experienced in a number of oil-exporting countries, coining the term 'resource curse' to describe how countries developing natural resources experienced growth rates below those that would have otherwise been predicted (Gelb, 1988). Subsequent studies (Auty, 1990; Sachs and Warner, 1995; 1997) drew similar conclusions to those of Gelb, firmly entrenching a shift in perception from natural resources providing development opportunities to one of an inverse relationship between mineral endowment and realised economic growth (McMahon and Moreira, 2014; Mien and Goujon, 2021).

The significant body of literature that has developed around the resource curse began with an economic focus, before expanding into analysis of the impact of natural resource wealth on sociopolitical development, including analysis of rent seeking, corruption, lack of democracy, conflict (McMahon and Moreira, 2014; Van der Ploeg, 2011) and the strength of institutions (Robinson, Torvik and Verdier, 2006; 2014). More recently, the accuracy of the resource-curse thesis has come under pressure, with leading proponents of the theory acknowledging that the question of whether an abundance of natural resources is a curse or blessing is a source of fundamental debate within economics (Collier, 2010; Van Der Ploeg and Poelhekke, 2017). McMahon and Moreira (2014) further this questioning through their examination of five low- and middle-income countries with long histories of mining, concluding each country experienced either a relatively high human development index (HDI) or a strong improvement in its HDI compared to those experienced by countries without minerals. While neither proving nor disproving the resource curse, the basis for its existence continues to be examined, and to inform debates on the role of minerals in national development.

Principal among those debates is the discussion around extractivism and neo-extractivism in Latin America and, increasingly, beyond. Referring to the predominance of economic activities primarily based on resource extraction and nature valorisation without distributive politics (Brand, Dietz and Lang, 2016), extractivism has formed the basis of much government policy in recent decades in Latin America. With economies dominated by the export of primary goods (including agriculture, forestry, hunting and mining) (Brand, Dietz and Lang, 2016), questions naturally arose in relation to the conversion from economic growth into poverty reduction (Burchardt and Dietz, 2014). More recently, a shift towards neo-extractivism—the use of surplus revenue from extractive activities to address poverty and enhance the material well-being of the population (Brand, Dietz and Lang, 2016)—is being considered as a new model for development in the region. However, much debate persists on how this model can be balanced with societal–nature relations, as articulated in the commitment to 'living well' (*buen vivir*) in the constitutions of Ecuador and Bolivia (Brand, Dietz and Lang, 2016; Gudynas, 2016; 2018; 2019; Van Teijlingen, 2016), the current social and political debate over extractivism in Europe (del Mármol and Vaccaro, 2020), and reflections on how different actors position themselves in relation to the 'multiplicity of effects of resource extraction' (Pijpers and Eriksen, 2019, 2).

Notwithstanding reservations or questions about the role of mining in development, many organisations and development initiatives have continued to focus on the development potential afforded by mineral development. These include the Australian-led International Mining for Development Centre (IM4DC, 2015), the World Bank's Extractive Sector Programmatic Support initiative (World Bank, 2021a), and material published by mining sector representative bodies (Cardno and MCA, 2018; ICMM, 2018).

Within the literature considering the potential for mining to generate either positive or negative development impacts, the vast majority of research has been focused on the national level. As highlighted by Horowitz et al. (2018), comparable analysis of the development contribution of mining to specific communities, such as Indigenous groups, is limited. Both regional-level analysis of Dutch Disease impacts (Papyrakis and Raveh, 2014) and community-level analyses in Indigenous communities (Langton and Mazel, 2008; O'Faircheallaigh, 2012) have been undertaken; they are, however, limited in number and have tended to be undertaken part way through the mining cycle. Hence, while such studies often foreshadow the impacts of mine closure, they do not necessarily convey the realised experience and impacts of closure when it occurs, and may therefore miss the aggregate development outcome achieved from hosting a mine.

3 Benefit Sharing with Indigenous Communities

Expectations around the sharing of benefits and compensation for damages generated by mining projects have increased in the past two decades due to a combination of widespread liberalisation of mining investment regimes, increased advocacy and empowerment of communities, the growth of corporate social responsibility, and demands for governments to be able to demonstrate a local positive impact from mining through a project's life cycle (Wall and Pelon, 2011). Mining projects can contribute to development through a number of benefit sharing channels, including: employment, procurement, value-adding beneficiation (the treatment of a raw material to improve its properties), project infrastructure, taxes, royalties, equity, community investment, and compensation (Wall and Pelon, 2011). Kung et al. (2022) and Bainton (2020) highlight a number of areas where expectations have grown and continue to increase—specifically around Indigenous equity participation and the transition from a focus on jobs and accumulation to a broader discussion around rights and long-term benefit.

While a company's obligations to compensate for or remedy identified impacts are typically legislated (with variable levels of enforcement), the nature of a mining company's relationships with the communities it directly affects (defined as 'affected communities' by the International Finance Corporation, IFC, 2012) and the sharing of benefits sit largely outside the remit of national legislation or policy (Parsons, Lacey and Moffat, 2014). In recognition of this gap, the concept of a Social Licence to Operate (SLO) was, in its contemporary usage, coined in 1997 by James Cooney, the then Vice President of External Relations for Placer Dome (Boutilier, 2014), comparing the need for community approval of projects with that of legal licences and permits (Boutilier, 2021). While much debate surrounds this concept, including over what it looks like, whether it is a veto, and how it can be achieved (Boutilier, 2021; Harvey, 2014; Kemp and Owen, 2016; Owen and Kemp, 2013; Parsons, Lacey and Moffat, 2014; Thomson and Boutilier, 2011), it has been pivotal in framing conversations about the roles and responsibilities of mining companies in communities. In more recent years the conversation has increasingly focused on the need to maintain a social licence throughout the duration of a mining project (Moffat and Zhang, 2014).

Negotiated agreements through which relationships between extractive companies and Indigenous landowners are formalised and governed have become increasingly prevalent (Adebayo and Werker, 2021; Kung et al., 2022; Sulyandziga, 2019; Tysiachniouk et al., 2018). Variously called benefit sharing agreements, local-level agreements, community development agreements, Indigenous land-use agreements (ILUAs), and impact and benefit agreements, they are referred to as benefit sharing agreements throughout this chapter.

In Australia specifically, ILUAs grew out of the landmark Mabo legal case recognising native title (the right of Aboriginal peoples to own their traditional lands and waters, as recognised by common law). ILUAs are voluntary agreements between native title parties and other people or bodies about the use and management of areas of land and/or waters, and many have been developed in relation to mining. By June 2022, over 1,400 ILUAs had been registered with the National Native Title Tribunal (NNTT, 2022). Figure 5.1 illustrates the geographic coverage of ILUAs that have been signed.

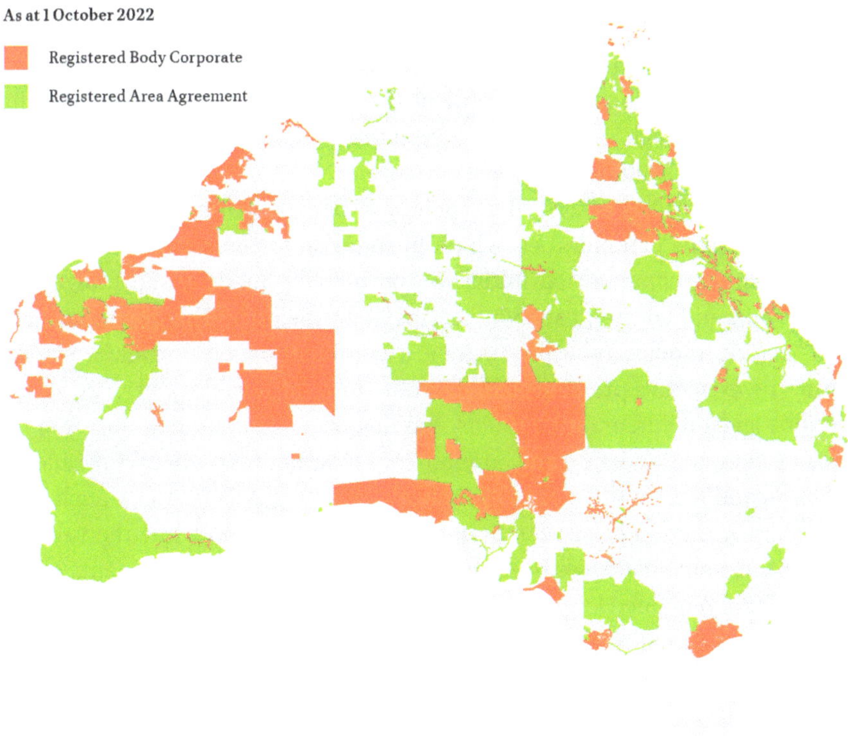

FIGURE 5.1 Indigenous land use agreements in Australia
SOURCE: AUTHORS, WITH DATA FROM NNTT, 2022

The optimal vehicle through which benefits can be shared has also been the subject of considerable analysis, with extensive critiques of different models such as community development agreements (CDAs), funds, trusts and foundations, public regulation, voluntary industry initiatives, and company discretion (O'Faircheallaigh, 2015; 2018; Wall and Pelon, 2011; World Bank, 2010; 2012).

There is a growing body of literature examining best practice in benefit sharing agreements (Cascadden, Gunton and Rutherford, 2021; Everingham et al., 2016; Gibson and O'Faircheallaigh, 2015; O'Faircheallaigh, 2015; 2018; 2012; Söderholm and Svahn, 2015; Sosa and Keenan, 2001; World Bank, 2012); most, however, has focused on the process and establishment of the conditions of agreements, with less focus on the outcomes they have achieved.

Moreover, expectations of what 'fair and equitable' benefit sharing should comprise vary significantly across jurisdictions and between various rights holders (Wilson, 2019). The rights of Indigenous and land-connected communities directly impacted by mining projects to participate in benefit sharing agreements have been enshrined in Australia and Canada (amongst other countries) through legislative requirements to develop ILUAs and Impact and Benefit Agreements (IBAs), respectively (O'Faircheallaigh, 2018). While legislation notes the requirement that such agreements should be developed, it largely leaves the content and value of the benefit sharing agreement to be determined through negotiation between the company and the affected community (O'Faircheallaigh, 2015; Wilson, 2019).

Wilson (2019) has described a typology of benefit sharing models for local and Indigenous communities, which includes state-controlled benefit sharing, voluntary company-led initiatives, partnership models, and Indigenous ownership and control, each with several subcategories. The dominant benefit sharing models typically include a combination of a revenue stream from the extractive project (possibly in the form of royalties), priority access to jobs and procurement contracts, training opportunities, cultural support, environmental protection and community investment initiatives (Cascadden, Gunton and Rutherford, 2021; O'Faircheallaigh, 2015; Wilson, 2019). Such benefit sharing models have been in use since the 1990s, and while the value of benefits in some instances have changed significantly, the components of the model have remained largely stable. The development contribution of specific parts of these models have come under scrutiny (Holcombe and Kemp, 2020; O'Faircheallaigh, 2018; Wilson and Istomin, 2019), but limited work has been undertaken to evaluate the aggregate development impact achieved by them, especially at the conclusion of the revenue producing activity.

Increasingly, the negotiation of project consent and associated benefits with Indigenous communities is framed in the context of free, prior and informed consent (FPIC) (MacInnes, Colchester and Whitmore, 2017; Southalan and Fardin, 2019; Tomlinson, 2019). This is not a new requirement, and it has been the subject of much deliberation since the World Bank commissioned the Extractive Industries Review in 2003 (MacInnes, Colchester and Whitmore, 2017; World Bank, 2003). The concept of FPIC derives from principles of equal rights and self-determination enshrined in the 1945 Charter of the United Nations, and reinforced through International Labour Organization Convention 169 (1989) and the United Nations Declaration on the Rights of Indigenous Peoples (UNDRIP) (2007) (Social Practice Forum, 2020; United Nations, 2007). Article 32 of UNDRIP specifically addresses the rights of Indigenous communities to determine and develop priorities for the development or use of their lands and territories. It requires states to consult and cooperate with Indigenous communities in good faith to seek their FPIC prior to the approval of any mining project affecting their lands or territories and other resources (United Nations, 2007). While widely referenced as a necessary condition for mining projects to proceed on Indigenous territory, there is no universally accepted definition of FPIC (IFC, 2012; Owen and Kemp, 2014).

Within this context, discussions on the contribution of mining projects to development in Indigenous communities are often focused on the pre-project approval period, with primacy increasingly given to considerations of FPIC and good faith negotiation of benefit packages. To the extent that development outcomes of agreed benefit packages have been assessed, as Söderholm and Svahn (2015) identified in their synthesised analysis of the literature on development impacts in four developed countries much of the analysis is based on assessments of inputs and outputs. Notable exceptions include the analysis of 'curse or opportunity' from mining for Aboriginal Australia by O'Faircheallaigh (2012), efforts to analyse the resource curse in Aboriginal communities neighbouring mining by Langton and Mazel (2008), case study research conducted by Altman and Martin (2009), empirical studies on regional well-being indicators among Western Australian Indigenous communities affected by mining by Taylor (2018; 2019), and Rodon's (2018) critique of development outcomes for Indigenous Peoples in Canada's Arctic.

Although failure to address impacts generated by mining will undoubtedly result in a poor or adverse development contribution, impact management and development contribution are generally not the same thing. Impact management is often described as mitigating or ameliorating the negative consequence of a project, with development contribution adding a positive contribution. During his tenure as the United Nations Special Rapporteur on the Rights of Indigenous Peoples, James Anaya investigated the experience of Indigenous communities living in close proximity to mining projects (Anaya,

2011), highlighting a number of severe adverse impacts. However, his observations extended beyond merely considering the extent to which impacts were mitigated, to also reflect on the level of benefit sharing that had occurred. Building on these observations, he noted that

> [the] prevailing model of resource extraction is one in which an outside company, with backing by the State, controls and profits from the extractive operation, with the affected Indigenous peoples at best being offered benefits in the form of jobs or community development projects that typically pale in economic value in comparison to profits gained by the corporation.
>
> ANAYA, 2013, 12

He went on to call for a new model that would prioritise Indigenous-controlled extraction (Anaya, 2013). In the intervening years, an increasing number of equity based agreements and Indigenous owned and controlled extractive projects (Denedeh Investments Corporation, 2021; First Nations Major Project Coalition, 2021; Gulkula, 2021; NRCAN, 2017; Suncor Energy Inc, 2021; TNDC, 2021) and associated contracting, infrastructure and financing projects (Carey Mining, 2021; First Nations Major Project Coalition, 2021) have emerged (although not all have been consummated; see, e.g., NAIF, 2021), but this is yet to become a dominant element of the mining industry.

While the mining industry has not necessarily fully embraced Anaya's call for a new model, and notwithstanding the limited empirical basis on which to claim success or failure in terms of development impacts from the existing model, mining companies and their representative bodies have been forthcoming in the ambitions they have set for themselves when working with Indigenous communities. The ICMM commits its 28 member companies (representing most of the largest and most influential global mining companies) to 'ensuring sustainable benefits and opportunities for Indigenous Peoples through the development of mining and metals projects' (ICMM, 2013). Similarly, the vision of one multinational mining company includes reference to 'shared, sustainable prosperity in our host communities' (Anglo American, 2021). While another states,

> Indigenous peoples will derive significant and sustainable benefit from BHP operations through the effective governance and management of land access, cultural heritage management, agreement making and benefit distribution processes […] BHP will contribute to improved quality of life for Indigenous peoples through voluntary social investment, support

> for reinforcement and promotion of Indigenous culture and building the Indigenous cultural awareness of our workforce.
>
> BHP, 2021

And a third sets out its commitment to 'work with Indigenous Peoples to achieve self-determined community goals that provide lasting benefits' (Teck, 2021).

4 The Perspective Gained from Mine Closure

The development outcomes of mining projects and their associated benefit sharing agreements are often evaluated during the operational phase of a project, when jobs and contracts are available, royalties are being paid and community investment initiatives are being implemented. However, the best time to assess the success of the existing model in achieving sustainable development outcomes is upon, or preferably after, mine closure. Mine closure has received considerably less attention as a research topic than other, arguably more optimistic phases of the mining cycle, and this lack of focus is evident in the small body of literature addressing the social aspects of mine closure (Bainton and Holcombe, 2018a). It was only at the turn of the millennium that significant focus started to be applied to this topic, through the World Bank Group's *Mine Closure and Sustainable Development* volume (Khanna, 2000) and the *Mining, Minerals and Sustainable Development* (MMSD) review (IIED, 2002). One of MMSD's nine key findings was that ensuring 'that improved health and education or economic activity will endure after mines close' required a level of planning that too often was not achieved (p. xvii). While mine closure is regulated in a growing number of countries, most regulation continues to focus on environmental and safety considerations, with very few standards set for the social outcomes to be achieved at mine closure. To the extent that social aspects of mine closure are anticipated in regulatory frameworks, requirements are typically limited to demonstrations of engagement with affected communities through closure planning (Kung, Everingham and Vivoda, 2020).

In the two decades since the appearance of the Bank's volume and of MMSD, many of the developments in this space have focused on closure planning from a practitioner perspective (Bainton and Holcombe, 2018a), including the development of good practice guides and frameworks (ICMM, 2020; MCA, 2015; Mining Association of Canada (MAC, 2008). These guides increasingly call for 'integrated mine closure planning', placing socio-economic considerations on a more equal footing with environmental and decommissioning considerations. However, few examples of successful mine closure and relinquishment have been documented (Bainton and Holcombe, 2018a). Early contributors to the field of social mine closure were particularly focused on the often vexing question of how to transition 'mine towns' (Neil, Tykkyläinen and Bradbury, 1992). Town 'normalisation' as it is often referred to has now developed into its own field (Littlewood, 2014; Marais et al., 2018). Subsequent researchers have focused on post-mining landscapes (Harvey, 2016; Kivinen, Vartiainen and Kumpula, 2018) and potential tension between environmental remediation and future economic occupation of post-mining environments.

Recognising the need for a central repository of knowledge, the Social Aspects of Mine Closure Research Consortium (2019) developed an e-library to capture the body of knowledge in this space. Most literature on social closure planning has sought to address challenges associated with 'transitioning' communities to a new socio-economic context. Such transitions can be complex, and can include impacts on local employment and business opportunities, the loss or transition of infrastructure and assets, loss of income (e.g. royalties and taxes), long-term or permanent changes to the landscape and environment, ongoing management of potentially hazardous infrastructure, and permanent impacts on cultural heritage. However, the experience evidenced in recent comparisons of mine closure plans (Kabir et al., 2015; Monosky and Keeling, 2021) indicates there remains a long way to go to adequately plan for and achieve success in the social aspects of mine closure.

Within the mine closure literature there is a small body of work focused on the impact of closure on Indigenous communities, and particularly on what a positive post-mining legacy might look like for these communities. In the operational closure context, there has been a temptation to reduce social closure to the cessation of an agreement, and to consider the cessation of an agreement an administrative exercise, neglecting mine closure's often significant economic, social and cultural impacts on Indigenous communities. The extent to which Indigenous communities have been involved in closure planning has tended to be driven by the need of the mining companies and their consultants to inform closure designs, rather than such involvement being a process via which to define and enable post-closure socio-economic legacies for the communities affected (Kung, Everingham and Vivoda, 2020; Monosky and Keeling, 2021). There is a growing chorus of calls for more work to be undertaken in this area (O'Faircheallaigh and Lawrence, 2019; Rodon and Levesque, 2015) and for an actor-oriented approach to mine closure, placing the knowledge, views and interests of Indigenous communities at the centre of the planning process (Chaloping-March, 2018).

Notably absent from most discussions of the social aspects of mine closure is a reflection on whether the expectations of communities have been met at the time of mine closure. This is not unsurprising given the often vague commitments made around economic growth and opportunity at the time of mine development and the considerable number of years that have typically passed from mine development to mine closure. This does, however, appear to constitute an obvious gap in which the assertions of 'sustainable benefits and opportunities' for host communities are yet to be fully tested. Questions asked of communities during engagement around mine closure tend to focus on whether they are satisfied with the closure process and specific details of the environmental remediation plan, but fail to ask or adequately assess whether the community is—and whether Indigenous communities in particular are—satisfied with the experience of having hosted a mine and the outcomes of the ILUAs and IBAs. Social impact assessments undertaken for mine closure are precisely as described, impact assessments of the experience of closure and its associated transitions, with little opportunity to address the more fundamental question of the impact of having hosted a mine, with mine closure representing only the final stage in this continuum.

5 Evaluating the Outcome

To quote UNDP, 'outcomes are developmental changes between the completion of outputs and the achievement of impact' (UNDP, 2002, 6). In the two decades since UNDP prepared its guidelines for outcome evaluators, outcome evaluation (and in some cases impact evaluation (Belcher and Palenberg, 2018)) has become a standard and critical element of most, if not all, development initiatives. While benefit sharing models are not always described as or considered to be development initiatives—and as with all analyses of outcomes and impact there can be a multitude of causal relationships (Belcher and Palenberg, 2018)—there is no obvious reason why an outcome evaluation approach should not be applied to them.

For the development outcomes achieved for an Indigenous community under a benefit sharing model to be assessed, a definition of what 'better off' means for that community and how it can be measured or evaluated is needed. Being 'better off' might better be considered to mean achieving some level of 'development'. As observed in the introduction of the first Human Development Report, 'the basic objective of development is to create an enabling environment for people to enjoy long, healthy, and creative lives' (UNDP, 1990, 9)—or, put simply, an improved level of well-being.

Prior to Amartya Sen's capability approach (CA) (Sen, 1979a; 1979b; 1985), the objectives of development focused primarily on utilitarian concepts of income and possession of commodities (Deneulin and McGregor, 2010). The CA instead placed the primary focus on an individual's freedom to achieve well-being, considering not what an individual has, but what individuals are able to do with what they have. Prioritising multidimensional approaches to progress and poverty, the CA is often credited with expanding the notion of well-being beyond 'objective' criteria such as life expectancy, rates of literacy and levels of unemployment (Manning, Ambrey and Fleming, 2016). As an approach, rather than a development theory the CA is focused on the informational basis for ethical judgements, and does not advocate some specific way of identifying what people might have reason to value (Deneulin and McGregor, 2010).

Utilitarian indicators of economic development were placed under further scrutiny in 2008 when the French Government commissioned its Report on the Measurement of Economic Performance and Social Progress (Stiglitz, Sen and Fitoussi, 2009). Bringing together a number of leading scholars, the Commission concluded that there was a need to 'shift [the] emphasis from measuring economic production to measuring people's well-being' (Stiglitz et al., 2009, 12). Rising to this challenge, the Organisation for Economic Co-operation and Development (OECD) and the European Union (EU) collated both objective and subjective data across countries to measure national well-being (Anderson and Mossialos, 2019), and a number of countries have also established well-being indicators and priorities (Caria and Domínguez, 2016; Dalziel, 2019; Thinley and Hartz-Karp, 2019). Specifically within the extractive sector, researchers have also started to probe relationships between the resource curse and happiness levels (Ali, Murshed and Papyrakis, 2020).

Embracing the expansion of well-being to go beyond indicators of economic growth, the set of eight Millennium Development Goals (MDGs) signed up to by all 189 UN Member States in 2000 (to be achieved by 2015) and the subsequent 17 Sustainable Development Goals (SDGs) specifically sought to establish global-level development targets, with associated indicators. Notwithstanding the holistic objectives of the MDGs and SDGs as global indicators, and the various national and regional initiatives to measure well-being, many are necessarily generic in nature and from their earliest inception questions were raised about how best to incorporate greater recognition of Indigenous concerns, interests and interpretations of development and well-being (Taylor, 2008).

Since its establishment in 2000, the United Nations Permanent Forum on Indigenous Issues (UNPFII) has been working to establish statistical profiles of the world's Indigenous peoples, and in 2004 a UNPFII workshop concluded, after reviewing the MDGs, that a conceptual framework for rights-based indicators was needed for Indigenous peoples (Taylor, 2008). UNDRIP (United Nations, 2007) further reinforced the importance of Indigenous peoples, defining its own indicators for well-being through articles 3 and 43, which assert that Indigenous peoples must be the agents of their own development and set the priorities that they value (Yap and Yu, 2016). A number of countries and Indigenous communities have sought to do precisely this, as seen in the Survey of Living Conditions in the Arctic (SLiCA), which focused on Innuit, Sammi and Indigenous peoples of Chukotka (Kruse et al., 2008), the development of a Maori Statistics Framework (Taylor, 2008), and the Australian Bureau of Statistics' National Aboriginal and Torres Strait Islander Social Survey (NATSISS) (Prout, 2012). These approaches break away from the pattern of identifying gaps between indicators for Indigenous communities and those for mainstream majority populations where the goal is one of equality of socioeconomic status, allowing space for conversations around self-determination (Taylor, 2008).

Indigenous well-being frameworks seek to ensure Indigenous voice and world views form the basis of an analysis of Indigenous well-being. For example, greater participation in the formal economy (through employment) would be considered an indicator of improved well-being in most analyses but may be considered negatively by Indigenous communities if it impinges on the maintenance of traditional cultural practices (Taylor, 2008). Existing indicators, and the CA in general, place considerable focus on individuals, which can often be inconsistent with more communal concepts of well-being held by Indigenous communities (Mero-Figueroa et al., 2020; Prout, 2012; Yap and Yu, 2016). Analysis of specific indicators can also fail to capture the highly interrelated nature of cultural, social and economic dynamics (Fonda and Anderson, 2009). Western models often fail to consider concepts of place and country and the need to ensure their protection (Barletti, 2016; Prout, 2012). Indicators of cultural autonomy and the strength of Indigenous governance also constitute a key gap (Prout, 2012). There are no 'off-the-shelf' models of Indigenous well-being that can (or should) be applied; there are, however, lessons from Australia (Prout, 2012; Yap and Yu, 2016) and Canada (Rixen and Blangy, 2016) upon which approaches can be built in collaboration with affected communities. This is an evolving field, with increasing pressure within Indigenous groups to take the lead in the development of environmental, social and governance (ESG) indicators (Podlasly, 2021).

6 Conclusion

Indigenous communities are present in more than 90 countries (United Nations, 2009), many of which have significant mineral resources.[1] Indigenous people represent approximately 5 per cent of the global population, but comprise approximately 15 per cent of the extreme poor (World Bank, 2021b). With mineral endowments located all over the globe, and most new mining development projects contingent upon community support, it is clear that the future expansion of the mining industry will be (or should be) dependent on being able to develop mutually beneficial relationships with Indigenous communities. In recent decades, the achievement of these mutually beneficial relationships has largely been assumed to be delivered through benefit sharing agreements between extractive sector companies and affected Indigenous communities. However, as highlighted by O'Faircheallaigh (1998; 2010; 2013a; 2013b; 2017; 2021) there remains a significant power imbalance in the negotiating positions of mining companies and Indigenous communities when such agreements are developed and implemented. While the development outcomes delivered by the extractive industry have been much assessed, the analysis has tended to focus on the national or regional levels, with a knowledge gap regarding the extent to which the effectiveness of existing benefit sharing agreements delivering on the expectations of in situ Indigenous communities has been realised.

This chapter reinforces the call for more case study–based research around the experience of Indigenous people hosting extractive sector projects on their lands and points to the vacuum around assessing this experience at mine closure, when the totality of the experience and final impact can be determined. Efforts are underway to begin to address that vacuum, as can be seen in a recent collaboration facilitated by the University of Queensland's Centre for Social Responsibility in Mining bringing together Indigenous communities in Australia, New Zealand and Canada to discuss their experiences of mine closure (CSRM, 2021). It is, however, acknowledged by all that this is only the beginning of the research and collaboration that is required. The chapter also highlights the critical importance of conducting assessments by working in collaboration with, if not led by, affected communities themselves, thus ensuring that any outcome evaluation is truly reflective of the values and priorities of those communities—that is to say, that it judges the experience against the host community's definition of 'success'. Such evaluation will also be critical

1 Of the 71 countries and territories reporting to the International Work Group for Indigenous Affairs (IWGIA), 86% also export mineral products (IWGIA, 2021).

to informing the structural causes of the success or failure of different benefit sharing agreements.

Mining in Australia generated over USD 140 billion (AUD 200 billion) in 2019 and 2020 combined (MCA, 2020), in a country in which more than 60 per cent of all mineral resources are located in proximity to Indigenous communities (Australian Government, 2016). In Canada, the government estimated in 2015 that then current and planned resource development projects would yield investments of approximately USD 514 billion (CAD 650 billion) over the following decade, with over 1,200 Aboriginal communities located within a 200 kilometre radius of producing mines or active exploration areas (Kielland, 2015). While these two countries may be somewhat extreme cases, they illustrate that there is a business and an ethical case, both compelling, for assessing whether current benefit sharing agreements are delivering on Indigenous expectations. While the level of rights of Indigenous peoples recognised by host governments varies considerably across jurisdictions, at both a local and a global level Indigenous peoples are key stakeholders in extractive sector development. With so many significant mine closures expected to occur in the coming decade or so, the time is ripe to evaluate the outcomes achieved under the existing benefit sharing model in order to better inform the models needed for future mineral development.

Disclosure statement

No potential conflict of interest was reported by the authors.

References

Adebayo, E., and E. Werker (2021) 'How Much are Benefit-sharing Agreements Worth to Communities Affected by Mining?', *Resources Policy*, 71, DOI: 10.1016/j.resourpol.2020.101970.

Ali, S., S.M. Murshed and E. Papyrakis (2020) 'Happiness and the Resource Curse', *Journal of Happiness Studies*, 21(2), pp. 437–464, DOI: 10.1007/s10902-019-00080-3.

Altman, J. and D. Martin (eds.) (2009) *Power, Culture, Economy—Indigenous Australians and Mining*, Research Monograph No. 30 (Canberra: Australian National University Press).

Anaya, S.J. (2015) 'Report of the Special Rapporteur on the Rights of Indigenous Peoples on Extractive Industries and Indigenous Peoples', *Arizona Journal of International and Comparative Law*, 32(1), pp. 109–142.

Anaya, S.J. (2013) *Report of the Special Rapporteur on the Rights of Indigenous Peoples, James Anaya: Extractive industries and indigenous peoples* (New York: United Nations), https://documents-dds-ny.un.org/doc/undoc/GEN/G13/152/49/PDF/G1315249.pdf?OpenElement (accessed on 30 November 2022).

Anaya, S.J. (2011) *Report of the Special Rapporteur on the Rights of Indigenous Peoples, James Anaya: Extractive Industries Operating within or Near Indigenous Territories* (New York: United Nations), https://undocs.org/A/HRC/18/35 (accessed on 30 November 2022).

Anderson, M., and E. Mossialos (2019) 'Beyond Gross Domestic Product for New Zealand's Wellbeing Budget', *The Lancet. Public Health,* 4(7), pp. e320–e321, DOI: 10.1016/S2468-2667(19)30109-4.

Anglo American (2021) *Communities* (London: Anglo American), https://www.angloamerican.com/sustainability/communities (accessed on 24 November 2022).

Australian Government (2016) *Working with Indigenous Communities* (Cambera: Commonwealth of Australia), https://www.industry.gov.au/sites/default/files/2019-04/lpsdp-working-with-indigenous-communities-handbook-english.pdf (accessed on 24 November 2022).

Auty, R.M. (1990) *Resource-Based Industrialization: Sowing the Oil in Eight Developing Countries* (Oxford: Oxford University Press).

Bainton, N. (2020) *Mining and Indigenous Peoples* (Oxford: Oxford University Press).

Bainton, N. and S. Holcombe (2018a) 'A Critical Review of the Social Aspects of Mine Closure', *Resources Policy,* 59, pp. 468–478, DOI: 10.1016/j.resourpol.2018.08.020.

Bainton, N. and S. Holcombe (2018b) 'The Social Aspects of Mine Closure. a Global Literature Review', *Centre for Social Responsibility in Mining* (Queensland: Sustainable Minerals Institute, University of Queensland).

Barletti, J. (2016) 'The Angry Earth—Wellbeing, Place and Extractivism in the Amazon', *Anthropology in Action,* 23, pp. 43–53.

Belcher, B. and M. Palenberg (2018) 'Outcomes and Impacts of Development Interventions: Toward Conceptual Clarity', *American Journal of Evaluation,* 39(4), pp. 478–495, DOI: 10.1177/1098214018765698.

BHP (2021) *Global Indigenous Peoples Strategy* (Australia: BHP), https://www.bhp.com/-/media/documents/ourapproach/operatingwithintegrity/indigenouspeoples/200619_bhpglobalindigenouspeoplesstrategy.pdf?la=en (accessed on 24 November 2022).

Boutilier, R.G. (2021) 'From Metaphor to Political Spin: Understanding Criticisms of the Social Licence', *The Extractive Industries and Society,* 8(2), 100743, DOI: 10.1016/j.exis.2020.05.022.

Boutilier, R.G. (2014) 'Frequently asked Questions about the Social Licence to Operate', *Impact Assessment and Project Appraisal,* 32(4), pp. 263–272.

Brand, U., K. Dietz and M. Lang (2016) 'Neo-Extractivism in Latin America—one Side of a New Phase of Global Capitalist Dynamics', *Ciencia Política*, 11(21), DOI: 10.15446/cp.v11n21.57551.

Burchardt, H.-J., and K. Dietz (2014) '(Neo-)extractivism—a New Challenge for Development theory from Latin America', *Third World Quarterly*, 35(3), pp. 468–486, DOI: 10.1080/01436597.2014.893488.

Cardno and MCA (Minerals Council of Australia) (2018) *Sustainable Development Goals—Sustainability in Action: Australian Mining and the United Nations Sustainable Development Goals* (Kingston ACT: MCA), https://minerals.org.au/wp-content/uploads/2022/12/Sustainability-in-Action-October-2018.pdf (accessed on 15 August 2023).

Carey Mining (2021) *Carey Mining* (Malaga WA: Carey Mining), https://careymining.com.au/ (accessed on 24 November 2022).

Caria, S. and R. Domínguez (2016) 'Ecuador's "Buen vivir": a New Ideology for Development', *Latin American Perspectives*, 43(1), pp. 18–33, DOI: 10.1177/0094582X15611126.

Cascadden, M., T. Gunton and M. Rutherford (2021) 'Best Practices for Impact Benefit Agreements', *Resources Policy*, 70, DOI: 10.1016/j.resourpol.2020.101921.

Chaloping-March, M. (2018) *Social Terrains of Mine Closure in the Philippines* (London: Routledge).

Cohen, T. (2017) 'Bringing Country Back?: Indigenous Aspirations and Ecological Values', in *Australian Mine-Site Rehabilitation* (New York: Routledge), pp. 137–150.

Collier, P. (2010) *The Plundered Planet: Why We Must—and How We Can—Manage Nature for Global Propserity* (Oxford: Oxford University Press).

CSRM (Centre for Social Responsibility in Mining) (2021) *Building Connections between First Nations Peoples who have Major Mines on their Lands*, 17 November, https://smi.uq.edu.au/article/2021/11/building-connections-between-first-nations-peoples-who-have-major-mines-their-lands (accessed on 29 November 2022).

Dalziel, P. (2019) 'Wellbeing Economics in Public Policy: a Distinctive Australasian Contribution?', *The Economic and Labour Relations Review*, 30(4), pp. 478–497, DOI: 10.1177/1035304619879808.

Del Mármol, C. and I. Vaccaro (2020) 'New extractivism in European rural areas: How Twentieth First Century Mining Returned to Disturb the Rural Transition', *Geoforum*, 116, pp. 42–49, DOI: 10.1016/j.geoforum.2020.07.012.

Denedeh Investments Corporation (2021) *DEMCO Limited Partnership.*

Deneulin, S. and J.A. McGregor (2010) 'The Capability Approach and the Politics of a Social Conception of Wellbeing', *European Journal of Social Theory*, 13(4), pp. 501–519, DOI: 10.1177/1368431010382762.

Everingham, J., D. Kemp, S. Ali, G. Cornish, D. Brereton, J. Parmenter, M. Langton and B. Harvey (2016) *Why Agreements Matter* (Queensland: Sustainable Minerals Institute,

University of Queensland), https://www.csrm.uq.edu.au/publications/why-agreements-matter (accessed on 30 November 2022).

First Nations Major Project Coalition (2021) *Stonger Together*, https://fnmpc.ca/ (accessed on 30 November 2022).

Fonda, M. and E. Anderson (2009) 'Diamonds in Canada's North: a Lesson in Measuring Socio-economic Impacts on Well-being', in *Canadian Issues* (Association for Canadian Studies), pp. 107–111.

Gelb, A. (1988) *Oil Windfalls: Blessing or Curse?* (Oxford: Oxford University Press).

Gibson, G. and C. O'Faircheallaigh (2015) *IBA Community Toolkit* (Toronto: The Gordon Foundation).

Gudynas, E. (2019) 'Value, Growth, Development: South American Lessons for a New Ecopolitics', *Capitalism, Nature, Socialism*, 30(2), pp. 234–243, DOI: 10.1080/10455752.2017.1372502.

Gudynas, E. (2018) 'Extractavism Tendencies and Consequences', in R. Munck and R.D. Wise (eds.) *Reframing Latin American Development* (Oxfordshire: Taylor & Francis Group).

Gudynas, E. (2016) 'Beyond Varieties of Development: Disputes and Alternatives', *Third World Quarterly*, 37(4), pp. 721–732, DOI: 10.1080/01436597.2015.1126504.

Gulkula (2021) *Gulkula—Advacing our Future*, www.gulkula.com (accessed on 30 November 2022).

Harvey, B. (2016) 'The eye of the Beholder—Utility and Beauty in Mine Closure', in A.B. Fourie and M. Tibet (eds.) *Mine Closure 2016: Proceedings of the 11th International Conference on Mine Closure* (Perth: Australian Centre for Geomechanics), pp. 17–23, DOI: 10.36487/ACG_rep/1608_0.3_Harvey.

Harvey, B. (2014) 'Social Development will not Deliver Social Licence to Operate for the Extractive Sector', *The Extractive Industries and Society*, 1(1), pp. 7–11, DOI: 10.1016/j.exis.2013.11.001.

Holcombe, S. and D. Kemp (2020) 'From Pay-out to Participation: Indigenous Mining Employment as Local Development?' *Sustainable Development*, 28(5), pp. 1122–1135, DOI: 10.1002/sd.2063.

Horowitz, L.S., A. Keeling, F. Lévesque, T. Rodon, S. Schott and S. Thériault (2018) 'Indigenous Peoples' Relationships to Large-scale Mining in Post/colonial Contexts: toward Multidisciplinary Comparative Perspectives', *The Extractive Industries and Society*, 5(3), pp. 404–414, DOI: 10.1016/j.exis.2018.05.004.

IM4DC (International Mining for Development Centre) (2015) https://www.im4dc.org/ (accessed on 28 November 2022).

ICMM (International Council on Mining and Metals) (2020) *Integrated Mine Closure: Good Practice Guide* (London: ICMM), https://guidance.miningwithprinciples.com/integrated-mine-closure-good-practice-guide/ (accessed on 28 November 2022).

ICMM (2018) *Role of Mining in National Economies, Mining Contribution Index 2018*, 4th Edition (London: ICMM), https://data.icmm.com/ (accessed on 30 November 2022).

ICMM (2013) *Indigenous Peoples and Mining: Position Statement* (London: ICMM), https://www.icmm.com/en-gb/our-principles/position-statements/indigenous-peoples (accessed on 30 November 2022).

IFC (International Finance Corporation) (2012) *IFC Performance Standards on Environmental and Social Sustainability*, https://www.ifc.org/wps/wcm/connect/topics_ext_content/ifc_external_corporate_site/sustainability-at-ifc/publications/publications_handbook_pps (accessed on 28 November 2022).

IIED (International Institute for Environment and Development) (2002) *Breaking New Ground: Mining, Minerals and Sustainable Development* (London: IIED), https://www.iied.org/9084iied (accessed on 28 November 2022).

IWGIA (International Work Group for Indigenous Affairs) (2021) *The Indigenous World 2021* (Copenhagen: IWGIA).

Kabir, S.M.Z., F. Rabbi, M.B. Chowdhury, and D. Akbar (2015) 'A Review of Mine Closure Planning and Practice in Canada and Australia', *World Review of Business Research*, 5(3), pp. 140–159.

Kemp, P.D. and D.J.R. Owen (2016) 'On the Limits of in-reach: a Reply to Harvey', *The Extractive Industries and Society*, 3(4), pp. 958–960, DOI: 10.1016/j.exis.2016.10.002.

Khanna, T. (2000) *Mine Closure and Sustainable Development, the World Bank Group, Mining Department* (London: Mining Journal Books).

Kielland, N. (2015) *Supporting Aboriginal Participation in Resource Development: the Role of Impact and Benefit Agreements* (Ottawa: Library of Parliament).

Kivinen, S., K. Vartiainen and T. Kumpula (2018) 'People and Post-Mining Environments: PPGIS Mapping of Landscape Values, Knowledge Needs, and Future Perspectives in Northern Finland', *Land*, 7(4), DOI: 10.3390/land7040151.

Kruse, J., B. Poppel, L. Abryutina, G. Duhaime, S. Martin, M. Poppel, M. Kruse, E. Ward, P. Cochran and V. Hanna (2008) 'Survey of Living Conditions in the Arctic (SLiCA)', in V. Møller, D. Juschka and A.C. Michalos (eds.) *Barometres of Quality of Life around the Globe: How Are We Doing?* (Heidelberg: Springer), pp. 107–134.

Kung, A., J. Everingham and V. Vivoda (2020) *Social Aspects of Mine Closure: Governance and Regulation* (Brisbane: Centre for Social Responsibility in Mining, University of Queensland), https://www.csrm.uq.edu.au/publications/social-aspects-of-mine-closure-governance-regulation (accessed on 30 November 2022).

Kung, A., S. Holcombe, J. Hamago and D. Kemp (2022) 'Indigenous Co-ownership of Mining Projects: a Preliminary Framework for the Critical Examination of Equity Participation', *Journal of Energy and Natural Resources Law*, 40(4), pp. 1–23, DOI: 10.1080/02646811.2022.2029184.

Langton, M. and O. Mazel (2008) 'Poverty in the Midst of Plenty: Aboriginal People, the 'Resource Curse' and Australia's Mining Boom', *Journal of Energy and Natural Resources Law*, 26(1), pp. 31–65, DOI: 10.1080/02646811.2008.11435177.

Littlewood, D. (2014) '"Cursed" Communities? Corporate Social Responsibility (CSR), Company Towns and the Mining Industry in Namibia', *Journal of Business Ethics*, 120(1), pp. 39–63, DOI: 10.1007/s10551-013-1649-7.

MAC (Mining Association of Canada) (2008) *Mine Closure Framework* (Ottawa: MAC), https://mining.ca/towards-sustainable-mining/protocols-frameworks/mine-closure-framework/ (accessed on 28 November 2022).

MacInnes, A., M. Colchester and A. Whitmore (2017) 'Free, Prior and Informed Consent: how to Rectify the Devastating Consequences of Harmful Mining for Indigenous Peoples', *Perspectives in Ecology and Conservation*, 15(3), pp. 152–160, DOI: 10.1016/j.pecon.2017.05.007.

Manning, M., C.L. Ambrey and C.M. Fleming (2016) 'A Longitudinal Study of Indigenous Wellbeing in Australia', *Journal of Happiness Studies*, 17, pp. 2503–2525, DOI: 10.1007/s10902-015-9704-y.

Marais, L., F. Haslam McKenzie, L. Deacon, E. Nel, D.V. Rooyen and J. Cloete (2018) 'The Changing Nature of Mining Towns: Reflections from Australia, Canada and South Africa', *Land Use Policy*, 76, pp. 779–788, DOI: 10.1016/j.landusepol.2018.03.006.

MCA (Minerals Council of Australia) (2020) *Mining is the Largest Contributor to Australian Economy in 2019–20*, press release, https://minerals.org.au/sites/default/files/201030%20Mining%20is%20the%20largest%20contributor%20to%20Australian%20economy%20in%202019-20.pdf (accessed on 15 August 2023).

MCA (2015) *The Enduring Value Framework: Voluntary Guidelines* (Australia: MCA), https://minerals.org.au/enduring-value-framework (accessed on 29 November 2022).

McMahon, G. and S. Moreira (2014) 'The Contribution of the Mining Sector to Socioeconomic and Human Development', *Extractive Industries for Development Series*, 30 (Washington DC: World Bank), https://minerals.org.au/resources/mining-is-the-largest-contributor-to-australian-economy-in-2019-20/ (accessed on 30 November 2022).

Mero-Figueroa, M., E. Galdeano-Gómez, L. Piedra-Muñoz and M. Obaco (2020) 'Measuring Well-Being: a Buen Vivir (Living Well) Indicator for Ecuador', *Social Indicators Research*, 152(1), pp. 265–287, DOI: 10.1007/s11205-020-02434-4.

Mien, E. and M. Goujon (2021) '40 Years of Dutch Disease Literature: Lessons for Developing Countries', *Comparative Economic Studies*, 64(3), pp. 351–383, DOI: 10.1057/s41294-021-00177-w.

Moffat, K. and A. Zhang (2014) 'The Paths to Social Licence to Operate: an Integrative Model Explaining Community Acceptance of Mining', *Resources Policy*, 39, pp. 61–70, DOI: 10.1016/j.resourpol.2013.11.003.

Monosky, M. and A. Keeling (2021) 'Planning for Social and Community-engaged Closure: a Comparison of Mine Closure Plans from Canada's Territorial and Provincial North', *Journal of Environmental Management*, 277, DOI: 10.1016/j.jenvman.2020.111324.

NAIF (Northern Australia Infrastructure Facility) (2021) *Australian Aboriginal Mining Corporation* (Australia: NAIF).

Neil, C., M. Tykkyläinen and J. Bradbury (1992) *Coping with Closure: an International Comparison of Mine Town Experiences* (London: Routledge).

NNTT (National Native Title Tribunal) (2022) *Statistics*, http://www.nntt.gov.au/Pages/Statistics.aspx (accessed on 28 November 2022).

NRCAN (Natural Resources Canada) (2017) *Orca Sand and Gravel Project—British Columbia* (Canada: Natural Resources Canada), https://www.nrcan.gc.ca/science-data/science-research/earth-sciences/earth-sciences-resources/earth-sciences-federal-programs/orca-sand-and-gravel-project-british-columbia/8820 (accessed on 30 November 2022).

O'Faircheallaigh, C. (2021) 'Explaining Outcomes from Negotiated Agreements in Australia and Canada', *Resources Policy*, 70, DOI: 10.1016/j.resourpol.2020.101922.

O'Faircheallaigh, C. (2018) 'Using Revenues from Indigenous Impact and Benefit Agreements: Building Theoretical Insights', *Candian Journal of Development Studies*, 39(1), pp. 101–118, DOI: 10.1080/02255189.2017.1391068.

O'Faircheallaigh, C. (2017) 'Shaping Projects, Shaping Impacts: Community-controlled Impact Assessments and Negotiated Agreements', *Third World Quarterly*, 38(5), pp. 1181–1197, DOI: 10.1080/01436597.2017.1279539.

O'Faircheallaigh, C. (2015) 'Social Equity and Large Mining Projects: Voluntary Industry Initiatives, Public Regulation and Community Development Agreements', *Journal of Business Ethics*, 132, pp. 91–103, DOI: 10.1007/s10551-014-2308-3.

O'Faircheallaigh, C. (2013a) 'Community Development Agreements in the Mining Industry: an Emerging Global Phenomenon', *Community Development*, 44(2), pp. 222–238, DOI: 10.1080/15575330.2012.705872.

O'Faircheallaigh, C. (2013b) 'Extractive Industries and Indigenous Peoples: a Changing Dynamic?' *Journal of Rural Studies*, 30, pp. 20–30, DOI: 10.1016/j.jrurstud. 2012.11.003.

O'Faircheallaigh, C. (ed.) (2012) *Curse or Opportunity? Mineral Revenues, Rent Seeking and Development in Aboriginal Australia* (Taylor & Francis Group).

O'Faircheallaigh, C. (2010) 'Aboriginal-Mining Company Contractual Agreements in Australia and Canada: Implications for Political Autonomy and Community Development', *Revue canadienne d'études du développement*, 30(1–2), pp. 69–86, DOI: 10.1080/02255189.2010.9669282.

O'Faircheallaigh, C. (1998) 'Resource Development and Inequality in Indigenous Societies', *World Development*, 26(3), pp. 381–394, DOI: 10.1016/S0305-750X(97)10060-2.

O'Faircheallaigh, C. and R. Lawrence (2019) 'Mine Closure and the Aboriginal Estate', *Australian Aboriginal Studies*, 1, pp. 65–81.

Owen, J.R. and D. Kemp (2014) '"Free Prior and Informed Consent", Social Complexity and the Mining Industry: Establishing a Knowledge Base', *Resources Policy*, 41, pp. 91–100, DOI: 10.1016/j.resourpol.2014.03.006.

Owen, J.R. and D. Kemp (2013) 'Social Licence and Mining: a Critical Perspective', *Resources Policy*, 38(1), pp. 29–35, DOI: 10.1016/j.resourpol.2012.06.016.

Papyrakis, E. and O. Raveh (2014) 'An Empirical Analysis of a Regional Dutch Disease: the Case of Canada', *Environmental and Resource Economics*, 58(2), pp. 179–198, DOI: 10.1007/s10640-013-9698-z.

Parsons, R., J. Lacey and K. Moffat (2014) 'Maintaining Legitimacy of a Contested Practice: How the Minerals Industry Understands its "Social Licence to Operate"', *Resources Policy*, 41, pp. 83–90, DOI: 10.1016/j.resourpol.2014.04.002.

Pijpers, R.J. and T.H. Eriksen (2019) 'Introduction: Negotiating the Multiple Edges of Mining Encounters', in *Mining Encounters* (London: Pluto Press), pp. 1–20.

Podlasly, M. (2021) *Indigenous Input Missing from Canada's ESG Investment Standards*, Business in Vancouver, 17 March, https://biv.com/article/2021/03/indigenous-input-missing-canadas-esg-investment-standards (accessed on 28 November 2022).

Prout, S. (2012) 'Indigenous Wellbeing Frameworks in Australia and the Quest for Quantification', *Social Indicators Research*, 109, pp. 317–336, DOI: 10.1007/s11205-011-9905-7.

Rixen, A. and S. Blangy (2016) 'Life after Meadowbank: Exploring Gold Mine Closure Scenarios with the Residents of Qamini'tuaq (Baker Lake), Nunavut', *The Extractive Industries and Society*, 3(2), pp. 297–312, DOI: 10.1016/j.exis.2015.09.003.

Robinson, J.A., R. Torvik and T. Verdier (2014) 'Political Foundations of the Resource Curse: a Simplification and a Comment', *Journal of Development Economics*, 106, pp. 194–198, DOI: 10.1016/j.jdeveco.2013.09.004.

Robinson, J.A., R. Torvik and T. Verdier (2006) 'Political Foundations of the Resource Curse', *Journal of Development Economics*, 79(2), pp. 447–468, DOI: 10.1016/j.jdeveco.2006.01.008.

Rodon, T. (2018) 'Institutional Development and Resource Development: the Case of Canada's Indigenous Peoples', *Revue canadienne d'études du développement*, 39(1), pp. 119–136, DOI: 10.1080/02255189.2017.1391069.

Rodon, T. and F. Levesque (2015) 'Understanding the Social and Economic Impacts of Mining Development in Inuit Communities: Experiences with Past and Present Mines in Inuit Nunangat', *Northern Review*, 41, pp. 13–39, DOI: 10.22584/nr41.2015.002.

Sachs, J. and A. Warner (1995) *Natural Resources Abundance and Economic Growth* (Cambridge, Massachusetts).

Sachs, J. and A. Warner (1997) *Natural Resource Abundance and Economic Growth* (Cambridge, Massachusetts: Harvard University Press).

Sen, A. (1985) 'Wellbeing, Agency and Freedom: the Dewey Lectures 1984', *Journal of Philosophy*, 82, pp. 169–221, DOI: 10.2307/2026184.

Sen, A. (1979a) 'Equality of What?' in J. Rawls and S.M. McMurrin (eds.) *Liberty, Equality, and Law: Selected Tanner Lectures on Moral Philosophy* (University of Utah Press).

Sen, A. (1979b) 'Issues in the Measurement of Poverty', *The Scandinavian Journal of Economics*, 81(2), pp. 285–307, DOI: 10.2307/3439966.

Social Aspects of Mine Closure Research Consortium (2019) *eLibrary*, https://www.mineclosure.net/elibrary (accessed on 30 November 2022).

Social Practice Forum (2020) *Free, Prior and Informed Consent (FPIC), a Primer: Lessons from the Field*, https://socialpracticeforum.org (accessed on 28 November 2022).

Söderholm, P. and N. Svahn (2015) 'Mining, Regional Development and Benefit-sharing in Developed Countries', *Resources Policy*, 45, pp. 78–91, DOI: 10.1016/j.resourpol.2015.03.003.

Sosa, I. and K. Keenan (2001) *Impact Benefit Agreements between Aboriginal Communities and Mining Companies: their use in Canada*, http://metisportals.ca/MetisRights/wp/wp-admin/images/Impact%20Benefit%20Agreements%20-%20Mining.pdf (accessed on 29 November 2022).

Southalan, J. and J. Fardin (2019) 'Free, Prior and Informed Consent: How and from Whom? an Australian Analogue', *Journal of Energy and Natural Resources Law*, 37(4), pp. 365–388, DOI: 10.1080/02646811.2018.1524436.

Stiglitz, J., A. Sen and J.-P. Fitoussi (2009) *Report by the Commission on the Measurement of Economic Performance and Social Progress* (Paris: The Commission on the Measurement of Economic Performance and Social Progress).

Sulyandziga, L. (2019) 'Indigenous Peoples and Extractive Industry Encounters: Benefit-Sharing Agreements in Russian Arctic', *Polar Science*, 21, pp. 68–74, DOI: 10.1016/j.polar.2018.12.002.

Suncor Energy Inc. (2021) 'Suncor Energy forms Partnership with Eight Indigenous Communities in the Regional Municipality of Wood Buffalo to Acquire an Equity Interest in the Northern Courier Pipeline', *Globe News Wire*, 16 September, https://www.globenewswire.com/news-release/2021/09/16/2298240/0/en/Suncor-Energy-forms-partnership-with-eight-Indigenous-communities-in-the-Regional-Municipality-of-Wood-Buffalo-to-acquire-an-equity-interest-in-the-Northern-Courier-Pipeline.html (accessed on 30 November 2022).

Taylor, J. (2019) *Change in Aboriginal Social Indicators in the East Kimberley: 2001–2016, a report to traditional owners of the Argyle Participation Agreement and Empowered Communities East Kimberly*, https://static1.squarespace.com/static/5a73dac1d0e62826b7a7521c/t/607e862d536e0517765ad5af/1618904677903/Taylor+Report+JULY.pdf (accessed on 29 November 2022).

Taylor, J. (2018) *Change in Wellbeing Indicators of Pilbara Aboriginal People: 2001–2016*, Report to the Regional Implementation Committee (Australian Government).

Taylor, J. (2008) 'Indigenous Peoples and Indicators of Well-Being: Australian Perspectives on United Nations Global Frameworks', *Social Indicators Research*, 87(1), pp. 111–126, DOI: 10.1007/s11205-007-9161-z.

Teck (2021) *Indigenous Peoples Policy*, https://www.teck.com/media/Indigenous-Peoples-Policy.pdf (accessed on 29 November 2022).

Thinley, J.Y. and J. Hartz-Karp (2019) 'National Progress, Sustainability and Higher Goals: the Case of Bhutan's Gross National Happiness', *Sustainable Earth*, 2(1), pp. 1–11, DOI: 10.1186/s42055-019-0022-9.

Thomson, I. and R.G. Boutilier (2011) 'Social License to Operate', in P. Darling (ed.) *SME Mining Engineering Handbook* (Engelwood: Society for Mining, Metallurgy, and Exploration), pp. 673–690.

TNDC (Tahltan Nation Development Corporation) (2021) *About TNDC*, https://www.tndc.ca/about (accessed on 28 November 2022).

Tomlinson, K. (2019) 'Indigenous Rights and Extractive Resource Projects: Negotiations Over the Policy and Implementation of FPIC', *The International Journal of Human Rights*, 23(5), pp. 880–897, DOI: 10.1080/13642987.2017.1314648.

Tysiachniouk, M., L.A. Henry, M. Lamers and J.P.M. van Tatenhove (2018) 'Oil and Indigenous People in sub-Arctic Russia: Rethinking Equity and Governance in benefit Sharing Agreements', *Energy Research and Social Science*, 37, pp. 140–152, DOI: 10.1016/j.erss.2017.09.004.

UN (United Nations) (2009) *State of the World's Indigenous Peoples* (New York: United Nations), https://www.un.org/esa/socdev/unpfii/documents/SOWIP/en/SOWIP_web.pdf (accessed on 29 November 2022).

UN (2007) *United Nations Declaration of the Rights of Indigenous Peoples* (New York: United Nations), https://www.un.org/development/desa/indigenouspeoples/wp-content/uploads/sites/19/2018/11/UNDRIP_E_web.pdf (accessed on 29 November 2022).

UNDP (United Nations Development Program) (2009) *Handbook on Planning, Monitoring and Evaluating for Development Results* (New York: UNDP), http://web.undp.org/evaluation/handbook/documents/english/pme-handbook.pdf (accessed on 29 November 2022).

UNDP (2002) *Guidelines for Outcome Evaluators: Monitoring and Evaluation Companion Series #1* (New York: UNDP), http://web.undp.org/evaluation/documents/HandBook/OC-guidelines/Guidelines-for-OutcomeEvaluators-2002.pdf (accessed on 30 November 2022).

UNDP (1990) *Human Development Report 1990: Concept and Measurement of Human Development* (New York: UNDP), http://www.hdr.undp.org/en/reports/global/hdr1990 (accessed on 29 November 2022).

Van der Ploeg, F. (2011) 'Natural Resources: Curse or Blessing?' *Journal of Economic Literature,* 49(2), pp. 366–420, DOI: 10.1257/jel.49.2.366.

Van der Ploeg, F. and S. Poelhekke (2017) 'The Impact of Natural Resources: Survey of Recent Quantitative Evidence', *The Journal of Development Studies,* 53(2), pp. 205–216, DOI: 10.1080/00220388.2016.1160069.

Van Teijlingen, K. (2016) 'The 'Will to Improve' at the Mining Frontier: Neo-extractivism, Development and Governmentality in the Ecuadorian Amazon', *The Extractive Industries and Society,* 3(4), pp. 902–911, DOI: 10.1016/j.exis.2016.10.009.

Wall, E. and R. Pelon (2011) 'Sharing Mining Benefits in Developing Countries: the Experience with Foundations, Trusts and Funds', *Extractive Industries for Development,* 21 (Washington DC: World Bank), https://openknowledge.worldbank.org/bitstream/handle/10986/18290/624980NWP0P116onsootrustsoandofunds.pdf?sequence=1&isAllowed=y (accessed on 30 November 2022).

Wilson, E. (2019) 'What is Benefit Sharing? Respecting Indigenous Rights and Addressing Inequities in Arctic Resource Projects', *Resources,* 8(2), DOI: 10.3390/resources8020074.

Wilson, E. and K. Istomin (2019) 'Beads and Trinkets? Stakeholder Perspectives on Benefit-sharing and Corporate Responsibility in a Russian Oil Province', *Europe-Asia Studies,* 71(8), pp. 1285–1313, DOI: 10.1080/09668136.2019.1641585.

World Bank (2021a) *Extractives Global Programmatic Support* (*EGPS*) (Washington, D.C.: World Bak), https://www.worldbank.org/en/programs/egps (accessed on 29 November 2022).

World Bank (2021b) *Indigenous Peoples* (Washington, D.C.: World Bank), https://www.worldbank.org/en/topic/indigenouspeoples (accessed on 29 November 2022).

World Bank (2012) *Mining Community Development Agreements: Source Book* (Washington, D. C.: World Bank), https://openknowledge.worldbank.org/handle/10986/12641?show=full (accessed on 29 November 2022).

World Bank (2010) *Mining Foundations, Trusts and Funds: a Sourcebook* (Washington, D. C.: World Bank), https://openknowledge.worldbank.org/handle/10986/16965 (accessed on 29 November 2022).

World Bank (2003) *Striking a Better Balance: the World Bank Group and Extractive Industries,* Ref. 84286 v1, (Washington DC: World Bank).

Yap, M. and E. Yu (2016) 'Operationalising the Capability Approach: Developing Culturally Relevant Indicators of Indigenous Wellbeing—an Australian Example', *Oxford Development Studies,* 44(3), pp. 315–331, DOI: 10.1080/13600818.2016.1178223.

PART 2

Scales of Space and Time

CHAPTER 6

Struggles over Resource Decentralisation: Legislative Reform, Corporate Resistance and Canadian Aid Partnerships in Burkina Faso

Diana Ayeh

Abstract

In attempting to counter the various negative correlations associated with the mining–development nexus in the global South (for example, the 'resource curse' or 'enclave economies'), the global mining sector experienced a mushrooming of ethical norms, practices and policies during the past three decades, many of them intended to strengthen local communities. In addition to the launch of various initiatives from the corporate world (ranging from multi-stakeholder partnerships on the global level to corporate social responsibility programmes in mining concessions), a number of West African countries have reformed their liberal mining legislation in recent years, thereby introducing new mechanisms for a more *just* local redistribution of mining revenues. In this spirit, the mining code of Burkina Faso, reformed in 2015, provides the implementation of a Mining Fund for Local Development (FMDL) to which multinational corporations are legally required to contribute 1 per cent of their national turnover (before tax).

This chapter investigates multi-scalar policies for decentralised mining revenue allocation in and around Burkina Faso's gold mining sector by engaging with and contributing to debates in post-structural geography and political ecology. It explores how 'resource decentralisation' became a priority of both the national government and of Canadian aid projects in Burkina Faso, while facing political resistance from mining companies. I argue that struggles for local profits from mining transcend specific scales ('the global', 'the national', or 'the local') in resource governance and focus either on promoting the various voluntary engagements of the corporate world or on calling for the state-centred enforcement of legal requirements. In Burkina Faso's mining areas this has ambivalent outcomes: It leads to a reshuffling of responsibility for the (re-) distribution of mining revenues from corporate agents to municipal decision makers, on the one hand. On the other, it serves to engineer (potential) community unrest, and thus to eventually make large-scale mining feasible in the first place.

 | DOI:10.1163/9789004685994_007

1 Introduction[1]

In the past decade, the ongoing gold mining boom in Burkina Faso has attracted a new wave of foreign direct investment to the country. With multiple global crises regularly pushing the international gold price to new record levels (that is, over USD 1,900 per ounce in the aftermath of the global financial crisis in 2007/08 and over USD 2,000 per ounce during the COVID-19 pandemic in 2020), a significant number of multinational companies listed on the Toronto Stock Exchange (TSX) have started to extract gold from its resource-rich subsoil. This has raised great hopes for socio-economic development both on a national and a local scale. Similar to other African contexts of extraction, this optimism has increasingly been questioned. Today, the national gold mining boom has the reputation of not (sufficiently) benefiting the country's citizens, and especially not those in the concessions directly affected by large-scale mining activities. According to some authors, the relatively recent engagement of foreign-based multinational companies in and with Burkina Faso even contributes to a deterioration of environmental, social and living conditions for mining-affected communities: the mines would 'make [people] poor' (Chouli, 2014; Drechsel, Engels and Schäfer, 2019; Drechsel and Groneweg, 2018). Others, such as many of the civil society leaders and government officials in the capital, Ouagadougou, do not question the presence of global mining capital and foreign direct investment as such, but increasingly call for a fairer distribution of access to, and benefits from, industrial mining activities (see, for example, ORCADE, PCQVP and Oxfam, 2018).

In addition to access to natural resources such as land, water and raw materials, actors in the capital, Ouagadougou, and in the concessions increasingly also request access to the political–economic and monetary resources, such as taxes and royalties, created by industrial mining. Central to these claims is the assumption that benefits for some are not equivalent to benefits for all, partly because mining revenues in the past were largely concentrated in the hands of the presidential family and a small economic elite of the country (Chouli, 2014; Drechsel and Groneweg, 2018; Werthmann and Ayeh, 2017). As this chapter discusses, struggles over mining revenue distribution involve a range of global, national and local actors that focus either on promoting the various voluntary engagements of the corporate world or on demanding the state-centred

1 The research underlying this chapter received funding from the German Research Foundation (DFG) within the framework of the Collaborative Research Centre (SFB) 1199 at Leipzig University.

enforcement of legal requirements. I call the different framing of their actions and goals, as well as their ability to enforce them 'scalar dimensions of agency' over mining revenue allocation and distribution. Drawing on the controversial implementation of the Mining Fund for Local Development (Fonds Minier de Développement Local, FMDL), it is shown how a decentralisation of mining revenues (or 'resource decentralisation') became a political tool with which to democratise the use and distribution of resources. As such, it not only figured as one of the most important projects of the reformed national mining code of 2015, it also became a priority for international donors and in particular for Canadian aid partnerships in the country. Between its operationalisation in 2017 and 2021, territorial units (municipalities and regions) have in total received over USD 166 million (West African CFA franc (XOF) 96 billion) through the FMDL. Of this amount, the mining municipalities of Houndé and Bagassi alone have each received more than USD 1.7 million (XOF 1 billion) (Kaboré, 2021).

This multi-sited ethnographic account retraces the recent history of mining reform in Burkina Faso. Inspired by debates in post-structural geography and political ecology on the different but entangled scalar practices involved in constructing and opposing global (mining) capitalism, it discusses how specific sites and topics of contention tell us something about 'the global' (Massey, 2005). To uncover the various local, national, and global negotiation practices and power relations that shape the global (mining) economy (Ayeh 2021; Engels, 2021; Martín, 2017), we are urged to look beyond Burkina Faso in the conventional ethnographic sense (Appel, 2019). These debates are simultaneously place-specific and global insofar as the transnational mining economy is 'linking the upstream mineralisation with the downstream money' (Miskelly, 2004): for example, investors, corporate executives and non-governmental organisation (NGO) representatives in the home countries of the global mining industry to government authorities, municipal actors and landowners in the host countries of foreign mining capital. A social engineering of extraction perspective reveals the different technologies and techniques 'from above' used by governmental, corporate and other elite actors in this regard, and how they shape and are shaped by (re)actions 'from below' (Brock and Dunlap, 2018; Verweijen and Dunlap, 2021). Making extraction feasible, its proponents contend, requires not only analysing how extraction is engineered physically (for example, through the use of specific technologies, fences, or the use of violence to smash protest). It is also based on the extensive use of social engineering practices aimed at 'preventing opposition to extractive projects from emerging in the first place' (Brock and Dunlap, 2018; Verweijen and Dunlap, 2021).

This chapter studies resource decentralisation through the prism of the mushrooming of ethical norms, practices and policies during the past three decades. It specifically addresses the role of different Canadian mining sector–related stakeholders (for example, corporate managers and NGO leaders) in promoting community–led mining governance initiatives. Implemented via legislative reform, corporate engagements and foreign aid partnerships, these emerging yet controversial policies have ambivalent impacts in areas of extraction: they lead to a reshuffling of authority over the allocation and distribution of mining revenues from the private, national and global to the public and local. The new emphasis on local participation and responsibilities, however, simultaneously comes with an engineering of community consent, and thus produces extractive expansion.

Methodologically, this can best be studied by tracing and looking into the various global, national and local arenas where ethics in mining are debated. As with other extraction contexts around the globe, the rather 'fuzzy field' (Nadai and Maeder, 2005) of the Burkinabè mining sector spans an indefinite number of social worlds, simultaneously anchored in the global mining economy and in national and local extractive relations and practices. None of these worlds exists independently from one another, which also means that (re)actions from 'below' and from 'above' mutually shape each other (Geenen and Verweijen, 2017; Verweijen and Dunlap, 2021). This requires us to extend the conventional lines of ethnographic inquiry (Ballard and Banks, 2003). The empirical foundation of this text is a total of 13 months of multi-sited ethnographic field research in Burkina Faso's capital, Ouagadougou, and two industrial mining municipalities in the western part of the country (Houndé and Bagassi). A variety of methods (e.g. document analysis and interviews) and modes of participation were used to follow the different ideas on ethics in mining. In specific sites some were used in more depth than others. For example, the participant observation in municipal council sessions, project workshops or corporate social responsibility (CSR) meetings in the concessions was supplemented by a two-week research stay in Canada's political and financial centres (Ottawa and Toronto) in November 2018, where semi-structured interviews were conducted with government, NGO and mining industry representatives. Research also entailed the regular attendance of online events dedicated to the Canadian (and African) mining investment world (quarterly investor calls, international mining fairs etc.). Rather than providing thick ethnographic descriptions, the chapter looks into the different sites of negotiation on resource decentralisation by analysing how they are connected.

Following the present introduction, I outline the theoretical framework of a multi-scalar approach to ethics in mining. The first section notably stresses how resource decentralisation evolved as a dominant ethical paradigm in global mining governance. This is followed by a section on the Canadian (corporate and donor-led) mining presence in Burkina Faso. More specifically, the third section discusses how the contested implementation of the respective mechanism (FMDL) comprises questions of holding corporations accountable through both voluntary codes of conduct and the legal domain of law. A last section highlights a Canadian public–private partnership (PPP) social engineering project implemented in two mining areas in western Burkina Faso. I end by discussing how, despite their promotion by global and relatively powerful coalitions, these projects also comprise windows of opportunity for local appropriation and resistance.

2 Global Partnerships, National Reform, Local Agency: a Multi-scalar Approach to Ethics in Mining

Whether natural resource endowment constitutes a 'curse' or a 'blessing' for governments and populations in African countries has been a prominent question in academia and policy discourse, and continues to be in even today. In the 'three decades of scholarship examining the link between mineral wealth and negative outcomes' (Elbra, 2017, 5), however, scholars increasingly questioned the very theories behind these concepts, such as that of analysing the curse as a mere technical and universal problem of revenue distribution. Anthropologists in particular explored 'the dynamic interplay of social relations, economic interests and struggles over power at stake in the political economy of extraction' (Gilberthorpe and Rajak, 2017) in that they highlighted how people respond to global discourses and concepts differently (see Behrends, Reyna and Schlee, 2013; Weszkalnys, 2010). Similarly to critical geography, there is a body of ethnographic literature on the global mining economy that increasingly uses spatial tropes to describe the implications of extraction's 'peculiar spatialities' (Himley, 2019, 31) for socio-economic development in the global South (see Bridge, 2015). One of the most prominent examples of this is the account of James Ferguson (2005; 2006), who observed in recent years the emergence of territorial mineral enclaves as enclosed spaces of extraction on the African continent. In summary, the enclave theory assumes that extractive activities are disarticulated from both local populations and national development projects, reinforcing the status of 'social thinness' inherent to mining capitalism.

What is absent from this 'highly simplified sketch', as Ferguson himself admits (2005, 381), is how 'the global', 'the national' and 'the local' as 'scalar dimensions of practices' (Mansfield, 2005, 468) are interrelated and shape one another. The scalar organisation in global capitalism has complex and contradictory effects on power relations, and the various scalar structures both shape and get challenged by social struggles (Dietz, 2017; Haarstad and Fløysand, 2007). Accordingly, 'the local' should not always be seen as a victim of globalisation; nor does it always represent a place of resistance. Yet those acting in the name of 'the local' shape 'the moments through which the global is constituted, invented, coordinated, produced' (Massey, 2004, 11). Therefore, the various ethical norms, principles and policies of the Burkinabè mining sector (ranging from corporate CSR initiatives and state-led policy reforms to community quests for more sustainable mining practices) cannot be analysed separately from one another. As the example of the reformed mining legislation of Burkina Faso illustrates, popular pressure must be considered very significant for the introduction of mechanisms for a more just and localised distribution of mining revenues (see Chouli, 2014; Engels, 2017; 2021). While scholarly attention paid to conflicting mining encounters in Burkina Faso (and beyond) has, to date, mainly focused on mobilisation against resource extraction 'from below' (see, for example, Ballard and Banks, 2003), this chapter retraces the implementation of a specific Canadian social engineering project in Burkina Faso's mining sector as a political (re)action 'from above'.

The latest trends regarding resource decentralisation in global mining governance have to be analysed against the backdrop of a number of (ambivalent) policy initiatives aimed at either promoting the voluntary engagements of multinational companies or at reinforcing the legal basis of foreign direct investment in host states of mining. Prominent examples are the neo-liberal turn in development since the 1970s (Verweijen and Dunlap, 2021), the ethical turn in corporate capitalism since the 1990s (Dolan and Rajak, 2016), and a growing pressure in African states to reform investor-friendly mining legislation. Altogether this gave rise to decentralised approaches and an emphasis on local participation to address the mining–development nexus and to counter enclaving. The understanding of how these agendas could be achieved varied greatly depending on the interests at stake. In the corporate world, for instance, we saw an emergence of new regimes of voluntary codes of conduct and responsibility, often designed as global or universal solutions for local problems (Dolan and Rajak, 2016; Sydow, 2016). The global rise of CSR as a 'semiformal, quasi-legal regulatory regime' (Barkan, 2013, 111) included the participation of corporations in multi-stakeholder partnerships (including in the Extractive Industries Transparency Initiative (EITI), launched in 2003) (Carbonnier, 2008; Fransen, 2017), the design of public–private donor projects (Zalik, 2004), and the implementation of the CSR programmes of individual companies in mining and oil extraction regions of the global South.

Against the backdrop of failed attempts to produce legal codes and requirements for multinational corporations from the 1960s onwards, these policies all shared an emphasis on normative agreements of corporate (self-)regulation instead of state intervention (Barkan, 2013; Jenkins, 2005). An exemplary case is the ambivalent role of the World Bank Group (WBG) in the reform of African mining regulations. Via the implementation of structural adjustment programmes (SAPs), the WGB contributed to a major shift in authority from government to industry actors in mining governance during the 1980s and 1990s, including the establishment of weakened mining legislation in terms of environmental protection and democratic participation. Yet from the new millennium on, it increasingly incorporated poverty alleviation and sustainability as main goals into its funding schemes (Jacobs, 2013; McMahon, 2010). In terms of mining governance, the neo-liberal turn comprised policies to redistribute mining rents to stakeholders other than African political elites that were largely perceived as corrupt and rent-seeking. Therefore, the increased promotion of fiscal decentralisation and local mineral revenue distribution were encouraged as important outcomes of mining reform in African countries (Ayeh 2021). In the following, it will be discussed how this more recent trend of decentralising mining revenue allocation and (re-)distribution is shaped by multiple forms of claims and fields of contention in Burkina Faso and Canada. As a result, the trend not only became a national government priority in Burkina Faso, but also one for Canadian foreign aid, notably via the implementation of public–private partnerships (PPPs) in the mining sector.

3 Canadian Corporate and Donor Presence in Burkina Faso's Mining Sector

The first location in which to discuss Canada's relations with and to Burkina Faso takes us neither to Toronto nor to Ouagadougou, but to Cape Town in South Africa. At an Investing in African Mining Indaba panel entitled 'Canada-Africa Session: Africa and Canada—a Win-Win partnership' the then Director General of the Pan-Africa Bureau of Global Affairs Canada, Paula Caldwell, emphasised Canada's 'unique' approach of partnering with African government, civil society, and private sector stakeholders:

> I would like to start by saying that [in] Canada, we're very proud of our African friends. Our mining companies play a very important role in our relationship, in reinforcing it. I will begin by talking about Canada's engagement, its mining presence and its commercial relationships. And then I would like to discuss what makes Canada's approach so unique

> beyond our technical expertise. And it's all about community collaboration and of course working hand in hand with governments.

Her political statement to the audience at the 2018 edition of 'the world's largest mining investment conference and the largest mining event in Africa' (Mining Indaba, 2021) continued with a reference to the financial and spatial extent of the commercial relationships between the Canadian nation and the African continent. In 2018, these comprised 130 mining and exploration companies operating in 29 countries and owning mining assets of more than 29 billion Canadian dollars (approximately USD 33.9 billion). Yet what makes of this a role model or a 'win-win partnership', she stated, is Canada's strong engagement in CSR policies, on the one hand, and the support of partner governments, on the other. The representative of the Burkinabè Ministry of Mines and Quarries (MMQ), who was also on the podium, vehemently agreed.

One year later, at the Prospectors & Developers Association of Canada's (PDAC) annual meeting, the Canadian government launched the Canadian Minerals and Metals Plan. 'To improve our Canadian competitive advantage', a representative stressed, goes hand in hand with helping mining communities [in the global South] 'to adapt to issues such as climate change, participation and innovation'. The stated purpose of this document is to reinforce Canada's leadership role in sustainable mining at home and abroad through 'building a Canada brand for mining'. These attempts at establishing Canada as 'the leading nation of responsible mining' must be analysed against the background of decades of activist and scholarly criticism of Canada's evolution as a 'mining superpower' in terms of financial capital for the minerals and metals industry (The McLeod Group, 2016, 1). Accordingly, Canada's role as a 'legal haven of choice for the world's mining industries' (Deneault and Sacher, 2012) implies multiple involvements of Canadian companies and their subsidiaries in human rights abuses and environmental destruction (Butler, 2015; Deneault, 2008; Dougherty, 2013, Thomas and Coburn, 2022). Also described as 'the global hub for mining finance' (Marshall, 2018, 6), the TSX and the TSX-Venture Exchange (TSXV) is 'home to more Mining companies than any other market in the world' (TSX, 2022). Interviewees in Ottawa and Toronto particularly highlighted Canada's role in creating favourable investment environments. This includes, for instance, government subsidised financing and tax inducements for (junior) companies and the relatively 'lenient' corporate tax requirements of the TSX (Dougherty, 2016). A coordinator of the NGO Mining Watch Canada stated in late 2017 that Canada's deep entanglements with the global mining industry could best be compared to what 'Panama or Liberia [are] for shipping'.

Another pillar of the Canadian state's direct and indirect assistance to its mining industry is reinforced diplomatic engagements with states with significant mineral resources (Thomas and Coburn, 2022). Taking advantage of Burkina Faso's investor-friendly mining legislation (at least until 2015) and the resource wealth of its subsoil, in 2021 Canada proudly claimed to be 'the largest mining investor in the country with mining assets of over 3 billion dollars' (approximately USD 3.5 billion) (GoC, 2021). According to Paula Caldwell, of the country's five biggest mining projects, three were 90 per cent owned and operated by Canadian companies in 2018. Their operation and trading activities were promoted by a bilateral foreign investment promotion and protection agreement (FIPA) that came into force in October 2017 (GoC, 2021). The Canadian presence in the country is not limited to mining companies, of course. In the domain of development and humanitarian assistance, one finds a flourishing network of Canadian-based NGOs and multi-stakeholder partnerships. It is no coincidence that their programmes are often implemented in the vicinity of producing gold mines. Traditionally Canadian foreign aid is linked to Canadian commercial interests and (notably) the extractive sector, for example through the choice of recipient countries, or the type of assistance provided (Brown, 2016a; 2016b; Goyette, 2016).

Burkina Faso was host to one of the three pilot projects of the so-called Devonshire Initiative (DI), criticised as 'an indirect subsidy to the Canadian private sector in the name of development' (Brown, 2016a, 23). Implemented by Plan Canada and the Mining company IAMGOLD, the project sponsored a USD 7.62 million (CAD 7.6 million) youth training initiative for the period 2011–17 (of which the Canadian International Development Agency contributed 75 per cent, the implementing NGO, Plan Canada, 12 per cent, and IAMGOLD only 13 per cent). With a strong focus on gender questions, it initially provided basic education and vocational training (in and beyond the mining sector) to 10,000 youth in southern Burkina Faso (Brown, 2016b; Butler, 2017). For the DI, one 'lesson learned' from the ensuing public criticism was that public–private partnerships should foster capacity-building, with an emphasis on helping communities (and local governments) set priorities for how to use and manage mining revenues (DI, 2017). From that point on, Canadian donors' work started to focus on a democratic and transparent use of mining funds, and a more decentralised approach to mineral revenue governance, thereby strengthening the decision-making power of local actors. This was in line with both general trends in the donor policies of the World Bank Group and the reform agenda of the Burkinabè state. Initially, however, multinational mining companies opposed these efforts, mainly because they felt that the visibility of their CSR programmes was at risk.

4 Legal Requirements vs. Voluntary Engagements: Contestations over the Implementation of a Mining Fund for Local Development (FMDL)

For many people in Burkina Faso, the reformed mining legislation of 2015 represents the spirit of the popular uprising that, in October 2014, overthrew the government of Blaise Compaoré, who had ruled the country for almost 30 years. The uprising not only paved the way for a democratic transition and for elections to be held in October 2015, democratisation also became one of the main demands of national civil society actors concerning an overdue reform of the mining code and a rupture with previous paternalistic modes of governance. Prior to these events the industrial gold mining sector (booming since 2008) had the reputation of being concentrated in the hands of a political elite close to Blaise Compaoré and his family. As one of the first political actions of the Conseil National de Transition (CNT), the subsequent reform addressed several scales and two main objectives: On the one hand, higher (national) government revenues from taxes and royalties were to be obtained (for example through an increase in corporate tax rates for industrial producers from 17.5 to 27.5 per cent). On the other hand, one of the main goals was to implement and intensify resource decentralisation, and thus to make the sector more profitable for populations living in the vicinity of mining projects. The mining code's most important provision in this latter sense was the establishment of a Mining Fund for Local Development (Fonds Minier de Développement Local, FMDL). Multinational corporations are now required to contribute 1 per cent of their national turnover (before tax) to the FMDL, of which equal shares are then administered by neighbouring municipalities and other decentralised units of political administration in line with regional and local development plans (Government of Burkina Faso, 2015; 2017).

In Burkina Faso and elsewhere, regional and local policy bodies, civil society organisations, private entrepreneurs and local populations have increasingly questioned the national government's monopoly in allocating mining rights and deciding about revenues. The formal process of decentralisation instigated by international development and financial organisations from the 1990s onwards added a further layer of authorities, institutions, and interests to the already complex spatialities of extraction (Martín, 2017). Elected local government bodies increasingly became part of the political arenas in which conditions for mining were negotiated. Extractive relations, in turn, shaped the relationships between local and central governments (Kesselring, 2018), and questions of voluntary and legal corporate responsibilities. In Burkina Faso the first political attempts to reshuffle authority in mineral revenue allocation and to strengthen local decision-making in mining governance can be traced back to 2006, when the first nationwide municipal elections took place (Côte, 2013; Côte and Korf, 2018). Since 2003 the mining code has provided for an annual surface tax (*taxe superficiaire*) to be paid by all industrial license holders to the local authority of the area in which their concession is located (Government of Burkina Faso, 2003; 2005). Since 2015, accounts of the mismanagement of these local budget lines by municipal actors have nurtured corporate concerns about (potential) municipal inefficiency regarding the FMDL. It is not surprising then that the FMDL's implementation has been both controversial and slow to materialise.

Contestation over its implementation reflects more general debates about both a redrawing of boundaries between corporate and state-centred regulation, and different scalar dimensions in mining governance. The FMDL law project, in this sense, provided for a reshuffling of certain decision-making powers from the national levels to municipalities. Paradoxically, the legislative project was supported by international donor communities (notably Canadian aid projects) on the one hand, and challenged by TSX-listed multinational corporations on the other. The companies' motivation derives from three factors: First, with respect to the interests of their shareholders and investors, they considered the amount of money to be paid as too large. Second, they expressed concerns about the management capabilities of local government in the municipalities, not resulting in serving the needs of local populations. Several corporate managers commented thus, that mayors and municipal councillors 'don't know how to use the money'. Third, and maybe most importantly, they feared a loss of the visibility with regard to their various voluntary engagements in the concessions, and therefore with regard to their 'social licence to operate'. The FMDL, as stated in a letter from the lobbying organisation Chambre des Mines du Burkina Faso (representing numerous TSX-listed multinational mining companies) to the Prime Minister in April 2019, 'does not resolve the issue of the population's expectations vis-à-vis the mining companies' (CMB, 2019, 4). During a workshop on the reformed mining legislation in March 2017, an executive of a Canadian-based corporation emphasised the danger of 'weakening' Burkina Faso's economy, but notably the (potentially) 'disastrous effects' on the companies' voluntary engagements due to the '1% law':

> I speak in the name of all companies in the mining sector; everyone undertakes CSR [programmes]. Some have foundations, others do it on their own. [...] The budgets are approved by the shareholders. Today, if you tell them 'we will conduct CSR [programmes]', the first thing that happens is [they say], 'but beware Mister [name], there is 1 per cent of

> taxes that turns up, but there is not enough money to undertake CSR'. Therefore, the first thing that happens with that fund is that the mining companies cut their CSR [budgets].

What the Burkinabè mining world contested was not only the amount of money to be paid, but also the question of who is entitled to decide on its use. In doing so they stressed their legitimacy with regard to having a certain monopoly on the control of resource governance. 'We want to know how the money is used', as a national director of a Canadian mining firm insisted in August 2017. Following the adoption of the new mining code in July 2015, individual mining companies and the Chamber of Mines thus lobbied for a reduction of their contribution from 1 to 0.5 per cent of turnover after tax. Another 0.5 per cent of the initial 1 per cent amount should be administered by the mining companies themselves within their existing CSR frameworks. In the letter to the Prime Minister they eventually accepted the 1 per cent figure 'as a sign of good faith', but only on their own terms, requesting the 'deduction' of already realised CSR expenses from the annual FMDL sum (CMB, 2019, 4). Ultimately, the Ministry of Mines and Quarries adopted this requirement for half of all FMDL payments of multinational corporations to their host municipalities and regions between 2017 and 2019 (MMQ, 2019).

This led to strong civil society resistance in the capital and in the mining regions (Bach, 2019; Kaboré, 2019). Notably, activists rejected threats expressed by corporate executives to cut their CSR budgets, or even to relocate their operations completely to other 'more investor-friendly' legal mining contexts. For these activists, multinationals in Burkina Faso should stop engaging in corporate publicity campaigns in the name of 'local development'. Ethical engagements were considered as both legal and moral obligations that the companies have to meet, and included the provision of appropriate compensation for the forced resettlement of populations. For a civil society leader in Houndé, a municipality hosting an operating mine since 2017, 'CSR is not an obligation. [And] Since it's not an obligation, it's not a responsibility'. Central government representatives and corporate agents alike—the same individual stated in early 2017—would perceive people in the provinces as 'idiots' who are unable to allocate and manage resources in a transparent and accountable way. To put pressure on the national government and the Ministry of Mines and Quarries to implement the FMDL, overdue since 2015, Houndé-based NGO leaders engaged in a social media campaign against the 'deductibility' of the FMDL for the benefit of CSR budgets. A civil society coalition organised, on 30 August 2019, a protest march to request the payment of the totality of FMDL funds to the municipality (Sanon, 2019).

5 Reshuffling Responsibility and Monitoring Community Unrest: How Ethics Shape Mining's Feasibility

Decentralised governance as a means of redistributing mining rents is also a prominent issue in regional policy frameworks (such as the African Mining Vision of 2009), sometimes implemented via development funds very similar to that of the FMDL in other West African host countries of large-scale mining. Examples include the reformed legislations of Guinea (in 2013) and Ghana (in 2014). As in Burkina Faso, however, these frameworks' implementation is often not yet completed or enforced (see, for example, Knierzinger (2016) for the Guinean Fonds de Développement Économique Local, adopted in 2013). To assist the (local) redistribution of mining revenues in these countries, the West Africa Governance & Economic Sustainability in Extractive Areas (WAGES) project was launched in 2016. It was financed by Global Affairs Canada and jointly implemented by two Canadian NGOs—the World University Service of Canada (WUSC) and the Centre for International Studies and Cooperation (CECI)—for a project period of seven years (2016–22). In Burkina Faso, the project was realised in two western mining areas, including seven municipalities where Canadian industry is located (with one company headquartered in Canada and one being TSX-listed).

With the strengthening of a decentralised mining revenue allocation being one of its main goals, the WAGES project was in line with both the new emphasis of Canadian aid policy on local resource governance and with targets for political reform in Burkina Faso. According to its implementers in Burkina Faso, the project's first and most important aim was to promote a more just distribution of mining benefits among local populations, especially women and young people. It therefore provided three different but interrelated areas of intervention, which consisted of (1) the strengthening of local governance, (2) the promotion of (sustainable and inclusive) local economies, and (3) the promotion of knowledge sharing concerning local community development (WAGES, 2017). The various training initiatives and programmes were implemented in more or less close collaboration with 'local and national governments, selected mining companies, as well as small and medium-sized businesses and civil society organizations' (WUSC, 2021). Journalists and NGO representatives more critical of the mining industry emphasised that WAGES was very similar in design to the highly criticised PPP pilot projects. However, the 'lessons learnt' from the past included that there were no longer any direct financial payments between Canadian NGO projects and the mining companies. Instead, a large portion of donor monies was paid directly to the respective municipality officially in charge of project implementation.

In its design, WAGES at least indirectly helped to legitimise the Canadian mining presence and the 'existing extractive order' (Hönke, 2018, 115) in western Burkina Faso. Philanthropic capacity-building programmes, for instance, obviously had the double effect of providing a 'skilled' workforce for the mining labour market and of reducing popular pressure on mining companies to provide access to jobs in mining for whole communities. The first pillar of their work (the strengthening of local governance) was intended to have an immediate impact on achieving the successful implementation of the FMDL. To enhance the credibility and management capacities of local states, for instance, WAGES organised training for municipal actors on accountability, planning, and budgeting. In 2017 and 2018 the programme (proportionally) financed a review of municipal development plans (Plans Communaux de Développement, PCDs). According to the reformed mining code, PCDs prescribe the criteria for the future allocation of monies derived from the Mining Fund for Local Development. While WAGES coordinators emphasised that their work was not equivalent to corporate social responsibility; they saw the FMDL as an opportunity to 'reduce the burden on behalf of CSR' in that it potentially 'mitigates' community pressure on mining companies. A lack of knowledge among local populations and notably among municipal councillors was identified as a key obstacle to peaceful business operations (see Hönke, 2018). Resource decentralisation, the coordinators admitted, enhances the social marketing of companies and reinforces the 'Canada brand' in extractive areas of TSX-listed companies. Finally, it facilitates 'the successful implementation of the mine'.

A social engineering perspective allows one to assess the extent to which these NGO projects represent '(re)actions from above' with the aim of securing community consent, disciplining dissent, and—eventually—making large-scale mining feasible (Brock and Dunlap, 2018; Brown, 2016b; Verweijen and Dunlap, 2021). Today, such and similar programmes in Canada are being referred to by some as 'token "corporate responsibility" initiatives [...] often implemented alongside [...] massive privatization programs' (Schalk, 2021). Thus, resource decentralisation not only creates (limited) scope for local governments to exercise control over mining revenues. For multinational corporations it also results in new ways of abdicating responsibility (Appel, 2019). The new trend of considering local socio-economic development as the task of municipalities could eventually allow Canadian policy bodies—(non-)governmental and corporate—to distance themselves further from certain responsibilities for 'local externalities' of large-scale mining in the global South, a Canadian NGO's leader stated in November 2017. While local governments are now held accountable for the fair distribution of mining revenues, this could consequently also be the case for all conflicts arising out of these new forms of distribution. In the eyes of that same representative of a civil society that is critical of mining, resource decentralisation could ultimately serve as a tool for engineering community consent in Canada and Burkina Faso, and therefore for preventing opposition to extractive (policy) projects from emerging in the first place.

6 Conclusion and Debate

The WAGES case is an example of multi-scalar strategies of actors in resource governance and different configurations of power that become (re)negotiated (Dietz, 2017; Haarstad and Fløysand, 2007). Far from solely representing mere technical questions of who is responsible for what (i.e. the roles of mining companies, national governments or municipalities in the mining revenue system), they have complex and contradictory effects on local, national and global power relations. No doubt community pressure in the mining areas and civil society engagement in Burkina Faso's capital city, Ouagadougou, had created important conditions for political change, legislative (mining) reform and the introduction of the FMDL in the first place (Ayeh 2021; Chouli, 2014; Engels, 2017). A social engineering perspective, however, is particularly useful in helping us to understand the underlying conditions for the (non-)implementation of such reform projects (e.g. why, how, when, and by whom). It 'entails looking at the less visible and long-term ways in which corporate actors and their allies obstruct, condition and attempt to shape (re)actions "from below"' (Verweijen and Dunlap, 2021). The present chapter's aim has been to contribute to these debates in political ecology and post-structural geography while emphasising the contestations around resource decentralisation in Burkina Faso and the implementation of the FMDL in specific mining regions. In Burkina Faso's mining sector, Canadian private and state-led initiatives served as an example of how the mining industry, foreign aid partnerships and the central government alike have an interest in preventing opposition to specific extractive projects from emerging in the first place, and thus in maintaining existing extractive orders. The decentralisation of mineral revenue allocation and distribution can play a significant role in this regard.

We have also seen, however, that the meaning and implementation of mineral revenue decentralisation as a powerful global idea and concept is disputed, not only locally and nationally, but also among actors from the globalised mining elites. One example of this are the multinational mining companies in Burkina Faso that want to avoid higher taxes and royalties, felt that the visibility of their CSR projects was at risk and that lobbied against the FMDL, which introduced a new mechanism for state-centred and localised resource governance. Although numerous Canadian-based and TSX-listed mining companies initially resisted the '1% law', evidence shows that in practice the increase in the importance of municipalities in the field of mining governance can also foster corporate practices of abdicating responsibility for the various environmental and social consequences of corporates' operations (see Appel, 2019). Furthermore, corporate executives are able to interpret reform measures to their benefit. One example of this is the deductibility (albeit only temporary) of their CSR expenses: ultimately, multinational mining companies successfully managed to avoid having to make full payments of their FMDL share to Burkina Faso's regions and municipalities between 2017 and 2019. During a corporate presentation in Houndé's municipal council in December 2019 'on the FMDL and investments for the benefit of populations', a mining firm was thus able to present its CSR projects and programmes of the years 2017 and 2018 (including the establishment of a youth training facility, and the purchase of an ambulance for the local hospital) as its good will participation in the '1% law' procedure. The municipal councillors', for their part, criticised this corporate interpretation of reform implementation, describing it as a mechanism by which they themselves were excluded from determining the use of large portions of the fund. Those are exclusion mechanisms that were not envisioned as such when the FMDL legislation was approved in 2015.

A multi-scalar approach to studying ethics allows us to develop a better understanding of old and new actor constellations and sites in the global mining sector. Instead of assuming a unidimensional increase in the importance of 'the local' in resource governance (Mansfield, 2005), or conceiving of national and global elites as dominant per se, it is necessary to analyse who has access to which resources and bargaining power in specific cases and circumstances. Therefore, it is worth taking a closer look at how actors in the concessions negotiate, reject and also appropriate, aid partnerships in different ways. An example of this is the municipality of Houndé, which received double funding, from a mining firm and the WAGES project (without their prior knowledge), for the revision of its municipal development plan (Ayeh 2021). Whether the engineering of 'inclusionary control' (Verweijen and Dunlap, 2021) succeeds or not also depends on who is part of the powerful alliances implementing 'ethical' projects, and which (multi-scalar) alliances mobilise against them. The Canadian mining industry, promoting resource decentralisation at home and abroad, points to important connections (and sometimes disruptions) between companies, home governments, and donors in the enforcement of legal reform in mineral-rich countries of the global South (Thomas and Coburn, 2022). While these alliances are often subject to contestation in home and host countries of mining, the make-up of the global and national mining sector itself is constantly changing. For several reasons the Canadian mining presence in Burkina Faso has been shrinking in recent years. In 2019, for example, a convoy of the Canadian mining company Semafo was attacked by armed groups, and at least 40 civilians died (van Praet and York, 2019). The company and its assets (the operating mine sites Boungou and Mana) were then acquired by the TSX-listed but Cayman Islands–registered multinational Endeavour Mining (Endeavour Mining, 2020). More empirical research is needed on whether Canada still occupies a dominant role in the global and Burkinabè mining sector, and what the answer to this question means for the role of resource decentralisation in public–private aid partnerships.

References

Appel, H. (2019) *The Licit Life of Capitalism: US Oil in Equatorial Guinea* (Durham: Duke University Press).

Ayeh, D. (2021) *Spaces of Responsibility: Negotiating Industrial Gold Mining in BurkinaFaso*, Dialectics of the Global 10 (Berlin, Boston: De Gryter Oldenbourg).

Bach, E. (2019) 'Fonds minier: une correspondance du ministre des mines à l'association des municpalités révolte des jeunes de Houndé', *LibreInfo*, https://libreinfo.net/fonds-minier-une-correspondance-du-ministre-des-mines-a-lassociation-des-municpalites-revoltent-des-jeunes-de-hounde/ (accessed on 10 October 2022).

Ballard, C. and G. Banks (2003) 'Resource Wars: the Anthropology of Mining', *Annual Review of Anthropology*, 32(1), pp. 287–313, DOI: 10.1146/annurev.anthro.32.061002.093116.

Barkan, J. (2013) *Corporate Sovereignty: Law and Government under Capitalism* (Minneapolis: University of Minnesota Press).

Behrends, A., S.P. Reyna and G. Schlee (eds.) (2013) *Crude Domination: an Anthropology of Oil* (New York, Oxford: Berghahn Books).

Bridge, G. (2015) 'The Hole World: Scales and Spaces of Extraction', *Scenario Journal*, 5, https://scenariojournal.com/article/the-hole-world/ (accessed on 10 October 2022).

Brock, A. and A. Dunlap (2018) 'Normalising Corporate Counterinsurgency: Engineering Consent, Managing Resistance and Greening Destruction around the Hambach Coal Mine and beyond', *Political Geography*, 62, pp. 33–47, DOI: 10.1016/j.polgeo.2017.09.018.

Brown, S. (2016a) 'The Instrumentalization of Foreign aid under the Harper Government', *Studies in Political Economy*, 97(1), pp. 18–36, DOI: 10.1080/07078552.2016.1174461.

Brown, S. (2016b) 'Undermining Foreign Aid: the Extractive Sector and the Recommercialization of Canadian Development Assistance', in S. Brown, M. den Heyer, and D.R. Black (eds.) *Rethinking Canadian Aid*, second edition (Ottawa: University of Ottawa Press/Les Presses de l'Université d'Ottawa), pp. 273–294.

Butler, P. (2015) *Colonial Extractions: Race and Canadian Mining in Contemporary Africa* (Toronto: University of Toronto Press).

Butler, P. (2017) 'Gold n' Girls: Why Canada Weds Gender Equality with Mining Capitalism in Burkina Faso', in R. Tiessen and S. Baranyi (eds.) *Obligations and omissions: Canada's ambiguous actions on gender equality, McGill-Queen's Studies in Gender, Sexuality, and Social Justice in the Global South*, Vol. 1 (Montreal, Kingston: McGill-Queen's University Press), pp. 141–164.

Carbonnier, G. (2008) 'Les négociations multi-parties prenantes: l'exemple de l' initiative de transparence des industries extractives', *Relations Internationales*, 4(136), pp. 101–113, https://www.cairn.info/revue-relations-internationales-2008-4-page-101.htm (accessed on 10 October 2022).

CDM (Chambre des Mines du Burkina) (2019) *Mémorandum sur les préoccupations du secteur minier* (Ouagadougou: Chambre des Mines du Burkina).

Chouli, L. (2014) *Le boom minier au Burkina Faso: Témoignages de victimes de l'exploitation minière* (Pantin: Fondation Gabriel Péri).

Côte, M. (2013) *What's in a Right? The Liberalisation of Gold Mining and Decentralisation in Burkina Faso*, LDPI Working Paper No. 25 (Brighton: The Land Deal Politics Initiative, LDPI), https://www.iss.nl/sites/corporate/files/LDPI_WP_25.pdf (accessed on 10 October 2022).

Côte, M. and B. Korf (2018) 'Making Concessions: Extractive Enclaves, Entangled Capitalism and Regulative Pluralism at the Gold Mining Frontier in Burkina Faso', *World Development*, 101, pp. 466–476, DOI: 10.1016/j.worlddev.2016.11.002.

Deneault, A. (2008) *Noir Canada: Pillage, corruption et criminalité en Afrique*, Éditions Écosociété (Montréal: Centre d'études sur l'intégration et la mondialisation, CEIM).

Deneault, A. and W. Sacher (2012) *Imperial Canada Inc.: Legal Haven of Choice for the World's Mining Industries* (Vancouver: Talonbooks).

DI (Devonshire Initiative) (2017) *Partnering and Partnerships: Lessons Learned in the DI* (Toronto: Devonshire Initiative), https://cfccdb0b-d93c-4fbf-bafe-f028554593ff.filesusr.com/ugd/420f7e_87897db997b349a1bfb0816bb9125bc7.pdf?index=true (accessed on 11 October 2022).

Dietz, K. (2017) 'Politics of Scale and Struggles over Mining in Colombia', in B. Engels and K. Dietz (eds.) *Contested Extractivism, Society and the State: Struggles over Mining and Land* (London: Palgrave Macmillan), pp. 127–148.

Dolan, C. and D. Rajak (2016) 'Introduction: Toward the Anthropology of Corporate Social Responsibility', in *The Anthropology of Corporate Social Responsibility* (New York, Oxford: Berghahn Books), pp. 1–28.

Dougherty, M.L. (2013) 'The Global Gold Mining Industry: Materiality, Rent-Seeking, Junior Firms and Canadian Corporate Citizenship', *Competition and Change*, 17(4), pp. 339–354, DOI: 10.1179/1024529413Z.00000000042.

Dougherty, M.L. (2016) 'Scarcity and Control: the New Extraction and Canada's Mineral Resource Protection Network', in K. Deonandan and M.L. Dougherty (eds.) *Mining in Latin America: Critical Approaches to the New Extraction* (Oxfordshire: Routledge Taylor & Francis Group), pp. 83–99.

Drechsel, F., B. Engels and M. Schäfer (2019) *"The Mines make us Poor": Large-scale Mining in Burkina Faso*, Glocon Country Report No. 2 February 2019 (Berlin: Glocon), https://www.land-conflicts.fu-berlin.de/_media_design/country-reports/country_report_EN_BURKINA-FASO.pdf (accessed on 11 October 2022).

Drechsel, F. and M. Groneweg (2018) 'Les mines nous appauvrissent : Impact de l'extraction aurifère industrielle au Burkina Faso et réponses de la société civile', *Ressources Naturelles*, 3 (Dakar: Rosa Luxemburg Stiftung, Afrique de L'Ouest), https://www.land-conflicts.fu-berlin.de/_media_design/Drechsel-Groneweg-RLS.pdf (accessed on 11 October 2022).

Elbra, A. (2017) *Governing African Gold Mining: Private Governance and the Resource Curse*, International Political Economy Series (London: Palgrave Macmillan).

Endeavour Mining (2020) *Endeavour to Combine with SEMAFO to create a leading West African Gold Producer*, News Release, 23 March, https://www.endeavourmining.com/media/news/endeavour-combine-semafo-create-leading-west-african-gold-producer (accessed on 11 October 2022).

Engels, B. (2017) 'Not All Glitter is Gold: Mining Conflicts in Burkina Faso', in B. Engels and K. Dietz (eds.) *Contested Extractivism, Society and the State: Struggles over Mining and Land* (London: Palgrave Macmillan), pp. 149–170.

Engels, B. (2021) 'All Good things Come from below? Scalar Constructions of the 'Local' in Conflicts Over Mining', *Political Geography*, 84, DOI: 10.1016/j.polgeo.2020.102295.

Ferguson, J. (2005) 'Seeing Like an Oil Company: Space, Security, and Global Capital in Neoliberal Africa', *American Anthropologist*, 107(3), pp. 377–382, DOI: 10.1525/aa.2005.107.3.377.

Ferguson, J. (2006) *Global Shadows: Africa in the Neoliberal World Order* (Durham: Duke University Press).

Fransen, L. (2017) 'Embedding the Multinational Corporation in Transnational Sustainability Governance', in G. Baars and A. Spicer (eds.) *The Corporation: a Critical, Multi-Disciplinary Handbook* (Cambridge: Cambridge University Press), pp. 257–267.

Geenen, S. and J. Verweijen (2017) 'Explaining Fragmented and Fluid Mobilization in Gold Mining Concessions in Eastern Democratic Republic of the Congo', *The Extractive Industries and Society*, 4(4), pp. 758–765, DOI: 10.1016/j.exis.2017.07.006.

Gilberthorpe, E. and D. Rajak (2017) 'The Anthropology of Extraction: Critical Perspectives on the Resource Curse', *The Journal of Development Studies*, 53(2), pp. 186–204, DOI: 10.1080/00220388.2016.1160064.

GoC (Government of Canada) (2021) *Canada—Burkina Faso Relations*, https://www.canadainternational.gc.ca/burkinafaso/bilateral_relations_bilaterales/Canada-Burkina_Faso.aspx?lang=eng (accessed on 11 October 2022).

Government of Burkina Faso (2017) *Décret N°2017-0024/PRES/PM/MEMC/MINEFI/MATDSI portant sur l'organisation, le fonctionnement et les modalités de perception du Fonds minier de développement local* (Ouagadougou: Government of Burkina Faso).

Government of Burkina Faso (2015) *Loi N° 036-2015/CNT portant Code Minier du Burkina Faso. JO N°44 du 29 Octobre 2015* (Ouagadougou: Burkina Faso, le Conseil National de la Transition), https://www.itie-bf.gov.bf/IMG/pdf/loi_no_036-2015_cnt.pdf (accessed on 16 August 2023).

Government of Burkina Faso (2005) *Décret n°2005-048/PRES/PM/MCE/MFB portant fixation des axes et redevances minières* (Ouagadougou: Government of Burkina Faso).

Government of Burkina Faso (2003) *Code minier: Loi n°031-2003/AN du 8 mai 2003, Modifié par la L.F.2009* (Ouagadougou: Burkina Faso), http://www.droit-afrique.com/upload/doc/burkina/Burkina-Code-minier-2009.pdf (accessed on 11 October 2022).

Goyette, G.C. (2016) 'Charity Begins at Home: the Extractive Sector as an Illustration of the Harper Governement's De Facto Aid Policy', in S. Brown, M. den Heyer and D.R. Black (eds.) *Rethinking Canadian Aid* (Ottawa: University of Ottawa Press/Les Presses de l'Université d'Ottawa), 2nd edition, pp. 255–271.

Haarstad, H. and A. Fløysand (2007) 'Globalization and the Power of Rescaled Narratives: a Case of Opposition to Mining in Tambogrande, Peru', *Political Geography*, 26(3), pp. 289–308, DOI: 10.1016/j.polgeo.2006.10.014.

Himley, M. (2019) 'Extractivist Geographies: Mining and Development in Late-Nineteenth and Early-Twentieth-Century Peru', *Latin American Perspectives*, 46(2), pp. 27–46, DOI: 10.1177/0094582X18820274.

Hönke, J. (2018) 'Transnational Clientelism, Global (Resource) Governance, and the Disciplining of Dissent', *International Political Sociology*, 12(2), pp. 109–124, DOI: 10.1093/ips/oly007.

Jacobs, J. (2013) 'An Overview of Revenue Flows from the Mining Sector: Impacts, Debates and Policy Recommendations', in B.K. Campbell (ed.) *Modes of Governance and Revenue Flows of African Mining* (London: Palgrave Macmillan), pp. 16–47.

Jenkins, R. (2005) 'Globalization, Corporate Social Responsibility and Poverty', *International Affairs* (Royal Institute of International Affairs 1944-), 81(3), pp. 525–540, https://www.jstor.org/stable/3569632 (accessed on 11 October 2022).

Kaboré, E. (2019) 'Fonds minier de développement local: Etat des paiements en 2017', *L'economiste Du Faso*, 3 June, https://www.leconomistedufaso.bf/2019/06/03/fonds-minier-de-developpement-local-etat-des-paiements-en-2017/ (accessed on 11 October 2022).

Kaboré, E. (2021) 'Fonds minier de développement local: 96,398 milliards FCFA au profit des collectivités en 3 ans', *L'economiste Du Faso*, 21 September, https://www.leconomistedufaso.bf/2021/09/21/fonds-minier-de-developpement-local-96398-milliards-fcfa-au-profit-des-collectivites-en-3-ans/ (accessed on 11 October 2022).

Kesselring, R. (2018) 'The Local State in a New Mining Area in Zambia's Northwestern Province', in J. Schubert, U. Engel and E. Macamo (eds.) *Extractive industries and changing state dynamics in Africa: Beyond the resource curse* (Oxfordshire: Routledge), pp. 129–147.

Knierzinger, J. (2016) 'Après le boom: la laborieuse mise en œuvre de nouvelles régulations dans le secteur minier guinéen', *EchoGéo*, 38, pp. 1–15, DOI: 10.4000/echogeo.14758.

Mansfield, B. (2005) 'Beyond Rescaling: Reintegrating the 'National' as a Dimension of Scalar Relations', Progress in Human Geography, 29(4), pp. 458–473, DOI: 10.1191/0309132505ph560oa.

Marshall, B. (2018) *Facts and Figures 2017: Facts and Figures of the Canadian Mining Industry* (Ottawa: The Mining Association of Canada), https://mining.ca/resources/reports/facts-and-figures-2017/ (accessed on 11 October 2022).

Martín, F. (2017) 'Reimagining Extractivism: Insights from Spatial Theory', in B. Engels and K. Dietz (eds.) *Contested Extractivism, Society and the State: Struggles over Mining and Land* (London: Palgrave Macmillan), pp. 21–44.

Massey, D. (2004) 'Geographies of Responsibility', *Geografiska Annaler: Series B, Human Geography*, 86(1), pp. 5–18, DOI: 10.1111/j.0435-3684.2004.00150.x.

Massey, D. (2005) *For Space* (Thousand Oaks: SAGE Publications Ltd.).

McMahon, G. (2010) *The World Bank's Evolutionary Approach to Mining Sector Reform*, Extractive Industries and Development Series No. 19 (Washington DC: World Bank).

Mining Indaba (2021) Institutional website: https://miningindaba.com/Home (accessed on 11 October 2022).

Miskelly, N. (2004) 'The International Mining Industry—Linking the Upstream Mineralisation With the Downstream Money', *PACRIM*, www.jorc.org/docs/miskelly3.pdf (accessed on 11 October 2022).

MMQ (Ministry of Mines and Quarries) (2019) *Objet: Validation des investissements socio-économiques réalisés par les sociétés minières dans les communes* (Ouagadougou : Ministère des Mines et des Carrières), https://libreinfo.net/wp-content/uploads/2019/07/lettre-ministre-1.pdf (accessed on 29 October 2022).

Nadai, E. and C. Maeder (2005) 'Fuzzy Fields. Multi-Sited Ethnography in Sociological Research', *Forum Qualitative Sozialforschung / Forum: Qualitative Social Research*, 6(3), DOI: 10.17169/FQS-6.3.22.

ORCADE, PCQVP and Oxfam (2018) *État des lieux de la mise en oeuvre du nouveau code minier du Burkina Faso* (Ouagadougou: Organisation pour le Renforcement des Capacités de Développement; Publiez Ce Que Vous Payez, Oxfam).

Sanon, A. (2019) 'Meeting de la coalition « Famu » à Houndé: « on veut profiter de l'argent de notre or »', *Ouest-Info.net*, 1 September, http://ouest-info.net/meeting-de-la-coalition-famu-a-hounde-on-veut-profiter-de-largent-de-notre-or/ (accessed on 11 October 2022).

Schalk, O. (2021) 'Canada's Colonies: Going for Gold (mines) in Africa', *People's World*, 15 September, https://www.peoplesworld.org/article/canadas-colonies-going-for-gold-mines-in-africa/ (accessed on 11 October 2022).

Sydow, J. (2016) 'Global Concepts in Local Contexts: CSR as 'Anti-Politics Machine' in the Extractive Sector in Ghana and Peru', in C. Dolan and D. Rajak (eds.) *The Anthropology of Corporate Social Responsibility* (New York, Oxford: Berghahn Books), pp 217–242.

The McLeod Group (2016) *The Extractive Sector and Development* (Ottawa: The McLeod Group), https://www.mcleodgroup.ca/wp-content/uploads/2016/04/REVISED-McLeod-Group-Policy-Brief-4-Extractive-Sector.pdf (accessed on 11 October 2022).

Thomas, D.P. and V. Coburn (eds.) (2022) *Corporate Canada at Home and Abroad* (Winnipeg: Fernwood Publishing).

TSX (Toronto Stock Exchange) (2022) *Mining* (Toronto: TSX). https://www.tsx.com/listings/listing-with-us/sector-and-product-profiles/mining (accessed 29 October 2022).

van Praet, N. and G. York (2019) 'Dozens Dead in Attack on Canadian Miner Semafo's Convoy in Burkina Faso', *The Globe and Mail*, 6 November, https://www.theglobeandmail.com/business/article-several-dead-in-attack-on-canadian-miner-semafos-convoy-in-burkina-2/ (accessed on 11 October 2022).

Verweijen, J. and A. Dunlap (2021) 'The Evolving Techniques of the Social Engineering of Extraction: Introducing Political (re)actions 'from above' in Large-scale Mining and Energy Projects', *Political Geography*, 88, DOI: 10.1016/j.polgeo.2021.102342.

WAGES (West Africa Governance & Economic Sustainability in Extractive Areas) (2017) *Guide de lecture du code minier burkinabè et des normes et standards de l'industrie minière* (Ouagdougou: WAGES), https://resources.wusc.ca/wp-content/uploads/2018/06/Guide-de-lecture-du-code-minier-AGCEDE-Burkina-Faso.pdf (accessed on 11 October 2022).

Werthmann, K. and Ayeh, D. (2017) *Processes of Enclaving under the Global Condition: the Case of Burkina Faso*, Working paper series of the SFB 1199 Universität Leipzig,

4 (Leipzig: Leipziger Universitätsverlag GmbH), https://research.uni-leipzig.de/~sfb1199/app/uploads/2017/05/WP4_Werthmann-Ayeh_final.pdf (accessed on 29 October 2022).

Weszkalnys, G. (2010) 'Re-Conceiving the Resource Curse and the Role of Anthropology', *Suomen Anthropologi*, 35(1), pp. 87–90, DOI: 10.30676/jfas.116662.

WUSC (World University Service of Canada) (2021) *WAGES: West Africa Governance and Economic Sustainability in Extractive Areas* (WAGES), https://resources.wusc.ca/project/wages/ (accessed on 11 October 2022).

Zalik, A. (2004) 'The Niger Delta: 'Petro Violence' and 'Partnership Development'', *Review of African Political Economy*, 31(101), pp. 401–424, https://www.jstor.org/stable/4006964 (accessed on 11 October 2022).

CHAPTER 7

The Promise of Gold: Gold and Governance in China's Borderlands, Then and Now

Eveline Bingaman

Abstract

Eagleback Village is located in Eya Naxi Autonomous Township, deep in the mountains of southern Sichuan Province, an area whose history has been intimately bound up in the search for gold since at least the Ming dynasty. In the People's Republic of China's Reform era, efforts to extract Eagleback's remaining gold resources have been fraught with controversy. Since 1984, reforms allowing individuals to pursue their own economic interests, combined with the difficulty of monitoring gold digging in such a remote area, have created a 'grey area' regarding ownership of the valley's gold resources. A gold rush began when speculators, villagers and township cadres alike began engaging in artisanal and small-scale mining for gold in the hope of being able to participate in China's growing economy and improve the standard of living of their families. At the county level in the early 2000s, efforts began to act on development and poverty alleviation policies, in particular the 'Three Connects' (三通) policy which aimed to connect every settlement in the county with roads, electricity, and water. County officials looking for contractors able to build roads made a deal with a Hunan gold mining multinational corporation (MNC) for mining rights throughout the county. However, when the project reached Eya Naxi Autonomous Township the damage done to the Longda River by the use of large-scale mining equipment led to a civil uprising in which villagers protested, eventually succeeding in bringing the mining to a halt in 2010. This chapter takes a historical approach while drawing on ethnographic fieldwork to present an example of 'rightful resistance' that offers a more nuanced understanding than that frequently offered with regard to state–society relations in China.

1 Introduction

After several years cutting through hundreds of kilometres of Muli County's virgin forest, in late 2009 'Boss Ho' and his mining equipment arrived on the bank of the Longda River a few miles upstream of Eagleback Village in Eya

© GENEVA GRADUATE INSTITUTE, 2024 | DOI:10.1163/9789004685994_008

Naxi Autonomous Township, Sichuan Province.[1] It was the first road to reach the township; it did not, however, lead to any of the township's villages or even to the township's government office. Under the auspices of Muli County's 'Three Connects' policy, this Hunan based multinational company had been promised that this river valley was rich in gold and that it would have a monopoly on rights to mine that gold if it contributed to the expansion of the county's infrastructure by building roads. What unfolded, however, was a series of cat and mouse disputes with local artisanal miners followed by a full-scale civil uprising that revealed the cracks in the state's ability to enforce its will on a local population.

Since the 1980s, mining and the issues surrounding resource extraction have become an explicit focus of anthropological investigation (Godoy, 1985). In recent decades, as technological advancement intertwines with a rising global demand for precious metals, as Jacka (2018) states we have entered the mineral age of the Anthropocene, in which resource extraction has become an imperative of the global economy. Along with this imperative come the creation of new and the enhancement of old dimensions of state–society relations, particularly in remote areas where state presence has historically been thin at times and non-existent at others. This has reopened questions about how to frame local agency (Lahiri-Dutt, 2018) in economically marginalised communities that are coming into contact with states in new ways.

In the People's Republic of China (PRC), state–society relations have been marked by both ruptures and consistencies as the context of these relations radically shifts as each generation comes of age. As Brandtstädter (2011) points out, since the 1980s the global neo-liberal agenda of the post-Maoist state and the country's increasing interaction with the global market have created an environment in which the parameters of legal–political citizenship have been recast. Yet for rural residents (i.e. the peasants that constituted the heroes of Mao's revolution) political citizenship remains 'rooted in rights to collective resources' (Brandtstädter, 2011, 266). This is perhaps even more true in areas where state rhetoric surrounding policies and promises of 'ethnic autonomy' intersects with geographic divisions.

This chapter takes a historical approach to gold mining to explore shifting state–society relations in one of China's borderlands and to examine how the process of domestic colonisation is less straightforward than other dimensions of China's authoritarian regime might lead one to believe. It reveals two things. The first is that while China may be characterised by a strong state and a weak

1 All personal names are pseudonyms.

society (Guo, 2003), this does not mean that the Chinese people are either unsophisticated or unsuccessful in their efforts to take a stand against the state. The second is that the durability of the Chinese state, which has allowed it to withstand such massive political and economic change, seems to come precisely from the diffusion of its authority rather than from a concentration of power among state officials.

At the same time, the actions taken by Eagleback Naxi in response to 'Boss Ho' and his mining efforts are consistent with indigenous responses to mining documented elsewhere. As a community already vulnerable due to its reliance on existing natural resources and its remoteness from economic alternatives, it was mining-caused environmental degradation that inspired this locally unprecedented political action (Martínez-Alier, 2002). Damage done to the river solidified the boundary between villager and township government (which in the past had frequently blurred) and delineated both in opposition to a new entity, the intruding corporation, reflective of the common 'three-legged' model of mining stakeholders (Ballard and Banks, 2003; 289). The event lead the community to consolidate its expression of and leverage its indigeneity (Golub, 2014) as a means of justifying both its opposition and its claim. Finally, these events demonstrate the presence of a dialectical relationship (Kirsch, 2014), in this case between community and local government, between society and state.

2 Life on the Periphery of China's Development

After decades of policy-induced economic disasters during the Maoist era (Li and Tao Yang, 2005) and massive environmental destruction (Shapiro, 2001), in 1978 there were 250 million Chinese citizens living in abject poverty (Park and Wang, 2001). That year China instituted its 'Reform and Opening' policy, carefully shifting the national economy away from the commune system and towards state run capitalism in an effort to deliver much needed development to its suffering population. However, China's subsequent efforts to economically rebuild itself were carefully rolled out in a piecemeal fashion, from tightly controlled Special Economic Zones, first opened in 1979, to the introduction of the Develop the West campaign of the 1990s. The goal was to introduce radical economic change while maintaining a firm grip on society, testing the waters in order to confirm that economic liberalisation could be achieved without leading to political liberalisation. As a result of geographically controlled reform, at the turn of the new millennium, while residents of the eastern seaboard had settled in to the *xiaozi* (petty bourgeoisie) indulgences that the new economy provided, populations in the western regions were still living hand-to-mouth existences, even as the dismantling of the commune system had made doing so much easier. For those populations, the message from the state had been that patience should be maintained: 'Relief is coming; we just haven't got to you yet'.

Observers have had dualistic impressions of the impact of China's form of economic mobilisation. From the economist's perspective, China's incredible growth has been nothing short of a 'miracle' (Page, 1994) given its remarkable progress through economically unorthodox means (Sylvie, 2001; Riedel, Jin and Gao, 2007; Cai, 2010). From the perspective of environmentalists and human rights advocates, the Chinese state appears to have continued to pursue development at any cost, much of those costs being both human and environmental (Chunli, 2008; Zhang et al., 2012; Fu et al., 2013; Dzonzi-Undi and Li, 2015; Zhao et al., 2015). It also appears incongruous that at the same time China was setting its sights beyond existing borders the nation continued to struggle with a domestic income disparity gap of massive proportions (Li, 2016; Shi, Guo and Sun, 2017; Zhou and Song, 2017). While China's new rich do not seem to know what to do with their newfound wealth (Osburg, 2013), there is still a large population—including a high percentage of the nation's ethnic minority populations—who are struggling to gain access the economic opportunities available to their Han counterparts (Barabantseva, 2009; Bhalla and Luo, 2013).

Eya Naxi Autonomous Township is nestled in the convoluted mountain ranges that break the landscape between the Tibetan and Yun-Gui plateaus in southern Sichuan Province. The township makes up the south-western most corner of Muli County running along the Yunnan–Sichuan border. Eya Township is divided into six administrative villages with a range of settlements varying in size from the largest, Eagleback—with over 230 households—to single-household 'villages' (Chinese (hereafter, 'Ch'.): *dujia cun*). Most of the settlements are located at around 2,500 meters above sea level; too high for growing rice and too low for raising yaks. There are two agricultural seasons: corn is grown in the summer, wheat in the winter, making up the two main crops. Food is supplemented with vegetable gardens, which each household maintains. Each household also practices animal husbandry, raising chickens, pigs and goats. Horses and oxen are mainly used for labour.

In addition to being geographically peripheral, under the system of ethnic autonomy operated in the People's Republic of China (PRC) Eya is also politically and administratively marginalised. Eya Naxi Autonomous Township is located within Muli Tibetan Autonomous County, which is in turn located within Liangshan Yi Autonomous Prefecture. What autonomy means in this situation is that leadership positions in local governments need to be filled by members of the majority nationality of the area. For Eya, this means that the position of township head (Ch. *xiangzhang*) needs to be filled by a member of the Naxi nationality. In practice, there are no Naxi from the local community qualified to hold the position, so the township head needs to be recruited from other Naxi communities of Muli County. The rest of the township government reflects the population balance in Muli County as a whole, with a majority of Tibetans, some Yi, and some Han.

The Naxi population of Muli, around 4,000 people, makes up only 3.47 per cent of the total population of the county. In turn, the predominant population in Muli, Tibetans, only makes up 1.39 per cent of the population of Liangshan Yi Autonomous Prefecture. While all of Liangshan Prefecture is struggling to pull its mountain populations out of poverty, this bureaucratic nesting of autonomy places Eya Naxi at the bottom of the list in terms of priority for receiving the benefits of government development policy. This makes a difference that can be demonstrated most starkly by comparing the Eya standard of living with that of the majority of those of Naxi nationality in China, who reside in and around the Lijiang basin, two days to the south in Yunnan Province. In Yunnan Province, Lijiang has long had the administrative level of 'City', placing Lijiang Naxi on the same level as Liangshan Yi Autonomous Prefecture in terms of power and sway in provincial actions. There have been several important politicians in Yunnan that have hailed from Lijiang, and thus Lijiang Naxi have been successful in having their voices heard. In Yunnan Province, the Naxi nationality is considered a shining example of a minority that has successfully developed to become a part of the PRC's mainstream (Su, 2013), while Eya Naxi in Sichuan remain largely invisible, hidden beneath politics involving the political sensitivity regarding Tibetans.

Until 2013 there was no road connecting Eya to outside markets, or even to the county government; all journeys in or out were made by foot or by horse caravan. In 2002 when I made my first trip to Eagleback Village, it took two days on foot to reach from the nearest market town. Reaching the county capital to deal with any kind of bureaucratic or administrative issue, including completing compulsory education, involved a ten-day trek. This was shortened in 2010 to five days when the road connecting Wachang to the county capital was completed. Now—and since 2013 when the road finally reached Eagleback—the county capital of Muli can be reached in a day as long as the roads are passable and not blocked by snow (in winter) or mudslides (in summer).

Despite these transportation difficulties, this does not mean that Eya has been so isolated as to be left unaware of the changes taking place in the world outside the Longda River valley, nor have Eya Naxi people been exempt from state policies since they were first incorporated into the PRC polity in 1957. These include economic and land reform policies (the collectivisation of agriculture, the Great Leap Forward, and finally de-collectivisation and the establishment of the household responsibility system), political policies (the Cultural Revolution), and policies regarding marriage, divorce and childbirth (from 1981 until recently, as members of an impoverished and rural ethnic minority community, they were subject to a limit of three births per woman).

Beginning in 1995 a variety of programmes were put in place, changing the population from taxpayers into recipients of various forms of welfare. Through the 'Reforestation of Fields' policy (Ch. *tuigeng huanlin*), which began in 2002, people were given walnut seedlings to reforest land that had been opened for cultivation during the commune era, and now receive an annual stipend for not farming that land until these walnut trees have matured enough to provide an income. They also receive subsidies to purchase 'improved' seeds for three kinds of crops, even though only one of the three is grown in Eya. They also receive subsidies for raising sows, and the township government receives an annual welfare subsidy (Ch. *dibao*), which it can allot to a small number of households.

However, these programmes have not been able to keep up with the population's growing needs. As the rest of China develops, a variety of desirable things have become available—things that cannot be acquired through trade but only with cash. This is not just store-bought items such as clothing and shoes, pots, pans, washing machines and TVs, but also includes opportunities for education and receiving healthcare.

A school was built in Eagleback Village in the late 1950s shortly after Muli Tibetan Autonomous County was established by the PRC. There is also a clinic that is able to treat minor illnesses and administer vaccines. Villagers are also active in their own attempts to improve their standard of living. Tired of waiting for the government to provide electricity, in the mid-1990s the residents of Eagleback Village all invested in purchasing and transporting the equipment necessary to build a small hydropower station, and since 1996 have had access (although minimal) to electricity.

Over the years that I had been visiting Eagleback, when I asked why no state project had had a noticeable impact on improving standards of living there the answer had always been the same: Eagleback Naxi had remained stuck in poverty because there was no road.

3 The History of Gold in Muli

Eya's history, for at least as long as the Naxi have been here, has been tied up in gold. Towards the end of the Ming dynasty, the power of the Naxi chieftains based in Lijiang—granted the surname Mu by the Ming court—was expanding.

The chieftain Mu Yi took on the appellation 'Heavenly King Mu' (Ch. *Mu Tian Wang*) and began expanding his reach up the Chong Tian River in search of gold that could be used to increase his legitimacy within the Tibetan Buddhist political system. It was said that he had a golden sword, and a 'golden' dog that helped him find the precious metal. Wherever the dog barked, he ordered his men to dig, and the dog was reputed to be incredibly accurate. At this point in history, gold was not a currency in China but was used as an offering between subjects and rulers, often related to religious legitimacy.[2] According to local legend, the gold collected by the Naxi chieftain is said to have been sent to Lhasa, where a golden pillar was built in honour of the Buddha. The more gold was harvested, the higher the pillar was built. Eventually the pillar became too tall, and the chieftain was ordered by Lhasa to make it shorter. According to local custom, this should be done by removing a section from the bottom. He, however, chose to remove a section from the top instead. This action, which angered the Buddha, is said to mark the beginning of the end of the power of the Mu Clan, eventually leading to the decline of Lijiang Naxi Kingdom as a whole.

In his expansion north from Lijang to Shuiluo, Mu Yi built several encampments close to rivers, the remnants of many of which can still be seen today. Eagleback is one such encampment, a settlement of Naxi settler-soldiers left behind to guard the point where Jinsha River, the Chongtian River, and the Dongyi River approach one another (Wang, 2008). However, Naxi dominance over the territory lasted less than fifty years. In 1647 Lijiang was conquered, and native chieftains were replaced by circulatory government officials (Ch. *gaituguiliu*), Lijiang being incorporated into the Qing central bureaucracy (MZZX, 1995, 9). Then, in 1675 control of the territory of Eya was granted to the Buddhist Kingdom of Muli by Lhasa as a reward for faithful service (MZZZD, 2002). From the end of the seventeenth century until Eya was officially 'liberated' by the People's Liberation Army (PLA) in 1957, Eya was governed by Muli Monastery. This governance operated through a local Naxi headman, a position inherited by principle of primogeniture by males of the Mugua (木瓜) clan (no relation to the Mu native chieftain based in Lijiang).

3.1 *Muli Kingdom Era, 1675–1957*

While the Mugua clan was the highest authority in Eagleback, it was relatively weak in terms of authority in comparison to Muli's monk officials. The Mugua

2 During the Ming dynasty, silver became the main currency, especially when the 'single whip' tax system (*yitiao bianfa* 一條鞭法) came into effect and taxes were to be paid in silver rather than in grain. This had a number of effects, including commercialisation of property, among other things. For more information, see Liu (2010).

had no authority to grant land as all land was officially owned by the head lama of the Muli Kingdom. The Mugua was not allowed to maintain a local army, and was not allowed to tax the local population, other than the nine houses that were officially designated to provide labour to support his rule. Both the Mugua family and all other houses paid tax directly to the Monastery.

Under the Muli Kingdom, the local population was governed as a Tibetan style polity. Taxpayer houses were the lowest unit of the bureaucracy and the main unit of property ownership. Part of Muli's taxation involved the number of days someone from each taxpayer household needed to spend digging for gold each year at various mines around Muli. The Mugua headman organised a rotation of responsibility through the different neighbourhoods so that every household was required to provide a labourer roughly once every three years. If a household had no men available, women would be assigned. Labourers were responsible for providing for all of their own needs—most importantly their food and tools—for their term performing corveé service. A quota was set for how many ounces of gold each individual needed to provide, and when that quota was reached the individual's service was deemed fulfilled for that occasion and he or she could return home. Often terms of service lasted for between three and six months. Occasionally people were able to steal gold. If caught, the punishment was death, but sometimes workers digging in the depths would find a solid nugget and swallow it before it could be seen by the foremen, recovering it later from their faeces. It could then be secretly sold to travelling tradesmen, who passed through the valley periodically.

With the arrival of the PLA, ownership of all of the gold yet to be mined in Eya shifted from the Muli Kingdom to the PRC.[3]

3.2 *Cooperative Era, 1957–84*

By the time the PLA arrived in Eya, the PRC had already begun carrying out economic reforms in Muli's Tibetan areas, so Eya was almost immediately collectivised. At the time, there were several communities in the Muli area that rebelled, leading to a series of temple bombings in order to pacify the region (Shakya, 1999). When the Muli Kingdom was overturned and Muli Tibetan Autonomous County was established by the PRC in 1955, the Mugua headman had already been taken to the prefectural capital for 're-education'. All

3 In the interim, there was a short period during which the Republican Army (1911–49) was present in Muli mining for metals to support the war effort. The presence of the Republic of China did not, however, mark a change in governance in this territory ruled by the Muli theocracy, and all the mining that was carried out by the Republic took place with the permission of, and was also taxed by, Muli.

accounts confirm that he became a strong advocate for the communist cause, returning only once to hand over all his property to the villagers. When the PLA headed for Eagleback in 1957, he sent word that the villagers should come to meet the army welcoming it with flowers, which they did. Eya was therefore 'peacefully liberated' and cooperated with all reforms.

This involved the collectivisation of all property into cooperatives. As was the practice throughout the rest of rural China, Eya was organised into production teams, each team led by a team head who had the job of assigning labourers to different tasks. As elsewhere, this move to collectivisation involved a massive change to family structure. During the Muli Kingdom era, taxpayer households were subject to a monk levy that limited the number of sons at home to two per generation (see Bingaman, 2021), keeping birth rates low and families relatively small. The abolition of Muli Monastery's monk levy combined with Maoist era policies encouraging births led family size to explode during this era as women had six, seven, even ten children.

Gold continued to be mined through the cooperative era. The labour for mining was organised by production team heads and overseen by the township's government. All gold recovered went to the collective—that is, to the state. According to local accounts, the collective essentially maintained the same method of recruiting labour as that used in the Muli Kingdom era—individuals were sent to dig in the mines on a rotation basis for periods of three to six months.

3.3 *'Household Responsibility' Policy, 1984—Present*

Beginning in 1982, policies allowing for the disbanding of the cooperatives began to be put in place in Muli and by 1984 the land in Eya had been redistributed and allotted to individual households. Under this new system, the household once again became the most basic production unit of a family's needs and households were encouraged to make efforts to maximise their economies.[4] Historically the main commodities that needed to be acquired from outside the valley through trade were tea, salt and cloth. By the 1980s, other products became available at the government-run store—cloth and yarn for making clothes and weaving, pots, pans, bowls, and blankets. Then, after

4 Previously, equality was emphasized, so families were discouraged from economic action that would only benefit their own household and not the whole community. For example, people were not allowed to have household gardens to supplement their family's diets. But after reform, there was no more fear of doing whatever you could to raise your own house's production. People were no longer accused of creating inequality if they produced more than other households.

Eagleback's power station was built, there was demand for TVs, refrigerators and lightbulbs. People needed money more and more, yet there were precious few ways of earning cash with which to gain access to all the things that only cash money could acquire.

Under the household responsibility system, mining on behalf of the state ceased and individual mining for gold became a grey area of economic opportunity. Technically, all the gold in the ground belonged to the state. Also technically, under the PRC's system of ethnic autonomy it belonged to the Naxi people of Eya Naxi Autonomous Township. Periodically township governments would get orders to tighten up on 'illegal' gold mining, and they would carry out surveys, dropping dynamite down mining pits to close them when they found them. But for the most part it was a free-for-all for whoever had the time and the ability to invest, and a miniature gold rush occurred. As with gold rushes everywhere, more people went bankrupt than actually turned a profit, but ongoing poverty and desperation kept hope in place and kept people heading out to the riverbed.

As described in detail below, by the late 2000s every household that had labourers to spare was involved in gold prospecting throughout the winter months. Men would get together in teams of three or four to invest in the equipment that was needed, and try their luck, sharing any profits between them. Some years some would be lucky, making a big enough return on their investment to buy some items for their households; other years they would suffer a loss. Even township officials and teachers who had been assigned to serve in Eagleback were involved in investing and digging for gold as a means of supplementing their meagre salaries. The promise that they might find gold was informally considered as compensation for officials from more connected areas being assigned to such a poor and remote place.

4 The Promise of Gold

As already stated, after the household responsibility system was put in place in 1984 giving individual households permission to do what they could to maximise their household economic holdings, opportunities to earn cash income were few and far between. The obvious first option—to invest in some kind of cash crop that would turn traditional agriculture into a profit-making activity—was impractical. The main obstacle remained transportation. Nothing that could be produced in the valley carried a market value high enough to offset the price of transporting it via horseback to distant markets. Additionally, during the collective era households had become accustomed to the white rice that had been shipped in at the state's expense; thus, the majority of households were already importing staples, making them reliant on external markets that they had no means to participate in. Two commodities that did have some potential were the Sichuan peppercorn and a type of orange that is particular to Muli, but transporting these by horseback was at best a means of making up some of the cost incurred on trading trips to buy staples to bring back.

The Longda River, which runs through the township and the surrounding mountains, did, however, offer two things that could be used to generate cash for households that were able to spare labour from normal agricultural activities: gold mining and matsutake mushrooms.[5]

4.1 *Eya's Gold Industry*

The Longda River Valley runs west to east through Eya Township. The largest settlement is Eagleback, located along the river at its eastern end. The settlement directly upstream is known as Suda Village. It is in the section of the Longda River that flows through Suda that Eya Township's richest gold reserves are found.

The relationship between Suda Village and Eagleback is one of convivial rivalry. The two villages have kinship ties between them, but in terms of economic development, Suda Village has been much more fortunate than Eagleback, leading to what is perhaps a reversal of historical relations (in the past the headman of Suda was subordinate to the headman of Eagleback in the Muli Kingdom's bureaucracy). To begin with, Suda's population is much smaller, and the majority of each house's fields are all close by, making agricultural work much easier. The villages' topographies also grant Suda's fields two hours more sunlight per day than those of Eagleback, resulting in higher yields. Also, considerably more forest land belongs to Suda Village, which means more reforested land, which brings in government subsidies per household. Lastly, Suda is a full day closer to the market town of Luoji, which was particularly fortuitous at the height of the matsutake mushroom trade. In the Reform era, all these elements have combined to offer the villagers of Suda many more

5 The matsutake mushroom market was a very important part of local economies throughout this mountainous region in the early reform period. Matsutake mushrooms grow wild in only a few places, and for about two decades they fetched an extremely high price in Japan, a phenomenon that connected some of China's most remote communities to an international market. The Japanese market has since dissipated, and matsutake mushrooms no longer represent the opportunities they once did. For more information on the area's mushroom industry, see Yeh (2000), Yang et al. (2008) and Arora (2008), and for a global scale view of the mushroom economy, see Tsing (2015).

opportunities to improve their economic standing, and these same villagers often brag that even though Eagleback's population is several times larger, their population on average is much more educated and financially secure.

When the collectives were disbanded and land redistributed in Suda, the riverbed, and thus gold mining areas, was not included in the redistribution. Still, the community had its own way of staking claims to areas and negotiating for mining rights. People would use paint to mark off the territory they wanted to claim, and such claims were respected by all, including the township government, a few members of which were eager to invest in the claims. Households that did not have the spare labour required to mine sought to attract speculators from outside the valley who would invest in the equipment needed and share in the wealth if any were found.

Bendi from Eagleback was one such ambitious investor, and he was intent on making a living from means other than agriculture once the household responsibility system had been put in place. Coming from a large family there were already two brothers capable of handling the farm work, releasing Bendi to try to 'find money' by whatever means possible. Immediately following decollectivisation, Bendi borrowed the funds to buy a few horses and started earning money as a transporter in the caravan trade. Then, later in 2003 he got his first job working as a labourer on a small-scale gold mining operation in a neighbouring township. Three years later, in 2006 he recruited three others from Eagleback to invest with him in buying the equipment necessary to set up a mining operation with a friend from Suda who had a claim ready for prospecting.

The initial investment in equipment was about USD 7,800 (CNY 50,000 by 2022's exchange rate). The main elements required were a water pump, motors, and diesel to run them. Once the operation was set up, labourers were hired—mostly from Eagleback—at a daily rate, and were paid at the end of the digging season from the profits made from any gold recovered. By 2009 there were three or four such operations going on during the winter months, providing sufficient labouring opportunities for every household in Eagleback that had labourers to spare to get involved.

Every local working as a labourer knew that this was no means to get rich. For local investors, labourers were contracted on the promise they would be paid at the end of the season when the year's take was sold, usually to travelling buyers who would visit each year at the end of the dry season. For village investors, every year was a gamble: some years would see a profit, others losses or break-even. For labourers, wages began at around USD 1.50 (CNY 10) per day, and had risen to around USD 7.50 (CNY 50) per day by the time mining operations were closed down in 2010. The best hope for day labourers was that they would be able to earn a bit of cash 'for tea and salt', and if they did well perhaps purchase a TV for their family.

5 The Three Connects Policy and the Arrival of 'Boss Ho'

In November of 2009 the first road reached Eya Naxi Autonomous Township, but this road did not go to any of the villages, or even lead to the township's government offices. Rather, it led straight to the riverbed in Suda, just upstream of Eagleback's power station. Soon, heavy earth-moving equipment arrived along with 'Boss Ho', who confronted the heads of the local mining operations announcing that the entire riverbed had been purchased by him and that all local small-scale operations were to stop immediately.

As surprising as his appearance was, Boss Ho and his mining equipment had not arrived on the banks of the Longda River out of nowhere. His company, a Hunan-based MNC, had been involved in gold mining all across China and as far away as Africa. Several years earlier it had won a contract with Muli County as part of the 'Connecting Villages' (Ch. *tongcun gonglu*) policy. Although unconfirmed, it appears that his ability to underbid his competitors centred on agreements made with the county government that part of the compensation would come from mining rights. By the time he arrived in Eya he already had several mining operations in progress across Muli County.

When the first confrontation between Boss Ho and villagers occurred, the heads of the local mining operations appealed to the township government. They were told that the government's hands were tied; this was part of a larger project to bring development to Eya that had begun at the county level, and the township had to cooperate. Still the villagers stood their ground. It is unclear who made initial moves to escalate the dispute, but efforts were made to disable Boss Ho's equipment, and dynamite was dropped down the pits of each of the local mining operations, damaging the villagers' equipment beyond repair. The culprits in both of these acts remain 'unknown', as no one has claimed responsibility and anyone who knew the truth has remained resolutely tight-lipped. Regarding the dynamite that destroyed the locals' mining equipment the township office appears to have made no efforts to investigate, which some have taken as an indication of its involvement, or at least its consent.

It was not, however, until Boss Ho's digging began in earnest that the conflict transformed from the relatively contained anger of local operators over the loss of their investments into a civil uprising involving the entire community of Eagleback. In comparison with the methods utilised by local mining operations, which left little visible surface impact and did not disturb the river,

FIGURE 7.1 Boss Ho's mining operation
SOURCE: AUTHOR, JANUARY 2010

Boss Ho's large-scale operation with heavy earth-moving equipment wreaked devastating environmental damage. The first step involved entirely altering the river's route through the area so that land that was once the riverbed could be accessed for dredging. Then, machines were set up to sift through the silt, dumping the excess back into the river (see Figure 7.1). As a result, the entirety of river water flowing through Eagleback and beyond became fouled and ran completely brown. The water canals running to the small hydroelectric power station that the villagers had built for themselves kept getting clogged with debris, causing wear and tear on the equipment and threatening its continued operation. Irrigation ditches drawing water from the river filled with silt, cutting off the water supply to the fields and livestock, causing a severe drop in production and a rapid spike in livestock deaths. All the fish in the river died. The villagers of Eagleback had no clean water to wash themselves, their food, or their clothing.

6 Collective Action

The damage to the river unified the community of Eagleback and at the same time divided the representatives of the township government. The villagers decided to sue the Muli County government, and with the help of a local advocate a letter stating the villagers' position was drafted:

> We, the Naxi people of Eagleback, Eya Township, wish to sue Muli County for allowing the mining of gold in the Longda River because of the destruction to forest resources and the erosion it has caused, which has severely polluted the Longda River, which we rely on for our livelihood, and for the severe economic losses and destruction to the environment it has brought upon the Naxi people of Eagleback, which has made it impossible for the people to survive.
>
> The mining resources of the Longda River should belong to the state, and be a part of the wealth of the people of Eya Township. If outside prospectors take all of it without compensation, what will we the people of Eya Township use to develop our economy?
>
> We, the Naxi people of Eagleback are grateful to the central party and the government for the 'Three Connections' preferential policy (connecting transportation, connecting water, connecting electricity) given to national minorities in the poor mountain areas; however the Naxi people of Eagleback have not only not enjoyed the benefits of these preferential policies, it has made it possible for outside gold miners to steal and destroy national resources.
>
> Author's field notes, August 2015

It was also decided to set up a roadblock on the mountaintop where Boss Ho's road entered the township and to not allow him or any more of his personnel or equipment entry. Every household in Eagleback sent people to camp on the mountain in rotation to guard the barricade; both young and old took their turns over a two-month period. The township government was unable to come to an agreement on how to proceed.

Finally, county level officials were sent in to resolve the problem. It is unclear which officials from which departments and which authorities were present, but it *is* clear that both township and county officials were split, some standing with Boss Ho, others in support of the villagers. Finally, the county and township governments decided to withdraw, removing themselves from the negotiating process. Boss Ho was told that to continue his mining, he would need to come to an agreement with the villagers of Eagleback regarding compensation for damage done to the river.

In the end it was Bendi who was chosen to represent Eagleback in the negotiations with Boss Ho. The villagers demanded an exorbitant amount in compensation, not actually in the belief that they would receive it, but to make their stand. Boss Ho made a counteroffer, to be paid directly to Bendi if he could get the villagers to agree to allow the digging to resume. Bendi replied that he could not carry such a burden in the knowledge that he had betrayed his village. Boss Ho finally threw up his hands and withdrew, claiming that he had previously assumed that the money he had paid to the county to secure mining rights would have been given to the villagers, thus pointing the finger at the county government. In March 2010, Boss Ho engaged a local family in Suda Village to look after his equipment, and departed.

7 Discussion

Unlike the 'resigned activism' observed by Lora-Wainwright (2017), the successful shutting down of Boss Ho's mining operations on the Longda River through village protests can be considered an example of what O'Brien (1996) and O'Brien and Li (2006) have termed 'rightful resistance'. Building on prior works by Herbst (1989) and Scott (1990) exploring various forms of popular resistance, O'Brien uses the term 'rightful resistance' to describe forms of protest in which groups 'dispute the legitimacy of certain political authorities and their actions while affirming (indeed relying upon) other authorities and established values to pursue their ends' (1996, 32). In other words, rightful resisters seek to use the state against the state by 'us[ing] a regime's policies and legitimizing myths to justify their defiance' (1996, 33).

In their study of rightful resistance in rural China, O'Brien and Li (2006) show that the rise of instances of this form of resistance indicate a growing fluency in the language of 'laws, regulations and other authoritative communications' (2006, 6) and of 'contractual ways of thinking' about state–society relations. O'Brien identifies three characteristics of 'rightful resistance': it '(1) operates near the boundary of an authorized channel, (2) employs rhetoric and commitments of the powerful to curb political or economic power, [and] (3) hinges on locating and exploiting divisions among the powerful' (O'Brien, 1996, 33).

In the debates going back and forth between villagers and township officials regarding the actual legality of Boss Ho's digging, the 'grey area' in policy that had previously given villagers and township officials alike the space to seek to create or supplement incomes with gold prospecting became a problem. Villagers cited policy that all natural resources belonged to the state, therefore arguing that the county had no right to sell mining rights to an outsider (and definitely not to a Han individual from Hunan). Township officials countered that according to this logic the villagers' own digging (and township officials' digging as well) was likewise illegal. Villagers countered again, arguing that although the Naxi people are also subjects of the Chinese state, Eya is recognised by the state as a Naxi minority autonomous township, and therefore that if any part of the state had a claim on Eya's natural resources it was the Naxi people. If anyone was going to benefit from these resources, it should be them.

None of these arguments ended up being particularly persuasive, and the final solution, which followed the county government's attempts at intervention, was the imposition of a county-wide ban on *all* gold mining in Muli, whether carried out by locals or by outside prospectors. The idea is that this ban will stay in effect until such a time that the county government is able to oversee environmentally friendly means of extraction and the 'fair' distribution of benefit, however that is to be calculated. The ban came into effect almost immediately following the Eagleback incident in 2010, but was not effectively enforced until 2012.

Secondly, the methods the villagers employed also demonstrated their sophistication in employing state rhetoric to bolster their cause. In the end, the letter that was drafted in preparation for their suing the county government was never submitted to higher authorities; it provides, however, an example of 'employ[ing] government commitments and established values to persuade concerned elites to support their claims' (O'Brien, 1996, 32). For example, the passage from the letter cited above is followed by a step-by-step description of how the 'Three Connects' promise made to minority populations has been violated by the county government:

> Connecting transportation: Eagleback is the largest settlement of Eya Township and is still not connected to a road, but in order to mine for gold the road has already been built through the virgin forest. The gold miners have done this for their own profit, causing major destruction to the virgin forest resources and massive erosion, which has led to the loss of the beautiful scenery on both banks of the Longda River.
>
> Connecting water: The Longda River has always been the mother river that the Naxi people of Eagleback rely on for their livelihood; the river water was originally clear and transparent, and is the water the Naxi people of the whole village use for their daily needs. But because of the pollution caused by gold mining, it is impossible for the Naxi people of Dacun to live.
>
> Connecting electricity: not only do the Naxi people of Eagleback not enjoy the benefits of the national preferential policies for the connecting

> of electricity, […] because of the erosion caused by gold digging the small electricity station we build ourselves has been severely damaged.
>
> Author's field notes, August 2015

Finally, there is no doubt that the villagers made full use of the divide between local township officials to build sympathy for their cause. After all, several officials were partner investors in the local mining operations and thus had also had their equipment destroyed. But ethnic divisions also undoubtedly played a role in alliance building. As already mentioned, although Eya is a Naxi autonomous township, the majority of the representatives of the township government, like those of the county government, are Tibetan. However, many Tibetan officials, particularly those who have/had been placed in Eya Township for a number of years, develop deep affections and commitments with regard to their Eagleback Naxi friends, putting them in a position to advocate on behalf of Eagleback Naxi across the ethnic—and particularly the linguistic—divide.

Much has been made of the resilience of the Chinese state, and particularly of how solidly the Chinese Communist Party (CCP) has managed to maintain its authority throughout periods of such incredible social and economic change (Nathan, 2003). The secret to this resilience seems to lie in the particularity of Chinese statecraft, and the character of that statecraft. One common feature of peasant protests in China is that they seem to always be directed at lower levels of bureaucracy, never at the system itself and never at the CCP. The key to understanding this perhaps lies in the institutionalised vagueness of PRC policy, in which 'policy' often takes the form of vague slogans such as 'Harmonious Society' or 'Chinese Dream' or in this case, the 'Three Connects'. The incident involving large-scale gold mining in Eya Township can be considered to be a result of the 'Develop the West' policy, which was launched in 2000 in an attempt to bring economic reforms to China's interior and particularly to its ethnic minority populations. Holbig (2004) refers to Develop the West as a 'soft policy', emphasising the diffused nature of decision-making with regard to how economic reform is to be carried out. Under this policy, local leaders are under huge pressure to bring about economic growth, with very little guidance as to how this should be done. In this way, it is the lower levels of the PRC bureaucracy (in this case, township and county level governments) that are left making the hard decisions and taking all the risks in their efforts to bring about change. If successful, the individuals involved may enjoy long and illustrious careers. If unsuccessful, they will be the ones to take the fall. What this demonstrates is that the Chinese state is not as 'authoritarian' as it seems, or at least not in the top-down manner that is usually imagined.

8 Epilogue

Looking back today on the incident at Eagleback, although the villagers were not happy to lose their means of scratching out a meagre income from gold mining, all agreed that a ban on any digging in the valley was a fair compromise. In recalling stories of the conflict, particularly the two months of camping on the mountain pass to barricade the road, villagers relived their anger and expressed their pride in their success in standing up for their village's welfare.

Although Boss Ho's digging had taken place on Suda Village's territory, the location was downriver from Suda's water supply, and thus Suda's villagers were not negatively impacted by the mining. They therefore did not actively take part in the protests or in mounting the barricade. It also appears that some from Suda continued to mine after the county-wide ban was put in place, which remains an issued of unsettled tension between Eagleback and Suda Village.

Not long after the incident, there was a reshuffling of officials at the township government, and the majority of those who were present at the time of the incident were replaced, being promoted to the county level or reassigned to other townships, or retiring. Current township officials have maintained a stricter distance from the villagers than had previously been the practice.

By 2013, a road suitable for passenger vehicles had finally reached Eagleback, with motorcycle paths connecting most other villages in the township. Since then—like in so many other rural areas China—seeking work outside the village and sending remittances has emerged as the preferred method of diversifying a household's economic holdings. As far as paid labour within the village goes, more and more opportunities are arising, usually related to state development projects, which are now in progress, fulfilling the promise of the 'Three Connects' policy to bring a reliable electricity supply to all communities.

References

Arora, D. (2008) 'The Houses That Matsutake Built', 62(3), pp. 278–290.

Ballard, C. and G. Banks (2003) 'Resource Wars: the Anthropology of Mining', *Annual Review of Anthropology*, 32, pp. 287–313, DOI: 10.1146/annurev.anthro.32.061002.093116.

Barabantseva, E.V. (2009) 'Development as Localization: Ethnic Minorities in China's Official Discourse on the Western Development Project', *Critical Asian Studies*, 41(2), pp. 225–254, DOI: 10.1080/14672710902809393.

Bhalla, A.S. and D. Luo (2013) *Poverty and Exclusion of Minorities in China and India* (New York: Palgrave Macmillan), DOI: 10.1057/9781137283535.

Bingaman, E. (2021) 'Measures and Countermeasures: Monk Levies and Kinship in the Sino-Tibetan Borderland', *Inner Asia*, 23(1), 51–78, DOI: 10.1163/22105018-12340162.

Brandtstädter, S. (2011) 'The Law Cuts Both Ways: Rural Legal Activism and Citizenship Struggles in Neosocialist China', *Economy and Society*, 40(2), pp. 266–288, DOI: 10.1080/03085147.2011.548944.

Cai, F. (2010) *Transforming the Chinese Economy* (Leiden and Boston: Brill), DOI:10.1163/ej.9789004184213.i-354.

Chunli, X. (2008) 'Autonomy and China's Ethnic Minorities: an Observation of Autonomous Legislatures', *Asia-Pacific Journal of Human Rights and the Law*, 9(2), pp. 11–46, DOI: 10.1163/157181509789025246.

Dzonzi-Undi, J. and S. Li (2015) 'SWOT Analysis of Safety and Environmental Regulation for China and USA : Its Effect and Influence on Sustainable Development of the Coal Industry', *Environmental Earth Sciences*, 74, pp. 6395–6406, DOI: 10.1007/s12665-015-4751-6.

Fu, J., Y. Luo, C. Liu and H. Zhu (2013) 'Studies on the Environmental Pollution of Huaihe River', *Journal of Environmental Protection and Ecology*, 14(4), pp. 1498–1505.

Godoy, R. (1985) 'Mining: Anthropological Perspectives', *Annual Review of Anthropology*, 14(1985), pp. 199–217, https://www.jstor.org/stable/2155595 (accessed on 22 November 2022).

Golub, A. (2014) *Leviathans at the Gold Mine: Creating Indigenous and Corporate Actors in Papua New Guinea* (Durham and London: Duke University Press).

Guo, X. (2003) *State and Society in China's Democratic Transition: Confucianism, Leninism, and Economic Development* (New York: Routledge).

Herbst, J. (1989) 'How the Weak Succeed: Tactics, Political Goods, and Institutions in the Struggle over Land in Zimbabwe', in F.D. Colburn (ed.) *Everyday Forms of Peasant Resistance* (New York: Routledge), pp. 198–220.

Holbig, H. (2004) 'The Emergence of the Campaign to Open Up the West: Ideological Formation, Central Decision-making and the Role of the Provinces', *The China Quarterly*, 178, pp. 335–357, DOI: 10.1017/S0305741004000207.

Jacka, J.K. (2018) 'The Anthropology of Mining: the Social and Environmental Impacts of Resource Extraction in the Mineral Age', *Annual Review of Anthropology*, 47, pp. 61–77, DOI: 10.1146/annurev-anthro-102317-050156.

Kirsch, S. (2014) *Mining Capitalism: the Relationship between Corporations and their Critics* (Oakland: University of California Press), DOI: 10.1525/9780520957596.

Lahiri-Dutt, K. (2018) 'Extractive Peasants: Reframing Informal Artisanal and Small-Scale Mining Debates', *Third World Quarterly*, 39(8), pp. 1561–1582, DOI: 10.1080/01436597.2018.1458300.

Li, S. (2016) 'Income Inequality and Economic Growth in China in the Last Three Decades', *The Round Table*, 105(6), pp. 641–665, DOI: 10.1080/00358533.2016.1246858.

Li, W. and D. Tao Yang (2005) 'The Great Leap Forward: Anatomy of a Central Planning Disaster', *Journal of Political Economy*, 113(4), pp. 840–877, DOI: 10.1086/430804.

Lora-Wainwright, A. (2017) *Resigned Activism: Living with Pollution in Rural China* (Boston: MIT Press).

Martínez-Alier, J. (2002) *The Environmentalism of the Poor: a Study of Ecological Conflicts and Valuation* (Cheltenham: Edward Elgar Publishing).

MZZX (Annals of Muli Tibetan Autonomous County Editorial Committee) (1995) *Muli Zangzu Zizhi Xianzhi* 木里藏族自治县志 [*Annals of Muli Tibetan Autonomous County*] (Chengdu: Sichuan renmin chubanshe).

MZZZD (Archives Office of Muli Tibetan Autonomous Prefecture) (2002) 'Muli Zhengjiaoshi de Neirong He Jiazhi 木里政教史的内容和价值 [The Contents and Significance of 'The History of the Muli Theocracy']', in W. 胡文明 Hu (ed.) *Pumi Yanjiu Wenji* 普米研究文集 [*Collected Pumi Research*] (Kunming: Yunnan Minzu Chubanshe 云南民族出版社), pp. 449–506.

Nathan, A.J. (2003) 'China's Changing of the Guard: Authoritarian Resilience', *Journal of Democracy*, 14(1), pp. 6–17.

O'Brien, K.J. (1996) 'Rightful Resistance', *World Politics*, 49(1), pp. 31–55.

O'Brien, K.J. and L. Li (2006) *Rightful Resistance in Rural China* (Cambridge and New York: Cambridge University Press).

Osburg, J. (2013) *Anxious Wealth: Money and Morality Among China's New Rich* (Stanford: Stanford University Press).

Page, J. (1994) 'The East Asian Miracle: Four Lessons for Development Policy', *NBER Macroeconomics Annual Review*, 9(1994), pp. 219–269.

Park, A. and S. Wang (2001) 'China's Poverty Statistics', *China Economic Review*, 12(4), pp. 384–398, DOI: 10.1016/S1043-951X(01)00066-9.

Riedel, J., J. Jin and J. Gao (2007) *How China Grows: Investment, Finance, and Reform* (Princeton: Princeton University Press).

Scott, J.C. (1990) *Domination and the Art of Resistance* (New Haven, Conneticut: Yale University Press).

Shakya, T. (1999) *The Dragon in the Land of Snows: a History of Modern Tibet Since 1947* (New York: Columbia University Press).

Shapiro, J. (2001) *Mao's War Against Nature: Politics and the Environment in Revolutionary China* (Cambridge: Cambridge University Press).

Shi, Y., S. Guo and P. Sun (2017) 'The Role of Infrastructure in China's Regional Economic Growth', *Journal of Asian Economics*, 49, pp. 26–41, DOI: 10.1016/j.asieco.2017.02.004.

Su, X. (2013) 'Tourism, Migration and the Politics of Built Heritage in Lijiang, China', in T. Blumenfield and H. Silverman (eds.) *Cultural Heritage Politics in China* (New York: Springer), pp. 101–14.

Sylvie, D. (2001) 'Infrastructure Development and Economic Growth : an Explanation for Regional Disparities in China?', *Journal of Comparative Economics*, 29(1), pp. 95–117, DOI: 10.1006/jcec.2000.1693.

Tsing, A.L. (2015) *The Mushroom at the End of the World: On the Possibility of Life in Captialist Ruins* (Princeton: Princeton University Press).

Wang, S.Y. (2008) 'An Investigation of Dacun of Eya Naxi Township, Muli', in W. Zheng (ed.) *Investigation on the Customs and Religion in Naxi Areas along the Yunnan-Sichuan Border* (Kunming: Yunnan Minority Publishing House), pp. 1–56 (in Chinese).

Yang, X., J. He, C. Li, J. Ma, Y. Yang and J. Xu (2008) 'Matsutake Trade in Yunnan Province, China: an Overview', *Economic Botany*, 62(3), pp. 269–277.

Yeh, E.T. (2000) 'Forest Claims, Conflicts and Commodification: the Political Ecology of Tibetan Mushroom-Harvesting Villages in Yunnan Province, China', *The China Quarterly*, 161, pp. 264–278.

Zhang, X., Z. Li, G. Zeng, X. Xia, L. Yang and J. Wu (2012) 'Erosion Effects on Soil Properties of the Unique Red Soil Hilly Region of the Economic Development Zone in Southern China', *Environmental Earth Sciences*, 67, pp. 1725–1734, DOI: 10.1007/s12665-012-1616-0.

Zhao, J., C. Liu, H. Yang and Y. Li (2015) 'Strategic Questions about China's Shale Gas Development', *Environmental Earth Sciences*, 73, pp. 6059–6068, DOI: 10.1007/s12665-015-4092-5.

Zhou, Y. and L. Song (2017) 'Income Inequality in China: Causes and Policy Responses', *China Economic Journal*, 9(2), pp. 186–208, DOI: 10.1080/17538963.2016.1168203.

CHAPTER 8

Spaces of Extraction in Europe: the Corporate–State–Mining Complex and Resistance in Greece and Romania

Konstantinos (Kostas) Petrakos

Abstract

Despite the widespread attention paid to the spatial expansion of extractive frontiers around the globe, the multiple ways in which states and extractive transnational corporations interfere with and exercise authority over local populations in spaces of extraction remain underexplored. Drawing on insights from the literature on critical geography and on current debates over extractivism and neo-extractivism, this chapter explores the corporate strategies and techniques of power used in spaces of extraction, and discusses how states promote the forcible appropriation of land for mining operations. While most critical perspectives on extractivism have mainly focused on Latin America, Africa and Asia, where the expansion of extractive activities has intensified and become widespread, my focus is on the expansion of extractive activities in Europe, which has attracted renewed interest from extractive capital in the wake of the financial crisis. Two mining investments—by Eldorado Gold and Gabriel Resources, in Chalkidiki and Roșia Montană, respectively—have been reactivated in crisis-ridden Greece and Romania. In each country, a whole range of neo-liberal state strategies have paved the way for the expansion of the extractive frontier. Through an in-depth exploration of the two European cases examined here, this chapter builds on recent critical scholarship on new enclosures, extractivism, and the permanence of primitive accumulation in order to survey the inter-articulation of extractivist projects and neo-liberal policies in crisis-scapes. Attention given to social mobilisation at the extractive frontier highlights that social opposition arises due to some common agents of oppression. This social resistance leads to the formulation of a critique of development and highlights the importance of contesting neo-liberal policies at the international level.

1 Introduction

Since the late 1960s or early 1970s, extractive projects have tended to be more 'capital-intensive' than 'labour-intensive'. This transition has attracted

 | DOI:10.1163/9789004685994_009

significant attention in the relevant literature (Kallis, 2015; Veltmeyer and Petras, 2014; Webber, 2017). The capital-intensive activities on which mining projects are based generate little employment after the construction stage, and the jobs that are created are typified by poor working conditions and almost entirely male labour, with all the usual consequences of gender segregation for women.

This study contributes to a growing literature on the roles of space and uneven geographical development (Harvey, 2005) in shaping extractive capitalism (Mezzadra and Neilson, 2019). Under capitalism, the appropriation of nature and the continuous search for raw materials is fuelled by capital accumulation (Smith, 1984), and the neo-liberal state assumes the role of a significant 'extra-economic' actor, enabling resource mobilisation and capital accumulation (Bridge, 2014) in this process. The reconfiguration of neo-liberalism started with the 2008 financial crisis, and has continued to shape the dominant paradigm of capitalist development since then. It is characterised, according to Svampa (2013), as the passage from the 'Washington Consensus' to a consensus of commodities based on the large-scale export of resources. As extractivism triumphs in many regions (Federici, 2019) it plays a crucial role in contemporary capitalism—a paradigmatic practice of twenty-first century neo-liberalism that provides, according to Mezzadra and Neilson (2019), a lens with which to understand the functioning and circulation of capital.

At a time of a crisis in capitalism, two mining investments, by Eldorado Gold and Gabriel Resources, in Chalkidiki and Roșia Montană respectively, were reactivated in the two crisis-ridden countries of Greece and Romania. These mega-development projects, just two of the many examples from all over the world, promote land-grabbing, marginalisation, contamination, dispossession and enclosures.

By shedding light on the current reconfiguration of neo-liberalism, this chapter seeks to address the multiple ways in which states and extractive transnational corporations interfere with and exercise authority over local populations in spaces of extraction. Throughout the study, I observe the close relations between extractive capital's strategies and those of the state.

Special emphasis is placed on the active role of states in strengthening the 'extractive imperative' (Arsel, Hogenboom and Pellegrini, 2016). The entanglement of states with extractive transnationals creates multilayered power relations that facilitate the extractive process. Across various countries and different land ownership regimes, capitalist accumulation and the incorporation of the state into the act of striving for development have pushed and expanded the spatial limits of extractive activities into national parks, environmentally protected areas, forests and highly populated zones.

States exercise authority through the modification of legal frameworks on land use and resource exploitation, which is usually expressed as 'flexibility', or as the 'simplification' of environmental regulations and of the spatial planning framework. Land dispossession and the active role of the state in it (Korfiati, 2020) is analysed in this chapter via a focus on the several amendments to environmental legislation, spatial planning policies and privatisation laws generated during the study period in Greece and Romania. This is rooted in McCarthy's (2004, 332) analysis of 'how neoliberal trade agreements impose an environmental governance model that attempts to expand private property rights claims while shrinking the public sphere'; Glassman (2006, 620) further expands on this idea. In each of the two countries examined here, a whole range of neo-liberal state strategies—including prolonged authoritarian governance, state corruption, greedy investors, deregulation of space, 'simplification' of environmental legislation, and socio-environmental disturbances (environmental destruction, pollution and social polarisation)—have paved the way for the expansion of the extractive frontier (Mezzadra and Neilson, 2017; Frederiksen and Himley, 2020).

Although there is a growing body of literature that has extensively explored the articulation between the extractive sector and state-led development strategies for the social redistribution of mineral wealth, these contributions have focused on a global South conceptualisation. Exceptions are the recent work 'The politicised ecologies of austerity: Anti-austerity environmentalism during and after the Greek crisis', which discusses how subaltern struggles in Greece, among them the Skouries movement, challenged 'austerity-driven development patterns' (Calvário, Kaika and Velegrakis, 2021), and a recent contribution on the 'socio-environmental injustices' (Velicu, 2020) generated by mining development and the actions of the Romanian and Bulgarian states and of market actors.

In the political framework of the aftermath of the 2008 financial crisis, an escalation of land dispossession in Europe to the benefit of extractive projects based on renewed corporate interests has been observed and analysed in the literature (Hadjimichalis, 2014; Tsavdaroglou, Petrakos and Makrygianni, 2017; Calvário, Velegrakis and Kaika, 2017; Velicu, 2020). With the present chapter, I seek to contribute to this literature by examining the corporate–state–mining complex in order to scrutinise the conflicting spatialities (Guzmán-Gallegos, 2012) in mining sites in a crisis framework.

By unfolding the complex ways in which extractive transnationals exercise their power in spaces of extraction, I investigate how both the financial crisis and the imperatives of extractive development (Verweijen and Dunlap, 2021) transform socio-spatial relations and how social resistance has responded to such processes of capital accumulation. The extractive transnationals focus their efforts on convincing the locals of the benefits of mining in order to secure a social license to operate (Svampa, 2012), as well as to tackle social opposition generated by their operations. For the purposes of this chapter, corporate social responsibility strategies employed by extractive transnationals are examined first through the close relations and partnerships that link them to the state, and second through the infiltration of corporations into almost all functions and areas of social activity. According to Welker (2009, 146), it is widely believed that corporations alone have the power to catalyse development; thus, they 'often assume a de facto state role, subsidising public transportation, education, health, utilities, and waste management infrastructure'.

At the local level, the expectation of development based on mining is often linked to the employment of local populations in economically deprived areas within the national territory. And this often creates expectations of local, regional and national development. Despite the frustration of these expectations, they tend to remain unchanged regardless of the lost opportunities to detach the economy from this specific activity and to deploy different forms of productive reconstruction. The basic, long-lasting problem in mining areas is the political priorities and choices that have imposed mining as the only route to economic survival, as the two cases presented here also show.

The local benefits of mining are, however, questioned both in the existing literature (Welker, 2009; 2014; Svampa, 2012; Gilberthorpe and Banks, 2012; Jacka, 2018) and on the ground, as seen in the proliferation of struggles against extractivist projects. The absence of 'any real socio-economic development at the grassroots' (Gilberthorpe and Banks, 2012, 185) contributes to the generation of conflicts between companies, states and local communities. As a counterbalance to this process of capital accumulation based on the joint efforts of extractive transnationals and host countries to expand the extractive frontier, powerful struggles against extractivism have emerged in both Romania and Greece. These began mainly as localised resistance to extractivist projects and to the environmental injustices (Velicu and Kaika, 2017; Velicu, 2020) provoked by them. Along with such local opposition, the defence of place (Escobar, 2001) and the construction of new materialities of space (Tsavdaroglou, Petrakos and Makrygianni, 2017) by social movements constitute what, according to Escobar (2001, 139), is seen as 'network-oriented subaltern strategies of localization'. That said, the present chapter also provides insights into the radical praxis of these struggles in the form of social opposition to extractivism on both the local and the national level and beyond, as they have achieved a significant international profile and garnered strong international support.

2 The Permanence of Primitive Accumulation: Expanded Extractivism in Crisis-Scapes

During the last decades of the twentieth century, various scholars, mainly from the Marxist perspective, reconsidered the discourse on primitive accumulation. In particular, autonomous Marxist scholars recognised that primitive accumulation is not only confined to the origins of capitalism, but is a continuous phenomenon (De Angelis, 2001; Glassman, 2006; Midnight Notes Collective and Friends, 2009) constitutive of capitalist relations at all times, eternally recurrent, and 'part of the continuous process of capitalist accumulation' (Federici, 2019, 15). Autonomous Marxists argue that enclosures are constantly expanding and therefore that they are not merely a pre-capitalist procedure. These contributions are complementary methodological tools that highlight Marxists' contribution to the interpretation of various urban and rural spaces and promote radical praxis. In this context, I also draw on scholars of political ecology who research struggles against the normalisation of austerity in Europe (Calvário, Kaika and Velegrakis, 2017; 2021).

In this framework I focus on insights from the literature on critical geography (Massey, 1994; Allen, 2016; Bridge, 2004; 2014) and on current debates over extractivism and neo-extractivism (Svampa, 2013; 2019; Acosta, 2011; 2016; Gudynas, 2013; 2018) in order to explore the corporate strategies and techniques of power used in spaces of extraction, and to discuss how states promote the forcible appropriation of land for mining operations.

The term 'extractivism' was first coined in Latin American critical thought with specific reference to the increasing extraction of minerals, hydrocarbons and other natural resources. According to Acosta (2016), the practice of extractivism began to emerge 500 years ago, and was maintained during the era of colonial and postcolonial looting and capital accumulation. Today, it has become prominent as a model of economic development in many Latin American countries and is expanding worldwide (Gudynas, 2013; Svampa, 2013; Fabricant and Gustafson, 2014; Gordon and Webber, 2016). In its most basic definition, extractivism is described as a type of natural resource extraction that is large scale, very intensive and oriented primarily towards export (Acosta, 2011; Gudynas, 2013), and subsequently as a mining trend–strategy that becomes prominent during a socio-economic crisis and facilitates the extraction of raw materials by transnational corporations, which develop close alliances with host countries and infrastructure companies. Extractivism differs from extraction geared towards endogenous needs (Webber, 2017) as it includes all the functions of both the capital and the industries activated for the exploitation, extraction and export of resources. Thus, it is associated with the orientation of national development strategies towards primary export, a colonial heritage reinforced by global neo-liberalism and maintained under progressive governments in Latin America (Brand, Dietz and Lang, 2016; Svampa, 2019). As a result, Latin American countries experienced an accelerated process of 're-primarization' (Lander, 2014) of their economies during the commodities boom of the early twenty-first century (de los Reyes, 2017).

As will become clear in the following analysis, this chapter aims to contribute to these discussions, and argues that the intensification of extraction worldwide reinforces the Latin American literature on extractivism. A growing body of literature focuses on the conflicts that emerge when the territorial logics of large-scale mineral mining are imposed through legislation and securitisation (Vélez-Torres, 2014) causing significant territorial reconfigurations (Warnaars, 2012; Vélez-Torres, 2014; Van Teijlingen, 2016). Illustrative of this is work on the processes that constitute the Colombian extractivist governmentality (Vélez-Torres, 2014), which places particular emphasis on the territorialisation of the government's juridical arrangements for the control of mining resources. Turning to the Ecuadorian Amazon, Van Teijlingen (2016) uses a governmentality approach to scrutinise the development discourses and practices that surround territorial struggles around mining. These two contributions to the literature suggest that state strategies have resulted in government-led mining dispossession and/or 'giving private actors privileged access while dispossessing local communities from their territorial control' (Vélez-Torres, 2014, 76). The argument here is that the mining–development nexus works as an essential element of the 'extractive imperative' (Van Teijlingen, 2016). In this respect, the present chapter examines the strategies, policies and tactics employed by states and private investors that reinforce the power relations present with regard to land and land-based resources (Vélez-Torres, 2014), and explores the subsequent social struggles that resist such power apparatuses.

Through an in-depth examination of the two European cases examined here, the present chapter underlines that mining sites' creation of environmental costs is not accidental and inadvertent, but is a result of the particular way in which production and its (constituent) social relations are organised at the local level, the sites' particular geography, the specific economic conditions, and the financialisaton of mining activities (Mezzadra and Neilson, 2017; de los Reyes, 2017). Thus, I build on recent critical scholarship on new enclosures, extractivism and the permanence of primitive accumulation in order to examine the inter-articulation of extractivist projects and neo-liberal policies in crisis-scapes.

3 Case Studies and Methodology

Located in northern Greece, the Chalkidiki peninsula is a popular tourist destination. The area of north-east (NE) Chalkidiki, meanwhile, is a departure from this tourism-based development model and is characterised by a long history of mining activities. Since the beginning of these activities, which go back to the time of the Ottoman Empire, the region and its local populations have been confronted with capitalist power relations, signified by the power exerted by national and international mining capital. The decision to locate mining facilities in NE Chalkidiki for the production of the materials and fertilisers needed by Greek industry for the post-WWII economic rebuilding activities of the Greek state gave the area its current character. Power alliances have changed over the years, but the power itself has shaped the region's extractive identity and has defined the labour relations around mining operations. During the past two decades, there has been renewed interest in mining investment in the region, targeting the further exploitation of its mineral wealth. In particular, the most recent period of mining exploitation is characterised by the development of a gold metallurgy infrastructure as the main target of the companies concerned. Prior to this, the production of mixed sulphide had been the main focus of mining activity in the region. The current investment phase began in 2006, and for the first time the region saw the introduction of new technologies, such as open-pit mining, which was introduced in Skouries—a pristine forest of rare biodiversity. Since February 2012, Eldorado Gold, which currently holds all of the share capital of Hellas Gold, has held the exploitation rights for 31,700 hectares in the area—43 per cent of Aristotle Municipality. This area, which has been earmarked as a possible mine, contains 16 villages and approximately 19,000 inhabitants.

Roșia Montană meanwhile, located in the Apuseni Mountains of western Transylvania (west-central Romania), is a mountain village that lies on a massive deposit of gold. The mining landscape of Roșia Montană is unique in Europe, as the visible results of its more than 2,000 years of continuous mining operations testify. But it is the open-pit mining that took place from 1971 onward—its production levels gradually decreasing until 2006—that is largely responsible both for the scale of the environmental degradation caused and for the most dramatic aspects of physical change. Those operations ultimately comprised both irreversible loss and unsustainable practice. After 2000, and mainly in the aftermath of the 2008 financial crisis, Canada's Gabriel Resources intended to implement Europe's largest open-pit mine in the region. The Roșia Montană project was planned to be four times larger than that of the exploitation that took place during the Ceaușescu regime, when gold and copper opencast mining took place.

At first sight these two mining projects have many features in common. Both regions have been officially declared mono-industrial, a fact that facilitates land speculation. Another common point is that both projects were reactivated during the financial crisis. Starting in 2009, the Romanian government entered into economic adjustment programmes with the World Bank, the European Union (EU) and the International Monetary Fund in exchange for its austerity measures with regard to public finances and salaries. Thus, the most recent attempt at mining exploitation in Roșia Montană began after the Romanian economy had been subjected to fiscal adjustment measures.

My research analysis regarding the project in Greece is based on document analysis and active participatory fieldwork research carried out specifically mainly in NE Chalkidiki, where the Kassandra Mines are run by multinational mining company Eldorado Gold. I draw on a fieldwork study conducted in the villages of Megali Panagia and Ierissos, both located in NE Chalkidiki. The study was spread intermittently over the five years from late 2013 to late 2018. In those years, I visited the site many times, and conducted extensive periods of fieldwork in the wider area. Around 20 semi-structured interviews with men and women between 25 and 55 years of age, and numerous face-to-face discussions with groups of participants in the Skouries movement, were conducted. The fieldwork employed an ethnographic approach to the case study, and participation in a wide range of activities, including everyday activities, informal discussions, local assemblies, protests, festivals and cultural ceremonies.

In parallel, yet not in the same detail, my research also considers the case of the Roșia Montană mining area in Romania, following a field visit conducted in May 2017. Here, the fieldwork included tours of the underground mining sites of past mining operations and of the open-pit mining sites of the Ceauşescu regime era, and trips to the wider area of the mining concession, alongside participating in local ceremonies and attending a meeting of the International Council on Monuments and Sites (ICOMOS). Following a visit to the Museum of Mining History, I had the opportunity to talk with members of the mining resistance movement, who guided me to the places that were being targeted for mining exploitation according to the investment plan of Gabriel Resources. I thus saw the scale of the mining concession area, and the wealth of the area under threat.

The aim of my research has been twofold: firstly, to trace the systems of oppression that seek to maintain inequality in extractive spaces; secondly, to highlight the variety of resistance strategies and actions that call into question the hegemonic reasoning of development projects.

4 Confronting the Expansion of Extractivism: Radical Praxis in Chalkidiki and ROȘIA MONTANĂ

When the mining investment plans for Chalkidiki were made public, several citizen initiatives (the so-called struggle committees) were formed in the surrounding villages, organising many mass demonstrations, occupying the local police station, and blocking the local road network in order to prevent the riot police from entering homes. In recent years, several acts of solidarity and sharing have been taking place, including popular assemblies, solidarity concerts–festivals, and summer camps in the forest of Skouries—in proximity to the open-pit mining site. The importance of this struggle and its unique characteristic is that participants act in the physical space, refusing to enter into endless, ineffective negotiations with institutional actors. At the same time, the struggle has spread to major Greek cities. Several solidarity initiatives, and protests in front of the Canadian embassy and Eldorado offices, were organised. The struggle also attracted international attention, as solidarity actions took place in many countries. The fight against gold mining in Skouries became one of the most emblematic socio-environmental struggles in Europe, alongside 'Save Roșia Montană', 'NO TAV' (*Treno ad Alta Velocità*) and 'ZAD' (Zone to Defend).

The gender dimension of daily life also came to the fore thanks to the involvement of women in this social movement against mining, and was identified by many participants as an important dimension of the struggle. Previous work (Tsavdaroglou, Petrakos and Makrygianni, 2017) has also emphasised the feminist perspectives that have emerged during the struggle against mining. On several occasions women tried to break the police blockade in order to approach the Skouries forest on the mountain at Kakavos, and successfully blocked the entrance of the construction site. This social mobilisation deregulated the patriarchal structures of local society, even temporarily, and caused ruptures that distorted the previous rhythm of everyday life (Tsavdaroglou, Petrakos and Makrygianni, 2017).

Company social infiltration tactics reproduce and reinforce power relations regarding land ownership and resources. According to the Megali Panagia struggle committee:

> Regardless of whether Eldorado, and every Eldorado, wants to, can or dreams of exploiting the resources, we do not share the Greek state's fantasies of 'gold' rights and surpluses in royalties. We are certain that extractivism and mega-exploitation have never served equal human well-being or satisfied real social needs, but have fostered and continue to foster voracious human greed, adventurism, speculation and the

> self-justification of the rulers. That is why we oppose mining investment development plans in general. 'Gold mining never and nowhere' remains our main slogan.
>
> Discussion with members of the struggle committee of Megali Panagia

In a similar manner, the Roșia Montană mining project faced social resistance from local communities and urban populations fighting for the protection of the environment and the preservation of their cultural heritage. As noted in the nomination dossier of ICOMOS WG for Roșia Montană,[1] the whole area is an outstanding cultural landscape with a rich diversity of different heritage components, constituting a unique mining landscape in Europe with regard to its characteristics of continuous mining operations. According to the resistance committees, the Roșia Montană valley in its entirety would be transformed into a lunar landscape.

At the local level in Roșia Montană, Gabriel Resources focused, as we shall see, on convincing the locals of the benefits of mining. Most residents, however, refused to enter into negotiations with the mining multinational or the Romanian state, deciding instead to form, in 2000, the non-governmental organisation Alburnus Maior to defend their right to property, preserve the natural landscape and cultural heritage of the area, and challenge the legality of permits. By confronting the 'legitimacy' of the state assuring the interests of extractive capital, residents of Roșia Montană refused to accept expropriation and won the 'recognition' of a place at the table in face-to-face discussions with Romania's president (Velicu and Kaika, 2017). During their struggles, they became involved in radical changes and ruptures in their everyday practices and livelihoods (Velicu, 2020).

In the village of Roșia Montană in particular, the situation was devastating, the place rendered a desert due to the expropriation of the inhabitants' houses by the mining company and these houses' gradual crumbling into ruin. Members of the mining resistance movement told me that this signified the point of no return for their action. They decided to intervene, and to focus their actions on the preservation of the built heritage and infrastructure, each of which was deteriorating.

The organisation of the 'FanFest', an annual cultural and ecological festival first held in 2004, has been the most visible expression of the struggle against this extractivist project. The aim of the Fest has been to promote the alternative development potential and preserve the cultural and natural landscape

1 A copy of the dossier is in the author's personal archive.

of Roșia Montană. Some years later, the resisting communities introduced the 'Adopt a House in Roșia Montană' campaign (launched in 2011), its aim to protect the historic site and its built heritage. Specifically, the campaign purpose is to restore buildings and religious sites and to establish a community centre dedicated to the struggle, contributing to social change through the empowerment of local communities in Roșia Montană and the surrounding area.

Despite the slow disappearance of communities (Velicu, 2020) from the region, an alliance of Alburnus Maior, Save Roșia Montană, and ICOMOS Romania made the struggle more effective and successfully prepared the nomination document for the inclusion of the mining landscape of Roșia Montană in the United Nations Educational Scientific and Cultural Organization's list of world heritage sites. On 27 July 2021, Roșia Montană was inscribed simultaneously in the World Heritage List and in the List of World Heritage in Danger, providing a successful conclusion to an effective struggle dedicated to the protection and conservation of a mining landscape.

Thus, despite the initial willingness of the Romanian state to foster, during the financial crisis, the exploitation of the mineral resources of Roșia Montană, the mining project was cancelled thanks to powerful struggles that developed against it.

5 Corporate Social Responsibility as a Means of Enhancing the Expansion of Extractivism

Having provided a brief description of two cases from the expanding resource frontier in Europe, with an emphasis on the characteristics of the social mobilisation that rose up against mining projects in these cases, I now move on to explore strategies as the means by which corporations seek to infiltrate society and promote their interests. Applied to the question of power imbalances, the ideology of 'senile developmentalism' (Martínez-Alier, 2010) in extractive spaces is, I argue in this chapter, supported and ensured by the concept of corporate social responsibility (CSR) and national developmental agendas. Building on the concept of CSR in extractive industries and its entanglement with sustainable development, Welker (2014) examines CSR as an extension of corporate knowledge and power and dissects the uneven and contingent ways in which capitalism is promoted and contested in particular places and among particular people. According to Welker (2014, 70), 'Talk of sustainable development in the mining industry—which by definition extracts nonrenewable resources, generating large-scale destruction and pollution in the process—sounds patently oxymoronic'.

The concepts of CSR and/or a 'social license to operate', combined with sustainable development and governance, configure the dominant discourse that aims to legitimise extractive economic projects. At the same time, as I will argue below, extractive multinational corporations seek to elicit acceptance of these projects through multifarious mechanisms of biopolitical control of the population (Svampa, 2012). In seeking a 'social license to operate', they aim to establish the legitimacy of the ongoing extraction in order to gain stable, long-term access to subsurface deposits (Frederiksen and Himley, 2020) despite the negative consequences of their projects for the social fabric and despite the degradation of the environment that these projects entail. I argue that soft power manifestations—or, as Allen (2016, 68) terms them, 'quieter registers of power'—such as incitement and manipulation, develop, occur and are implemented in combination with violent processes of dispossession around mining locations. On this topic, a growing body of critical literature (see Brock and Dunlap, 2018, and Verweijen and Dunlap, 2021) uses the notion of counter-insurgency in the extractive sector in order to emphasise the 'hard'-coercive and 'soft'-pacification techniques employed by corporate–state networks. 'Participatory' and 'community-oriented' interventions deployed in CSR initiatives constitute, according to Verweijen and Dunlap (2021), the 'soft' tools of counter-insurgency that operate next to and overlap with techniques of overt violence (Brock and Dunlap, 2018). According to the analysis of Brock and Dunlap (2018), the use of counter-insurgency techniques demonstrates a continuation of repressive tactics and social manipulation, revealing the efforts of corporations and governments to socially engineer the political terrain and normalise socially and ecologically damaging practices. In this context, my focus lies on elucidating the political (re)actions 'from above' (Verweijen and Dunlap, 2021) in these two extractive spaces in Europe.

With regard to those local communities affected by extractivist projects, multinational mining corporations financially support specific economic sectors and settlements in order to achieve a more effective infiltration into society.

In the case of Chalkidiki, quieter registers of power include Eldorado Gold's infiltration into local authorities and communities, supported by the pretext of the jobs created by its activities, and exacerbated by its exploitation of the concept of CSR. In particular, Eldorado Gold rewarded the former (until 2014) municipal authority of NE Chalkidiki for its support by subsidising public services and the police. Simultaneously, the company was promoting its investment in the schools of the region and created a 'tourism organisation' in order to demonstrate the compatibility of extraction and cultural tourism. In addition, in certain settlements it emphasised the strengthening of the region's economy, creating an imaginary picture of a society that prospers. Whereas for settlements close to the mining operations the economic viability of their populations is threatened by the forced abandoning of the forest and other primary sector activities, as well as by their geographic proximity to the mining operations, in a process that has led to spatial and social deprivation. As a result, local conflicts between the inhabitants of different settlements become part of daily life, social discord is spreading through the local community, and tensions arising from the spatial separation generated are exacerbated.

In this context, it is worth mentioning that promises of local employment and of preferential treatment for the local workforce contributed decisively to the driving of a wedge between the locals, and between settlements—a corporate strategy that continues to shape the area today. 'What is interesting with Eldorado Gold', the struggle committee of Megali Panagia stressed,

> is that the Canadian multinational company acts as a typical example of [...] so-called cowboy capitalism [...] a company that was not afraid to make aggressive moves. Having acquired a partial social consensus, [it] targets citizens who opposed mining and turns its employees against their fellow villagers. Look at the facts ... on March 20, 2012, 400 hundred miners led the attack on the mountain with the company's vans, and burned the guardhouse built by the struggle committees three years earlier.
>
> Discussion with members of the struggle committee of Megali Panagia

With regard to the struggle against the Eldorado Gold mining project, a variety of repressive techniques have been documented, including the burning of the guardhouse, police harassment and brutality, surveillance techniques, vandalising homes and illegal detainment by the police. At the same time, Eldorado Gold collaboration in repressive/violent operations in the Skouries forest interacts with sensitive social development initiatives and public relations strategies (Verweijen and Dunlap, 2021).

The above indicates that the dialectic relationship between soft power tactics/quieter registers of power and violent processes of dispossession—a point I made earlier in this chapter—takes on particular visible forms. It is precisely these repetitive tactics of multinational companies that, as Maria—a member of the struggle committee of Megali Panagia—points out, create this 'nerve-racking' environment:

> In the first stage, mining multinationals promise jobs, compensation benefits, infrastructure projects and training programs for the population. In

> the second stage, when these means do not work, they attempt to acquire control over all the resources of the area via force, through expropriations of land and savage repression, in collaboration with the state. States are passing laws prohibiting people from suing companies for environmental disasters and declaring that the area is in a state of emergency. The companies' strategy is driven by the 'divide and rule' doctrine, since social discord has been spreading in the local community and social conflicts have become part of daily life.
>
> Discussion with Maria, member of the struggle committee of Megali Panagia

What emerges is that in contrast to the area's reputation as a pristine forest region of rare biodiversity and possessed of a rich cultural history (known worldwide as the birthplace of the Greek philosopher Aristotle), transformed regimes of access to land and resources create accumulation by a process of dispossession (Harvey, 2003). The reputation of the region is currently at risk due to the ensuing environmental degradation and the undermining of different forms of productive reconstruction. That said, another repeating pattern in the area's mining history is the emergence and bankruptcy of mining companies, and shifts between job security and growing unemployment at the local level. Here, a fine example is the village of Stratoni. According to the New Investment Agreement signed by the Greek government while COVID-19 lockdown measures were in place, the village appears to be of diminished importance for Eldorado Gold due to the elimination of certain of the company's activities. For the population of Stratoni, the non-inclusion of a metallurgical plant and port facilities in the new Agreement could mean a future characterised by unemployment and poverty.

A mining monoculture has therefore emerged, which signifies an economic weakness for the settlement due to the banning of any other development in the area. While the company's plan to move its offices and administrative services from Stratoni to Thessaloniki may have been temporarily frozen[2] due to the negative reaction of its employees' unions, the existence of such a plan per se rather reinforces arguments of economic weakness. Further, a significant change in the new Agreement is that the 90:10 quota in favour of hiring employees from local communities has been abolished. The company has thus now been given the opportunity to take any action it deems to be in its own

2 Eldorado Gold announced the move in May 2019. Its employees warned that if the company stuck to this decision, it would be a 'cause of war with uncontrollable consequences'. See https://antigoldgr.org/blog/2019/06/18 (accessed in November 2021).

interest and to employ a local workforce only where it wishes to do so. As Elli and Giannis put it,

> A company that for years has been polluting and destroying the land, looting the mineral wealth of the area, manipulating and trying to mislead the residents of the Municipality of Aristotle. A company that, we would remind you, advertises itself as a low-cost gold producer. For us, this means high environmental and social costs and certainly not local development and prosperity.
>
> Discussion with Elli and Giannis, members of the struggle committee of Megali Panagia

Eldorado Gold is a low-cost gold producer and the open-pit mining sub-project at Skouries forest is ranked first in the top ten lowest-cost gold mining projects in the world, at a cost of only USD 215 per ounce.[3]

In Romania, meanwhile, Gabriel Resources, the parent company of Roșia Montană Gold Corporation (RMGC), took over the management of the Museum of Mining History in Roșia Montană to promote and advance its message of corporate sensitivity and social responsibility with regard to the preservation of cultural heritage. Simultaneously, it spearheaded the relocation of the inhabitants of Roșia Montană and the forced expropriation of their legally owned property. With a mining monoculture imposed, the local agricultural sector deteriorated. Thus, the case illustrates how local communities are manipulated in ways that allow multinational extractive capital to operate amid specific cultural and economic sensitivities, in a process that obscures dominant relations regarding access to land.

As Eugen pointed out,

> Through these years, mining representatives when they came they never talked about the project itself, they were just lying about their mission. Our area is at risk of total destruction as it lies squarely in the path of today's hazardous mining practices.
>
> Discussion with Eugen David, president of Alburnus Maior

'What they [...] proposed to us', stresses Irina, a member of ICOMOS Romania, 'was to blow up four mountains to create Europe's largest opencast mine,

3 See 'Top 10 lowest cost gold projects on the globe', https://www.mining.com/ranked-top-10-lowest-cost-gold-projects-on-the-globe/ (accessed on 13 March 2023).

to eliminate 2,000 years of continuous mining history, [and] to destroy the archaeological landscape, the underground mining network that remains unexplored'.

This analysis shows that, in the region of Roșia Montană, 'hard'-coercive spatial instruments were deployed, but coexisted with 'soft' tactics aimed at making possible the apparatus of extractive development as it is 'genetically determined throughout the population' (Gudynas, 2018, 68).

6 The Logic of Extractivism Shapes State Policies

At the nexus of finance and mining there is a growing literature (Gago and Mezzadra, 2017; de los Reyes, 2017; Mezzadra and Neilson, 2017; 2019) in which the notion of extraction is extended to include the articulation of mining operations with other operations of capital, apart from and beyond the site of physical mining. With regard to the question of finance, an important factor of the revival of research interest in mining and extraction is the fact that the operators pursuing these mining and extraction activities display a surprising level of corporate concentration (Mezzadra and Neilson, 2017). In the mining sector, a limited number of companies control an increasing share of the industry globally (Ericsson, 2012). Regarding gold in particular, de los Reyes (2017) skilfully focuses on some of the biggest gold mining corporations and underscores the new manifestations of financialisation in the mining industry. Her work presents systematic research into the changing landscape of the mining industry and the internal financial processes of mining companies and shows how mining investment decisions are made in places far away from the site of extraction (Rodríguez-Labajos and Özkaynak, 2017).

The aforementioned extension of the notion of extraction is used as a way of analysing and understanding the current moment of contemporary capitalism, at a time when economic growth is increasingly shaped and controlled by financial institutions. It is important to understand the current dominant forces driving the intensification of extraction. Extractive operations—which are highly dependent on globalized capital—severely limit national governments' choices as to how to handle them. Rather than replacing the state, extractive capital complements it, so that together they shape the development framework of a country. In a recent interesting contribution on this topic, Brock's (2020) analysis reveals the interconnection between the fracking industry and the British state, exposing the state's extractive interests at the fundamental level, and highlighting the interplay between extractivism and statism.

In various cases, the effects at the local level are repeated under all property regimes involved in extraction, whether private, public, or mixed (Gudynas, 2018). That said, it is of crucial importance that we focus our attention on the state's policies in fostering the spatial expansion of the extractive frontier. These policies, although diversified, all end up supporting and enhancing the expansion of extractive operations, as I shall argue below.

Extractive operations are not applied in the same way everywhere. Extractive transnationals take into account and adapt to the specificities of host countries and their mining regions, targeting national governments and—as I have already shown—local authorities and communities. Regarding host countries, extractive multinational corporations implement a range of different strategies depending on the national government's willingness to approve the licensing of mining projects. Often, the involvement of states in corporate schemes is the most appropriate way of ensuring that a mining project can be carried out.

In Romania for example, Minvest Deva, a state-owned mining company, holds a 20 per cent stake in mining projects in Roșia Montană and Certej. When operating in Certej, Eldorado Gold concluded an agreement with the same state-owned company, but the Greek state never claimed a share of the profits of Eldorado Gold from its related activities. According to the new investment plan for the Kassandra Mines in Chalkidiki, Eldorado Gold 'is recognized as the absolute manager, holder and owner of all natural resources in the area' (Struggle Committee of Megali Panagia, 2021).

By analysing processes of state intervention in the mining areas of Chalkidiki and Roșia Montană, this study shows that the logic of extractivism continues to shape the model of economic development in these two countries and beyond. At each site, the respective national government has implemented an orthodox, neo-liberal-oriented policy regime in order to attract foreign direct investment. The dominant forces of this neo-liberal orientation are inherited power relations (resulting from the interregional and transnational division of labour), the lucrative environment for speculative capital (Hadjimichalis, 2014) in the context of socio-economic crisis, and the economic adjustment programmes—imposed by each country's creditors—to which the economy has been subjected in a phase of economic crisis. In each country, the state has revised existing or adopted new mining regulations in an attempt to attract foreign investment to the mining sector (Bridge, 2004).

In the case of Greece, several amendments to spatial legislation were accelerated in the aftermath of the 2008 financial crisis. Spatial planning policies were characterised by an overproduction of legislation, and spatial arrangements to facilitate land privatisation and the exploitation of public property. Two of these laws (4262/2014 and 4280/2014), passed in 2014, are directly related to the specific mining project studied here. In particular, Law 4280/2014 (Article 54) permitted the construction of buildings serving the needs of mining investment in the forest of Skouries. Giorgos Zoumpas, former mayor of Aristotle Municipality, argues that 'the construction of industrial plants in forest areas was allowed, since the Law was made for this, mainly for our mines and those that will come later, in other areas of Northern Greece'.

Such types of legislative amendments have set a new paradigm in the relation between fiscal policy and spatial policy (Klabatsea, 2012), following a process that has been applied since the preparation for the 2004 Athens Olympiad, in which the establishment of projects involved derogation of the legislation then in force (Kalatzopoulou and Belavilas, 2014). This new approach to jurisprudence has created the precedent upon which decision-making in the aftermath of 2008 has been based.

In Chalkidiki, the alliance between extractive capital and the indebted state resulted in several amendments to spatial legislation that purposely precluded the introduction of any alternative proposals with regard to regional planning. Thus, the Greek state, which has been subjected to neo-liberal structural adjustment programmes imposed by its creditors, is extremely willing to entertain foreign investment in the form of extractive capital. Contesting this process of capital accumulation, members of the struggle committee of Megali Panagia stress:

> To the timeless blackmail of [...] mining exploitation, we counter-propose the declassification and restoration of the area by the Greek state. [...] [I]n a beautiful and fertile place, but [one] neglected, abandoned and trapped due to mining activity and the inability of the Greek state to solve any serious social and economic problems, our counter-proposal is economic and productive reconstruction based on the primary sector, with small-scale agricultural and tourist activities, with social control, for the harmonisation of ourselves with the natural environment. We remind the Greek governments, which are probably not aware of the spatial planning of the region[,] that its sustainability could be ensured by the proper and rational management of the primeval forest of Skouries rather than by [the] mining project of a low-cost gold-producing company trying to implement the world's cheapest mining investment.
>
> Discussion with members of the struggle committee of Megali Panagia

In a process similar to that mentioned above, the Romanian government and the local administration of Roșia Montană allowed, through the modifications of legislation, Gabriel Resources to expropriate hundreds of local properties and dispossess citizens of their private property. According to Velicu (2020), the authorities repeatedly plan in favour of the corporation. By banning any other economic activity in the area, they forced relocation; by failing to provide basic services such as medicine or education, they created impoverishment. Under this sociopolitical framework, almost 600 houses were abandoned by farming families—in total, 80 per cent of the 800 families then present (Velicu, 2020) sold their lands and properties to the corporation. As Eugen David, President of Alburnus Maior, puts it, the local and national authorities were 'behaving like representatives of the mining company, and as a consequence they have lost the trust of the residents'.

All this became evident in the state's intervention to facilitate the extractive project. Claudia, a member of Arhitectură. Restaurare. Arheologie (Architecture. Restoration. Archaeology (ARA[4])), argued during one of our discussions that the representatives of the Parliamentary Committee on Cultural Heritage had abandoned their previous position and were now at the disposal of the mining company: '[T]hey visited the site under the protection of the miners, instead of meeting directly with the young people who have worked voluntarily for the restoration of the old houses in Roșia' (this, a reference to the 'Adopt a House' project).

After the visit, the local movement's resistance escalated, encompassing outward-facing actions and successfully mobilising Romanian citizens to participate in marches the like of which had not been seen in Romania since the fall of the oppressive Ceaușescu regime in 1989. Apart from cultural heritage, Romanians' criticism focused on political corruption, the failure of state commissions to preserve this historic site, and the social infiltration tactics that the mining company was employing in order to exploit poor local residents. In particular, local activists referred to the predicament that many of the residents found themselves in when they accepted the company's offer to resettle. These residents saw their property pass into the hands of the company and their material and emotional ties with their land disappear.

In this sense, the difficulties in compiling the management plan for the site were underlined during discussions with members of the 'Save Roșia Montană' social movement concerning the lack of a coordinated legislative framework to safeguard the area of protection, as was the fact that settlements are now largely abandoned as a result of the multinational mining corporation's grabbing of housing. As noted in the nomination dossier of ICOMOS WG for

4 ARA is an NGO dedicated to research into and the preservation and enhancement of cultural heritage for the benefit of communities.

Roșia Montană, the 'authenticity of the villages is threatened in its absolute [because] the properties are turned into ruins', but still there is space for the development of a model of a mixed local economy 'based upon the sustainable preservation and enhancement of Roșia Montană settlements and mining landscape'. This condition is necessary for an appropriate management of the historical tangible and intangible values of the heritage of the site and its environment, as well as for the quality of life of the site's inhabitants.

7 Conclusion

In contributing empirical evidence to an emerging area of research that identifies extractive operations and projects as key drivers of land dispossession and environmental degradation, the purpose of my research has been twofold. First, I have tried to clarify the reasons for the expansion of resource frontiers in crisis-ridden countries of Europe and for the escalation of the land dispossession exercised by extractive projects based on renewed corporate interests. Second, I have sought to analyse the social struggles against such enclosures and how they have generated what is an ongoing crisis.

Extractivism in its current form is a prominent developmental model of capital accumulation that allows us to explain the prevalence and strategic role of extractive operations in contemporary capitalism (Mezzadra and Neilson, 2017). This argument is aligned with a growing discourse on the power imbalances between multinational mining companies, state actors and local populations. In this chapter, I have focused my attention on the close relations that connect extractive capital strategies to state strategies. Through an examination of the two cases presented, I have also shown how the concept of corporate social responsibility is employed by corporations in extractive spaces.

According to Brenner (2000), the state operates as the most crucial institutional mediator of uneven geographical development (Smith, 1984) under capitalism. As the case of the mining project in NE Chalkidiki shows, the Greek state is engaged in juridical and territorial negotiations that precede the licensing and expansion of mining operations. In Roșia Montană, the Romanian state is directly involved in partnerships with multinational corporations through state-owned enterprises. These entanglements often involve multifarious and changing forms of patronage. And direct corruption and political complicity with transnational corporations and large private infrastructure companies are both, for example, observed.

The infiltration of extractive capital and its dynamics into different regimes of ownership of land and/or resources is based on the ability to take advantage of the specificities of conditions of production (Massey, 1994), such as mining legacy, degraded land and spaces, and marginalised communities. All of the above are, in the context of extractive expansion, transformed into opportunities for capital accumulation. And in each of the two cases studied here, this occurs under a range of different ownership statuses, whether this be through full control over access to the resource including possession (privately owned Eldorado Gold mines) or through foreign investors entering into joint ventures with state-owned mining enterprises (RMGC is a joint venture between Gabriel Resources and the state-owned company Minvest Deva). Thus, the extractive frontier is constantly expanding under different ownership regimes (Gudynas, 2018, 64), whether these be private companies (such as Eldorado Gold), or joint ventures (such as RMGC).

I have analysed struggles against the expansion of extractivism, but have also explored the mining–development nexus in terms of a variety of socio-spatial implications. Given the spatial scope of extractive operations (Mezzadra and Neilson, 2019), this concept led me deeper into how power dynamics unfolded in spaces of extraction in the aftermath of the 2008 financial crisis. First and foremost, these social struggles centre their opposition on issues related to the spatial dimension, such as the imposed mining monoculture and the resulting transformations in the productive sectors. I have shown that the implementation of spatial policies that are harmful and disruptive for the environment, the local economy, and social relations is a tool for 'regulating' corporate demands on space and leads to communities being dispossessed of their lands and places. These state-led transformations, which produce spatial enclosures, demonstrate how the 'spatializing powers' (Glaab and Stuvøy, 2021, 38) of governments–corporate actors and 'the spatialized juridical mechanisms of mining management' (Vélez-Torres, 2014, 77) facilitate the expansion of the extractive frontier.

Based on the above observations, what becomes clear from this research is that the politico-economic transformations brought about by extractive processes are produced both within the countries concerned and in new or emerging international relations. Thus, this chapter contributes to the documentation and critical theorisation of the interconnections between capital, corporations, states, and local communities, and does so by revealing how corporations and their allies push through extractive operations (Verweijen and Dunlap, 2021). In this light, I argue that the states' support for the private accumulation of capital that takes place through the foreign exploitation of mining resources (Vélez-Torres, 2014) is implemented through 'soft' power manifestations that operate alongside techniques of overt violence. And that these manifestations and techniques reconfigure spatial relations, displace previous land uses (Frederiksen and Himley, 2020), and diminish access to land and resources for nearby populations.

In the two preceding sections, I have discussed how corporate social responsibility strategies and national developmental agendas converged to generate social discord, and how large-scale mining is portrayed as an opportunity for the respective countries to overcome the crisis in question and for the respective regions to develop. In both Greece and Romania, the narrative that seeks to promote the expansion of extractivism is based on a vague 'national interest', or on an even more questionable 'public interest'. Whatever the argument is, the costs are borne by the local population in terms of both spatial deprivation and environmental degradation.

In such a context, it is also crucial to analyse the systems of oppression that seek to maintain inequality in extractive spaces. Power imbalances require that we focus on social mobilisation at the extractive frontier. In this sense, social opposition arises based on certain common agents of oppression, which leads to the formulation of a critique of development, and highlights power imbalances and the importance of contesting neo-liberal policies at the international level. As discussed here, the specific opposition to mining in Greece and Romania, respectively, decisively contributed to highlighting the negative impacts of extractivism, and the social movements concerned developed a creative criticism of the positive role of mining in the development processes of a country. In their struggles, these movements introduced a variety of resistance strategies and actions, and questioned the hegemonic reasoning of development projects.

The literature that lends support to my analysis focuses mainly on cases from Latin America, Africa and Asia. The expansion of extractive operations in European countries demonstrates, however, that the act of pushing through extractive operations is occurring everywhere. In particular, I argue that the case of such extractivist projects in Europe has come to the fore and has been intensified in the aftermath of the 2008 financial crisis. This chapter illustrates how the literature from Latin America is in dialogue with the European context of mining in the context of the financial crisis and accompanying austerity measures.

Since then, as a study of the EU's list of critical raw materials (EU, 2020) clearly shows, the logic of extractivism has continued to shape European policies and strategies. That study includes raw materials of high importance to the EU's economies and of high risk with regard to their supply, and more research is planned to ensure the security of supply of critical raw materials to EU industries, giving priority to domestic resources.

But political and corporate pressure for exploration and the exploitation of new mining sites is expected to increase in the coming years. In such a context, social resistance to extractivist projects, while apparently fruitful, may yet become more complicated, as 'the geography of global capitalism embraces all scales and spaces, in complex ways' (Glassman, 2006, 617).

What I have personally witnessed, perceived, and experienced is that social mobilisation against the expansion of the extractive frontier in Europe produces unique social struggles able to re-territorialise resistance (Psimitis, 2016) to globalised capitalism while adopting strategies and tactics rooted in specific sites. Such social resistance constitutes prefigurative movements that take the form of a peculiar hybrid of community organisation and international action. Instead of centrism, hierarchy, and authority (Springer, 2016), they adopt decentralised radical praxis and implement locally focused collective efforts (Psimitis, 2016), aiming to generate powerful resistance spaces with which to counteract the hegemonic reasoning of development projects.

References

Acosta, A. (2016) 'Post-Growth and Post-Extractivism: Two Sides of the Same Cultural Transformation', *Alternautas,* 3(1), DOI: 10.31273/alternautas.v3i1.1027.

Acosta, A. (2011) 'Extractivismo y neoextractivismo: Dos caras de la misma maldición', in M. Lang and D. Mokrani (eds.) *Más allá del desarrollo—Grupo Permanente de Trabajo sobre Alternativas al Desarrollo* (Quito: Fundación Rosa Luxemburg), pp. 83–121.

Allen, J. (2016) *Topologies of Power: Beyond Territory and Networks* (London: Routledge).

Arsel, M., B. Hogenboom and L. Pellegrini (2016) 'The Extractive Imperative in Latin America', *The Extractive Industries and Society*, 3(4), pp. 880–887, DOI: 10.1016/j.exis.2016.10.014.

Brand, U., K. Dietz and M. Lang (2016) 'Neo-Extractivism in Latin America—One Side of a New Phase of Global Capitalist Dynamics', *Ciencia Política,* 11(21), pp. 125–159, DOI: 10.15446/cp.v11n21.57551.

Brenner, N. (2000) 'The Urban Question: Reflections on Henri Lefebvre, Urban Theory and the Politics of Scale', *International Journal of Urban and Regional Research,* 24(2), pp. 361–378, DOI: 10.1111/1468-2427.00234.

Bridge, G. (2014) 'Resource Geographies II: the Resource-state Nexus', *Progress in Human Geography*, 38(1), pp. 118–130, DOI: 10.1177/0309132513493379.

Bridge, G. (2004) 'Mapping the Bonanza: Geographies of Mining Investment in an Era of Neoliberal Reform', *The Professional Geographer,* 56(3), pp. 406–421, DOI: 10.1111/j.0033-0124.2004.05603009.x.

Brock, A. and A. Dunlap (2018) 'Normalising Corporate Counterinsurgency: Engineering Consent, Managing Resistance and Greening Destruction around the Hambach Coal Mine and Beyond', *Political Geography*, 62, pp. 33–47, DOI: 10.1016/j.polgeo.2017.09.018.

Calvário, R., M. Kaika and G. Velegrakis (eds.) (2021) *The Political Ecology of Austerity: Crisis, Social Movements, and the Environment* (London: Routledge).

Calvário, R., G. Velegrakis and M. Kaika (2017) 'The Political Ecology of Austerity: an Analysis of Socio-environmental Conflict under Crisis in Greece', *Capitalism Nature Socialism*, 28(3), pp. 69–87, DOI: 10.1080/10455752.2016.1260147.

De Angelis, M. (2001) 'Marx and Primitive Accumulation: the Continuous Character of Capital's Enclosures', *The Commoner*, 2(1), pp. 1–2.

De los Reyes, J. A. (2017) 'Mining Shareholder Value: Institutional Shareholders, Transnational Corporations and the Geography of Gold Mining', *Geoforum*, 84, pp. 251–264, DOI: 10.1016/j.geoforum.2016.12.004.

Ericsson, M. (2012) *Mining Industry Corporate Actors Analysis*, POLINARES Working Paper No. 16, http://pratclif.com/2015/mines-ressources/polinares/chapter4.pdf (accessed on 28 February 2023).

Escobar, A. (2001) 'Culture Sits in Places: Reflections on Globalism and Subaltern Strategies of Localization', *Political Geography*, 20(2), pp. 139–174, DOI: 10.1016/S0962-6298(00)00064-0.

EU (European Union) (2020) *Critical Raw Materials*, https://ec.europa.eu/growth/sectors/raw-materials/areas-specific-interest/critical-raw-materials_en (accessed on 28 February 2023).

Fabricant, N. and B. Gustafson (2014) 'Moving Beyond the Extractivism Debate, Imagining New Social Economies', *NACLA Report on the Americas*, 47(4), pp. 40–45, DOI: 10.1080/10714839.2014.11721813.

Federici, S. (2019) *Re-enchanting the World: Feminism and the Politics of the Commons* (Kairos: PM Press).

Frederiksen, T. and M. Himley (2020) 'Tactics of Dispossession: Access, Power, and Subjectivity at the Extractive Frontier', *Transactions of the Institute of British Geographers*, 45(1), pp. 50–64, DOI: 10.1111/tran.12329.

Gago, V. and S. Mezzadra (2017) 'A Critique of the Extractive Operations of Capital: Toward an Expanded Concept of Extractivism', *Rethinking Marxism*, 29(4), pp. 574–591, DOI: 10.1080/08935696.2017.1417087.

Gilberthorpe, E. and G. Banks (2012) 'Development on Whose Terms?: CSR Discourse and Social Realities in Papua New Guinea's Extractive Industries Sector', *Corporate Social Responsibility in the Extractive Industries: Experiences from Developing Countries*, 37(2), pp. 185–193, DOI: 10.1016/j.resourpol.2011.09.005.

Glaab, K., and Stuvøy, K. (2021) 'The Politics of Violence in Extractivism: Space, Time, and Normativity', in *Our Extractive Age*. (London: Routledge).

Glassman, J. (2006) 'Primitive Accumulation, Accumulation by Dispossession, Accumulation by 'Extra-Economic' Means', *Progress in Human Geography*, 30(5), pp. 608–625, DOI: 10.1177/0309132506070172.

Gordon, T. and J. Webber (2016) *Blood of Extraction: Canadian Imperialism in Latin America* (Winnipeg: Fernwood Publishing).

Gudynas, E. (2018) 'Extractivisms: Tendencies and Consequences', in R. Munch and R. D. Wise (eds.) *Reframing Latin American Development* (London: Routledge), pp. 61–76.

Gudynas, E. (2013) 'Debates on development and the alternatives in Latin America. A brief heterodox guide', in M. Lang and D. Mokrani (eds.) *Beyond Development: Alternative visions from Latin America* (Amsterdam: Transnational Institute and Rosa Luxemburg Foundation), pp. 15–39.

Guzmán-Gallegos, M. A. (2012) 'The Governing of Extraction, Oil Enclaves, and Indigenous Responses in the Ecuadorian Amazon', in H. Haarstad (ed.) *New Political Spaces in Latin American Natural Resource Governance* (Palgrave Macmillan), pp. 155–176.

Hadjimichalis, C. (2014) 'Crisis and Land Dispossession in Greece as Part of the Global "Land Fever"' *City*, 18(4–5), pp. 502–508, DOI: 10.1080/13604813.2014.939470.

Harvey, D. (2005) *Spaces of Neoliberalization: towards a Theory of Uneven Geographical Development* (Stuttgart: Franz Steiner Verlag).

Harvey, D. (2003) *The New Imperialism* (Oxford: Oxford University Press).

Jacka, J. K. (2018) 'The Anthropology of Mining: the Social and Environmental Impacts of Resource Extraction in the Mineral Age', *Annual Review of Anthropology*, 47(1), pp. 61–77, DOI: 10.1146/annurev-anthro-102317-050156.

Kalatzopoulou, M. and N. Belavilas (2014) 'From the Olympiad to Memorandum: Establishing "Stage of Exception" in Spatial Planning', *Geographies*, 23, pp. 3–6.

Kallis, G. (2015) '"Extractivism", the Greek Way', *The Press Project*, 31 March, https://thepressproject.gr/extractivism-the-greek-way/ (accessed on 28 February 2023).

Klabatsea, I. (2012) *Spatial Planning as a Means of Managing the Crisis in Greece*, paper presented at the 3rd Panhellenic Conference of Urban Planning and Regional Development, Volos, Greece.

Korfiati, I. P. (2020) 'Classifying Like a State: Land Dispossession on Eastern Crete's Contested Mountains', *Antipode*, 52(5), pp. 1331–1350, DOI: 10.1111/anti.12640.

Lander, E. (2014) *El neoextractivismo como modelo de desarrollo en América Latina y sus contradicciones*, Paper presented at the conference '(Neo)extractivismo y el futuro de la democracia en América Latina: Diagnóstico y retos', Berlín, 13–14 May (Berlin: Heinrich Böll Stiftung), http://mx.boell.org/sites/default/files/edgardolander.pdf (accessed on 6 March 2023).

Martínez-Alier, J. (2010) 'No sé si hay un ecologismo infantil pero sí creo que hay un desarrollismo senil', *Le Monde Diplomatique*, 14 February, https://rebelion.org/no-se-si-hay-un-ecologismo-infantil-pero-si-creo-que-hay-un-desarrollismo-senil/ (accessed on 4 November 2021).

Massey, D. (1994) *Space, Place, and Gender* (Minneapolis: University of Minnesota Press).

McCarthy, J. (2004) 'Privatizing Conditions of Production: Trade Agreements as Neoliberal Environmental Governance', *Geoforum*, 35, pp. 327–41, DOI: 10.1016%2Fj.geoforum.2003.07.002.

Mezzadra, S. and B. Neilson (2017) 'On the Multiple Frontiers of Extraction: Excavating Contemporary Capitalism', *Cultural Studies*, 31(2–3), pp.185–204, DOI: 10.1080/09502386.2017.1303425.

Mezzadra, S. and B. Neilson (2019) *The Politics of Operations: Excavating Contemporary Capitalism* (Durham: Duke University Press).

Midnight Notes Collective and Friends (2009) 'Promissory Notes. From Crisis to Commons', http://www.midnightnotes.org/Promissory%20Notes.pdf (accessed on 15 January 2022).

Psimitis, M. (2016) *Relocalization and Prefigurative Movementsas Social Networks Against Globalization: the Construction of Local Alternatives to Global Capitalism* (Mytilene: University of the Aegean), http://icconss.soc.uoc.gr/images/ecp/ICCONSS_16_8_1.pdf (accessed on 1 March 2023).

Rodríguez-Labajos, B. and B. Özkaynak (2017) 'Environmental Justice through the Lens of Mining Conflicts', *Geoforum*, 84, pp. 245–250, DOI: 10.1016/j.geoforum.2017.06.021.

Smith, N. (1984) *Uneven Development: Nature, Capital, and the Production of Space* (Oxford: Basil Blackwell).

Springer, S. (2016) 'Fuck Neoliberalism', *ACME*, 15(2), pp. 285–292.

Struggle Committee of Megali Panagia (2021) *Ten Days of Struggle and Freedom*, 8 July, https://epitropiagonapanagias.blogspot.com/2021/07/ten-days-of-struggle-and-freedom.html (accessed on 4 November 2021).

Svampa, M. (2019) 'Neo-extractivism in Latin America: Socio-environmental Conflicts, the Territorial Turn, and New Political Narratives', in *Elements in Politics and Society in Latin America*, (Cambridge: Cambridge University Press), DOI: 10.1017/9781108752589.

Svampa, M. (2013) Consenso de los commodities y lenguajes de valoración en América Latina. *Nueva Sociedad*, 244, pp. 30–46, http://sedici.unlp.edu.ar/handle/10915/96101 (accessed on 28 February 2023).

Svampa, M. (2012) 'Resource Extractivism and Alternatives: Latin American Perspectives on Development', *Journal Für Entwicklungspolitik*, 28(3), pp. 43–73, DOI:10.20446/jep-2414-3197-28-3-43.

Tsavdaroglou, C., K. Petrakos and V. Makrygianni (2017) 'The Golden 'Salto Mortale' in the Era of Crisis', *City*, 21(3–4), pp. 428–447, DOI: 10.1080/13604813.2017.1331563.

Van Teijlingen, K. (2016) 'The "Will to Improve" at the Mining Frontier: Neo-extractivism, Development and Governmentality in the Ecuadorian Amazon', *The Extractive Industries and Society*, 3(4), pp. 902–911, DOI: 10.1016/j.exis.2016.10.009.

Vélez-Torres, I. (2014) 'Governmental Extractivism in Colombia: Legislation, Securitization and the Local Settings of Mining Control', *Political Geography*, 38, pp. 68–78, DOI:10.1016/j.polgeo.2013.11.008.

Velicu, I. (2020) 'Prospective Environmental Injustice: Insights from Anti-Mining Struggles in Romania and Bulgaria', *Environmental Politics*, 29(3), pp. 414–434, DOI: 10.1080/09644016.2019.1611178.

Velicu, I. and M. Kaika (2017) 'Undoing Environmental Justice: Re-imagining Equality in the Roșia Montană Anti-mining Movement', *Geoforum*, 84, pp. 305–315, DOI:10.1016/j.geoforum.2015.10.012.

Veltmeyer, H. and J. Petras (2014) *The New Extractivism: a Post-Neoliberal Development Model or Imperialism of the Twenty-First Century?* (Bloomsbury Publishing).

Verweijen, J. and A. Dunlap (2021) 'The Evolving Techniques of the Social Engineering of Extraction: Introducing Political (Re)actions "from above" in Large-scale Mining and Energy Projects', *Political Geography*, 88, DOI: 10.1016/j.polgeo.2021.102342.

Warnaars, X. S. (2012) 'Why Be Poor When We Can Be Rich? Constructing Responsible Mining in El Pangui, Ecuador', *Resources Policy*, 37(2), pp. 223–232, DOI:10.1016/j.resourpol.2011.10.001.

Webber, J. (2017) 'Social Theory from the South', *New Left Review*, *103*, pp. 151–160.

Welker, M. (2014) *Enacting the Corporation: an American Mining Firm in Post-Authoritarian Indonesia* (University of California Press).

Welker, M. (2009) '"Corporate Security Begins in the Community": Mining, the Corporate Social Responsibility Industry, and Environmental Advocacy in Indonesia', *Cultural Anthropology*, 24(1), pp. 142–179, DOI: 20484533.

CHAPTER 9

Muddled Times: Temporality and Gold Mining in Colombia and Venezuela

Jesse Jonkman and Eva van Roekel

Abstract

In current social theorising there is a burgeoning interest in the 'afterlife' of resource extraction. In this chapter, we maintain that while the assumption of a post-extractive afterlife might grasp certain social and extractive dynamics of mining areas, it is not necessarily indicative of how people in mining sites themselves conceive of being in time. To this end, we explore how different temporal experiences coincide and converge with one another in two informal gold-mining regions in Colombia and Venezuela. In particular, we reveal that during our fieldwork in these regions the extractive present was imagined as an afterlife and/or a thing of the past. In other words, miners who were extracting in the present nevertheless experienced and described their work through tropes of anteriority (of being stuck in an earlier time) and posteriority (of being stuck after history). In the gold rush of the Venezuelan Arco Minero region, miners encountered their ongoing mining practices as if having descended into a messy hereafter they had never imagined becoming part of. In the Colombian Chocó region, residents of post-boom towns and villages returned to pre-boom extractive practices, and described these practices as the tragic aftermath of a rich gold rush, while simultaneously relating them to pre-boom years of poverty. We couple both cases to highlight how lived experiences in present-day gold country cannot be analysed without considering previous booms and busts, as one resource frontier's life is often another frontier's afterlife. We present 'muddled times' as an alternative way to conceive of the temporality of the gold mine.

1 Time and Again

In current social theorising on human ecologies and the exploitation of land and people, there is a burgeoning interest in the 'afterlife of destruction' (Gordillo, 2014), with scholars wrestling with the question of what happens to life when extractive industries come to an end. Various authors in this debate have made the case for studying the empirical characteristics and political potentialities of people and places that are situated 'after capitalism', 'after dispossession', or in 'capitalist ruins' (Morton, 2010; Salemink and Rasmussen, 2016; Tsing, 2015). In this chapter, we likewise address the interface of the lives and afterlives of resource frontiers, putting ethnographic emphasis on political and social potentialities. Specifically, we maintain that while the assumption of a post-extractive afterlife might grasp certain social and extractive dynamics of mining areas (Avango and Rosqvist, 2021), it is not necessarily indicative of how people in mining sites themselves conceive of being in time.

Time and again, notions such as 'afterlife' and 'post-extraction' assume, more or less explicitly, demarcated temporalities such as 'before', 'during' and 'after' in order to address how landscapes and communities are affected by resource extraction. Yet the lived experience of time and space at resource frontiers is often much more cyclical in nature. Such regions are subject to appearing, disappearing, and reappearing extractive practices, and are characterised by overlapping resource potentialities. Indeed, quite unlike the successive chronology of national mining legislation—whereby miners explore, then exploit, then close down—time in mining sites is messy and multiple; it consists of coexisting temporalities of people, lands, policies, and things. Just as the afterlife of one mine may give birth to future mining desires and activities, so present-day extraction is sometimes experienced as an aftermath of earlier boom years of the same or another resource. Time is, for the most part, a muddled matter.

Following scholars who emphasise the presence of multiple temporalities of mining (D'Angelo and Pijpers, 2018; Jaramillo, 2020; Luning, 2018), and others who have challenged the finality of the mining cycle (Cater and Keeling, 2013; Halvaksz, 2008), this chapter explores how different temporal experiences coincide and converge with one another in two informal gold-mining regions in Colombia and Venezuela. In particular, we reveal that during our fieldwork in these regions the extractive present was imagined as an afterlife and/or a thing of the past. In other words, miners who were extracting in the present nevertheless experienced and described their work through tropes of anteriority (of being stuck in an earlier time) and posteriority (of being stuck after history). As such, rather than following the scholarly convention of using time as an analytic to describe harm inflicted on vulnerable populations—as 'slow violence' (Nixon, 2011), 'a state of uneventfulness' (Hetherington, 2020, 37), or surely, as 'afterlife' (Gordillo, 2014)—our analysis seeks to foreground, as Chloe Ahmann (2018, 144) puts it, 'how affected groups *work time* to emphasize their vulnerability'. While the muddled temporalities we describe are by no means a monopoly of informal mining zones, we consider that they are especially pronounced there. Previous booms and busts of mineral markets, drastic changes to landscapes, steep rises in the arrival of newcomers, and political shifts towards either the criminalisation or the toleration of gold miners jointly result in a constant reshuffling of economic and social practices in these regions, and by extension in a constant reshuffling of local experiences of time.

Time is a classical object of anthropological inquiry and runs through almost all social analysis. As Ernest Gellner (1964, 1) asserts, 'the way in which time and its horizons are conceived is generally connected with the way the society understands and justifies itself'. How extractive communities understand and justify their own temporal and social make-up is thus key here. In gold country, expectations of future extraction often emerge as rapidly as they go bust, nostalgia about previous resource booms intersects with present opportunities and future misfortunes, former mine infrastructures become an integral part of contemporary mines, state-of-the-art technology gets replaced by older and cheaper equipment in the event of an unlucky mining streak, and both the new and older work techniques are described to the passing anthropologist as 'our traditional culture'. In short, the past, present, and future are all over the place in the goldfields.

In building our case, we draw on ethnographic fieldwork in Venezuela and Colombia. Eva van Roekel lived in Venezuela on and off between 1998 and 2008. In 2019, she made a research trip to the Venezuelan border with Brazil. Due to the pandemic, since 2020 she has conducted collaborative fieldwork with a local anthropologist who lives in this mining region located in Bolívar State. Jesse Jonkman has conducted over 14 months of fieldwork since 2016 in Colombia, mostly in Chocó, a vast rainforest region that covers roughly half of Colombia's Pacific lowlands. At first glance, these two mining cases seem somewhat at cross purposes. In Venezuela, a former leading global oil producer, both small- and large-scale goldmining have played a smaller part in the national economy since the discovery of rich oil fields in the early twentieth century, whereas Colombia has been an important gold producer since colonial times, the result of which is a legacy of placer- and tunnel-mining regions scattered throughout the country.[1] In recent years, the Colombian government has opened up the country to the large-scale mining industry, promoting neoliberal legislation that has gone hand in hand with the persecution and subsequent demise of small-scale mining activities. In turn, since 2012 the socialist government of Venezuela has begun to endorse informal mining activities in the wake of economic sanctions, falling oil prices, and its own negligence of

1 In placer mining, extraction takes place in stream beds and adjacent alluvial landscapes. Most of such extraction takes place above the Earth's surface.

the oil industry (Bull and Rosales, 2020). This endorsement has partly resulted in a great expansion of informal mining in what is now known as the Arco Minero del Orinoco (Orinoco Mining Arc), largely located in Bolívar State in the south of Venezuela (Ebus, 2019; Peters, 2019).

Yet on closer inspection, there is plenty that connects the two cases. In Venezuela and Colombia alike, gold mining is a controversial activity, whereby most mines lack the necessary paperwork, non-state armed groups regulate and tax miners, state authorities (by defect or default) have partly forsaken their task of enforcing legislation, and Indigenous and Afro-descendant populations suffer environmental and social destruction at the hands of wildcat miners from other regions. What is more, as we explain below, these contentious mining dynamics coincide in both cases with muddled temporal experiences that sit uneasily with a simple linear model of extractive life-becoming-afterlife.

To make this shared argument tangible, we divide our analysis into four sections. First, we engage in conversation with classical readings in the anthropology of time and temporality, which help us to conceptualise time differently from a single and straight narrative of life preceding afterlife—or extraction preceding post-extraction. Second, we zoom in on the Arco Minero region in Venezuela, and highlight that despite an unfolding gold rush, some miners experienced their wants and ongoing mining practices as if they had descended into a messy hereafter they had never imagined becoming part of. Third, we focus on Chocó (Colombia), where residents of post-boom mining towns and villages returned to pre-boom extractive practices, and described these practices as the tragic aftermath of a rich gold rush, while simultaneously relating them to pre-boom years of poverty. Lastly, we couple both cases to highlight how lived experiences in present-day gold country cannot be analysed without considering previous booms and busts, as one resource frontier's life is often another frontier's afterlife. As such, we present 'muddled times' as an alternative way to conceive of the temporality of the gold mine, and more precisely, to look at how miners are caught up in the middle of various temporalities of resources, people, policies, and lands that co-constitute gold extraction in Venezuela and Colombia.

2 Extraction and Time

In recent years, the social analysis of mining has increasingly drawn attention to the so-called afterlife of extraction. Most of such analysis concerns studies that explore the ecologies and socialities that emerge once mines are abandoned. Among other things, these studies have shown that the social and environmental influence of mines outlives their actual extraction phase (Avango and Rosqvist, 2021; Mazzeo, 2018; Long, 2020; Oakley, 2018), that former mines shape contemporary attitudes to new extraction (Cater and Keeling, 2013; Halvaksz, 2008), that mining results in a post-extractive situation of abandonment, loss, dispossession and lingering responsibilities and new hardships (Askland, 2020; Silva, 2020), and conversely, that the afterlife of mining is also productive of new forms of economic and social life (Keeling and Sandlos, 2017; Robertson, 2006). Another strand of research, more specific to Latin America, has conceptualised the afterlife of mining as less an empirical condition than a possible political project to emancipate national economies from their extractive leanings. Put differently, the 'after' experience of mining is the onset of conceiving new ways of diversifying the economy. This research outlines several reasons 'to design and implement a strategy that will lead to a post-extractivist economy' (Acosta, 2013, 80), such as the need to prevent the inevitable exhaustion of resources, the social conflicts surrounding mineral, oil, and gas extraction, the low economic benefits of extraction for local populations and national governments, and the contributions of the extractive industries to local environmental degradation and global climate change (Acosta, 2013; 2015; Gudynas, 2013; Moreno, 2015; Svampa, 2013).

In a nutshell, both strands of research firmly acknowledge that post-mining and the afterlife of extraction is rather the beginning of new social practices and new political potentialities for local communities and territories. While describing extractive practices and mining communities in terms of afterlife and pre- or post-extractive booms—or writing against such terminologies—we are tacitly playing with notions of time and temporality from the outset (Browne Riberio, 2019, 47). This burgeoning acknowledgment of temporal messiness within the extractive present, we believe, requires a deeper engagement with the actual experience of time and its relation to the environment. As Richard Irvine (2014, 158) rightly observes, 'conceptualizations of time emerge from social interests, activities, and relations'. Stated otherwise, how we understand time depends on for whom and what we think we are responsible, as well as on with whom and what we interact. Tim Ingold (1993) likewise invites us to ponder how past and future always gather into the present in numerous ways, and how multiple timescales of the various elements that co-constitute an empirical reality (e.g. a tree, a person, a path, a valley, and so on) interact with one another. Our struggle therefore is not to determine which temporality a priori works best, but to do justice to a much more undetermined relationship of multiple social representations of temporality and the many varieties of experience of being-in-time (Jackson, 2018, xv). Life and afterlife of mining may, for instance, easily exist side by side. Likewise, temporal experiences that correspond with a linear progression of past, present, and future may very well coexist with circular or spiralling temporalities.

People's experiences of time are largely related to a jumble of biological rhythms, daily routines, seasonal practices, and social calendars. The influence of time on people's everyday lives is contingent on these competing or coexisting relations between natural and social tempos, cyclical and linear time, and repetition and irreversibility (Gell, 1992). Recently, a 'temporal turn' in anthropology has emphasised the heterogeneity of temporal experience under financial capitalism, and has called attention to alternative orientations to futures and pasts (Bear, 2016; Bryant and Knight, 2019). Long before this research, in his classical work on how the Nuer understood time, Evans-Pritchard (1939, 189–190) already argued that, while all time concepts are social notions, we should distinguish between time concepts that involve people's relations with their physical environment and time concepts that relate to interpersonal affiliation. Albeit both social and interrelated, these are distinctive time concepts: the first is occupational and the second is moral. In the latter, for instance, the Nuer understood and experienced when events took place not in numbers of years, but in their structural relation to a limited group of people (Evans-Pritchard, 1939, 210–211). After various generations time got lost, so to speak.

How people reckon the beginning and ending of a certain time and how they experience the passage of time in their lives thus vary greatly. That being said, Fabian (1983) warned us that we should not deny the 'coevalness' of the time of the ethnographer and that of their so-called Other. In other words, alternative experiences of time should never become a device that exoticises people. There is simply not *one* way of being in time. Anthropological critique against favouring a single temporality (often a linear one) fits a relative temporal disposition, including in Das (2006) Desjarlais (1997), van Roekel (2020), and Vargas-Roncancio (2017). These authors acknowledge that being in time is always a mix-up of different temporalities that converge and overlap, just as the busts and booms in mining settlements evidence. Miners may very well experience the 'post' and 'after' of extraction differently, but we should not dismiss coexisting linear temporalities while trying to make an effort at understanding the empirical realities we are interested in.

The renewed debate on Bakhtian chronotopes (i.e. the representation of time and space) in anthropology furthermore sensitises us to the intrinsic connectedness of various temporal and spatial relations (Bakhtin, in Boletsi et al., 2021, 5). The chronotope highlights how our experiences and subjective understandings of time and place emerge through meaning-making processes that can generate different kinds of historicity (Wirtz, 2016). We should, therefore, not only look at different ways of conceiving time-space, but also accept that different chronotopes converge in people's lives. For instance, in the case of Amazonian rubber tappers that Browne Ribeiro (2019, 55) describes, one chronotope emerges from a small and rural settlement that is organised primarily through kinship and seasonal agro-extractivist activities, while another emerges from global capitalist markets that are organised through the accumulation and movement of goods and capital. Ethnographies that explore Amazonian soils similarly point out that binaries and juxtapositions—such as living and non-living—'trouble modern temporal divides between past, present, and future' (Lyons, 2020, 62). The impermanence of Amazonian lands, with their ever-changing existence, makes soils inextricable from an entangled web where every element is always implicated in the existence of the other (Lyons, 2020, 99). Multiple temporalities converge likewise in Amazonian resources frontiers. As this shows, people and lands can then sometimes become awkwardly trapped between multiple chronotopes that rely simultaneously on different kinds of pasts and different claims for the future (HadžiMuhamedović, 2018).

It follows, then, that in the following sections on the extractive present in Venezuela and Colombia our interest lies not so much in analysing what life looks like after destruction—or if the afterlife has arrived (or not) for the people and lands that are implicated in mining practices. Rather, we want to analyse how local ideas about life and afterlife intersect in resource extraction (see also D'Angelo and Pijpers, 2018), and how such ideas mesh with the concrete experiences, memories, and expectations of miners, as well as the formations, residues, and adaptations of extractive landscapes.

3 The Venezuelan Gold Rush: the Afterlife Within

In March 2018, whilst the national economy was spiralling down fast and the majority of Venezuelans increasingly faced hunger and deprivation, President Nicolás Maduro smooched a gold bar on national television. With a complacent smile he looked into the camera and said that the gold is of *la patria* (the 'fatherland') and of *el pueblo* (the people).[2] His kiss was a performative act during a national communique in which the Minister of Mining and President Maduro declared a new mining area in the Orinoco Mining Arc in Bolívar State in the southern part of Venezuela. A potential of eight thousand tons of new gold, they claimed, would become the new motor to reform the economy and

2 See https://www.youtube.com/watch?v=zarI307Yb6Q (accessed on 8 September 2021).

endorse the new national cryptocurrency, the 'Petro', bringing prosperity and happiness to all Venezuelans.

Not so long ago, similar promises saturated national broadcasting and the future of Venezuela was brighter than ever: abundant oil would bring affluence to all Venezuelans. This promise of 'sowing the oil' to strengthen agricultural and industrial activity has existed in the national imaginary and political discourse since the 1930s (Coronil, 1997). Yet, due to low oil revenues, in the last decade the Venezuelan extractive imaginary has in some way taken a 'resource turn'. The Maduro government now aims to stabilise the steep crisis and diversify the economy through the extraction of minerals, such as gold, diamonds, coltan, iron and bauxite. Particularly, gold has become the new promise of wealth for all Venezuelans and a way to survive a complex humanitarian crisis (van Roekel and de Theije, 2020). These social imaginaries have had far-reaching political outcomes. In 2016, the government issued a decree to create the Orinoco Mining Arc, a special development zone for the mining of minerals that is ruled by flexible monetary arrangements and malleable labour and environmental policies—the Orinoco Mining Arc was evidently not created to encourage foreign investments, but to legalise existing informal mining activities in protected areas and formalise alliances between the government and the irregular armed groups that largely control the extraction of minerals in the south of Venezuela (Bull and Rosales, 2020, 125–126). The Amazonian forests and rivers and the southern savannahs soon turned into highly profitable assets, and violent land disputes, deforestation, water contamination, and rising crime have increasingly been harming people and lands (UNHCHR, 2020). In 2020, the disputed extractive region, which covers approximately 110,000 square kilometres, was expanded towards new potential mining areas in important rivers in the Venezuelan Amazon.

The policies that formalised small-scale mining in the Venezuelan south were infused with linear mining cycles of prospection, exploration, extraction and closure (Gobierno Bolivariano de Venezuela, 2018, 22). The Plan Sectorial Minero of 2018 likewise emphasised a prospective mineral abundance of its national territories and the promise of extraordinary profits, and its words fitted perfectly with the temporal make-up of global extractive markets and notions of pre-boom, post-mining, and the life-preceding-afterlife in the current mining literature. While reading the report, it was difficult to ignore the previous oil bust and present crisis that have confronted the country for almost a decade. Temporally speaking, Venezuelan miners seemed awkwardly trapped between these promising reports, previous booms and busts, and present crises—different chronotopes that depended on different kinds of pasts and different claims for the future simultaneously. We should not ignore such temporal muddles, which are part and parcel of an experiential world of the extractive present and the current gold rush in Venezuela.

Late in 2019, I (Eva van Roekel) travelled to the Venezuelan and Brazilian border area and learned how Venezuelan refugees and internally displaced people had turned to artisanal gold mining as a way to survive the humanitarian crisis. Thousands of newcomers had flocked to old and new gold mining sites that had recently boosted a local economy of food, gasoline, and banknotes to make the extraction and exchange of gold possible. Although I hardly saw any gold during my stay, it appeared to be everywhere, for the good and the bad. The omnipresence of gold was similar to what I knew from my previous years of living in Venezuela, when the blessing and curse of oil had always been dauntingly present in everyday life.

When I had just decided to continue fieldwork on the emergency extraction of gold that was sustaining the livelihood of thousands of Venezuelans, the global pandemic hit. So, instead of a subsequent fieldtrip, I started collaborating with Morelia Morillo, a colleague who lives in the mining region, which used to be a thriving hotspot for ecotourism. One extractive industry had replaced the other, and the practical workings of the gold rush had built upon existing social and material infrastructures. For the past twelve months, my first-hand experiences from 2019 have fused with the field diaries of Morelia and my interrogations of her personal experiences, observations and casual conversations with villagers and newcomers. The experience of being in an afterlife often appeared right in middle of the current gold rush in her hometown. One life story of a villager helped me to perceive how previous booms and busts of many resources (not only oil) were all part of the 'extractive present' in the Venezuelan south that further muddled my ideas of the life and afterlife of mining—or any social activity really.

Tariq[3] had arrived at the border town a decade ago and had soon started a household appliances business. According to Morelia, the burgeoning of Tariq's business was due to the rising shortages in Venezuela, and their local border economy was in its 'pre-boom climax' back then. The growing economy of scarcity up north soon became highly profitable in this border area, with Brazilian supplies nearby. Tariq was doing well in his personal life too. He fell in love with a girl whose father belonged to the Pemón, a local Indigenous community, and they got married and had two daughters. But his prosperous shop went bankrupt soon after a procedure called 'controlled sales' was introduced—that is, forced sale at cost price, which was controlled by the

3 The authors use pseudonyms when referring to research participants.

national armed forces. Tariq's bankruptcy was part of a larger economic bust at the border.

Many of his colleagues found refuge in artisanal gold mining, but Tariq continued to resist going to the mines. He became a taxi driver first. Soon gasoline became a scarcity too and Tariq turned to the resale and smuggling of fuel for a while. Then he started a makeshift shop in basic goods next to the road leading to the village of his in-laws. But he had to close his new business down following a violent mining dispute in 2019 in which he lost several friends. His wife became the main provider. Then she lost her job too. Tariq was in despair and saw no other option than the gold mines. For many newcomers, and residents like Tariq, gold mining became the ultimate recourse and was a kind of afterlife that was paradoxically generated by previous booms and current economic effervescence.

Early in 2021, Tariq visited Morelia in the afternoon. He told her again that he had long refused to go to the mines. 'Going to the mine is not something that makes me proud', he said.

He emphasised once more that he had tried to subsist with any job other than gold mining. He thought, just like Morelia had been told by previous research participants, that working in the gold mines was too dirty and insecure a job due to rising crime in and near the mines. Two years earlier, a small-scale mining area near his in-laws' village had sprung up. Tariq told Morelia that he was granted entrance because his wife's family belonged to the indigenous community.

> The mine gives me to live. In a week I take out … three to three point five [grams] each. Already on Thursdays, I have bought everything we need for the house. What we [extract] between Friday and Saturday, we save for any emergency. I feel good because my girls are eating well, they have milk, their Toddy [chocolate drink], their cereals, their clothes, their shoes.

While the green savannahs turned into red mud, Tariq and the others all worked in an artisanal manner, each one their own piece of land, approximately two by two metres, from which each took the gravel and the sand mixed with pebbles. This was, according to Morelia, supposedly the layer that was rich in gold, which they washed in a *suruca* (a sieve) and a wooden pan, in which the gold remains. Grams of gold that were just enough to subsist on.

Like other emergency miners, Tariq seemed hardly concerned with the prospection, exploration, extraction and closure of the expanding Orinoco Mining Arc he had unwillingly become part of. Both he and Morelia rather describe their presence in the current gold rush as an afterlife within. As already mentioned, overlapping extractive realities coexist; past and present booms and busts of oil and gold easily subsisted with other resource commodity booms and busts that made life (a bit more) liveable at a resource frontier (see also D'Angelo, 2018). Like in many Amazonian contexts, gold cycles are just one of the many booms and bust cycles that characterise the *longue durée* of colonial and postcolonial presence in this part of the world (Browne Riberio, 2019, 48). Extraction, in its many arrangements, holds a form of permanence at these resource frontiers. The afterlife of one form of extraction, cultivation, and commerce often intersperses with other lives and afterlives that are about to appear. Each element of life, as Ingold (1993) notes, has its own timescale and rhythm that we should consider in our intent to make sense of empirical realities. These different chronotopes of resources, exposed lands, mining policies and opposing communities evidently intersect in how individuals like Tariq and Morelia experience and make sense of the extractive present in gold country. Tariq and the green savannahs in the Venezuelan south have become awkwardly trapped between different resource chronotopes that depend on different historical pasts and different entitlements for the future simultaneously. The experiences of small-scale gold miners in the current post-mining boom in Chocó prove the same.

4 Mining in the Ruins of the Chocó Gold Rush

The starting point of Chocó's resource extraction lies somewhere in the early 1700s, when Spanish colonisers began to bring enslaved Africans and their descendants to the region and forced them to work in placer mines (Sharp, 1975). Chocó soon became an archetypical example of colonial extractivism: gold travelled from its rainforest outwards, whereas investments in local infrastructure were scarce and restricted to mining operations (Wade, 1993). Colonial rule ended in 1821; slavery in 1851. Yet this combination of gold extraction and social abandonment has, in different guises, remained. Today, many of the region's Afro-descendant inhabitants continue to work in placer mining. Meanwhile, official statistics designate Chocó as Colombia's poorest region (DANE, 2020), while grassroots leaders have repeatedly organised mass protests that condemn the perceived 'abandonment of the state' (Tubb and Rojas, 2020).

Of course, continuing abandonment notwithstanding, many things did change. Mining companies came and went, villages transformed into towns, asphalt and motorboats increased the speed of travel, miners increasingly complemented wooden mining gear (pans, sticks, sluice boxes) with diesel-powered pumps, and local prices of gold and platinum fluctuated in tandem with the shifting demand for minerals elsewhere in the world. In recent decades change has accelerated. In the 1980s, paramilitaries, guerrillas, and state forces enveloped Chocó in the wider Colombian conflict—whose violence, until then, had largely skirted the region (Wouters, 2001). At more or less the same time, wildcat miners from other parts of Colombia began arriving in the region in search for gold. Their migration was piecemeal until it took on dramatic proportions in the late 2000s, when the gold price skyrocketed in the aftermath of the financial crisis. A mining boom ensued, swallowing up the rainforest. These new miners relied on heavy machinery, such as excavators and pontoons, that turned rivers into sandbanks, streams into puddles, plots of crops into piles of rocks, gold-bearing forests into worthless moonscapes. The gold rush wreaked havoc on traditional economies of artisanal mining, farming, fishing and hunting (Jonkman, 2021; Tubb, 2020).

The boom years did not persist. After half a century of war, Colombia was cruising to a peace deal with the FARC guerrillas, and the national government deemed 'illegal miners' enemies of the upcoming peace. Apart from destroying the natural environment, miners supplied rents (or extortion money, as they themselves said) to paramilitaries and guerrillas, and thereby thwarted the government's efforts to re-establish military control over the Colombian countryside. What's more, the Santos Administration (2010–18) had envisioned 'post-conflict' development as revolving around large-scale extractive industries, and this endorsement coincided with the criminalisation of small-scale miners, who worked not only without the proper papers but sometimes also on the concessions of the desired multinationals. And so, in the course of the 2010s the government increasingly attempted to eradicate unlicensed extraction by means of police operations that incarcerated miners and dynamited their machinery. In Chocó, such persecution, along with the declining accessibility of gold reserves, resulted in the end of the mining boom. When I (Jesse Jonkman) did fieldwork in 2017, excavator mines had drastically decreased in number.

At the same time that the government began penalising unlicensed mining, four *chocoano* grassroots organisations filed a lawsuit against various state agencies for permitting the deterioration of the Atrato river, Chocó's main artery, mostly as a consequence of such mining. The lawsuit resulted in the Colombian Constitutional Court declaring the Atrato a 'legal entity', and assigning specific tasks to state agencies to decontaminate the river and persecute 'illegal' miners. The court presented the ruling as a historical turning point toward the 'sustainable exploitation of resources in the present and the future' (Corte Constitucional, 2016). The leaders of the four grassroots organisations largely shared the court's position on extraction. In meetings with state officials, they criticised the excavator and dredge mines for denying them future livelihoods. One of these meetings ended with a song with the following refrain: '*Atrato es, Atrato soy, Atrato somos y debemos seguir siendo*' ('It's the Atrato; I'm the Atrato; we're the Atrato and we should continue being it'). *Chocoano* leaders and Bogotá bureaucrats agreed: the future of the region depended on making the wildcat mines history.

But this view was hardly hegemonic in the mining villages where I did fieldwork. The controversial miners had provided local households with land rents, jobs, and *bareque*; a form of placer mining whereby artisanal miners work in the pits of excavator mines—where gold is more abundant than in stream beds. These economic opportunities had allowed families to improve their homes, pay for their children's education, and help out less fortunate family members. Against this backdrop, popular opinion was that by removing the excavators, the government was not so much bringing peace as hunger, delinquency, and disorder.

Mercedes was among those who shared this opinion. The first time I met her, she was working in a water pump mine alongside her friends Yoser and Ernesto. The operation, called *chorreo*, consisted of hosing down a wall of gold-bearing earth, transforming it into a brownish stream that snaked towards a subjacent sluice box, in which gold specks were trapped from the surrounding sediment. Yoser manned the hose, Ernesto threw away larger pebbles from the sluice's entry point, and Mercedes discarded the gravel, using two hand-sized wooden boards to rake, bundle, and finally sweep it away in a lateral direction. All three of them were past their thirties and had worked in *chorreo* before the excavator miners had conquered the rainforest a few years earlier. They had abandoned *chorreo* in the heyday of the more lucrative *bareque*, but now that the excavators were mostly gone, they had once more picked up their former labour. Economic hardship even required them to work during the Holy Week of Easter, a fact they did not take lightly.

'The government might save the environment, but if mining ends, we end', Mercedes said after I acquainted the miners with my study on mining politics. Once she had finished one more routine of collecting, bundling, and dumping gravel, she began to elaborate:

> Look, [the police operations] affect the excavator miners the most, but we are living off them. So, if they don't work, what are we going to live off? Here we make 10, maybe 20 thousand pesos a day [3, maybe 6 US dollars]. With the three of us! So, I have 5, 6 thousand pesos to buy food for my children.

Before I could ask, she added, 'I have five children'.

Her friend Ernesto cut in: 'The only reason why we're here is that there is no other work'.

'This is just for your daily utilities, for your food', Mercedes underscored. 'But sometimes we have to stop eating to pay for utilities. We'll die of hunger here. What can you do if the government decides to make the mines disappear? You die of hunger. What else? Who would have thought, to have to shovel (*echar pala*) during Easter?'

While walking towards the exit point of the sluice box, and away from the conversation, she repeated three times over a single sentence in a hushed voice: 'Hunger is killing us. Hunger is killing us. Hunger is killing us'.

Her mantra-like lament was a far cry from the aforementioned hopes of activists and legislators for a future free of 'illegal mining'. Unlike them, Mercedes did not see the end of the excavators as a precondition for a sustainable tomorrow. Rather, she seemed to equate it with the end of her own time—'if mining ends, we end'—thereby denying the possibility of that extractive hereafter that critical scholars of Latin America have so often imagined and celebrated (e.g. Acosta, 2013; Gudynas, 2013). For her and other miners, post-extraction was no option whatsoever. That said, along with their rejection of a non-extractive hereafter, they simultaneously described their current labour as a sort of extractive afterlife itself, meaningful only in relation to a rosier economic past. Herein they were not so different from Tariq in Venezuela. But while in his case the afterlife equalled the gold rush itself, in Chocó it connoted the mining labour that persisted despite the end of the boom years. *Chocoano* miners were panning in stream beds and hosing in pits after being employed as excavator conductors, after receiving land rents, after the *bareque*. And so, even if they praised wholeheartedly their traditional mining for granting them a sense of labour autonomy (Jonkman, 2022), many also described it as a residual economy that produced merely a pittance compared to excavator mines.

Cabello, for one, reckoned that with his current *matraqueo* operation (shovelling sand on a sluice box) he made only one-tenth of what he used to earn as an excavator driver at a pit that had closed a few years previously. In an interview, he made no attempt to sugar-coat his contempt for the government's police operations. 'The government has ended everything; Chocó is one of the departments that will disappear. Just imagine, we lived so much more *sabroso* [richly] with the machines. Here we have a plot of land, but we can't have it worked because the [excavator] miners don't want to run the risk'. His concern, though, was the disappearance not just of the excavators but also of the prospects of working in an artisanal manner now that the excavators had mined away most of the surface gold. 'Look, the problem here is that artisanal mining has ended. It's so difficult right now, even with heavy machinery you can't do anything'.

Miners like Cabello and Mercedes presented their work as existing after history—or more specifically, after prosperity. After all, the excavators of migrant miners had emptied their local lands of gold and laid waste to crops and fertile soil. And they were now left behind looking for scraps in a leftover landscape, using equipment whose horsepower was only a fraction of that of the migrants' machinery. Yet peculiarly enough, Chocó's local miners spoke of themselves not only as if being in an afterlife, but also as if being stuck in the past. Theirs, after all, was a special kind of afterlife, one that was associated with pre-boom poverty. They regarded their contemporary labour practices as an afterthought of the gold rush, precisely because these were said to belong to a previous day and age. Traditional forms of mining (panning, tunnelling, pump mining) had been the labour of parents and ancestors (reaching as far back as colonial times), and felt to many contemporary miners out of place in today's era of mechanised extraction. What's more, under current environmental circumstances, most miners agreed that low-tech equipment was no longer suitable. The recent removal of surface gold by excavators demanded more of the same heavy-handed excavation, not the surface-scraping of pans and pumps.

While the national government had focused its formalisation efforts on traditional forms of mining, many of those working the traditional methods regarded them as being hopelessly outdated. They had already passed the technological stage (pans, pumps) they once more found themselves in, as had the landscape they were labouring in. As community leader Moisés said, 'The state wants us to do traditional mining: a batea, a bar, and a spade. All legislation focuses on this. But this is only going backward. Artisanal mining is no longer possible. We have passed that stage. We also want to progress. That's what they're denying us: progress'.

All this demonstrates that *chocoano* miners recurred to muddled conceptions of time to make sense of their contemporary precarity—even though the terminology being used was often not shy of a good dose of linear promise (or 'progress', to use Moisés's phrasing). Indeed, by designating their modest techniques as both the aftermath and the antecedent of what they considered to be the technological present, they underlined that their work was, extractively speaking, awfully out of time. Surely, such temporal experiences cannot be reduced to theoretical and legislative arguments that understand mining in a neatly divided pre, intra, and post phase. At resource frontiers like Chocó—and the Venezuelan Arco Minero for that matter—swift booms and busts give shape to a much more muddled experience of time, whereby the extractive present is rarely only experienced as one temporal phase, as miners may understand and present themselves through local time concepts of posteriority (of living an afterlife) or anteriority (of living in the past), and sometimes both.

5 Muddled Times as Afterthought

Mining codes and concomitant legislation often frame extraction as a linear process with neatly delimited temporal phases; that is, as exploration preceding exploitation preceding mine closure. The burgeoning scholarly literature on resource extraction challenges the assumptions of finality and linearity that such narratives uphold, and instead shows that (ex-)mining sites produce multiple experiences of time and land. Phrased otherwise, the actual workings of time clearly depend on whom and what people think they are responsible for, as well as on with whom and what they interact on a daily basis in past, present, and future. Now, while current theorising on temporal multiplicity has mostly led to analyses that have as their 'starting point the potential conflict and non-synchronicity of mining temporalities' (D'Angelo and Pijpers, 2018, 215), we have shown that in gold-mining regions in Venezuela and Colombia it is quite difficult to put coexisting timeframes in such sharp juxtaposition, insofar as overlapping and converging chronotypes result in a muddled experience of temporality. To be precise, by spending time with small-scale miners we have learned that being a miner may very well be considered to be somewhat of an afterlife itself, that the lingering death of one resource frontier (the Venezuelan oil industry) may give birth to another (Venezuelan gold mining), that former extractive practices can suddenly resurface in new guises in the aftermath of a resource boom, and that environmental devastation might be at once the effect and cause of resource extraction (as for some *chocoanos*, the destruction wrought by excavators has led to pragmatic desires for more excavator mining). In effect, temporal notions such as 'pre-boom climax' materialise the ongoing muddling of time in South American mining frontiers where gold appears, disappears, and reappears together with other resources. In this scenario of constant change and resource frontiers overlapping or even cannibalising each other, the experience of time is a jumbling phenomenon. Amid the continuing reshuffling of the old and the new, residents of mining settlements continually invoke the past and future to give meaning to the present, in which they incorporate multiple temporalities that move with different rhythms.

In light of such temporal multiplicity, here we have understood the afterlife of mining less as some neutral or objective posterior phase in an extraction timeframe than as one of the many cultural categories (or chronotopes) that residents of mining regions themselves invoke to make sense of the extractive present. To our thinking, a single and rigid demarcation between life and afterlife, or any temporal demarcation for that matter, falls flat when touching ground in mining frontiers. The experience of time is much more muddled than this. In both Venezuela and Colombia, some miners experienced current extraction activities as an extractive hereafter to some richer past. When taken at face value, the notion of life-becoming-afterlife proposes a chronological process in which non-extraction (as in the afterlife) succeeds extraction (as in the extractive life). The way we see it, this consecutive conceptualisation says precious little about the larger historical and overlapping resource cycles in which these moments of (non-)extraction occur. If anything, the idea of an afterlife glosses over the fact that the so-called *pre*-afterlife phase (the boom years) follows and feeds on preceding exclusions and crises or afterlives, if you will. Our point is that mining booms and extractive lives may very well exist as the aftermath of other economic and social realities (e.g. oil recessions, hyperinflation, political abandonment, colonialism). One resource frontier's life is another frontier's afterlife.

The coexistence of these intersecting activities and traversing expectations further muddles the progression of past, present, and future. By analytically confining the transformative transition of life-becoming-afterlife to one specific resource, or to one specific historical conjecture, we ignore the cyclical and overlapping resource trajectories in Venezuela and Colombia. Both Bolívar State and Chocó are archetypical manifestations of what Michael Watts (2012) calls 'the permanent frontier', which captures the fact that global extractive capitalism continually incites both the creation of new spaces of accumulation and the reconfiguration of old ones. In this regard, what was *before* the afterlife in Chocó and what surfaces from the mining activities in Bolívar State is not some homogenous life or afterlife. If we simply suggest that first there was life and now there is none, we end up setting 'afterlives'—such as non-extractive periods or economic crises—apart from the wider booms and busts from which they emerge and to which they give shape. This runs the serious risk of ignoring how gold miners like Tariq, Mercedes and Cabello understand their present work and future expectations for labour and land through memories of prior booms and exclusions, and may conceive of their current mining lives as the afterlife of earlier affluent economic epochs. Life and afterlife, pre and post, circularity and linearity, and immanence and indeterminacy all muddle in without the need for one temporal imperative in how miners experience the extractive present.

References

Acosta, A. (2015) 'Después del Saqueo: Caminos hacia el Posextractivismo', *Perspectivas América Latina*, 1, pp. 12–15.

Acosta, A. (2013) 'Extractivism and Neoextractivism: Two Sides of the Same Curse', in M. Lang and D. Mokrani (eds.) *Beyond Development: Alternative Visions from Latin America* (Quito: Fundación Rosa Luxemburg), pp. 61–86.

Ahmann, C. (2018) '"It's Exhausting to Create an Event out of Nothing": Slow Violence and the Manipulation of Time', *Cultural Anthropology*, 33(1), pp. 142–171, DOI: 10.14506/ca33.1.06.

Askland, H.H. (2020) '*Mining Voids*: Extraction and Emotion at the Australian Coal Frontier', *Polar Record*, 56(e5), pp. 1–10, DOI: 10.1017/S0032247420000078.

Avango, D. and G. Rosqvist (2021) 'When Mines Go Silent: Exploring the Afterlives of Extraction Sites', in D.C. Nord (ed.) *Nordic Perspectives on the Responsible Development of the Arctic: Pathways to Action* (Cham: Springer), pp. 349–368.

Bear, L. (2016) 'Time as Technique', *Annual Review of Anthropology*, 45, pp. 487–502, DOI: 10.1146/annurev-anthro-102313-030159.

Boletsi, M., N. Lemos Dekker, K. Mika and K. Robbe (eds.) (2021) *(Un)timely Crises: Chronotopes and Critique* (Cham: Palgrave MacMillan).

Browne Ribeiro, A. (2019) 'Ragtime, Clockwork: Community Work, Mobility, and Chronotope Production in Amazonian Communities', *Signs and Society*, 7(1), pp. 38–67, DOI: 10.1086/701149.

Bryant, R. and D.M. Knight (2019) *The Anthropology of the Future* (Cambridge: Cambridge University Press).

Bull, B. and A. Rosales (2020) 'Into the Shadows: Sanctions, Rentierism, and Economic Informalization in Venezuela', *European Review of Latin American and Caribbean Studies*, 109, pp. 107–133, DOI: 10.32992/erlacs.10556.

Cater, T. and A. Keeling (2013) '"That's Where Our Future Came From": Mining, Landscape, and Memory in Rankin Inlet, Nunavut', *Études Inuit Studies*, 37(2), pp. 59–82, DOI: 10.7202/1025710ar.

Coronil, F. (1997) *The Magical State: Nature, Money, and Modernity in Venezuela* (Chicago: The University of Chicago Press).

Corte Constitucional (2016) *Sentencia T-622/16*, https://www.corteconstitucional.gov.co/relatoria/2016/t-622-16.htm (accessed on 24 September 2021).

D'Angelo, L. (2018) 'Diamonds and Plural Temporalities: Articulating Encounters in the Mines of Sierra Leone', in R.J. Pijpers and T.H. Eriksen (eds.) *Mining Encounters: Extractive Industries in an Overheated World* (London: Pluto Press), pp. 138–155.

D'Angelo, L. and R.J. Pijpers (2018) 'Mining Temporalities: an Overview', *The Extractive Industries and Society*, 5(2), pp. 215–222, DOI: 10.1016/j.exis.2018.02.005.

DANE (2020) 'Boletín Técnico: Pobreza Monetaria Departamental (Año 2019)', http://www.dane.gov.co/files/investigaciones/condiciones_vida/pobreza/2019/Boletin-pobreza-monetaria-dptos_2019.pdf (accessed on 16 June 2021).

Das, V. (2006) *Life and Words: Violence and the Descent into the Ordinary* (Berkeley: University of California Press).

Desjarlais, R.R. (1997) *Shelter Blues: Homelessness and Sanity in a Boston Shelter* (Philadelphia: University of Pennsylvania Press).

Ebus, B. (2019) 'Venezuela's Mining arc: a Legal Veneer for Armed Groups to Plunder', *The Guardian*, 8 June, https://www.theguardian.com/world/2019/jun/08/venezuela-gold-mines-rival-armed-groups-gangs (accessed on 06 September 2022).

Evans-Pritchard, E.E. (1939) 'Nuer Time-Reckoning', *Africa Journal of the International African Institute*, 12(2), pp. 189–216, DOI: 10.2307/1155085.

Fabian, J. (1983) *Time and the Other: How Anthropology Makes Its Object* (New York: Columbia University Press).

Gell, A. (1992) *The Anthropology of Time: Cultural Constructions of Temporal Maps and Images* (Oxford: Berg).

Gellner, E. (1964) *Thought and Change* (London: Weidenfeld and Nicolson).

Gobierno Bolivariano de Venezuela (2018) *Plan Sectorial Minero 2019–2025* (Caracas: Ministerio del Poder Popular para Desarrollo Minero Ecológico), http://www.desarrollominero.gob.ve/wp-content/uploads/2019/03/plan-sectorial-minero2019-2025_reducido.pdf (accessed on 29 September 2021).

Gordillo, G.R. (2014) *Rubble: the Afterlife of Destruction* (Durham: Duke University Press).

Gudynas, E. (2013) 'Debates on Development and its Alternatives in Latin America: a brief Heterodox Guide', in M. Lang and D. Mokrani (eds.) *Beyond Development: Alternative Visions from Latin America* (Quito: Fundación Rosa Luxemburg), pp. 15–39.

HadžiMuhamedović, S. (2018) *Waiting for Elijah: Time and Encounter in a Bosnian Landscape* (New York: Berghahn Books).

Halvaksz, J.A. (2008) 'Whose Closure? Appearances, Temporality, and Mineral Extraction in Papua New Guinea', *Journal of the Royal Anthropological Institute*, 14(1), pp. 21–37, DOI: 10.1111/j.1467-9655.2007.00476.x.

Hetherington, K. (2020) *The Government of Beans: Regulating Life in the Age of Monocrops* (Durham: Duke University Press).

Ingold, T. (1993) 'The Temporality of the Landscape', *World Archeology*, 25(2), pp. 152–174, DOI: 10.1080/00438243.1993.9980235.

Irvine, R. (2014) 'Deep Time: an Anthropological Problem', *Social Anthropology*, 22(2), pp. 157–172, DOI: 10.1111/1469-8676.12067.

Jackson, M. (2018) *The Varieties of Temporal Experience: Travels in Philosophical, Historical, and Ethnographic Time* (New York: Columbia University Press).

Jaramillo, P. (2020) 'Mining Leftovers: Making Futures on the Margins of Capitalism', *Cultural Anthropology*, 35(1), pp. 48–73, DOI: 10.14506/ca35.1.07.

Jonkman, J. (2022) 'Extracting Empirically: a Ground's-Eye View of Small-Scale Mining in Colombia', *Anthropological Quarterly*, 95(3), pp. 649–680.

Jonkman, J. (2021) 'Underground Multiculturalism: Contentious Cultural Politics in Gold-Mining Regions in Chocó, Colombia', *Journal of Latin American Studies*, 53(1), pp. 25–52, DOI: 10.1017/S0022216X2000098X.

Keeling, A. and J. Sandlos (2017) 'Ghost Towns and Zombie Mines: the Historical Dimensions of Mine Abandonment, Reclamation, and Redevelopment in the Canadian North', in S. Bocking and B. Martin (eds.) *Ice Blink: Navigating Northern Environmental History* (Calgary: University of Calgary Press), pp. 377–420.

Long, A. (2020) 'The Afterlife of Extraction in the Coal Region: an Exploration into the "Land of the Living Dead"', *Anthropocenes—Human, Inhuman, Posthuman*, 1(1), DOI: 10.16997/ahip.8.

Luning, S. (2018) 'Mining Temporalities: Future Perspectives', *The Extractive Industries and Society*, 5(2), pp. 281–286, DOI: 10.1016/j.exis.2018.03.009.

Lyons, K.M. (2020) *Vital Decomposition: Soil Practitioners and Life Politics* (Durham: Duke University Press).

Mazzeo, A. (2018) 'The Temporalities of Asbestos Mining and Community Activism', *The Extractive Industries and Society*, 5(2), pp. 223–229, DOI: 10.1016/j.exis.2018.02.004.

Moreno, C. (2015) 'El Posextractivismo y el Reto de Repensar el Metabolismo de la Economía Mundial', *Perspectivas: América Latina*, 1, pp. 18–21.

Morton, T. (2010) 'Ecology after Capitalism', *Polygraph*, 22, pp. 46–59.

Nixon, R. (2011) *Slow Violence and the Environmentalism of the Poor* (Cambridge: Harvard University Press).

Oakley, P. (2018) 'After Mining: Contrived Dereliction, Dualistic Time and the Moment of Rupture in the Presentation of Mining Heritage', *The Extractive Industries and Society*, 5(2), pp. 274–280, DOI: 10.1016/j.exis.2018.03.005.

Peters, S. (2019) 'Sociedades Rentistas: Claves para Entender la Crisis Venezolana', *European Review of Latin American and Caribbean Studies*, 108, pp. 1–19, DOI: 10.32992/erlacs.10505.

Robertson, D. (2006) *Hard as the Rock Itself: Place and Identity in the American Mining Town* (Boulder: University Press of Colorado).

Salemink, O. and M.B. Rasmussen (2016) 'After Dispossession: Ethnographic Approaches to Neoliberalization', *Focaal—Journal of Global and Historical Anthropology*, 2016(74), pp. 3–12, DOI: 10.3167/fcl.2016.740101.

Sharp, W.F. (1975) 'The Profitability of Slavery in the Colombian Chocó, 1680–1810', *The Hispanic American Historical Review*, 55(3), pp. 468–495, DOI: 0.2307/2512376.

Silva, L. (2020) 'El Ciclo de las Des-re-territorialización en el Antes y Después de la Minería', in G. Espinosa Damián and A. Meza Velarde (eds.) *Reconfiguraciones*

Socioterritoriales: Entre el Despojo Capitalista y las Resistencias Comunitarias (Mexico City: UAM), pp. 201–221.

Svampa, M. (2013) 'Resource Extractivism and Alternatives: Latin American Perspectives on Development', in M. Lang and D. Mokrani (eds.) *Beyond Development: Alternative Visions from Latin America* (Quito: Fundación Rosa Luxemburg), pp. 117–143.

Tsing, A.L. (2015) *The Mushroom at the End of the World: On the Possibility of Life in Capitalist Ruins* (Princeton: Princeton University Press).

Tubb, D. (2020) *Shifting Livelihoods: Gold Mining and Subsistence in the Chocó, Colombia* (Seattle: University of Washington Press).

Tubb, D. and D.E. Rojas (2020) '"We Voted for Your Peace Santos; Now It Is Our Turn": a General Strike, Conflict, and the State in the Chocó, Colombia', *Canadian Journal of Latin American and Caribbean Studies*, 45(2), pp. 155–173, DOI: 10.1080/08263663.2020.1744285.

United Nations High Commissioner for Human Rights (UNHCHR) (2020) *Independence of the Justice System and Access to Justice in the Bolivarian Republic of Venezuela, including for Violations of Economic and Social Rights, and the Situation of Human Rights in the Arco Minero del Orinoco Region,* Report of the United Nations High Commissioner for Human Rights, A/HRC/44/54 (Geneva: United Nations).

van Roekel, E. (2020) *Phenomenal Justice. Violence and Morality in Argentina* (New Brunswick: Rutgers University Press).

van Roekel, E. and M. de Theije (2020) 'Hunger in the Land of Plenty: the Complex Humanitarian Crisis in Venezuela', *Anthropology Today*, 36(2), pp. 8–12, DOI: 10.1111/1467-8322.12561.

Vargas-Roncancio, I.D. (2017) 'Nomadic ecologies: Plants, Embodied Knowledge, and Temporality in the Colombian Amazon', *Boletín de Antropología,* 32(53), pp. 255–276, DOI: 10.17533/udea.boan.v32n53a14.

Wade, P. (1993) *Blackness and Race Mixture: the Dynamics of Racial Identity in Colombia* (Baltimore: Johns Hopkins University Press).

Watts, M.J. (2012) 'A Tale of Two Gulfs: Life, Death, and Dispossession along Two Oil Frontiers', *American Quarterly*, 64(3), pp. 437–467, DOI: 10.1353/aq.2012.0039.

Wirtz, K. (2016) 'The Living, the Dead, and the Immanent. Dialogue across Chronotopes', *HAU: Journal of Ethnographic Theory*, 6(1), pp. 343–369, DOI: 10.14318/hau6.1.019.

Wouters, M. (2001) 'Ethnic Rights Under Threat: the Black Peasant Movement Against Armed Groups' Pressure in the Chocó, Colombia', *Bulletin of Latin American Research*, 20(4), pp. 498–519, DOI: 10.1111/1470-9856.00027.

PART 3

Extractive Frontiers: Narratives and Discourses

CHAPTER 10

Exploration, Storytelling and Frontier-Making in the Colombian Andes

Anneloes Hoff

Abstract

This chapter shows how the speculative (pre-)lives and afterlives of resource extraction are put together through corporate narrative and imaginative practices. It shows that the expansion of extractive frontiers is not merely driven by abstract and asocial market forces, but that deeply social practices of storytelling and imagination are also vital for making mining exploration possible. Drawing on 15 months of fieldwork in Colombia, it discusses the spectacular narratives surrounding the exploration campaign of South African gold mining corporation AngloGold Ashanti (AGA) across the Colombian Andes. The chapter examines how corporate storytelling unfolds through corporate processes and individual narratives, and shows it to be integral to conjuring Colombia as the 'last Andean frontier' for gold exploration in the international investor's imagination. Corporate narrative and performative practices were not only crucial to attracting and sustaining investor interest, but also served an important internal function in shaping the professional identity of exploration geologists and corporate identity more broadly. At the same time, the chapter shows that frontier expansion and the capitalisation of mineral finds are uneven and speculative processes, with room for alternative stories.

1 Introduction[1]

Minerals are critical for the transition to a post-carbon future. They are crucial for renewable energy technologies, such as wind turbines, solar panels and batteries, which require significant amounts of copper, lithium, nickel, zinc, rare earths and other minerals (IEA, 2021; World Bank, 2020). The rising demand for these 'transition minerals' has led analysts to anticipate a 'next

1 The chapter is based on fieldwork funded by the Economic and Social Research Council (ESRC award no. ES/J500112/1).

mining boom' (*The Economist*, 2022), in which the mineral requirements of meeting global carbon reduction targets will spur the search for new deposits, leading to a further expansion of mining frontiers into areas once considered too difficult or dangerous to invest in (Ali et al., 2017; Bebbington et al., 2018). Growing demand and rising commodity prices are a key part of what shapes and sustains the imperative for further mineral exploration and extraction. Yet to understand how such abstract and asocial market forces drive frontier expansion, we should be careful not to overlook the deeply social practices that enable them. In this chapter, I draw particular attention to the ways in which storytelling and imagination render mining exploration possible.

In studying 'the narrative and performative aspects of corporate practice' (Rajak, 2011a, 93), this chapter draws on and contributes to anthropological work on corporations that seeks to shed light on the social and moral practices and sentiments that animate them (Dolan and Rajak, 2016; Foster, 2017; Rajak, 2011a; Sawyer, 2018; Welker, 2014). Attention to the social dimensions of corporate practice is crucial for advancing a grounded understanding of the functioning of corporate capitalism. Furthermore, in attending to the performative nature of the processes through which geological substances in the subsurface are rendered into exploitable resource deposits, and territories are rendered into extractive frontiers, the chapter contributes to scholarship on the politics of geology, in particular work on 'resource making' (Kama, 2020; Richardson and Weszkalnys, 2014; Weszkalnys, 2015).

This chapter focuses on the exploration campaign of AngloGold Ashanti (AGA) in Colombia during the early 2000s, and on the narratives surrounding this campaign at the time and afterwards. AGA is a South African transnational mining corporation listed on the Johannesburg, New York, Australian and Ghanaian stock exchanges, and one of the world's leading gold producers. I draw on my ethnographic study of AGA in Colombia (Hoff, 2020), for which I conducted 15 months of fieldwork, in part 'inside' the company, and in part among members of an anti-mining movement that had formed in resistance to the company's activities. In this chapter, I particularly draw on my fieldwork with the personnel of AGA's so-called Greenfields department, the section of the company focused on the discovery of new deposits. This fieldwork involved informal conversations and semi-structured interviews with employees, most of which were exploration geologists of varying levels of seniority. In addition, I base my analysis on a large number of publicly available corporate presentations and industry-oriented publications. The dynamics of mining exploration described in this chapter are characteristic of greenfields exploration, which is the exploration of previously unexplored or underexplored terrain, as opposed to near-mine or 'brownfields' exploration. This process typically starts with a broad regional outlook and narrows down to smaller target areas on the basis of findings in previous stages. At the beginning of the process, the probability of success is low and the risk for investors very high. With each step, this risk decreases, though only a very small proportion of prospecting programmes—geologists typically speak of less than 1 or less than 0.1 per cent—eventually become mines. This type of exploration is most commonly carried out by 'juniors': smaller mining companies focused on resource speculation and exploration, rather than on extraction. If successful, juniors usually sell their discoveries to 'majors' for further development. For majors, working with juniors is a means of isolating or mitigating the substantial risks associated with greenfields exploration, financial as well as political, and of leveraging previous findings. Anthropological work on mining exploration has typically focused on juniors (Gilbert, 2020; Kneas, 2020; Tsing, 2005), and this chapter contributes a more unusual account, of a major's approach to greenfields exploration.

In the chapter, I examine the stories surrounding AGA's greenfields campaign in Colombia to show how narrative, imaginative and performative practices are integral to the making of resources and mining frontiers, as well as that of corporate and professional identity in the extractive industries. In the first part, I focus on the 'outward-oriented' narratives that, I argue, helped conjure Colombia as the 'last Andean frontier' in corporate, shareholder and investor imagination. In the second part, I provide insight into 'internal' practices of storytelling in AGA's Greenfields department, and show the importance of these practices to the self-understanding and identity of exploration geologists, as well as to corporate identity more broadly. In these different ways, the chapter elaborates how extractive activity is rendered possible through narrative and imagination. At the same time, it highlights that the capitalisation of exploration success is not a given, and that in the highly uneven and speculative process of frontier expansion (see Weszkalnys, 2015), alternative stories are also possible.

2 New Frontiers

At the turn of the millennium, AGA sought to expand its global portfolio.[2] The price of gold and other minerals on the global market was on the rise, driven by

2 AGA in its current form was formed in 2004, when AngloGold, a subsidiary of the South African transnational corporation Anglo American, merged with Ashanti Goldfields Corporation, a company partially owned and largely controlled by the Ghanaian government. For clarity, I use the name AGA throughout this chapter, but events I describe prior to

the demand of China and India's growing middle classes for gold jewellery, as well as gold's appeal as a hedging investment at a time of global political uncertainty (see also Ferry, 2020). AGA's reserves, however, were in decline, as were those of many of their industry peers (Danielson, 2005). In order to ensure it would be able to continue operating in the long term, therefore, the company sought to shift its focus away from its dwindling South African reserves to 'new areas with potentially higher risk profiles' (AGA, 2005, EP9). It developed a globe-spanning exploration programme, which it called its 'New Frontiers' strategy, targeting jurisdictions as diverse as the Philippines, Mongolia and the DRC (AGA, 2004).

The term 'New Frontiers' invokes the idea of uncharted territory, 'empty land' awaiting discovery and development, reminiscent of Turner's (1921) depiction of the nineteenth century American West as a wilderness to be colonised and civilised. Such an imagination of frontier lands often has an erasing effect, as critical scholarship on resource frontiers has noted: it strategically overlooks the presence of people with a long-standing relationship to the land and its subsoil minerals, a relationship that existed long before the entrance of new forms of exploration and exploitation (Luning, 2018). The frontier concept nevertheless continues to be widely used in mining scholarship, but in a 'post-Turnerian' way, to critically examine the changing territorial dynamics following the arrival of new forms of extraction (Rasmussen and Lund, 2018). In this chapter, I build on the idea that resource frontiers are not simply 'out there' to be discovered, but that they are actively 'made'. As Mattias Rasmussen and Christian Lund put it, a frontier is 'not space itself', but rather 'something that happens *in* and *to* space' (2018, 388).

Anna Tsing describes the frontier as a 'zone of not yet'—'an edge of space and time [...] not yet mapped, not yet regulated' (2005, 28). One such 'zone of not yet', which AGA's 'New Frontiers' strategy targeted, was Colombia. In contrast to other Andean nations, it had not been explored with modern technology due to the protracted armed conflict that had plagued the country since the 1960s. An industry journal referred to Colombia as the 'last Andean frontier', which 'in the international race by majors to replace their reserves [...] represents a true elephant hunting opportunity' (Global Business Reports, 2011, 80, 82). 'Elephant', here, is industry lingo for 'major long-life orebodies with reserves of at least five million ounces', the type of mineral deposits AGA's exploration strategy targeted (AGA, 2005, EP9). In this chapter, I explore how Colombia came to be imagined as this 'last Andean frontier' for gold exploration.

---

the 2004 merger concern AngloGold, which was the part of AGA that first became active in Colombia.

Anthropological work on exploration and speculation in the extractive industries highlights that narrative and imaginative practices play a crucial role in the making of extractive frontiers. Frontier-making, this scholarship reveals, is animated by the imagination of resource potential. In her analysis of oil exploration in São Tomé and Príncipe, Gisa Weszkalnys considers speculation about resource potential 'an observation of potentiality' through which exploration becomes possible (2015, 623). For a site to become a resource frontier, the possibility of future discovery must be made imaginable. Companies involved in exploration play a key role in marking out these 'conceptual fields of space and time within which potential exists and exploration can occur', as David Kneas notes in his analysis of copper exploration and the junior mining sector (2020, 277). While eventual mineral extraction depends on the actual resources present in the subsoil, what is most important during the exploration phase is not the material deposit, but the imagined one—the 'articulation of resource potential rhetorically instead of empirically' (Kneas, 2020, 277). This resonates with Tsing's characterisation of frontiers as 'both material and imaginative' (2005, 29): the frontier brings together the materiality of the resource and the imagination of its potential.

Mining exploration starts as a speculative enterprise, which requires significant investment before the presence of a mineral deposit can be reliably confirmed. To attract this investment, greenfields exploration programmes seem to need to emit an air of promise, opportunity and adventure. As Tsing puts it, 'the possibility of economic performance must be conjured like a spirit to draw an audience of potential investors' (2005, 57). Gold, in particular, seems to possess a 'mythic power' to inspire excitement and incite a 'gold fever' in investors (Ferry, 2020; Taussig, 2010; see also Weszkalnys, 2013). In her discussion of the Bre-x scandal, which involved a gold prospecting company fraudulently claiming an enormous gold find in Kalimantan (Indonesia), Tsing highlights the speculative drama the company cultivated around its (non-existent) discovery to attract investment for further exploration. Such 'self-conscious making of a spectacle', 'a performance, a dramatic exposition of the possibilities of gold', she argues, is 'a necessary aid to gathering investment funds', not only for a sham such as Bre-x, but also for non-fraudulent endeavours, as a 'regular feature of the search for financial capital' (Tsing, 2005, 57). The mining exploration industry thus involves what she calls an 'economy of appearances', in which dramatic performance serves as a prerequisite for economic performance. In Marieke de Goede's words: 'the magical storytelling of investment opportunities [...] performatively constitutes "real" economic performance, in the form of measured international capital flows, investments, stock prices, etc'. (2005, 8). While this is particularly true for junior mining companies, dependent as they are on the attraction of venture capital, in the following sections I show that the greenfields exploration programme of mining major AGA involved a similar generation of hype, which served to legitimise investment in high-risk exploration strategies and to entice investment in further exploration.

Corporate meaning-making in the production of extractive frontiers involves the imagination not only of potential, but also of its counterpart: risk. Typically, companies and investors assess the risk of investing in a certain frontier territory on the basis of tools such as 'political risk' rankings and ratings. In his ethnographic account of London's junior mining market, Paul Gilbert (2020) discusses the imaginative work that goes into the construction of such rankings and ratings. Rather than viewing them as purely calculative devices, he treats them as 'technologies of the imagination' (see also Bear, 2015; Sneath, Holbraad and Pedersen, 2009), and highlights their capacity to produce images of territories as stable or unstable in the investor's imagination. For Gilbert such technologies 'animate speculative activity oriented towards opening up new resource frontiers' (Gilbert, 2020 18), and serve to attract and allocate capital to speculative projects. In the next sections, I draw on his insights to explore the role of corporate storytelling in the imagination of both potential and risk in Colombia.

3 País minero

A team of AGA geologists first visited Colombia in early 1999 (AGA, 2016). At the time, only a handful of foreign gold mining companies were active in the country, all of them juniors. Even though no large-scale industry players were active, artisanal, small- and medium-scale gold mining was an important economic activity in Colombia, and has been throughout its history (Álvarez, 2016). In the country's recent history, mining has played a significant role in fuelling Colombia's armed conflict, as illegal gold mining and drug trafficking were the most important source of income for various illegal armed groups (Rettberg and Ortiz-Riomalo, 2016). This conflict had also prevented large corporations from entering the country.

In November 1999, AGA established its first joint venture in Colombia, with US-based junior Conquistador Mines, which had been active in the country since 1996 (AngloGold, 1999). Working with juniors was a central aspect of AGA's 'New Frontiers' strategy, enabling the company to share financial risk, leverage previous exploration findings made by junior companies, and attract experienced geologists previously employed by these juniors (AGA, 2004).

AGA's decision to become active in Colombia had industry-wide significance, as it diverged from the common practice of majors leaving the risk to juniors. It signalled to the wider international investment community that a reassessment of the perception of Colombia as a 'no-go area' might be warranted (see Harris, 2006a). As a director of Greystar Resources (now Eco Oro), another of the few juniors active in Colombia in the late 1990s, stated when AGA's move to Colombia first became public: '[t]he fact that Anglo, the world's largest gold miner, is prepared to put its money into Colombia sends a positive sign to the investment community at large. [...] With more exploration there will be more investment, and more interest in the country' (*BN Americas*, 1999). His statement calls attention to the important role the behaviour of industry peers plays in corporate risk assessment. In Colombia in 1999, the security situation on the ground had not changed substantially, and would in fact worsen over the next few years, but the fact that a mining major signalled that the country was stable enough to risk a major investment started to change the image of Colombia in international investors' imagination, and placed the country more firmly on their radar.

As early as in the second quarter of 2000, AGA reported to shareholders it had obtained 'highly encouraging results' in Colombia (AngloGold, 2000). Similar excitement speaks from a corporate report on an early field visit to the area in the department of Tolima where the company would later make its most significant discovery. It narrates how two North American AGA geologists gathered rocks along a creek near an old artisanal mine that was no longer operational, where they found several boulders that indicated the presence of another gold source further upstream. They were keen to continue following the creek, but Conquistador's security guards, who accompanied them, urged them not to go any further (AGAC, 2008, 10). At the time, the guerilla movement FARC controlled the area, and North American white men gathering rocks in a remote rural area were likely to attract suspicion. They risked being kidnapped, as had indeed happened to personnel of Canadian junior Greystar Resources in another part of the country two years earlier (Harris, 2006a). The geologists would have to wait for over five years before they could visit the area further upstream.

In the meantime, while the company still considered field visits too dangerous the Greenfields team prepared its Colombian exploration strategy on the basis of desk research, drawing on its initial field visits as well as geological information from the Colombian government and Canadian juniors. Even though the team had hardly been able to spend time on the ground, at the end of 2003 'the decision was made to focus the majority of the South American exploration budget on the "new frontier" of Colombia, given the interpreted high prospectivity of the country' (Lodder et al., 2010, 23). AGA also moved its exploration office for the Americas from Lima to Bogotá (Harris, 2006b).

Political and policy changes following the turn of the millennium were also of great significance to making Colombia imaginable as a mining frontier. During the 1990s, in the wake of the 'Washington Consensus', many Latin American countries reformed their mining legislation (Bury and Bebbington, 2013; Hogenboom, 2012). The current Colombian Mining Code (Law 685 of 2001) is a late product of this neo-liberal wave. It prioritised international investment through tax incentives and by opening the process of obtaining mining titles to foreign corporations (Echavarría, 2014; Vélez-Torres, 2014). In a newspaper interview on the subject of the legislative reform, the Minister of Mining argued that 'if good mining conditions are not put in place soon, [Colombia] will no longer be competitive, and natural rivals, especially within the region, will attract the capital that Colombia will definitively lose' (*El Tiempo*, 2000). His statements echoed the findings of a World Bank report, which concluded that in order to attract international investment Colombia needed to follow neighbouring countries and reform its mining legislation (World Bank, 1996, 7). Under the new mining law, the Colombian state remained the owner of the subsoil and its resources, but handed over control over production to the (international) private sector, while taking on the dual role of regulator as well as facilitator and promotor of extractive activity (UPME, 2006). Especially in this latter role, the state's narrative and performative practices, in conjunction with those of companies such as AGA, were crucial to conjuring Colombia as a gold mining frontier.

When AGA started its Colombian exploration campaign, Colombia had just elected a new president. Álvaro Uribe would be in power from 2002 to 2010. He sought to change Colombia's image as a country plagued by narco-violence and guerilla kidnappings to that of a stable and attractive investment destination, in particular for mining corporations (UPME, 2006). Uribe implemented a conservative security policy aimed at weakening the FARC through a systematic, US-backed military counter-insurgency operation. The policy successfully weakened the FARC and, in the eyes of many Colombians, restored security and stability in many parts of the country. This increased stability, however, came at the expense of marginalised communities. Many vulnerable people, in particular from peasant, indigenous and Afro-Colombian communities, fell victim to extrajudicial killings and forced displacement by the Colombian army and paramilitary groups (Isacson, 2010; Rojas, 2009).

Uribe actively sought to present Colombia as a '*país minero*' ('mining country') to international investors. To reassure investors, and mitigate the risk that the presence of armed groups constituted from an investor perspective, his government offered military protection to mining, oil, energy and construction companies—the industries most frequently targeted by guerilla groups (O'Connor and Bohórquez Montoya, 2010). Uribe also gave several performances aimed at the international mining investment community, which were crucial to making Colombia imaginable as an investment destination. In 2005, he gave a long speech at the '*Feria Internacional Minera*', an internationally oriented mining conference in Medellín, telling investors how he sought to make Colombia 'a country of great investment attraction, which will be fashionable not briefly, but for a long time' (Uribe, 2005, author's translation). A Canadian newspaper noted how Uribe 'wasn't on the official conference program, but showed up to deliver a remarkable three-hour discourse, challenging delegates to tell him what needs to be done to make Colombia more attractive for miners' (Harris, 2006a).

The way the narrative on Colombia in the international investor community gradually started to shift is illustrated by international mining industry journals from this period. Articles from around 2005 to 2010 typically highlight the country's great gold mining potential alongside an improving security situation for foreign miners, with headings such as 'Colombia's troubles pale next to golden opportunities' (Harris, 2006a) or 'Colombia's untapped gold potential lures wary miners' (Danielson, 2008). In an often spectacular tone, they talk about Colombia, a 'country once dangerous from civil war' and 'a pariah for most mining investors' (Harris, 2006a), now 'rapidly becoming a sought-after destination for mining investment' (Harris, 2007), and quote mining analysts speaking of it being 'very probable that there exist large undiscovered reserves' and 'gigantic potential to develop gold mining activity' (Harris, 2006b). In the words of Canadian industry journal *The Northern Miner*, 'One of South America's historically richest gold-producing nations appears poised to regain a crown that was stolen by years of endemic corruption, crime and warfare. Colombia is finally awakening from the social and political nightmare that robbed it of foreign direct investment for the last many decades' (Vaccaro, 2009). The interest Colombia was generating was, for instance, clear at the Prospectors & Developers Association of Canada conference in 2007, one of the largest international mining exploration conferences, where a presentation on Colombia was 'standing room only' (Hoffman, 2007). According to a Canadian embassy representative, 'Colombia is the poster child of the mining world and people are excited to come and work here now' (quoted in Harris, 2007).

A further indication of the shift in the way investors imagined Colombia was the country's inclusion in the Fraser Institute's Annual Survey of Mining Companies in 2006. This survey ranks a selection of countries based on their 'attractiveness' in terms of geological potential and regulatory framework, based on the perceptions of industry professionals, and plays a significant role in making new 'frontier territories' legible to international investors (Gilbert, 2020). Colombia did not rank highly, according to the survey likely due to 'years of turmoil and bad publicity' (Fraser Institute, 2007, 6), although it topped its regional competitors Venezuela and Bolivia. One of the analysts leading the survey commented that he was 'personally not sure whether this reflects today's situation, or whether miners with memories of the recent past are not aware of the very great improvements that have taken place in Colombia' (McMahon in Hill, 2010). Even so, the fact that Colombia was considered of sufficient interest to be included in itself indicates a significant shift in the investor imagination.

4 Mining Title Bonanza

The reform of the Mining Code, combined with the growing interest in Colombia, led to a strong surge in applications for mining titles—the concessions through which the state gives a person or company the right to explore the subsoil of a certain area. The state agency in charge of granting and controlling these titles at the time was the Colombian Geology and Mining Institute, Ingeominas. Before 2001, Ingeominas granted 80 to 100 mining permits per year. Under the Uribe Administration, it granted 7,869 mining titles in a period of eight years, thereby increasing the number of hectares of land under mining concession from 1.13 million to 8.53 million (Osorio, 2010). Colombian media referred to this fast-paced process of title applications, and the speculation that ensued, as the 'mining titles bazaar' (*feria de títulos mineros*).

As the first mining major to invest in Colombia, and aided by the timing of the legislative reform, AGA was in an ideal position to stake its claim for mining titles. It referred to this position as its 'first mover advantage'. In what an industry publication called a 'blitzkrieg staking program' (Harris, 2006b), AGA applied for a very large number of titles. Exact figures are unclear, but according to a 2007 corporate report, AGA applied for an area covering 13 million hectares, which it reduced to 3.7 million hectares after initial exploration activities (AGA, 2008a, 2). An article by the lead geologists involved speaks of systematic reconnaissance exploration 'covering about 10.5 million hectares' (Lodder et al., 2010, 19).

AGA obtained its titles through a complex web of tax haven–based holding companies and Colombia-based subsidiaries, as well as separate subsidiaries created for joint ventures with other mining companies, which together provided the capital needed for its exploration activities in Colombia. From 2003, it operated through a Colombian subsidiary called Sociedad Kedahda, in 2007 renamed AngloGold Ashanti Colombia. Critics claim that AGA used a different name 'to acquire a large number of mining concessions throughout the country, while keeping a low profile', as the name of a well-known multinational would attract more societal scrutiny (Colombia Solidarity Campaign, 2013, 32). The company denied that it used a different name 'to operate in secret' (AGAC, 2013), although elsewhere, in a more general sense, it recognised that 'we went through a phase with a lot of silence, in which we sent the message that the project was secret. The reason we did not speak was that the information [on AGA's discoveries] was still very preliminary, not because it was confidential' (Celedón, 2014, author's translation).

At the time of my fieldwork, which took place around 15 years later, the exceptionally large area to which AGA had access for exploration continued to inspire stories about AGA's dominant position during its early days in Colombia. Greenfields employees, for instance, described the early exploration years to me as a time when AGA employed 'almost all field geologists in Colombia' to conduct a systematic exploration across the Colombian Andes. A corporate report speaks of 'employing as many as 127 field geologists at a time' (Lodder et al., 2010, 23), and an industry journal from this period notes with fascination how, '[h]aving taken a huge land position in Colombia', AGA was 'in the process of turning over every rock in the country' (Harris, 2006c). 'When we first came to Colombia', a senior geologist told me, 'they just had this new legislation for staking land. What we did was basically stake the whole country'. The idea that Colombia was 'AGA's for the taking' was also echoed by Tim Coughlin, AGA's former chief geologist for South America, in an interview with a mining news website:

> We walked into the old licensing department, and people thought we were crazy. 'Where did you guys come from? People don't invest in our country'. We had the place to ourselves, it was ludicrous. There were immeasurable amounts of opportunity and resources all over the place.
>
> KWANTES AND HUMPHREYS, 2015

In its communications to investors and shareholders, AGA frequently prided itself on its 'first mover' position and the mining titles it was able to acquire as a result. 'AGA will continue to push its first-mover advantage and dominant land position, particularly as major competitors realise the potential of Colombia, which has not seen a major gold mine development for decades', the multinational's 2010 annual report states (AGA, 2011, 131).

Within the wider international mining community, 'AGA's bullish entry' (Harris, 2006b) was generally regarded with admiration. Clive Johnson, the

CEO of B2Gold, one of AGA's joint-venture partners in Colombia, commented in an industry journal:

> AngloGold did a very bold thing by going into Colombia several years ago, when it was still a very dangerous place. They were able to tie up so much ground because many other companies feared to tread there. I tip my hat to them for that.
>
> Global Business Reports, 2011, 91

The quote further illustrates how, in the 'first mover' narrative of boldness and bravado that surrounds AGA's entry into Colombia, even the company's decision to enter the country during a particularly violent period of internal armed conflict was regarded with admiration rather than reservation. Rather than questioning the ethical and political sensitivity of AGA's decision, industry peers seemed to admire exactly this ostensible ruthlessness regarding the political and security implications of its arrival. An analyst's note written two decades after AGA's move to Colombia still reflects this sentiment:

> AGA [...] came in in the early 2000's and staked all the good bits, this even as the war was in full swing [and] bombs were going off in Bogotá. The people at the mine office thought the Anglo people were crazy, which might not have been too far from the truth.
>
> POLLITT, 2020, 7

AGA's own public narrative about its decision to start exploring during the conflict did not highlight this 'boldness', but framed it, in a seemingly politically naive way, as a contribution to greater stability in the region:

> Given the internal conflict in Colombia, AGA was well aware of the risks it faced when it entered Colombia. [...] Our objective is to find viable projects in Colombia, projects that can be developed into mines which will form an economic hub in the areas where they are situated. It is our hope that this will lead to other commercial ventures being established, bringing greater stability and improved living standards to the communities concerned.
>
> AGA, 2008a, 2

Nevertheless, AGA's sweeping entry also had a flip side, as my conversations with AGA officials made clear. Many employees I spoke to retrospectively saw the mass accumulation of mining titles as a strategic mistake. They considered that it had reinforced the public image of the 'voracious multinational', strengthening anti-mining sentiments that continue to hinder the company's activities in Colombia to this day. In the words of a senior geologist, 'Lots of mining titles are worth absolutely nothing when you don't have access to the land'.

5 Speculation and Superlatives

In 2006, the Greenfields team returned to the area where, as I described earlier, AGA geologists had previously found indications of a mineral source but had not been able to continue their fieldwork due to security concerns. In its report on the second quarter of 2007, the company started to make cautiously optimistic announcements about its find, named 'La Colosa', calling its interim drilling results 'encouraging' (AGA, 2007). La Colosa would become AGA's most important discovery in Colombia.

While AGA executives spoke to investors about their drilling results, only very few locals living near the company's exploration site were aware of the activities taking place in the steep mountains surrounding their town, Cajamarca. This changed in December 2007, when not AGA but the national newspaper *El Tiempo* announced the discovery to the Colombian public with an article entitled 'Gold reserve that would be among the ten biggest in the world, discovered in Cajamarca (Tolima)'. According to the article, a South African multinational, AGA, had discovered 'a supremely large deposit', which it had announced to President Uribe and the Minister of Mining in a private meeting. AGA executives had asked Uribe to keep the information confidential, but 'he could not resist the urge to talk about the discovery, and said that the deposit would require investments of over two billion dollars' (*El Tiempo*, 2007). The company confirmed the 'supreme' size of the La Colosa deposit several months later. The first resource estimate it released, in May 2008, estimated the deposit held 12.9 million ounces of gold (AGA, 2008b). This more than doubled the estimated resources of its greenfields portfolio at the time. AGA's Colombian discovery made waves on a global scale, as its share price on the New York Stock Exchange peaked following the company's declaration (see AGA, 2011, 7). Over the following years the company would continue to announce higher and higher estimates. In 2012, when the company almost doubled its initial estimate to 24 million ounces, an excited analyst commented:

> La Colosa, AGA's flagship project in Tolima, has gone from big to huge. [...] The size of the gold resource is astonishing: less than 2% of gold projects

> have a resource of over 10 Moz Au [million ounces of gold], and La Colosa has now grown to become one of the most important gold projects in the world, and the most important discovery in recent times, making it by far Colombia's largest and most important gold project.
>
> Colombia Gold Letter, 2012

The size of the deposit would eventually be estimated at over 28 million ounces (AGA, 2021), making La Colosa a key symbol of AGA's conquest of the 'new frontier'.

AGA executives frequently presented their exploration activities in Colombia at large international mining industry conferences. These conferences gather large numbers of mining companies, investors and analysts, and constitute an important place for the creation and promotion of industry narratives. This makes them a key venue for corporate storytelling. The presentations companies give at these conferences may be seen as ritualised performances that serve to attract mining investment and sustain investor confidence (see also Rajak, 2011b). AGA's presentations on Colombia typically figure slides with a map of the country, on which the company's large 'area of interest' is marked out, visualising the company's territorial dominance by showing its widespread presence across the Western and Central Cordillera of the Colombian Andes (see, e.g., AGA, 2006; AGA, 2012a). Other common elements in these conference presentations are an emphasis on the company's 'first mover advantage' and its resulting 'strong position in the world's most prospective new gold district' (AGA 2012a). La Colosa in particular is often discussed in superlative terms, for instance as 'the most significant new gold discovery of the current era' (AGA, 2009), or 'a global tier-one deposit […] a large world-class gold resource [that is] getting bigger, and is only the tip of the iceberg given a wealth of targets in Colombia' (AGA, 2012b). AGA's presentations at industry conferences illustrate how, through spectacular language and visuals, the company fostered a dramatic narrative of conquest and discovery to entice investors and sustain its high-risk greenfields strategy in Colombia.

6 Greenfields Mythologising

AGA's narrative practices were not only directed towards investors and shareholders, but also played a vital role inside the company, especially for the Greenfields department. As I have already discussed, during my fieldwork inside the company Greenfields employees recounted legends of the early days of AGA's greenfields exploration campaign in Colombia. This was striking, as most of these employees had not personally been involved in the heyday of this campaign, which perhaps made this period seem all the more mythical to them. In this section, I discuss two aspects of this internal 'corporate mythologizing' (Rajak, 2014, 259): the myth-making among Greenfields employees around large discoveries, and the internal narratives on what it means to be an exploration geologist. Both are integral to shaping corporate and professional identity.

Discovering a deposit viable for exploitation is what makes or breaks the career of an exploration geologist. This makes the fact that AGA's exploration team made three discoveries that could be developed into mining projects all the more exceptional. In addition to La Colosa, the team made two smaller but substantial discoveries: Gramalote, in 2007, and the more recent find of Nuevo Chaquiro or Quebradona, in 2014. On its web page on exploration, AGA proudly cites a report that recognises the AGA Greenfields team as the world's most successful, with 'a proven track record that includes the discovery of world-class ore bodies in Colombia at La Colosa, Gramalote and Nuevo Chaquiro' (AGA, n.d.), showing the great relevance of the Colombian discoveries to the business at the global level.

Large greenfields discoveries lend themselves well to mythologising. Geologists who have been involved in important discoveries typically develop a 'discovery history', which they disseminate in geological publications (for La Colosa, see, e.g., Lodder et al., 2010), and at exploration-focused industry conferences. Some of these events even specifically focus on storytelling, by gathering geologists who have been involved in recent discoveries to tell the exploration community about their discovery process. An example is the Australian 'NewGenGold' conference, which promotes itself as 'consistently featur[ing] the case histories of most of the world's more important gold discoveries' (NewGenGold, n.d.). The importance of these discovery histories shows how corporate mythologising is not only integral to attracting investment at the stage when a discovery is no more than a promise, but is a key part of the business of mining exploration in a broader sense. Stories of successful discovery contribute to sustaining the quest for new frontiers by making exploration success tangible.

Inside AGA's Greenfields department in Colombia, its discoveries were also the object of extensive myth-making, and employees avidly told and retold these tall tales among themselves. One such greenfields legend concerned the name 'La Colosa'. Mining projects are traditionally named by exploration geologists after a landmark in the area of discovery, such as the name of a creek, estate, or mountain. This also appears to be the case for La Colosa, which is named after the creek from which the first rock samples were collected. Was it a coincidence that this 'colossal' discovery was made in a creek with such a fitting name? According to a greenfields legend I was told by various employees, it was not in fact the discovery that was named after the creek, but the creek that was named after the discovery. This story revolves around a Colombian geologist who was part of the exploration team that returned to Cajamarca in 2006 to take further samples, whom I will refer to using the pseudonym Santi(ago). A Greenfields employee told me (interview, 2 May 2017):

> Santiago has an exceptional instinct. He is *un terco* [someone stubborn] but knows when something is worth going after. In Cajamarca, he could tell from the first rocks they analysed that they were after something gigantic. Did you know that they say that he was the one who gave the creek where they were prospecting the name of La Colosa? They were using an old map of the region, on which the name of the creek was not legible. All they could make out was 'La Col'. Santi felt that they were after something colossal, so he took a pen, and changed the name of the creek on the map by scribbling 'La Col.-osa'. Since then, everyone has called the creek La Colosa.

The story is a true tale of conquest, in which the gifted exploration geologist not only discovers the deposit, but, in an ultimate act of appropriation, even renames the creek where he made the discovery. According to an article by the geologists involved in the La Colosa discovery, the creek was originally named 'La Cólogan', 'later renamed by AngloGold Ashanti La Colosa Creek' (Lodder et al., 2010, 26).

AGA's more recent greenfields discovery in Colombia, 'Nuevo Chaquiro', was also the subject of many stories I was told by Greenfields employees, as many workers employed at the time of my fieldwork had been involved in this find. The discovery had been much anticipated, as it had come after several years of unsatisfactory drilling work, and was referred to by Greenfields employees as 'the miracle of Quebradona' (interview, 2 May 2017):

> We had been exploring for several years but did not find anything significant. The process was coming to a close and we knew that eventually, we all would lose our jobs. The envelopes with our termination letters were ready, so to say. One afternoon, the Australian lead geologist came into the office, and said, 'Everyone, stop what you are doing, I have a big announcement to make'. We all thought, there it is, we are all getting sacked. But he said, 'Let's go out, we're going to celebrate. We have made an important discovery!'

In this story, again, Santi is a heroic character:

> The company had been on the brink of shutting down the project for a while, but Santi had insisted that there was something there. He managed to convince the company to start one last round of drilling to a deeper level than had previously been performed in Colombia: over one kilometre deep. It turned out that all this time, we simply had not gone deep enough. The deposit had been there all along, but it was covered under a thick layer of rock without mineralization, and we had to drill deeper to get to the mineral.

As the heroic stories about Santi show, among the Greenfields personnel, exploration geologists who were considered responsible for key discoveries were elevated to the rank of almost mythical figures. Another revered geologist was AGA Colombia's first president, who had played a leading role in the La Colosa discovery. The geologist who led the exploration team in Colombia at the time of my fieldwork, for instance, looked up to him as a 'very inventive geologist', who had 'convinced Anglo to go to Colombia'. Interestingly, whereas modern mining exploration involves complex scientific procedures and the use of advanced technologies, the mythology around individual 'hero' geologists centres on their instinctive ability to sense opportunity and their audacity in pursuing these intuitions. These epic stories maintain the age-old image of greenfields exploration as a magical process of gold seeking, in which intuition and boldness are eventually rewarded.

The stories told and retold among Greenfields personnel are central to shaping a distinct 'greenfields identity'. Amid engineers, managers, lawyers and other bureaucrats, they allowed exploration geologists to think of themselves as the bold pioneers who venture into remote mountain areas to look for gold. A senior Greenfields manager described exploration geologists to me as 'the adventurous types [...] who dare to get on a plane and go to a country they don't know, even if there is a war'. The performance of this greenfields identity extended beyond stories to the way Greenfields personnel presented themselves. In the Bogotá office, for instance, they walked around in sturdy mountain boots, in sharp contrast to the smart business attire worn by most of their colleagues from other departments. The Greenfields desks were also easily recognisable in the open plan office space, as Greenfields employees typically decorated their desks with mineralised rocks and fragments of drilling samples—greenfields symbols in an otherwise corporate space. Thus, narrative and performance were key to shaping greenfields identity.

Notably, these greenfields stories are also deeply gendered. They involve a celebration of particularly 'male' qualities, such as being bold and unabashed, and are typically centred around a male hero figure. In contrast, the greenfields vernacular uses terms of a female origin to describe the pristine character of greenfields discoveries. Greenfields finds are, for instance, referred to as 'virgin' discoveries (e.g., AGA, 2011, 45), and the initial resource estimate a company releases after discovery the 'maiden resource' (e.g., AGA, 2014). This way, the 'greenfields identity' shaped through corporate storytelling is a gendered identity.

The gendered identity of the exploration geologist was also reflected in the gender distribution of the Greenfields department, which employed very few women, most of whom worked in social roles, for instance as community liaisons, rather than in geology. At the time of my fieldwork, the department did have one female geologist, whom I will call Adriana. When she was not on field trips, she worked in the Bogotá office, where I got to know her. Whereas most women in the office dressed in a more stereotypically feminine way, Adriana had bright pink hair and a tomboyish style. When I asked her what it was like to work as the only woman on the team, she told me, 'I already don't notice it anymore. In my team, there is not much machismo. When you work together, it doesn't matter if you are a man or a woman, I don't feel it'. It seemed to me that Adriana's way of dealing with the male dominance of the Greenfields department was by conforming to the greenfields identity of being cool, bold and adventurous, downplaying her femininity in the way she presented herself, in the way she talked, and seemingly even in the way she thought about this. This involved a constant tension between her ignoring or even 'undoing' gender difference, and acting and speaking in particularly gendered ways (see also Smith, 2014, Chapter 5).

Greenfields identity was not only shaped from the inside, but also by other actors in the company, outside the Greenfields department. While they shared the reverence for geologists who had made important discoveries, other employees tended to highlight the cowboy reputation of these geologists. A former manager of government relations, for instance, described Lodder to me as 'brilliant' but '*un bruto*' (a rogue) because 'he went to very dangerous parts of the country without any form of protocol' (see Welker (2014, 47) for a similar narrative on greenfields geologists by Newmont's CSR personnel). The executive talked to me at length about how he saw 'the greenfields geologist', whom he found difficult to manage and spoke of as if he were discussing an exotic species: 'a greenfields geologist is, by nature, independent, and does not want to be restricted by too many limits. To be successful, he needs to be as flexible and quick as possible'. Another manager described greenfields geologists as 'very keen on maintaining their independence', and had found that they tended to resist managers who attempted to impose rules and protocols. Greenfields geologists themselves saw such characterisations as a misunderstanding of what greenfields exploration really involves, and argued that colleagues who criticised the 'greenfields way of working' had not properly understood that 'the skills explorationists need to have are to be agile, flexible, adaptive'. These various and sometimes incompatible stories from inside and outside the Greenfields department shaped the understanding people inside the company had of greenfields identity, which formed a controversial but essential part of the company. This identity, in turn, corresponded to the company's image in the wider sector as a bold, visionary and at times perhaps reckless greenfields explorer.

7 Suspended Capitalisation and Alternative Stories

In this chapter, I have argued that the study of extractive frontier expansion requires attention to narrative, imagination and performance, as this allows us to see how seemingly abstract market dynamics are embedded in, and enabled by, deeply social practices. AGA's exploration campaign in Colombia illustrates how storytelling and imagination were key to making mining exploration possible. This chapter has illustrated how Colombia was actively conjured as the 'last Andean frontier' for gold exploration in the corporate, shareholder, and investor imaginations through narrative and performative practices, by both state and industry. To AGA specifically, this imagination of Colombia's subsurface potential and the generation of hype around it were key to attracting the investment required for its extensive exploration campaign, which yielded important mineral discoveries.

Yet the case of AGA in Colombia also crucially illustrates the other side of this argument: storytelling is crucial for advancing mining exploration and exploitation, but alternative stories to extractive frontier expansion are also possible. The spectacular narratives I have discussed in this chapter did not go uncontested, but competed with other imaginations for the country's future. AGA's performance of greenfields bravado on the one hand earned the company a competitive advantage as 'first mover' and admiration from industry peers, but the hype it generated around its exploration campaign also exposed the company to intense public scrutiny from an early stage. This turned La Colosa into a flagship project not only for AGA and the Uribe Administration, but also for a growing anti-mining movement of concerned peasants, national and local politicians, and environmental activists in alliance with international NGOs.

The opposition to La Colosa continues to be one of the most prominent cases of mining resistance in the country. In March 2017, a coalition of anti-mining groups successfully organised a municipal referendum to ban mining in Cajamarca, the town where the project is located (*BBC Mundo*, 2017). A month later, AGA decided to indefinitely suspend the project, citing uncertainty in the permitting process as well as the result of the anti-mining vote (AGAC, 2017). The project remains suspended to this day. At its other projects in Colombia, the company also continues to struggle to obtain the environmental licences and permits it needs to advance into the exploitation phase (Jamasmie, 2022). This illustrates how the capitalisation of subsurface resource potential, the transformation of a discovery into an extractive operation, is not a given, even after a deposit has been found.

Narrative, imaginative and performative practices are integral to the making of resources and extractive frontiers. While these practices are interconnected with a mining project's viability, they do not necessarily or straightforwardly enable the actual realisation of a mining operation. Whether or not extractive frontier expansion materialises is the result of an uneven and speculative process involving (temporary) deferrals and disruptions, competing anticipations of financial gain and environmental damage, and a complex interaction of geological substances with the imaginations of geologists and financiers, assessments of financial, environmental and political risk, legal arrangements and volatile commodity prices. As Gisa Weszkalnys characterises it, the process through which resources and frontiers are made is 'simultaneously ethically charged, materially grounded, and temporally extended into an uncertain future' (2015, 633). In Colombia, stories and imaginations alternative to an extractive future are central to a polarised public debate on whether and in what way there is a place for large-scale mining in the country's future, reinvigorated by the growing demand for transition minerals, on the one hand (ANM, 2021), and the election of an outspoken opponent of the extractive industries as president, on the other. Whether or not Colombia will indeed turn out to be the last Andean frontier for industrial gold mining is a story still being written.

Acknowledgements

For valuable feedback on earlier drafts, I am grateful to Filipe Calvão, Matthew Archer, Asanda Benya, Kuntala Lahiri-Dutt, Paul Gilbert, and two anonymous reviewers.

References

AGA (AngloGold Ashanti) (n.d.) *Exploration*, (Johannesburg: AGA) http://www.anglogoldashanti.com/operations/exploration/ (accessed on 18 September 2020).

AGA (2021) *Mineral Resource and Ore Reserve Report 2020* (Johannesburg: AGA).
AGA (2016) *Discovery and Geology of the Nuevo Chaquiro CU-AU (AG-MO) Porphyry Deposit*, Corporate presentation by Nick Winer at ADIMB—Simexmin, Ouro Preto, Brazil, 16 May.
AGA (2014) Release of Maiden Resource for Nuevo Chaquiro Deposit, press release, 3 November.
AGA (2012a) *AngloGold Ashanti: 'Delivering Sustainable Value'*, Corporate presentation by Mark Cutifani at Denver Gold Forum, Denver, CO, 11 September.
AGA (2012b) *Compelling Value: the AngloGold Ashanti Story*, Corporate presentation by Mark Cutifani at Scotiabank Latin American Mining Conference, October.
AGA (2011) *Annual Financial Statements 2010: Pure Gold* (Johannesburg: AGA).
AGA (2009) *Macquarie Gold Rush Conference*, Corporate presentation at Macquarie Gold Rush Conference, Sydney, 2 June.
AGA (2008a) *Country Report Colombia 2007* (Johannesburg: AGA).
AGA (2008b) AngloGold Ashanti Announces Significant Exploration Results at 100% Owned La Colosa Project in Colombia, press release, 6 May.
AGA (2007) 'Q2 2007 Anglogold Ashanti Limited Earnings Conference Call', 31 July (Johannesburg: AGA).
AGA (2006) *Denver Gold Forum*, Corporate presentation by Bobby Godsell and Richard Duffy at Denver Gold Forum, Denver, CO, 26 September.
AGA (2005) *Report to Society* (Johannesburg: AGA).
AGA (2004) *Managing Risk Beyond Mature Gold Regions*, Corporate presentation by Richard Duffy and Gordon Wylie at Gold Investment Summit (London), 5 November.
AGAC (AngloGold Ashanti Colombia) (2017) Comunicado Oficial Sobre La Colosa: AngloGold Ashanti Acepta Resultados de La Consulta Popular y Reduce al Mínimo Sus Actividades En Cajamarca, press release, 27 April, https://www.anglogoldashanticolombia.com/comunicado-oficial-la-colosa/ (accessed on 26 June 2022).
AGAC (2013) '*Consideraciones de AnlgoGold Ashanti Colombia Sobre El Documento de Colombia Solidarity Campaign Titulado 'La Colosa: Una Muerte Anunciada'*', Company response in Business & Human Rights Resource Centre portal.
AGAC (2008) *Estudio Socioeconómico y Ambiental de Cajamarca Área de Influencia del Proyecto de Exploración Minera La Colosa Fase III* (Bogotá: AGAC).
Ali, S.H., D. Giurco, N. Arndt, E. Nickless, G. Brown, A. Demetriades, R. Durrheim, M.A. Enriquez, J. Kinnaird, A. Littleboy, L.D. Meinert, R. Oberhänsli, J. Salem, R. Schodde, G. Schneider, O. Vidal and N. Yakovleva (2017) 'Mineral Supply for Sustainable Development Requires Resource Governance', *Nature*, 543(7645), pp. 367–372, DOI: 10.1038/nature21359.
Álvarez, J.D. (2016) 'Governing Mining Resources in the History of Colombia: Between Official Institutions and Resistance', *Law and Development Review*, 9(1), pp. 29–67, DOI: 10.1515/ldr-2015-0022.

AngloGold (2000) *AngloGold Results for the Quarter and Six Months Ended 30 June 2000*, Quarterly report (Johannesburg: AngloGold), 27 July, accessed through London Stock Exchange Aggregated Regulatory News Service.

AngloGold (1999) AngloGold South America Limited Takes Stake in Colombian Exploration Project, press release, 19 November.

ANM (Agencia Nacional de Minería) (2021) "Colombia Tiene Potencial Minero Para Aportar a La Transición Energética": Presidente de La ANM, press release, 21 April, https://www.anm.gov.co/?q=colombia-tiene-potencial-minero-para-aportar-la-transicion-energetica-presidente-de-la-anm (accessed on 11 June 2022).

BBC Mundo (2017) 'Cajamarca, el pueblo de Colombia que le dijo no a la explotación minera', *BBC News*, 27 March, https://www.bbc.com/mundo/noticias-america-latina-39407877 (accessed on 18 September 2020).

Bear, L. (2015) 'Capitalist Divination: Popularist Speculators and Technologies of Imagination on the Hooghly River', *Comparative Studies of South Asia, Africa and the Middle East*, 35(3), pp. 408–423, DOI: 10.1215/1089201X-3426265.

Bebbington, A.J., D. Humphreys Bebbington, L.A. Sauls, J. Rogan, S. Agrawal, C. Gamboa, A. Imhof, K. Johnson, H. Rosa, A. Royo, T. Toumbourou and R. Verdum (2018) 'Resource Extraction and Infrastructure Threaten Forest Cover and Community Rights', *Proceedings of the National Academy of Sciences*, 115(52), pp. 13164–13173, DOI: 10.1073/pnas.1812505115.

BN Americas (1999) *Greystar Says AngloGold Move Good for Colombia*, Business News Americas, 24 November.

Bury, J. and A. Bebbington (2013) 'New Geographies of Extractive Industries in Latin America', in A. Bebbington and J. Bury (eds.) *Subterranean Struggles: New Dynamics of Mining, Oil, and Gas in Latin America* (Austin, TX: University of Texas Press), pp. 27–66, DOI: 10.7560/748620-004.

Celedón, N. (2014) *'Esperamos que La Colosa tenga licencia ambiental en 2020'*, Portafolio, 6 November, https://www.portafolio.co/negocios/empresas/esperamos-colosa-tenga-licencia-ambiental-2020-63888 (accessed on 18 September 2020).

Colombia Gold Letter (2012) *La Colosa Goes World Class*, Colombia Gold Letter No. 10.

Colombia Solidarity Campaign (2013) *La Colosa: a Death Foretold* (London: Colombia Solidarity Campaign), https://www.colombiasolidarity.org.uk/wp-content/uploads/2013/12/attachments_article_612_LA-COLOSA_A-Death-Foretold.pdf (accessed on 18 September 2020).

Danielson, V. (2008) *Colombia's Untapped Gold Potential Lures Wary Miners*, The Northern Miner, 3 March, https://www.northernminer.com/news/colombia-s-untapped-gold-potential-lures-wary-miners/1000220367/ (accessed on 25 January 2023).

Danielson, V. (2005) *A Good Gold Mine Is Hard to Find*, The Northern Miner, 23 May, https://www.northernminer.com/news/a-good-gold-mine-is-hard-to-find/1000169305/ (accessed on 25 January 2023).

Dolan, C. and D. Rajak (eds.) (2016) *The Anthropology of Corporate Social Responsibility* (Oxford: Berghahn).

Echavarría, C. (2014) *'What Is Legal?' Formalising Artisanal and Small-Scale Mining in Colombia* (London: International Institute for Environment and Development), https://pubs.iied.org/sites/default/files/pdfs/migrate/16565IIED.pdf (accessed on 18 September 2020).

El Tiempo (2007) *Hallan En Cajamarca (Tolima) Reserva de Oro Que Estaría Entre Las 10 Más Grandes Del Mundo*, El Tiempo, 21 December, https://www.eltiempo.com/archivo/documento/CMS-3871744 (accessed on 18 September 2020).

El Tiempo (2000) *Es Urgente Modernizar Legislación Minera*, El Tiempo, 9 October, https://www.eltiempo.com/archivo/documento/MAM-1285528 (accessed on 18 September 2020).

Ferry, E. (2020) 'Speculative Substance: 'Physical Gold' in Finance', *Economy and Society*, 49(1), pp. 92–115, DOI: 10.1080/03085147.2019.1690254.

Foster, R.J. (2017) 'The Corporation in Anthropology', in G. Baars and A. Spicer (eds.) *The Corporation* (Cambridge: Cambridge University Press), pp. 111–133.

Fraser Institute (2007) *The Fraser Institute Annual Survey of Mining Companies, 2006/2007* (Vancouver: The Fraser Institute), https://www.fraserinstitute.org/studies/annual-survey-mining-companies-2006-2007 (accessed on 30 November 2021).

Gilbert, P.R. (2020) 'Speculating on Sovereignty: 'Money Mining' and Corporate Foreign Policy at the Extractive Industry Frontier', *Economy and Society*, 49(1), pp. 16–44, DOI: 10.1080/03085147.2019.1690255.

Global Business Reports (2011) 'Mining in Colombia: Exploring the Last Andean Frontier', *Engineering and Mining Journal*, pp. 79–118, https://www.gbreports.com/wp-content/uploads/2014/12/Colombia_Mining2011.pdf (accessed on 18 September 2020).

Goede, M. de (2005) *Virtue, Fortune and Faith: a Genealogy of Finance* (Minneapolis, MN: University of Minnesota Press).

Harris, P. (2007) *Colombia Poised for Project Startups*, The Northern Miner, 7 October, https://www.northernminer.com/regulatory-issues/colombia-poised-for-project-startups/1000214876/ (accessed on 25 January 2023).

Harris, P. (2006a) *Colombia Gold Again Luring Miners*, The Globe and Mail, 3 January.

Harris, P. (2006b) *Going for Gold in Colombia*, The Northern Miner, 6 March, https://www.northernminer.com/news/going-for-gold-in-colombia/1000201703/ (accessed on 25 January 2023).

Harris, P. (2006c) *Colombia Attracting Mining's Heavy Hitters*, The Northern Miner, 23 October, https://www.northernminer.com/regulatory-issues/colombia-attracting-mining-s-heavy-hitters/1000206632/ (accessed on 25 January 2023).

Hill, L. (2010) 'Mining industry eyes Colombian policy under post-Uribe government', *Mining Weekly*, 23 June.

Hoff, A. (2020) *Power, Fragility and Corporate Social Responsibility: an Ethnography of a Mining Corporation in Colombia*, PhD dissertation (Oxford: University of Oxford), https://ora.ox.ac.uk/objects/uuid:033609d0-6705-4fe5-8695-d72480adb0d9 (accessed on 11 June 2022).

Hoffman, A. (2007) *Mineral Frenzy Tips Risk Scale in Colombia's Favour*, The Globe and Mail, 7 March, https://www.theglobeandmail.com/report-on-business/mineral-frenzy-tips-risk-scale-in-colombias-favour/article20394552/ (accessed on 25 January 2023).

Hogenboom, B. (2012) 'Depoliticized and Repoliticized Minerals in Latin America', *Journal of Developing Societies*, 28(2), pp. 133–158, DOI: 10.1177/0169796X12448755.

IEA (International Energy Agency) (2021) *The Role of Critical Minerals in Clean Energy Transitions* (Paris: IEA), https://www.iea.org/reports/the-role-of-critical-minerals-in-clean-energy-transitions (accessed on 30 November 2021).

Isacson, A. (2010) *Colombia: Don't Call It a Model* (Washington, DC: Washington Office on Latin America), https://www.wola.org/2010/07/colombia-dont-call-it-a-model (accessed on 18 September 2020).

Jamasmie, C. (2022) *Colombia Rejects AngloGold's Appeal over Quebradona License Shelving*, MINING.Com, 2 May, https://www.mining.com/colombia-rejects-anglogolds-appeal-over-quebradona-license-shelving/ (accessed on 11 June 2022).

Kama, K. (2020) 'Resource-Making Controversies: Knowledge, Anticipatory Politics and Economization of Unconventional Fossil Fuels', *Progress in Human Geography* (SAGE Publications Ltd), 44(2), pp. 333–356, DOI: 10.1177/0309132519829223.

Kneas, D. (2020) 'Placing Resources: Junior Mining Companies and the Locus of Mineral Potential', *Geoforum*, 117, pp. 268–278, DOI: 10.1016/j.geoforum.2020.05.007.

Kwantes, J. and T. Humphreys (2015) *Mine-Finder Tim Coughlin Returns to Gold Exploration in Colombia*, MINING.Com, 20 December, https://www.mining.com/web/dow-divide-and-conquer/ (accessed on 18 September 2020).

Lodder, C., R. Padilla, R. Shaw, T. Garzón, E. Palacio and R. Jahoda (2010) 'Discovery History of the La Colosa Gold Porphyry Deposit, Cajamarca, Colombia', in R.J. Goldfarb, E.E. Marsh and T. Monecke (eds.) *The Challenge of Finding New Mineral Resources: Global Metallogeny, Innovative Exploration and New Discoveries* (Littleton, CO: Society of Economic Geologists), DOI: 10.5382/SP.15.1.03.

Luning, S. (2018) 'Mining Temporalities: Future Perspectives', *The Extractive Industries and Society*, 5(2), pp. 281–286, DOI: 10.1016/j.exis.2018.03.009.

NewGenGold (n.d.) 'History of NewGenGold', https://www.newgengold.com/about/history-of-newgengold/ (accessed on 18 September 2020).

O'Connor, D. and J.P. Bohórquez Montoya (2010) 'Neoliberal Transformation in Colombia's Goldfields: Development Strategy or Capitalist Imperialism?', *LABOUR, Capital and Society*, 43(2), pp. 85–118.

Osorio, C. (2010) *El legado minero de Uribe*, La Silla Vacía, 14 October https://archivo.lasillavacia.com/historia/18648 (accessed on 18 September 2020).

Pollitt, D. (2020) *Mind the Gaps* (Toronto: Pollitt & Co).

Rajak, D. (2014) 'Corporate Memory: Historical Revisionism, Legitimation and the Invention of Tradition in a Multinational Mining Company', *PoLAR: Political and Legal Anthropology Review*, 37(2), pp. 259–280, DOI: 10.1111/plar.12074.

Rajak, D. (2011a) *In Good Company: an Anatomy of Corporate Social Responsibility* (Stanford: Stanford University Press).

Rajak, D. (2011b) 'Theatres of Virtue: Collaboration, Consensus, and the Social Life of Corporate Social Responsibility', *Focaal*, 2011(60), pp. 9–20, DOI: 10.3167/fcl.2011.600102.

Rasmussen, M.B. and C. Lund (2018) 'Reconfiguring Frontier Spaces: the Territorialization of Resource Control', *World Development*, 101, pp. 388–399, DOI: 10.1016/j.worlddev.2017.01.018.

Rettberg, A. and J.F. Ortiz-Riomalo (2016) 'Golden Opportunity, or a New Twist on the Resource–Conflict Relationship: Links between the Drug Trade and Illegal Gold Mining in Colombia', *World Development*, 84, pp. 82–96, DOI: 10.1016/j.worlddev.2016.03.020.

Richardson, T. and G. Weszkalnys (2014) 'Resource Materialities', *Anthropological Quarterly*, 87(1), pp. 5–30, DOI: 10.1353/anq.2014.0007.

Rojas, C. (2009) 'Securing the State and Developing Social Insecurities: the Securitisation of Citizenship in Contemporary Colombia', *Third World Quarterly* (Routledge), 30(1), pp. 227–245, DOI: 10.1080/01436590802622631.

Sawyer, S. (2018) 'Corporations', in H. Callan (ed.) *The International Encyclopedia of Anthropology* (Hoboken, NJ: Wiley).

Smith, J.M. (2014) *Mining Coal and Undermining Gender: Rhythms of Work and Family in the American West* (New Brunswick, NJ: Rutgers University Press).

Sneath, D., M. Holbraad and M.A. Pedersen (2009) 'Technologies of the Imagination: an Introduction', *Ethnos*, 74(1), pp. 5–30, DOI: 10.1080/00141840902751147.

Taussig, M. (2010) 'The Corn-Wolf: Writing Apotropaic Texts', *Critical Inquiry*, 37(1), pp. 26–33, DOI: 10.1086/656467.

The Economist (2022) 'Between a Rock and a Hard Place: the Energy Transition Is Sparking America's next Mining Boom', *The Economist*, 19 February, https://www.economist.com/united-states/the-energy-transition-is-sparking-americas-next-mining-boom/21807704 (accessed on 11 June 2022).

Tsing, A.L. (2005) *Friction: an Ethnography of Global Connection* (Princeton, NJ: Princeton University Press).

Turner, F.J. (1921) *The Frontier in American History* (New York City, NY: Henry Holt).

UPME (Unidad de Planeación Minero Energética) (2006) *Colombia País Minero: Plan Nacional Para El Desarrollo Minero, Visión al Año 2019* (Bogotá: UPME).

Uribe, Á. (2005) *Feria Internacional Minera*, Speech, 18 November, https://alvarouribevelez.com.co/discursos-2005-65677/ (accessed on 11 June 2022).

Vaccaro, A. (2009) *Colombia Braces For Renaissance In Gold Mining*, The Northern Miner, 21 September, https://www.northernminer.com/news/colombia-braces-for-renaissance-in-gold-mining/1000341376/ (accessed on 25 January 2023).

Vélez-Torres, I. (2014) 'Governmental Extractivism in Colombia: Legislation, Securitization and the Local Settings of Mining Control', *Political Geography*, 38, pp. 68–78, DOI: 10.1016/j.polgeo.2013.11.008.

Welker, M. (2014) *Enacting the Corporation: an American Mining Firm in Post-Authoritarian Indonesia* (Berkeley, CA: University of California Press).

Weszkalnys, G. (2015) 'Geology, Potentiality, Speculation: On the Indeterminacy of First Oil', *Cultural Anthropology*, 30(4), pp. 611–639, DOI: 10.14506/ca30.4.08.

Weszkalnys, G. (2013) 'Oil's Magic: Contestation and Materiality', in S. Strauss, S. Rupp and T. Love (eds.) *Cultures of Energy: Power, Practices, Technologies* (London: Routledge).

World Bank (2020) *Minerals for Climate Action: the Mineral Intensity of the Clean Energy Transition* (Washington, DC: World Bank), https://pubdocs.worldbank.org/en/961711588875536384/Minerals-for-Climate-Action-The-Mineral-Intensity-of-the-Clean-Energy-Transition.pdf (accessed on 30 November 2021).

World Bank (1996) *A Mining Strategy for Latin America and the Caribbean*, Technical Paper No. 345 (Washington, DC: World Bank), https://documents.worldbank.org/en/publication/documents-reports/documentdetail/650841468087551845/a-mining-strategy-for-latin-america-and-the-caribbean (accessed on 18 September 2020).

CHAPTER 11

(Im)mobility Economies: Extractivism of the Refugee as a Human Commodity

Julia C. Morris

Abstract

This chapter advances a resource extractive framework for understanding the expansion of extraction and capitalist activity into the governance of human mobility. I utilise a theoretical framework centred on resource extraction to argue that the figure of the refugee is entangled in extractive capitalism. Understanding the expansion of extractive industries into 'frontiering' practices requires attention to asylum as a form of governance, powered by a heavily racialised and liberal-positioned performative economy. Asylum is one means of entry across the hardened nation state borders of the current racialised global order. In putting forward an asylum claim, migrants (largely the Black and brown poor from the global South) must perform within a particular objectified narrative, making claims on their bodies to move between sovereign states. This performative dimension can allow for agency, but it is also a mode of subjectification that creates immense power imbalances, while profiting a vast industry of corporate, non-governmental, government, and other actors. Arguing that value is extracted from migrants as resources, I also probe the power of liberal-leftist representations, which help sustain this (im)mobility economy. Tropes of refugee suffering have gained popularity, leading to the fetishisation and durability of refugee extractivism, all while obscuring the massively consequential impacts of the industry. By moving outside of state and industry categorisations, we might better imagine alternative systems of free movement that go beyond adjudicating human worth and solidifying hierarchies of suffering.

1 Introduction

'Each of us has a dollar sign on us. That's how they see us. Just like commodities', Alexia sighed as we sat down at Nauru's boat harbor.[1] She kept a close

1 Pseudonyms are used throughout this chapter to maintain confidentiality.

© GENEVA GRADUATE INSTITUTE, 2024 | DOI:10.1163/9789004685994_012

eye on her children while they played in the water under the heat of the sun, but grew noticeably more frustrated as she described 'the industry' that she saw operating around refugees. 'Without us, this country would go bankrupt again, and look at all these Australian companies contracted here. Do you know how much they're getting? *Multi-millions*. And it's only a few of us here'. Alexia was not exaggerating. By the time I arrived to conduct my fieldwork in the small Pacific island nation of the Republic of Nauru in 2015, the Australian government had spent USD 314 million[2] (AU$415 million) on its Nauru operations that fiscal year alone: almost USD 243,000 (AU$350,000) for each asylum seeker or refugee held on the island. Along with Papua New Guinea's Manus Island, Nauru was at that time the principal seat of the Australian government's 'regional processing arrangements'. As is the case with similar offshored and outsourced 'frontiering' arrangements worldwide, these offshoring operations play out along the fault lines of colonialism (Morris, 2021a). Nauru has a colonial history of phosphate extraction, when the island operated as a company town under the British Phosphate Commission and Australian administrative control (Williams and MacDonald, 1985). After a brief post-independence heyday of local phosphate boom wealth under the new government's Republic of Nauru Phosphate Corporation (RONPhos), the island's new-found billion-dollar economy crashed dramatically. Now, Nauru is neo-colonially restructured in line with processing and resettling refugees for Australian political and organisational profit (Morris, 2019a). On an on-and-off-again basis, anyone who makes their way by boat and claims asylum to Australia is automatically sent to Nauru or Manus for processing and indefinite resettlement.[3]

Alexia was all too aware of the industry dynamics that made her subject to immense profiteering from zealous right-wing and liberal prospectors alike. She, like so many others I spoke with, trying to make their way from global South regions (Afghanistan, Bangladesh, Iran, Iraq, Pakistan, Somalia, Sri Lanka) to Australia, was imbricated in the gruelling process of making her asylum claim. It was this labour-intensive process of making an asylum claim that entangled her and other migrants in the industry's circuits of value. At that time in Nauru's resource frontier, the Australian company Transfield Services held a USD 1.04 billion (AUD 1.5 billion) contract for refugee managerial provisions at the regional processing centres, or 'RPCs', over a period of three

2 Currencies were converted using the exchange rate on 22 July 2022, when 1 AUD = USD 0.692782.

3 As of writing, just over 100 migrants remained living in the country under refugee visas. However, Nauru continues to be financed by the Australian government with the understanding that this operation might be restarted in the future.

years; Save the Children had a contract of USD 25.4 million (AUD 36.7 million) for child welfare activities over one year, and another of USD 53.9 million (AUD 77.8 million) was held by Connect over two years: a consortium of a Melbourne and Brisbane-based NGO contracted into resettling migrants in Nauru. These contracts were not withstanding the immense array of international and Australian medical, legal, interpreting, security, food, goods, housing, construction and transportation contractors, coupled with the local land leasing and entrepreneurial practices, that pushed these human extractive operations into an almost USD 595,523 (AUD 860,000) a person a day industry. Many organisational names were familiar to me before arriving on the island, having already conducted extensive fieldwork into the industry that circulates around migrants and, I soon found, asylum seekers and refugees. In fact, a range of Australian and transnational non-governmental, intergovernmental and corporate providers were active in Nauru's localised business operations, revealing quite how institutionalised the 'refugee business' (Franck, 2018) has become, 'modulating' (Appel, 2019) to new extractive sites in response to frontiering activity. By 2020, the Australian government had spent over USD 8.31 billion (AUD 12 billion) on Nauru and Manus as so-called third country resettlement sites since the operations restarted in 2012: industry 'boomtowns' flourishing on migrants as commodities. Yet, during my fieldwork, only 1,300 asylum seekers and refugees were living on the island: the maximum the country ever reached at one time. Nauru demonstrates the extent to which the realities of numbers are irrelevant to the accumulation of capital.

This chapter explores the power that a resource extractive framework provides for understanding the expansion of extraction into ever-growing resource frontiers globally. It extends previous arguments I have made in relation to the Nauruan context (Morris, 2019a; 2019b) to consider the bio-economic dimension of refugee legal systems as an extractive practice. In my overall work, I advance a provocative framework centred on extractivism to argue that the figure of the refugee is entangled in extractive capitalism. My scholarship contributes to the debates advanced in this thematic volume by arguing that extractivism is a logic that pervades spheres beyond more typically thought of resource extractive sectors, such as mining. Moving beyond extraction, I see extractivism as an ideological construct, an analytical and political concept, connected to deep logics of exploitation and subjectification (Arboleda, 2020). Extractivism is not just defined by, as Mezzadra and Neilson (2017, 188) put it, the 'forced removal of raw materials and life forms from the earth's surface, depths, and biosphere', but also by the opening of new frontiers and the urge to 'find untapped substances to turn into commodities'. In examining the changing character of 'hyper-extractivism' (Watts, 2021) in the twenty-first century, I trace resource frontiers into forms of migrant extraction. Extractive processes are the forces that push many people to move from homeland regions. This includes massive land grabs, ecological destructions from mining, and the implementation of neo-colonial development programmes, all of which generate migrations (North and Grinspun, 2016; Sassen, 2016). But extractivism does not stop there. People are then subject to the extractive systems of legal technologies that track their movements across territories (Morris, 2019b; 2021a).

Asylum seekers like Alexia discussed the grueling process of making an asylum claim with me. She—and others—described it as a form of dehumanising exploitative labour. She was required to recount intimate experiences and narratives of trauma in order to move elsewhere. What is extracted then is people's vital energies, time, and material resources, all of which profit a vast industry of corporate, non-governmental, government, and other actors. Yet Nauru is not unique; rather, the island is simply microcosmic of extractive racial dynamics that I have noticed elsewhere (Morris, 2019a; 2021a). Nauru is worryingly symptomatic of the political penchant for Western governments, in particular, to outsource and offshore border enforcement on a global scale through all manner of blatantly repressive and humanitarian devices, including, but by no means limited to, border personnel training (Bialasiewicz, 2012), containment regimes and militarised border technologies (Besteman, 2020), development and conservation programmes (Kröger and Nygren, 2020) *and* the international refugee legal system (Morris, 2019b; 2021b).

Over the last near decade, I have been tracking new fronts of extraction emerging related to human (im)mobility. This chapter draws on prolonged periods of fieldwork in two extractive 'patches' (Ferguson, 2006, 204)—Nauru and Jordan—to trace the connections between capitalist activity and expansive extractive logics in the domain of migration governance. I conducted ethnographic fieldwork in Australia, Switzerland, Fiji, and Nauru for a total of fifteen months between 2015 and 2016, and then in Jordan for three months across 2018–19. Certainly, these diverse geographical contexts have their own particularities. By bringing these sites together, I do gloss over many social, political, and economic specificities. But in so doing, my intention is to more expansively consider the global trend towards offshored and outsourced frontiering models as they zig-zag from global North to South (Besteman, 2020).

I am certainly conscious of my role within the processes of extraction, also deriving capital from following zones of continual extractivism. In this regard, my methodological approach takes its inspiration from social scientists focused on addressing carceral logics (Davies et al., 2021). Drawing on the pioneering work of abolitionist activist-scholars like Angela Davis and Ruth

Wilson Gilmore, this approach focuses on advancing transformative changes by meaningfully engaging with the unequal distribution of power, rather than centring practices such as mass incarceration, policing, and borders as societal givens. By naming the asylum system as a form of extractive capitalism, I look to disrupt these forms of administrative governance over majority Black and brown poor migrant populations. Through this analysis, I hope to offer analytically useful conceptualisations of human extractive frontiers in socio-spatially broader areas, even as I play a role in extractive industries.

This chapter proceeds in three parts. The first section lays out my theoretical framework in conversation with work on the migration industry and on new bio-economies that sees commodities not as reified 'things'—or indeed people as innately 'refugees'—but as brought into being by social relations. I ask what it means to understand refugees as commodities in a context where people's own labour power is directed towards asserting themselves as refugees. The second section draws on my fieldwork in Jordan to reveal the expanding webs of infrastructure, labour, and activist struggle that drive new resource-based industries in the twenty-first century. In the final section, I argue that forms of pro-refugee activism and cultural practices, such as images, media, and other productions, work to harden the refugee economy. When examined closely, calls for rescue and welcome contribute to—rather than disrupt—these new extractive arrangements and the colonial relations of power that undergird them. The push to circulate migrants to offshored and outsourced sites raises questions about how these economies come to be advanced and enacted and, importantly, how they are challenged and continuously reopened again.

2 The Economies of (Im)mobility

Frontier expansions around human extractive regimes can be powerfully examined through political economic approaches. Recent scholarship in critical migration studies unpacks the political and economic profit extracted from migrants by a spectrum of institutional actors (Andersson, 2018; Coddington et al., 2020; Gammeltoft-Hansen and Sørensen, 2013). From the symbolic purchase of discourses of 'illegality' (De Genova,2013) to lucrative organisational contracts (McGuirk and Pine, 2020) and the feel-good value of 'missionary-esque' altruism (Morris, 2022), a range of state and non-state actors have a stake in the governance of migration. Borders are, Mezzadra and Neilson (2013) point out, at the very heart of global capitalism. Global capitalism rests upon exploited labour within which practices of border-making and maintenance are a crucial part of producing labour power as a commodity (Rajaram, 2018;

Samaddar, 2020). Populations are put to work as a reserve army of informal low-wage labour to support global supply chains of commodities, such as in construction labour (Kathiravelu, 2016), the care and entertainment industries (Cheng, 2010) and forms of entrepreneurship (Bhagat, 2020).

But while border practices are well recognised as significant to current ruling relations, understandings of this exploitation all too often rely upon caricatures of passive workers. Indeed, much of the migration industry focus still distances migrants from the institutionalised governance industry through theories of abjection: as 'wasted' (Bauman, 2004) or 'expelled' populations rendered irrelevant and invisible (Sassen, 2014). Racialised migrants are framed as displaced victims who are subject to immense 'profit and predation' (Andersson, 2018). Even as scholars critique state institutional classifications, such as the 'asylum seeker' and 'refugee', many still utilise them to make normative claims about intrinsic suffering and the overall benevolence of the international refugee system. So too, the process of making an asylum claim is not taken to be a form of intimate labour in its own right, one that contributes to value generation. Yet, as I see it, migrants, as racialised refugee bodies in capitalism, are not only pushed 'to turn themselves into productive members of society – through employment or entrepreneurship – in order to survive' (Bhagat, 2020, 3). They are *also* entangled in the intimate labour of making an asylum claim. The process of appropriating people's bodies depends increasingly on individuals' personal capacities to adjust their emotions and concepts of self, body and intimacy to the rationalities of the market. Poor migrants of colour are encouraged to subordinate themselves through an 'embodied performance of trauma' (Pine, 2020, 212), while the white subject is presented as empathetic, caring and good, offering 'protection' to the stranger (Danewid, 2017).

Yet despite mounting criticism in other fields relating to bodily substances (Scheper-Hughes and Wacquant, 2002; Vora, 2015) and intimate labour (Mahdavi, 2011), the international refugee regime is remarkably resistant to challenge. Migrants advancing or having received asylum claims are still taken to be outside the industry in terms of the biopolitical function of their labour power. Debates around extraction are usually limited to the generation of migration, not to the extractivist logics that incorporate migrants into—and pervade—migration governance systems, such as asylum. A major difficulty in making these arguments is that many critics and publics have uncomfortable, mixed feelings in approaching people—saturated by morally charged representations—as commodities. Those who object to the idea of refugee commodification do so because it 'implicitly includes a type of objectification; converting something or someone into a good that can be traded' (Hofmann and Moreno, 2016, 7). It is thus not the commodifying argument per se that provokes the objections, but the uncomfortable realities of how people are objectified, and at times utilise objectifying discourses themselves. My intention here is to flag up how people *are* treated—and indeed traded—as objects in a capitalist market system in highly demeaning and intimately extractive ways. Extractivism as an analytical category then captures not just the processes that push people to move (Sassen, 2014; Stefoni Espinoza et al., 2021), but also the institutional assemblage that extracts value from those migration pathways.

Anthropologists have long pointed out the myriad cultural settings in which 'the human body and its parts' are targets for commodification (Sharp, 2000). In the context I will go on to describe, migrants are pushed to translate their body power into valorised labour through forms of 'refugee performativity' (Häkli et al., 2017). These forms of refugee embodiment are harnessed to the marketplace and profitability for migrants and workforces alike. Organisations receive large contracts for all aspects of the asylum process, exerting forms of control and rule over people's lives (Morris, 2021b). Meanwhile, terms such as 'refugee economies' (Betts et al., 2017) are entering into normative vocabulary, tying migrant use to capitalist extraction. Refugees are also traded around the world for their geopolitical utility and, at times, financial currency. In mainstream economics, this tradability in a capitalist market is known as 'fungibility'. It is a crucial characteristic of commodities in a capitalist sense: a form of market value that Kelberer (2017) describes in this context as 'refugee rentierism'. States leverage their position as host states of displaced communities, extracting revenue from other states for maintaining migrant groups within their borders on the basis of ascribing prices to refugee bodies (Morris, 2020).

Migrants are also subject to an immense moral economy where 'exchange is not motivated by profit, but by an identification with abstract moral values' (Erevelles, 2001, 8), such as philanthropy and civil society galvanised by white empathy discourses of #RefugeesWelcome (Picozza, 2021). In turn, these discourses are entangled in migrant desires for mobility and consumption (Cabot, 2013). People potentialise the logic of commodity in their self-appreciation as capital in ways that are related to their labour power and fulfilling their onwards goals. The performative and ethical dimensions here constitute the fetishistic power of refugees, in particular, as commodities. As Marx described, fetishism is about concealing production relations, but also about permeating products with an objectified mystical dimension. In their particular imaginings, #RefugeesWelcome movements and migrant practices may deepen this mystical character through a 'refetishization' (Adams and Raisborough, 2008).

By grounding the shifts towards migrant extractivism in the operations of capital, we might better understand the enormity of this planetary phenomena and the violence it produces.

In addition to objectification, another major concern around the commodification framework is that it appears to discount the very real violence that many migrants might have experienced. By saying that migrants are performing demeaning identities, my critique of the international refugee system could be misinterpreted as questioning the authenticity of people's experiences. This is by no means my intention, and making these arguments is not to claim that migrants are not suffering. Rather, it is to say that asylum is one means of entry across the hardened nation state borders of the current racialised global order. In putting forward an asylum claim, migrants (largely the Black and brown poor from the global South) must perform within a particular objectified narrative, making claims on their bodies to move between sovereign states. Here, I draw on Miriam Ticktin's (2006) work in understanding the consequences of a new 'biosocial' space that pushes people towards drawing on their biology as a resource for mobility. Alongside these concerns, it might be said that in emphasising the inequalities of this governance regime I may undermine a key legal mechanism that many have benefited from in decades past to the present day. I do so with the understanding that the international refugee regime is inherently problematic. I want to challenge and pull back the veil of mystification regarding asylum as benevolent and the racist, capitalist, classist, sexist, misogynist systems that place demands and regulations on certain bodies to bring their suffering to bear in order to move elsewhere. The focus on hierarchies of suffering strengthens a 'victim-villain binary' (Pupavac, 2008) that forestalls critical reconsiderations of free movement across borders, and creates human divisions in the process. This 'technology of antirelationality' is, Ruth Wilson Gilmore (2002, 261) points out, intrinsic to racial capitalism. Collective life in humanity is 'partitioned' and then 'interconnected' in ways that feed capital and wealth.

The next section draws on my fieldwork in Jordan, almost 14,000 kilometres away from Nauru, to consider asylum as a hyper-extractive system. Moving towards an understanding of the expansion of extraction into spheres of human activity also requires recognising the complications of the performative dynamics of this industry, an aspect that my previous work has not adequately captured. But while accounting for individual agency in 'reshaping and refusing dominant images of deservingness, victimhood, and vulnerability' (Cabot, 2013, 453), the bodily dissemination of sociolegal terminologies and processes can ensure that extractive activities continue unhindered.

3 Jordan: Asylum as a Hyper-extractive System

I am at the United Nations High Commissioner for Refugees' (UNHCR) registration centre in Amman. A dusty waiting room is packed with new Syrian arrivals to the Jordanian capital. Individuals, friends, couples, families, young and old, mingle about. Some wear T-shirts and jeans, but many are also in kaftans and abayas marked in distinctive traditional patterns specific to far-flung rural regions. They are unable to afford the freedom of movement that has seen the wealthy Syrian elite more easily migrate on a global scale. Instead, many patiently wait to register as asylum seekers with UNHCR. Others await their refugee status determination (RSD) interviews to decide whether they are formally classified as refugees and could potentially apply for residency elsewhere. Many of the latter clutch folders filled to the brim with the countless documents they require to prove the authenticity of their persecution, and eligibility to move from their home regions. Some have told me that this complicated and drawn-out process involved months, if not years, of painstaking work. Collating documents from bygone pasts, calling family and friends that might remain, combines with the often re-traumatising effect of rehearsing one's life stories prior to arrival in Amman. The technical and labour-intensive process of 'asylum labour' means locating verifiable proof that your residence was subject to devastation, medical reports documenting physical and mental health distress, evidence of past employment showing you to be a target of Syrian state violence, to proof of sexuality that might substantiate your maltreatment in the country. These forms of intimate extraction are undeniably invasive and form part of the labour-intensive process of claiming asylum (Harper et al., 2015).

Specialised methods of intimate extraction require increasingly specialised labour. The side rooms that splinter off from the main waiting room are all staffed by international and Jordanian UNHCR officials who consider the credibility of each applicant in detail: a model that I have likened elsewhere to 'assembly line' assessment practices (Morris, 2019b) premised on, as Anna Tsing (2013, 21) describes with familiar capitalist commodities, 'creating commodity value from non-capitalist value forms'. In asylum adjudication, migrants are sieved out as 'worthy' from 'unworthy' based on being 'sorted' and 'regraded' as a 'refugee' or not. As a result, migrants must utilise gendered, racialised, and class-based discourses to produce 'pictures' of lives eligible for protection that fit templates of victimhood and vulnerability (Cabot, 2013). 'Trauma', writes Adrienne Pine (2020, 211), 'only has value in the asylum industry [...] if it's the right *kind* of trauma'. How asylum applicants dress, how they comport themselves, their overall appearance are all stereotyped assumptions that are taken to signal possible victimhood. When summoned to perform their life histories in the asylum interview, many migrants actively strive to meet their audiences' expectations. This performance of 'idealized refugeeness' (Fiddian-Qasmiyeh, 2014) resonates with what Giddens (1991) famously described as the 'commodification of self'. In late modernity, Giddens argues, personal lives are, to a greater or lesser degree, reorganised on the model of market relations. He writes how the 'narrative of the self' is 'constructed in circumstances in which personal appropriation is influenced by standardized influences on consumption' (201). Knowing how to act and represent oneself is a mediated process, under the influence of sources such as images in advertising and media entertainment, which act as 'substitutes for real satisfactions unobtainable in normal social conditions' (199). The consumptive influences Giddens describes are clear here when set against discussions of NGO moral economies and the political economic utility of 'the refugee'. Suffering itself is commodified (Kleinman and Kleinman, 1996), but also reworked for strategic ends (Cabot, 2013). In this sense, self-definition depends on personally branding oneself to meet the demands of the marketplace.

I discussed this with Imran, a younger Syrian man from Idlib, working on the front desk at my hotel. He was interested in my research and keen to talk about his asylum legal experience. Over coffee downtown, Imran and his friend Georg, also from the same heavily bombed northern Syrian region, both in their mid-twenties, described their experiences to me. Highly fluent in the refugee legal system, Imran and Georg were well aware of how to meet the demands of the asylum performative context, describing it together jokingly, yet with conviction, as a form of 'self-marketing'. Imran commented that he knew from conversations with friends of his who had been through the system, as well as NGO workers, and his own online media and legal aid website research, that 'tears were very helpful'. He continued, 'I was told make sure you *at least* shed a tear in your interview'. Imran's life history was meticulously planned out and, he shared, part of his success. 'I thought about it like writing and acting out a story. A sort of fictionalised account of my life, like if I was working with a movie director and wanted to shock the audience through some of those techniques they use'.

The 'techniques' that Imran describes are the narrative conventions of asylum, which include incorporating such emotionally charged aspects as tropes of violence and flight (Malkki, 1995). This is not to imply that Imran is somehow not a 'real refugee', but reveals the intensive work that he and other applicants had to put into becoming recognisable as such. Certainly, each person's narrative might reflect some of these broadly shared experiences. However, asylum applicants must figure out how to present their experiences in a compelling manner resonant with the cinematic account that Imran describes. In fact, not just Imran and Georg, but other asylum applicants also told me how they polished their life histories to meet racialised arcs of white salvation: a European promise of winning a universal crusade against a regressive Orientalised and transhistorical Taliban barbarism. These forms of self-representation invoked normative ideas of race, class, and gender within the overarching narrative of fleeing Taliban persecution for the safety and protection of the liberal democratic core. They all form part of the work of presenting—and often strategically degrading—oneself as worthy of capitalist state insertion within notions of civility, wealth, and Europeanness (Cabot, 2013). In this sense, it is not only explicitly commercial practices that have interpenetrated the lifeworld and selfhood, but also the predictable attributes about 'who a refugee is' (Shacknove, 1985), which are 'floated' onto the public marketplace, and reworked by individuals for their restricted mobility goals.

This is the system of 'unfree labour' whereby poor brown and Black migrants from the global South, in particular, are channelled into making an asylum claim in order to move elsewhere. Imran and Georg were both of a lower socioeconomic status, and unable to afford the time and expense of finishing their high school education, instead entering straight into apprenticeship professions. Unlike those of the mobile elite class, and without the sponsorship of a foreign employer, their abilities to move from Syria were restricted to the demeaning process of proving their suffering by making asylum claims. Aihwa Ong (1999, 58) describes this differential access to mobility as 'graduated sovereignty', whereby racialised segments of the population are differentially governed according to how they relate or do not relate to global markets, 'and in the process assigned different social fates'. These forms of differential mobility governance were certainly the case with Imran and Georg, whereby their devaluation as 'low-skilled' and 'low-income' workers restricted their freedom to move.[4]

Yet, Imran and Georg were by no means disposable populations, not 'relevant' to global markets. Rather, their alleged 'disposability' brought them into the folds of capital accumulation in their struggle to survive. In fact, it is through the unfree and precarious employment relations of the asylum system that state and non-state actors alike ensure levels of profitability. The refugee

4 The division of people into 'low-skilled' and 'high-skilled' workers is immensely problematic. Such binaries all too often map neatly onto race as a way to legitimise lower wages, more intense schedules, and institutional segregation, and a never-ending low-wage exploitable labour force (Appel, 2019).

industry relies on migrants making asylum claims, while state and organisational modes of investment profit from suspending people in conditions of precarity (Coddington et al., 2020). But in the process, migrants are subject to the 'precaritization of labor and life' (Allison, 2013, 7) symptomatic of forms of unfreedom, as they make their asylum claims. Imran and Georg described the limitations on their abilities to work during this time, outside of working on their asylum claims. While under the asylum process, they were barred from formal employment, and instead cobbled together cash-in-hand jobs coupled with piecemeal NGO support in order to survive. Their exploited labour as asylum claimants and low-wage 'illegal' workers made them subject to multiple modes of accumulation.

3.1 *Jordan: a Resource Boom Frontier*

The effects of these industry investments are unmistakable as Jordan is identified as a resource frontier region. As Syrian migrants are harnessed to the marketplace and profitability, organisations have mushroomed across Amman to provide all aspects of humanitarian care within the refugee and wider market economy, in much the same way as I found in Nauru. Local coffee shops are filled with humanitarian aid workers; researchers, such as myself, fly in-and-out of this new extractive frontier, as the (im)mobility of people enables the mobility of others. Local organisations that once focused on quite different priorities segue towards the new human resource boom. Many NGO heavyweights in Jordan focused on the great Syrian commodity boom hold benchmark quotas for the number of Syrian refugees they match to local employment: part of the economic metrics tied to a new human commodity (Morris, 2020). In exchange for employing targeted numbers of Syrian refugees in various industry sectors (agriculture, construction, manufacturing, and so forth), the Jordanian government received humanitarian and development funding and concessional loans of USD 1.9 billion, and the opening up of tariff-free trade in the European market to Jordanian goods.

Yet, in the process of this resource grab, the economic 'worthiness' assigned to Syrian refugees also leads to the exclusion of non-Syrian migrants.[5] Because of these prerogatives, many migrants, in particular those from Sudan, Somalia and Yemen, who also have their own backgrounds of terrifying experiences, are unable to access the same levels of socio-economic support. Some are subject to increased violence, and events include the shooting of a Sudanese man in

5 Time, place, and context all strongly influence who is determined to be a refugee; often relating to the geopolitical zeitgeist (Morris, 2021b), illustrating how valuation varies over time and space, and is situated in particular sociocultural contexts.

Amman's Ashrafiyeh neighbourhood in October 2014: part of a string of violent acts targeting African refugees, which go unreported (Verduijn and Al Majali, 2020). So too, regional migrants seeking economic stability, predominately from Egypt, who depend on daily work in Jordanian construction, farming, retail and the restaurant industry, are also sidelined in favour of the boom sector centred on Syrian refugees. As a result, such forms of refugee fetishisation create racialised, classed, and ethnic divisions centred on the monopolisation of resources.[6] Meanwhile, many of the Syrian asylum applicants I spoke with will be unable to move beyond Jordan, even with their refugee status. Instead, they are explicitly entangled in the structural impediments of the wider (im) mobility economy and its spectacular modes of accumulation. They are made commercially viable as a low-wage exploitable labour force benefiting local and global economies, while also hardening the conceptual frontiers of the EU through the spectacle of borders (De Genova, 2013). In effect, racialised peoples simultaneously facilitate capital accumulation through their labour and their representation as racialised 'risky' or 'at risk' bodies (Gray and Franck, 2019).

Imran was lucky, he told me, more so than friends of his, who were only able to find work in manufacturing plants on the fringes of the city as part of the Jordanian government's limitations on employment sectors (see Morris (2020)). He was well aware that his hotel work—his immobilised labour of hospitality (Duncan et al., 2013)—tied him into *mobile* global tourism, and more specifically once again, the humanitarian industry, much of which came in the scramble for the human extractive boom. Migrants such as Imran may be physically excluded from European and western shores, but they are by no means outside of global spheres of production and consumption. Rather, contemporary consumer cultures are directly connected to the wealth generated by frontier regimes, one premised on their low-wage labour and their bodily currency. However, Imran had by no means lost control of his labour power. Rather, he navigated the forms of value extracted from his refugee figuration to further his own mobility agenda. As an accomplished tailor who had previously owned his own business, working in a hotel was not high on Imran's list of priorities. But, without the sponsorship of a local employer, owning his own business was out of the question: an explicit stipulation of Jordanian labour laws. Imran remained upbeat though and stressed to me that at least he *had* employment thanks to the drive the employ Syrian refugees. Moreover, it was a respectable hotel chain and the work covered his living expenses and might

6 Although I did not directly meet anyone who had done this, I heard numerous anecdotal reports of migrants adopting a Syrian identity in the hope that they could receive residency and work permits in Jordan or ultimately in European countries.

mean one day that he could utilise the transferable skills to access a more exciting position elsewhere. While he all too clearly felt his imbrication in the (im)mobility economy, performing within supply chains was an important strategy of securing onward goals.

It is not only goods and commodified labour that circulate in the global economy, but also the consumption of suffering of distant others. The final section of this chapter zooms back out to global liberal advocacy movements focused on 'welcoming refugees'. Although well meaning in their attempts, pro-refugee activism is also part of the 'hyper-extractive assemblage' (Watts, 2021) premised on continued racial subordination. Simultaneously, campaigns centred on white hospitality and rescue are strategically manipulated by migrants, who draw on the idiom of international organisations for their tremendous profit potential. Yet in the process, these forms of self-representation bolster an extractive system premised on exclusion and exploitation and the boom sector of (im)mobility economies.

4 Conclusions: #RefugeesWelcome and Hyper-Extraction

The summer of 2021 brought an inordinate humanitarian #RefugeesWelcome push. The high-profile Taliban takeover in Afghanistan and large-scale movements of Haitian and Central American migrants to the Mexican-Texan border spurred on humanitarian groups and their allies to galvanise campaigns in empathy and solidarity with 'refugees'. In fact, over the last decade activism campaigns led by organisational representatives, scholars, artists, politicians and migrants have relied on the left-liberal and multicultural #RefugeesWelcome framing. Stock images of poor Black and brown migrants in excruciating pain and desperation bombard Western publics on a perennial basis. In the wake of the Russian invasion of Ukraine, humanitarian depictions of 'white like us' Europeans galvanised the European Union and global publics in solidarity.[7] Racialised migrants are alternatively cast as threats or objects of sympathy or through an affinity based on whiteness, whereby national boundaries are

7 Ukrainian citizens are eligible for temporary protection in any EU country, including the right to work, housing, healthcare, and education for children. These efforts are certainly to be applauded; however, they operate in stark contrast to the border regimes experienced by migrants from the Middle East and Africa. Reports also detail how Black and Asian Ukrainian citizens and long-term residents have experienced overwhelming discrimination (Bajaj and Stanford, 2022). Overall, though, Ukraine is still denied access to the European Union, which Ivan Kalmar (2022, 248) argues is symptomatic of a racialised West-to-East axis where each nation is 'deemed more white than the next'.

constantly defined through a racialised politics. From the women like Alexia to the young men like Imran and Georg, migrants are presented—and at times present themselves—as fleeing the suffering of despotic third-world regimes for the salvation of democracy and global North protectionism. Their diverse stories are plastered together under generalised representations of third-world suffering that see majority white western nations positioned as havens of democracy, liberty, and universal rights.

Critical political economists call attention to the linkages between Northern consumption practices and livelihoods elsewhere as part of extractive operations (Pickren, 2014). Colonial countries benefited disproportionately from wealth accumulation, transforming regions into purveyors of raw materials and cheap labour, and facilitating massive out-migrations. Dramatic #RefugeesWelcome campaigns reveal the practices of consumption through which value is continuously extracted from racialised migrants as a renewable resource. Liberal human rights discourses centred on rescue narrative sentiments are heavily implicated in the cyclical production of migration (Morris, 2019a). Left liberal responses bolster the authority of the international refugee system, while simultaneously justifying all manner of Western military interventions premised on liberation from barbaric regimes, which in turn pushes more people to migrate. In recognising these circuits of consumption, it becomes evident how the work of activists and social movements is crucial to the constitution of raced markets in the trade, production, and consumption of migrants.

Applying an extractivism lens—drawing on the terminologies of the extractive mining industries—starkly captures the extent of global capital in human (im)mobility economies. Migrants are not expelled or pushed out to society's margins. Rather, people are made valuable to the global political economy. The fetishised figure of the refugee has well solidified with the explosive growth of the humanitarian industry, where organisations and individuals extract value from suffering refugee Others. The matter thus becomes not one of protecting people per se. Indeed, scanty support and suspension as dependent and impoverished subjects is what many asylum recipients actually do face in global North regions (Morris, 2021b). Migrants within the asylum system are often reliant on meagre welfare handouts, limited employment, haphazard social housing, and patronising NGO programming as 'social difference, legal categories, and destitution come together to make [populations] valuable to contractors and states in specific ways' (Coddington et al., 2020, 1429). Instead, the matter becomes one of extracting moral value that 'sanctions a white(washed) sense of self and satisfied way of being in the world' (Danewid, 2017, 1681). People are reduced to objects with their meaning connected to marketability and feel-good philanthropy, perpetuating racial capitalism's logics and sustaining racial injustice through what Jodi Melamed (2011) calls 'race-liberal orders'. The concept of extractive logics thus helps us understand how people are reduced to profit, even through liberal international legal orders.

The resistances to recognising commodification are no clearer than in the refugee industry. As scholars have shown more broadly in extractive industries (Huber, 2013), the entwinement of grassroots culture and political power signals just how integral the refugee is to the global cultural imagination, shaping contemporary ways of being and of imagining acceptable movement across borders. The obstacles become even greater when migrants are being pushed to identify as refugees and to perform what Liisa Malkki (1995) has referred to as 'refugeeness' in order to legalise their movement across borders. In fact, the performative demands particular to this form of intimate extraction make it difficult to demystify the social relations that go into the violent production of refugees. It is challenging to separate migrants from the products of their labour when it is an activity of production premised on translating oneself towards market demands. Yet unlike Marx's model of alienation, whereby workers lose control over the production process, many migrants interact and perform within consumer culture to construct new identities compatible with absorbing societies, and as tools for social, cultural, and political mobility. While the status of 'refugee' places one in imbalanced power relations, these legal structures also allow for some degree of political power at times *because of* representations of vulnerability. Performing oneself as a refugee and rejecting one's position as 'illegal' by making an asylum claim 'operates as both a mode of subjectification and as a site of active resistance' (McNevin, 2011, 2). It enables new kinds of organising, even as these forms of self-capitalisation and subjectification can create immense power imbalances and divisions between populations.

Examining the asylum and refugee industry in Jordan or Nauru hardly captures the enormity of this form of frontiering across the globe, or the larger cosmos of which it is part. The last decade and a half have seen a dramatic increase in the outsourcing and offshoring of asylum processing and resettlement to developing countries. The US has adopted these operations in Central America, using regional asylum seekers and refugees to fuel the Guatemalan government's economy (Morris, forthcoming). This is similarly the case with the EU in Eastern Europe, Turkey, North Africa, and Central Asia, and the UK's recent arrangement with Rwanda (Achtnich, 2021). So too, Australia uses migrants as a form of economic development with Pacific island nations and across South Asia (Morris, 2019a). Many of the regions where western countries have financed border enforcement projects exhibit continuities from histories of colonial resource extraction through to the extractive projects of the contemporary era (Morris, 2021a).

How then might we disrupt these models of perennial extractivism? A more productive approach is to ask how we can move towards a collective flourishing where people have the freedom to live, love, and work where they choose. This is by no means utopic, but can be directly accomplished by attention to representation and social justice goals. We can move towards using a more egalitarian language of solidarity, coalitions, and commonality, rather than one of suffering, salvation, and #RefugeesWelcome valuation. A first step is to see the international refugee regime as an extractive process; from there we can choose to collectively shift our attention to amplify future analyses and responses.

References

Achtnich, M. (2021) 'Bordering Practices: Migrants, Mobility, and Affect in Libya', *American Ethnologist*, 48(3), pp. 314–326, DOI: 10.1111/amet.13030.

Adams, M. and J. Raisborough (2008) 'What Can Sociology Say About Fair Trade? Class, Reflexivity, and Ethical Consumption', *Sociology*, 42(6), pp. 1165–1182, DOI: 10.1177/0038038508096939.

Allison, A. (2013) *Precarious Japan* (Durham: Duke University Press).

Andersson, R. (2018) 'Profits and Predation in the Human Bioeconomy', *Public Culture*, 30(3), pp. 413–439, DOI: 10.1215/08992363-6912115.

Appel, H. (2019) *The Licit Life of Capitalism: US Oil in Equatorial Guinea* (Durham: Duke University Press).

Arboleda, M. (2020) *Planetary Mine: Territories of Extraction under Late Capitalism* (London: Verso).

Bajaj, S.S. and F.C. Stanford (2022) 'The Ukrainian Refugee Crisis and the Pathology of Racism', *British Medical Journal*, 376, o661, DOI: 10.1136/bmj.o661.

Bauman, Z. (2004) *Wasted Lives: Modernity and Its Outcasts* (Cambridge: Polity Press).

Besteman, C. (2020) *Militarized Global Apartheid* (Durham: Duke University Press).

Betts, A., L. Bloom, J. Kaplan and N. Omata (Eds.) (2017) *Refugee Economies: Forced Displacement and Development* (Oxford: Oxford University Press).

Bhagat, A. (2020) 'Governing Refugee Disposability: Neoliberalism and Survival in Nairobi', *New Political Economy*, 25(3), pp. 439–452, DOI: 10.1080/13563467.2019.1598963.

Bialasiewicz, L. (2012) 'Off-shoring and Out-sourcing the Borders of EUrope: Libya and EU Border Work in the Mediterranean', *Geopolitics*, 17(4), pp. 843–866, DOI: 10.1080/14650045.2012.660579.

Cabot, H. (2013) 'The Social Aesthetics of Eligibility: NGO Aid and Indeterminacy in the Greek Asylum Process', *American Ethnologist*, 40(3), pp. 452–466, DOI: 10.1111/amet.12032.

Cheng, S. (2010) *On the Move for Love: Migrant Entertainers and the US Military in South Korea* (Philadelphia: University of Pennsylvania Press).

Coddington, K., D. Conlon and L. Martin (2020) 'Destitution Economies: Circuits of Value in Asylum, Refugee, and Migration Control', *Annals of the American Association of Geographers*, 110(5), pp. 1425–1444, DOI: 10.1080/24694452.2020.1715196.

Danewid, I. (2017) 'White Innocence in the Black Mediterranean: Hospitality and the Erasure of History', *Third World Quarterly*, 38(7), pp. 1674–1689, DOI: 10.1080/01436597.2017.1331123.

Davies, E.J., J.M. Jackson and S. Streeter (2021) 'Bringing abolition in: Addressing Carceral Logics in Social Science Research', *Social Science Quarterly*, 102(7), pp. 3095–3102, DOI: 10.1111/ssqu.13022.

De Genova, N. (2013) 'Spectacles of migrant 'Illegality': the Scene of Exclusion, the Obscene of Inclusion', *Ethnic and Racial Studies*, 36(7), pp. 1180–1198, DOI: 10.1080/01419870.2013.783710.

Duncan, T., D.G. Scott and T. Baum (2013) 'The Mobilities of Hospitality Work: an Exploration of Issues and Debates', *Annals of Tourism Research*, 41, pp. 1–19, DOI: 10.1016/j.annals.2012.10.004.

Erevelles, N. (2001) 'Disability and the Political Economy of Place: Case Study of a Voluntary Organization in South India', *Disability Studies Quarterly*, 21(4), pp. 5–19, DOI: 10.18061/dsq.v21i4.313.

Ferguson, J. (2006) *Global Shadows: Africa in the Neoliberal World Order* (Durham: Duke University Press).

Fiddian-Qasmiyeh, E. (2014) *The Ideal Refugees: Gender, Islam, and the Sahrawi Politics of Survival* (Syracuse: Syracuse University Press).

Franck, A.K. (2018) 'The Lesvos Refugee Crisis as Disaster Capitalism', *Peace Review*, 30(2), pp. 199–205, DOI: 10.1080/10402659.2018.1458951.

Gammeltoft-Hansen, T. and N.N. Sørensen (eds.) (2013) *The Migration Industry and the Commercialization of International Migration* (London: Routledge).

Giddens, A. (1991) *Modernity and Self-Identity* (Stanford: Stanford University Press).

Gilmore, R.W. (2002) 'Race and Globalization', in R.J. Johnston, P.J. Taylor and M.J. Watts (eds.) *Geographies of Global Change: Remapping the World* (New York: Wiley-Blackwell), pp. 261–274.

Gray, H. and A.K. Franck (2019) 'Refugees as/at Risk: the Gendered and Racialized Underpinnings of Securitization in British Media Narratives', *Security Dialogue*, 50(3), pp. 275–291, DOI: 10.1177/0967010619830590.

Häkli, J., E. Pascucci and K.P. Kallio (2017) 'Becoming refugee in Cairo: the Political in Performativity', *International Political Sociology*, 11(2), pp. 185–202, DOI: 10.1093/ips/olx002.

Harper, I., T. Kelly and A. Khanna (2015) *The Clinic and the Court: Law, Medicine and Anthropology* (Cambridge: Cambridge University Press).

Hofmann, S. and A. Moreno (eds.) (2016) 'Introduction: Global Intimate Economies: Discontents and Debates', in *Intimate Economies: Bodies, Emotions, and Sexualities on the Global Market* (New York: Palgrave Macmillan), pp. 1–30.

Huber, M.T. (2013) *Lifeblood: Oil, Freedom, and the Forces of Capital* (Minneapolis: University of Minnesota Press).

Kalmar, I. (2022) *White but Not Quite: Central Europe's Illiberal Revolt* (Bristol: Bristol University Press).

Kathiravelu, L. (2016) *Migrant Dubai: Low Wage Workers and the Construction of a Global City* (London: Palgrave Macmillan).

Kelberer, V. (2017) 'Negotiating Crisis: International Aid and Refugee Policy in Jordan', *Middle East Policy,* 24(4), pp. 148–165, DOI: 10.1111/mepo.12313.

Kleinman, A. and J. Kleinman (1996) 'The Appeal of Experience; the Dismay of Images: Cultural Appropriations of Suffering in Our Times', *Daedalus,* 125(1), pp. 1–23, http://www.jstor.org/stable/20027351?origin=JSTOR-pdf (accessed on 17 October 2021).

Kröger, M. and A. Nygren (2020) 'Shifting Frontier Dynamics in Latin America', *Journal of Agrarian Change,* 20(2), pp. 364–386, DOI: 10.1111/joac.12354.

Mahdavi, P. (2011) *Gridlock: Labor, Migration, and Human Trafficking in Dubai* (Stanford: Stanford University Press).

Malkki, L.H. (1995) *Purity and Exile: Violence, Memory, and National Cosmology among Hutu Refugees in Tanzania* (Chicago: University of Chicago Press).

McNevin, A. (2011) *Contesting Citizenship: Irregular Migrants and New Frontiers of the Political* (New York: Columbia University Press).

McGuirk, S. and A. Pine (eds.) (2020) *Asylum for Sale: Profit and Protest in the Migration Industry* (Oakland: PM Press).

Melamed, J. (2011) *Represent and Destroy: Rationalizing Violence in the New Racial Capitalism* (Minneapolis: University of Minnesota Press).

Mezzadra, S. and B. Neilson (2017) 'On the Multiple Frontiers of Extraction: Excavating Contemporary Capitalism', *Cultural Studies,* 31(2–3), pp. 185–204, DOI: 10.1080/09502386.2017.1303425.

Mezzadra, S. and B. Neilson (2013) *Border as Method, or, the Multiplication of Labor* (Durham: Duke University Press).

Morris, J. (forthcoming) 'Resource Frontiers: Frontiering through Development in Guatemala', *Anuac.*

Morris, J. (2022) 'Strange Bedfellows?: NGOs and Offshore Asylum', in G. İnanç and T. Lewis (eds.) *Forced Displacement and NGOs in Asia and the Pacific* (London: Routledge), pp. 190–206.

Morris, J. (2021a) 'Colonial Afterlives of Infrastructure: from Phosphate to Refugee Processing in the Republic of Nauru', *Mobilities*, 16(5), pp. 688–706, DOI: 10.1080/17450101.2021.1961289.

Morris, J. (2021b) 'The Value of Refugees: UNHCR and the Growth of the Global Refugee Industry', *Journal of Refugee Studies*, 34(3), pp. 2676–2698. DOI: 10.1093/jrs/feaa135.

Morris, J. (2020) 'Extractive Landscapes: the Case of the Jordan Refugee Compact', *Refuge: Canada's Journal on Refugees*, 36(1), pp. 87–96, DOI: 10.25071/1920-7336.40623.

Morris, J. (2019a) 'Violence and Extraction of a Human Commodity: from Phosphate to Refugees in the Republic of Nauru', *The Extractive Industries and Society*, 6(4), pp. 1122–1133, DOI: 10.1016/j.exis.2019.07.001.

Morris, J. (2019b) 'Refugee Extractivism: Law and the Mining of a Human Commodity in the Republic of Nauru', *Saint Louis University Law Journal*, 64(1), pp. 59–90.

North, L.L. and R. Grinspun (2016) 'Neo-extractivism and the New Latin American Developmentalism: the Missing Piece of Rural Transformation', *Third World Quarterly*, 37(8), pp. 1483–1504, DOI: 10.1080/01436597.2016.1159508.

Ong, A. (1999) *Flexible Citizenship: the Cultural Logics of Transnationality* (Durham: Duke University Press).

Pickren, G. (2014) 'Political Ecologies of Electronic Waste: Uncertainty and Legitimacy in the Governance of E-Waste Geographies', *Environment and Planning a: Economy and Space*, 46(1), pp. 26–45, DOI: 10.1068/a45728.

Picozza, F. (2021) *The Coloniality of Asylum: Mobility, Autonomy and Solidarity in the Wake of Europe's Refugee Crisis* (Lanham: Rowman & Littlefield).

Pine, A. (2020) 'An "Expert" View of the Asylum Industry', in S. McGuirk and A. Pine (eds.) *Asylum for Sale: Profit and Protest in the Migration Industry* (Oakland: PM Press), pp. 203–218.

Pupavac, V. (2008) 'Refugee Advocacy, Traumatic Representations and Political Disenchantment', *Government and Opposition*, 43(2), pp. 270–292, DOI: 10.1111/j.1477-7053.2008.00255.x.

Rajaram, P.K. (2018) 'Refugees as Surplus Population: Race, Migration and Capitalist Value Regimes', *New Political Economy*, 23(5), pp. 627–639, DOI: 10.1080/13563467.2017.1417372.

Samaddar, R. (2020) *The Postcolonial Age of Migration* (London: Routledge).

Sassen, S. (2016) 'A Massive Loss of Habitat: New Drivers for Migration', *Sociology of Development*, 2(2), pp. 204–233, DOI: 10.1525/sod.2016.2.2.204.

Sassen, S. (2014) *Expulsions: Brutality and Complexity in the Global Economy* (Cambridge: Harvard University Press).

Scheper-Hughes, N. and L.J.D. Wacquant (eds.) (2002) *Commodifying Bodies* (London: Sage Publications Ltd.).

Shacknove, A.E. (1985) 'Who Is a Refugee?', *Ethics*, 95(2), pp. 274–284, DOI: 10.1086/292626.

Sharp, L.A. (2000) 'The Commodification of the Body and its Parts', *Annual Review of Anthropology*, 29, pp. 287–328, DOI: 10.1146/annurev.anthro.29.1.287.

Stefoni Espinoza, C., F. Stang Alva and P. Rojas Varas (2021) 'Extractivismo y migraciones: Expresiones cambiantes de una desigualdad histórica. La gran minería del cobre en la región chilena de Antofagasta', *Rumbos TS*, 26(26), DOI: 10.51188/rrts.num26.549.

Ticktin, M. (2006) 'Where Ethics and Politics Meet: the Violence of Humanitarianism in France', *American Ethnologist*, 33(1), pp. 33–49, DOI: 10.1525/ae.2006.33.1.33.

Tsing, A. (2013) 'Sorting out Commodities: How Capitalist Value is Made through Gifts', *HAU: Journal of Ethnographic Theory*, 3(1), pp. 21–43, DOI: 10.14318/hau3.1.003.

Verduijn, S. and S. Al Majali (2020) 'Somalis and Yemenis of Mixed Origin Stranded and Struggling in Jordan's Capital', *Mixed Migration Centre*, 23 July, https://mixedmigration.org (accessed on 14 October 2021).

Vora, K. (2015) *Life Support: Biocapital and the New History of Outsourced Labor* (Minneapolis: University of Minnesota Press).

Watts, M.J. (2021) 'Hyper-Extractivism and the Global Oil Assemblage', in J. Shapiro and J.-A. McNeish (eds.) *Our Extractive Age: Expressions of Violence and Resistance* (Abingdon: Routledge), pp. 207–248.

Williams, M. and B. MacDonald (1985) *The Phosphateers: a History of the British Phosphate Commissioners and the Christmas Island Phosphate Commission* (Melbourne: Melbourne University Press).

CHAPTER 12

Anti-extractive Rumouring in the Russian North-East

Sardana Nikolaeva

Abstract

This chapter discusses the potentiality of alternative Indigenous politicised discourses, arguing that diverse public narratives can reveal more subtle, yet still effective forms of agency, and, most importantly, highlight the plurality of Indigenous anti-extractive discourses. Building on ethnographic materials, I address the neglected subject of rumours that can open a specific productive space for alternative forms of evidence to understand, write, and most importantly, experience resistance. I demonstrate how localised rumours can mirror uneven power relations between local community, extractive company, and the state. Through the production and reproduction of certain rumouring narratives, the community expresses its fears and anxieties over changing environmental conditions (especially water pollution and radiation), concerns over health, and its members' precarious and marginalised position within the extensive discourses on economic development, extractive profits and government interventions. Under these conditions of marginality, the community members resist with the only resource they have—rumours—reacting to and, sometimes, subverting their precarious positions.

1 Introduction

It was a cold November day in Djelinde. Diana and I were having a casual conversation and discussing the village news while waiting for Diana's friend, who had agreed to be interviewed for this research. We were sitting on the old couch in Diana's office in the local cultural centre. Suddenly, Diana asked me: 'Do you know if there are bison in Canada?' I confirmed that there were indeed bison in Canada though I had never seen them myself. Diana then excitedly shared: 'We saw a bison here last summer. One of the old hunters shot it; he thought it was a bear but when he got closer and couldn't recognise the animal, he brought it to the village; and because we were having problems with the Anabar-Diamonds company at the time, I told others not to consume

© GENEVA GRADUATE INSTITUTE, 2024 | DOI:10.1163/9789004685994_013

it because it might have been poisoned'. The statement was baffling; I observed closely Diana's face, trying to figure out if she was joking, then cautiously asked if she really thought that the company would poison the meat of the bison. Unfazed, she exclaimed: 'Of course, I do! There were so many things happening at that time in the village, you know; there were also a lot of rumours about the company workers causing harm and intimidating our own people with weapons on our territory! That's why I believed that the company had poisoned that bison and dropped it off for us to find and eat it'. This was a bizarre and hard-to-believe story that came up several times during my visit to Djelinde. In fact, there were similar fantastical rumours told and actively circulated by the villagers, the rumours that I listened to, empathised with, and even sometimes shared myself. This ubiquity of rumours (and of rumouring) within the public sphere intrigued me, and, considering the specific context of the community's ongoing conflict with the extractive company, made me realise the complex, contradictory nature of these rumours, as well as their political potentiality.

The extractive company Anabar-Diamonds specialises in exploration, mining, and the manufacturing of diamonds and rare metals; since 2014, the company had been planning to expand its activities on the river Malaya Kuonamka, which served as the primary fresh water source for the villagers (Figure 12.1 and 12.3). The Tomtor massif, a rare metals deposit site in the Olenyek district, licensed by the extractive company Vostok-Engineering, has recently become a focus of heated debates in the central Sakha Republic and locally because of speculation that the rare metals extractive activities projected for 2025 are to be particularly environmentally destructive and radioactively pollutive. Evidently Djelinde residents found themselves in a precarious situation that engendered highly contextualised rumours.

In the following discussion, I will illustrate that these local rumours are not mere fantasies of the marginalised and powerless community. Rather, they represent the complexity of events I have witnessed during my fieldwork. Moreover, the rumours embodied everyday experiences of members the local community, revealing their concerns about local social and political events, and are used as covert tactics to manoeuvre within the ambiguous contexts between alterity and opposition outside of government and corporate discourses. In addition, I theorise rumouring as an unorthodox strategy utilised mostly by the Djelinde residents to enforce themselves into the local political and public sphere by creating specific emotional and powerful narratives, hence legitimising their anti-extractivist position. Specifically, the activists in Djelinde strategically used their verbal skills to shape public opinion and alter local discourses through intimate and private channels of communication that are only accessible in informal settings. More precisely, in the context

FIGURE 12.1 Billboard with the names of the companies operating in the Olenyek District
SOURCE: AUTHOR, 2017

of Djelinde the rumours became weaponised as a politicised tool for opening up a public sphere to make sense of, and privately (and publicly) discuss, the local ambiguous circumstances in relation to impending mining projects, as well as to confront and resist corporate power. It is, however, also important to note that the same very rumours came to provide an insidious way of exercising governmental power since their ultimate effect was the creation of a misinformed, frightened and intimidated community. Thus, it is this conjecture created by rumours and rumouring that I want to explore in this chapter, by analysing the complex web of rumours and other stories (poisoned meat, 'fixed' radiation meter, forced relocations, and such) that permeated the day-to-day experiences and interactions of Djelinde community members, illuminating historically constructed structures and techniques of power, and how—sometimes—it is possible to subvert them.

2 Situating the Research: Location and Methodologies

Sakha Republic, the far north-eastern region of the Russian Federation, presents an excellent geographical site for exploring conditions and mechanisms through which Indigenous peoples become involved in local (and global) politicised struggles and mobilisations. The Republic, perpetually exploited for its abundance of natural resources, was developed as a colony by the Soviet state; the region also came to be seen as an important object of a larger policy to 'master' the North and its resources wealth (Hicks, 2011; Tichotsky, 2000). This rhetoric of exploitation and dependence was preserved after the collapse of the Soviet Union; the resource extraction industry was kept under the new Russian state's control, excluding the local Indigenous and non-Indigenous population from the large-scale extractivist profits, causing political and economic anxiety within the region. Additionally, the extractive activities, along with a disregard for land rights, further politically and economically disadvantaged the region's most vulnerable communities, particularly rural Indigenous groups (Hicks, 2011; Maj, 2012). According to Susan Hicks (2011, 88), Russia maintains that it supports Indigenous rights in theory; however, it also characterizes the issues of land and natural resources as 'a problem of compensation and redress', promoting the rhetoric of cultural rights but overall rejecting the idea that cultural rights might imply political and economic rights. Therefore, an inquiry into the state and corporate politics targeting Indigenous communities and Indigenous politics in Sakha Republic generally and in the Olenyek district specifically has the potential to provide fertile ground for an analysis of the complex discourses of Indigenous political, as well as for reconsidering simplified and essentialised notions of Indigeneity, Indigenous experience, and how local articulations of Indigeneity interact with global power structures and practices.

This project was an ethnographic inquiry built on participant observation, a combination of oral histories and semi-structured interviews, and field notes collected in 2017 in the Olenyek district of Sakha Republic. The Olenyek Evenki National district is the north-west territory of Sakha; the district was established in 1934 by the new Soviet government. The population of the Olenyek district are predominantly the Indigenous Evenki; the Evenki or Evenks are one of five regionally and federally recognised Indigenous groups. The total Olenyek population is 4,127 with the Indigenous Evenki's population totalling 3,117 (the 2010 Russian Census). In the Olenyek district, I split my fieldwork between three villages. In this chapter, I rely on materials from my fieldwork encounters in Djelinde (Figure 12.2), a rural village with a population of around 664. The village residents practice a mixed economy, mostly being employed in wage labour but also practicing traditional modes of subsistence of hunting, fishing and gathering, with a few involved in reindeer herding. The participant observation data were supplemented by 32 interviews with local government officials, Indigenous activists, and other community members.

Considering the main focus on the issues surrounding extractive activities, confidentiality and anonymity were enforced and maintained throughout the

FIGURE 12.2 My host, her friend, and I taking a stroll around the village of Djelinde
SOURCE: AUTHOR, 2017

project duration. In this chapter, I use pseudonyms for individual Indigenous people (unless they are public figures and do not object to their names appearing in the research documents); this is not necessarily for fear that the individuals will face any danger or risks (individual, professional, financial or otherwise) should their identities be exposed, but to protect their privacy.

3 Theoretical Considerations: an Act of Rumouring

There is a large body of anthropological and sociological literature that addresses the subject of rumours as orally transmitted information, produced and reproduced at specific times with specific reasons (DiFonzo and Bordia, 2007; Rosnow, 1988), representing unofficial historical narratives of political abuse (Bolten, 2014; Kirsch, 2002; Masquelier, 2000; Perice, 1997; White, 1997; 2000), historically shaped imaginations of powerlessness, and economic exploitation (Taussig, 1980), but most importantly, as a discursive field that could 'control some people, terrorize others, damning and enabling, shoring and subverting power at the same time' (Stoler, 1992, 75).

One of the earlier scholars of rumour, Ralph Rosnow (1988, 12), defines rumours as 'public communications that reflect private hypotheses about how the world works. Embellished by allegations or attributions based on circumstantial evidence, they are attempts to make sense of uncertain situations'.

Since rumours are based on unconfirmed information and represent attempts at sense-making of uncertain and ambiguous situations and positions, they necessarily occupy particularly thin line between imagination and reality. In his work, Rosnow (1988, 14) underscores that the important factor in rumour is the context in which it occurs, arguing that the nature of rumour is contextual, which requires a more situated interrogation of '*who was saying what to whom*'. Further, Rosnow (1988, 16) builds on Tamotsu Shibutani's (1966) influential work on rumours, which viewed rumour construction as a communication process through which individuals seek for other perspectives concerning what is happening—repeating, and circulating rumours to initiate and perpetuate a problem-solving process. This emphasises the ideas of uncertainty and anxiety as implicit in rumour construction and circulation, arguing that the repetition of rumours allows for the communal imagination of their conceptual framework and 'new ways of coping with perceived threats to the existing order' (Rosnow, 1988, 16). Therefore, when people pass on fantastical, hard-to-believe rumours, they mediate their anxieties and uncertainties in order to dissipate their discomfort.

Similarly, Glen Perice (1997, 1) argues that, in violent and dangerous situations, specific rumours are constantly repeated 'to calcify them into accepted representations of social reality and political life'. In his study, Perice (1997, 4) focuses on the rumours circulated during Francois Duvalier's political reign in Haiti, including 'gruesome tales of the severed head packed on ice, the heart taken from the dead man, the children stolen from their families'. He argues that these are not only scary, blood-chilling, fantastical stories but imaginations of those who suffer within the authoritarian state—the terror and power of terror are spread and mediated by this specific discursive practice. Rumours, then, 'are not a collection of unverified reports and fantasies of the marginalized and powerless, but a speech form used by speakers to maneuver into spaces of alterity and opposition' (Perice, 1997, 9). This two-sidedness of rumours suggests the intimate relation of rumour to authority, creating circumstances where rumours can be strategically instrumentalised by the government to strengthen its power and inflict political violence on its own citizens. In his research on the intersection between the state's political violence and rumours in West Papua, Stuart Kirsch (2002) confirms that rumours and other 'fictionalized' narratives could enable and reproduce oppressive regimes. Examining how rumours can contribute to the experiences and expressions of state-sponsored terror, Kirsch (2002, 70) states that rumours can provide important historical readings of state power and its abuses, and the reproduction of inequality and exploitation, 'promot[ing] acts of violence', through constructions of cultural and gendered difference. He argues that rumours reflect and reproduce political violence, specifically determining the margins of the Indonesian state as well as constructing 'the Other' with hegemonic governmental discourses. Drawing on his fieldwork with political refugees from West Papua, Kirsch (2002, 61) focuses on the political properties of rumours and argues that rumours of epidemic diseases (particularly those about the prostitutes infected with HIV/AIDS) represent not only the 'penetration of political violence into the most private and intimate areas of life' but also the vulnerability of West Papuans before the Indonesian state terror. As Kirsch (2002, 63) puts it, '[t]error moves silently beneath the skin, embodying the violence of the state'. Kirsch further describes how remote areas, predominantly inhabited by 'the lost tribes', become specifically designated for developmental projects, and rumours are used as rationale for taking over the land and reifying the state power. Most importantly, Kirsch points out that even though rumours continually transform as they circulate, because of their collective, organic, and subjective nature, they can also be easily appropriated and manipulated by the state, eventually intensifying, and reproducing political violence and state terror rather than critiquing and potentially subverting existing unequal power relations.

In another analytical take on rumours, James Scott (1990, xiii) suggests that rumours, gossip, folktales, songs and jokes of the powerless represent an anonymous critique of power, which he calls the 'infrapolitics of the powerless' or 'hidden transcripts'. This sort of politics occurs in the space between overt collective defiance and complete hegemonic compliance, concealing the identity of the powerless, largely because of the potential absence of state retaliation (Scott, 1990, 138). In this sense, rumours, as well as other forms of oral traditions, provide 'seclusion, control, and even anonymity' (Scott, 1990, 160), which makes them easily transmittable, and therefore ideal for grassroots resistance. Here, anonymity of rumouring is of particular interest, because as Scott (1990) argues the unstable and changeable forms of rumours (and of other oral culture) represent them as a collective production without specific origins with multiple authors, which provides an opportunity to constantly transform them. Precisely because of this anonymous nature of folk culture (including rumours), Scott (1990, 200) notes that this form of oral communication can be understood as an elementary mode of political practice that exists within 'the realm of informal leadership and nonelites, of conversation and oral discourse, and of surreptitious resistance'. However, Scott (1990, 201) also points out that 'infrapolitics' are indeed real politics and that they are 'always pressing, testing, probing the boundaries of the *permissable*', threatening at any moment to turn into strikes, overt resistances, and even revolutions. Similarly, David Samper (2002, 2)—noting that the previous scholarly work on rumours, gossip and contemporary legends neglects the theme of resistance and social movements—argues that '[r]umors [...] affect the solidarity of a group, creating a public that can then participate in collective action. As counter-hegemonic discourse, rumors may lead to resistance'. Samper echoes Scott's analysis of practices of hidden resistance, disguised 'ideological insubordination' to the hegemonic ideology, which reveals a false compliance. As such, rumours and similar covert discursive practices may become 'tactics' with the potential of transforming into more overt politicised strategies, or as Samper (2002, 20) puts it, 'rumors do not begin from a posture of resistance, but rather describe the moment when hegemony is first understood as a cultural construct. [...] rumors may mark the shift to community resistance, may signal the moment that hegemonic ideology is questioned'.

Therefore, since rumours are often collectively generated, reimagined, and circulated primarily by those deemed powerless, it may be useful to suggest that rumours are a special form of politicised narratives that presuppose political action, precisely because they facilitate vocalisation of local concerns and anxieties and express the potentiality of action. In this sense, rumours present 'a first step in challenging, and possibly rejecting, hegemonic ideologies as alternative discourses to officialdom. [...] rumors are covert tactics that facilitate overt strategies' (Samper, 2002, 25).

4 Rumours in Action

Liya was from an extended reindeer-herding family; she spent her childhood between the village (attending a boarding school during autumns, winters and early springs) and the tundra (herding reindeer with her parents and siblings during the summer months). Liya was referred to me as a potential interviewee by multiple people because her family was one of the most highly respected in the village, and she had first-hand knowledge of issues faced by the local reindeer herders, hunters, and fishers. Liya was also one of the most active members of the community, organising and participating in local social and cultural events, as well as political meetings as an elected representative of her administrative division (the village was divided into several administrative clusters; the residents of each of these clusters elect their own representative at the local administrative centre). One afternoon, she agreed to meet with me at the local school. The school was located in the central street, and was hard to miss as it was in the largest building in the village. I arrived 30 minutes before the agreed time with the intention of looking around the school without disturbing any ongoing classes. Liya showed up a little later and invited me to one of the classrooms so we could converse uninterrupted. The reason for me seeking an interview with Liya was her participation, with other ten residents, in a trip to extractive sites, organised by Anabar-Diamonds in September of 2016. The summer of the same year was a critical period for the village; the local administrative centre had just reached an agreement with the company after two unsuccessful legal proceedings at the Republic Court, in 2015 and 2016. I asked Liya to elaborate on her impressions from the trip, and she recounted:

> There were ten of us, all village residents, you remember Margarita, she was there as a community elder, Ivan [a local paramedic], Taras [a veteran hunter], Mikhail [the village leader], and several others. The company used its own helicopter for this trip, and we managed to visit three sites of their past and current operations: Talakhtaakh was an important site, however they showed it only from the air, from the helicopter; Mayat was another location but with fully completed extraction activities; they showed us the patches of land where they had recultivated, but also from afar. We wanted to see it close up, but the representative assured us it was not possible. I wish I could visit that place now and see how nature is recovering … Finally, the helicopter brought us to 'Pentagon', a newly built company workers' settlement: several buildings make up a pentagon shape and that is why everyone calls it Pentagon. It was nice, it looked like the company workers were provided all necessities, most of the workers were fly-in fly-out *nuuchcha* migrants, there were also Sakha boys, and we saw several young men from our village. At the end of the trip, the company's representative made us all sign several documents with statements that we had indeed visited all the sites and were satisfied with their environmental conditions. We had to sign a bunch of other documents back at the administrative centre. It was bizarre to me, and I did not like that when we came back to the village and told others that we [had] had to sign some documents; some people started spreading rumours that we had actually sold ourselves and everyone else in the village to the company. You see, the company was really smart [in] taking us there, but you know they did not show us the sites that we actually wanted to see. No surprise that people here share information that sounds more like rumours rather than proper news
>
> Conversation with Liya, a Djelinde resident

Liya and her story about this trip, so historically important to the village, and about after-trip rumours about her and other community activists 'selling out' echo the arguments made by numerous scholars of rumour, that the power of rumouring and rumour-mongering is not in delivering information but in exchanging it, simultaneously criticising and debating issues and concerns. In this sense, troubling elements of the trip organised by the company's management, and the fact that the invited residents were not permitted to see the sites in as much detail as they would have wanted, generated more anxiety, and strengthened the residents' mistrust of the company. The rumours about the trip spread almost immediately. Liya was clearly upset about the villagers spreading rumours about her involvement in the trip, but those rumours so perfectly embodied the concerns of the people, revealing a dire lack of appropriate information (about the company's true intentions, extracting sites, their environmental conditions, etc.), that even she rationalised the existence of those rumours. Liya and many others in the village accepted the rumours because these rumours' historical and temporal context 'made sense' precisely because of their current situation.

Interestingly enough, some village residents confided in me their proactive stance within this complex situation, proposing a potentially actionable plan; yet these proposals were also based on specific rumours. Aida was an employee of the local cultural centre; in addition to her busy work schedule, she was a known cultural activist in the village. The following excerpt is from my interview with her, recorded during one of my last days in Djelinde. Aida and I met at her workplace, and I requested she share her thoughts on the public meetings organised by the administrative centre and the extractive company many of which Aida attended, as well as on the infamous trip to the extraction sites—a direct outcome of one of those public meetings. Aida detailed some aspects of the plan she proposed to her fellow activists right after the trip:

> You know, I wanted to ask some of our boys who work for the company to take pictures of the sites to see what they are actually extracting there and, most importantly, how they do that. We were taken to those extracting sites, but were not permitted to visit the most important locations and observe extracting and other processing activities; we were simply told that everything was fine and [that] there was nothing to worry about. But someone posted some comments and pictures on WhatsApp that it was all lies and in fact everything looks damaged and dead there. I have myself heard a rumour that if a reindeer wanders on[to] that extraction site, it drops dead just like that right there. Conversation with Aida, a Djelinde resident.

Having recognized an importance of concrete evidence rather than relying on numerous rumours about the extractive site, Aida and several other villagers suggested taking advantage of the access to the sites of interest granted to several village youths employed by the company. However, they also frequently added that it would not be particularly fair to these youths since their employment status was highly precarious and unemployment was one of the major issues in the village. In this instance however, rumours and rumouring provided a specific public space where illegitimate discourses and actions of contestation (otherwise radically circumscribed) became potential. Aida's plan of action was envisioned after the dissemination of rumours of dangerous and harmful environmental conditions on the extractive sites of unreliable information having been provided by the company representatives to the community Having considered the plan as risky, primarily to the youths in question, Aida and the other activists never attempted to implement it. Evidently, rumours did not necessarily provide resolution to many of the problems or the deeply precarious situation of the Djelinde residents; yet their constant circulation provided an opportunity to re-explore and renegotiate communal fears and anxieties, as well as to challenge official discourses.

5 Contaminating Rumours

One of the important analytical tools to think about and think with while attempting to understand the state, the nation, and power imbalances within particular social systems is an intense focus on 'small places' and 'small things'. Michel-Rolph Trouillot (1988) suggests that seemingly marginal and unimportant people and small communities with less visible manifestations of inequality might tell us more about power and engender a different perspective on understanding the local and the global. Building on Trouillot's discussion, Vanessa Agard-Jones (2013, 188) turns to the body and its parts as the objects of analysis, exploring 'how people understand the small—even microscopic—objects that are ingested into and that meld with their bodies', and looking in particular at 'the circulation of a hormone-altering pesticide called chlordecone' in rural Martinique. According to Agard-Jones (2013, 190), Martinique is known to be the country most contaminated by chlordecone, a recognised carcinogen and an endocrine disruptor linked to male infertility and prostate cancer. These particular effects of chlordecone generated local discussions of emergent gender and sexual politics on the island as a response to rumours of 'genocide by sterilization' and high rates of 'intersex births'. Here, Agard-Jones (2013, 192) argues that the rumours of local environmental contamination came to be seen as the issues of gender, sexual, and reproductive politics, ultimately insisting that taking a molecule of chlordecone as a unit of analysis

FIGURE 12.3 A view of the river Malaya Kuonamka
SOURCE: AUTHOR, 2017

encouraged the action of 'scaling outward to the world, but in doing so [...] also enabled our efforts to scale inward, recognizing the multiple levels at which our material entanglements—be they cellular, chemical or commercial—might be connected to global politics'.

Similar to those affected by chlordecone in Martinique, Djelinde's residents were deeply concerned about the radioactive threat of the Tomtor deposit and its damaging contaminating effects on the environment as well as their health. These concerns were reflected in several pervasive rumours. In fact, the planned extractive activities in the Tomtor massif were the dominant topic of most of my conversations with Djelinde residents during my fieldwork in 2017; it seemed that the conflict with Anabar-Diamonds had exhausted itself and community leaders had already started negotiations about the

company's financial contributions to the district budgetary fund. During my conversation with Liya, I asked her if she was concerned about the Tomtor as the company Vostok-Engineering was projected to start extraction in near future. Liya became very agitated:

> Apparently, there was such a crazy auction process for the Tomtor massif because it is a federal development project, but, here, we heard nothing about that. We were getting all the updates and news from the outside people or through rumours. You know, my family used to herd in [the] Tomtor area when I was a child; but one cannot go there these days

> because some of our herders started losing [their] hair and their health worsened. That's why we do not believe when the company experts say that everything is fine, and [that] we will not be impacted by extractions. How come will we not be impacted?! People say that that area is all dug up through and through. But our biggest concern is water, our river seems to be so polluted now. There used to be so many fish, we used to fish by buckets but now if you catch a few, you feel lucky. And you know yourself how we survive here, we depend on fish since we have not had wild reindeer game crossing our territory for almost a decade. Who would bring fish to us if we cannot fish ourselves? A lot of unemployed people and families with many children in the village depend on fish as their primary food source. What will happen with our river when they start with the Tomtor extraction? I cannot even imagine what will happen.
>
> Conversation with Liya, a Djelinde resident

Radiation, a constant concern for Djelinde's residents, is a highly ambiguous phenomenon to detect (it is invisible and odourless) and evaluate (its effects on health are undisputed), but studying it can be complicated if the necessary data—including type of exposure, level of exposure, temporality of exposure, specific circumstances, and so forth, preferably collected through longitudinal studies—are missing. In his research on uranium mining in Meghalaya, India, with a predominantly Indigenous population, Bengt Karlsson (2009, 44) argues that despite most countries having their own regulations regarding permissible doses or levels of radioactive exposure, 'all types of environmental or health regulations are settled politically, reflecting a compromise or balance between safety concerns and the economic and other interests involved in pursuing the activity in question'. In this sense, if extraction projects with potential radioactive contamination risks are tied to the military and/or are highly profitable, both the industry concerned and the government are responsible for making decisions as to how safety standards are set and enforced. Mineral mining and the nuclear industry appear, therefore, to be the most contentious areas, often resulting in public distrust and opposition. In such cases, Karlsson (2009, 46) notes that the primary strategy of industry becomes 'to convince people of the benefits of nuclear-driven development'. A similar strategy of 'benefits' persuasion was employed by Vostok-Engineering, the company responsible for the Tomtor massif extraction project. The village residents were, however, not convinced. In addition to rumours about radioactive pollution, some activists told me stories about cases of worsening health in the local population, including more cases of various types of cancer (particularly among young women), the sudden deaths of otherwise healthy people, unexpected heart attacks among both elders and youths, and so on. During my conversation with four kindergarten employees, the women shared the following:

> People say that the Tomtor extraction site is *very* radioactive. We had several people die suddenly after visiting that place, and some of the herders had strange sores on their skin, and some of them lost all of their hair. There was one hunter, Danilov, he visited the site in the 90s and opened the covered-up pit in the Tomtor, he got sick and died soon after!.
>
> Conversation with four kindergarten employees, Djelinde

This and similar stories about herders' and hunters' experiences with radiation in Tomtor were repeated by the local maternity nurse, Khristina. Khristina arrived in Djelinde as a young professional in the 1960s from another district. Having lived in Djelinde most of her life, she had come to see herself as a local, and had become a passionate and vocal advocate for local cultural and environmental rights. Khristina's opinion of the rumours about radiation and its effects was of particular interest to me because she was a medical professional, and I wondered if those stories about the people affected could be medically (and scientifically) verified. Nancy Scheper-Hughes (2000, pp. 203–204) points out that studying rumours, especially in medical field, requires practical and material explanations, because '[e]ven the most preposterous of the organ-stealing rumors […] finds some basis in lawsuits and criminal proceedings, some still unresolved or pending'. Therefore, upon learning about potential radiation and health issues, I sought interviews with local medical professionals, who would be aware of both the rumours and the specific contexts that engendered them. I met with Khristina at the local hospital; she was eager to talk to me, and when I asked her about radiation and herders' health problems, she emphatically ranted:

> I think that they [the Vostok-Engineering company] are lying to us; they say that it does not have any radiation, but it is a lie—Tomtor is very radioactive. Why then [do] the workers take off and disinfect their clothes after being there, huh?! They make our own village people work there because it is already polluted. People say some herders lost their hair, and they were camping close to Tomtor; nowadays no one dares to go to that area. And if anyone asks any questions, they twist your words and state the opposite. Last year, they sent some doctors here, but they were all sell-outs (*prodazhnie*); after examining several community members, they announced that everyone was healthy here. It is ridiculous! How come people would be healthy here? Half of the population have problems

> with joints, some are not even able to walk, everyone's blood pressure is abnormally high, there are lot of people with heart defects ... We did have cancer patients before but nowadays we have more of them and with 'unusual' and 'atypical' cancer types, especially among younger women.
>
> Conversation with Khristina, a Djelinde resident and local maternity nurse

According to Nancy Scheper-Hughes (1996, 7), actual events, and the rumours based on them, reflect 'poor people's perceptions, grounded in a social and in a biomedical reality'; in her research, the residents of shanty towns easily believed rumours and bizarre stories about organ theft because they are 'fundamentally, *existentially* true' (Scheper-Hughes, 1996, 9). Likewise, Liya, Khristina, and the kindergarten employees' fears over radiation exposure and the deteriorating health of the village's residents should be perceived as *fundamentally* true and as evidence of local complex experiences of conflict, injustice, and violent social reality. Moreover, intense and widely practiced rumouring revealed the deep concerns of Djelinde residents with regard to contamination that they were potentially being exposed to and its harmful toxic effects.

Furthermore, the power of rumours seemingly coincided with the insidious power of the government, which was paradoxically expressed through a lack of governmental intervention and an absence of official clarifications and explanations regarding local communal concerns about the projected extractive activities of Vostok-Engineering. This governmental invisibility in Djelinde invigorated more intense and frantic rumouring. Yet it must also be noted that several community activists managed to vocalise their grievances and fears with regard to radiation during a handful of public hearings with the environmental researchers hired by the Vostok-Engineering. Katya, an elderly local activist, attended those meetings and recounted to me afterwards:

> I was at the hearings with Vostok-Engineering; they talked a lot about nanotechnology, niobium, other rare metals, [the] periodic table, ore, and so much more. Apparently, they have been working there for a long time, but they still claim that there is no radiation. I do not believe that; if there are so many metals there, it is bound to have *some* radiation.
>
> Conversation with Katya, a Djelinde resident

Fabiana Li (2015, 186) argues that the strategic language of science and expertise frequently implemented by extractivist corporations in their dealings with affected communities 'prioritize[s] mining interests and enable[s] corporations to define the standards of performance that governments will use to establish compliance', disadvantaging activists and NGOs since they rarely have the resources necessary to produce 'accurate and scientific' counterarguments (Li, 2015, 207). Considering Katya's description of the public hearings and of the company representatives' deliberate deployment of overtly scientific language (nanotechnology, niobium, rare metals, the periodic table, ore, etc.), it must, as well, be argued that this corporate strategy not only managed to limit the informed participation of Djelinde's residents in critical discussions about their futures and the future of their environment, it also further rendered them as 'ignorant', 'irrational', 'misinformed' and 'biased', making them appear deficient and in need of external 'developmental' interventions.

To alleviate public mistrust and fears of possible radioactive contamination, the company installed a radiation meter on the main administrative building; the villagers, however, immediately circulated another rumour, alleging that the meter was actually 'set up' to only show the numbers 8 and, occasionally, 9—supposedly the acceptable radiation emission range and believed to be harmless for humans. During one of our many conversations in the library, I specifically mentioned the radiation meter to my friend Aida, and asked her what she thought of it; Aida replied:

> I attended the recent meeting with the company representatives; the local people were very concerned about radiation, but the company people assured us there was nothing to worry about and they put that radiation meter on the administrative building. But you know what people say? They say it is fixed (*zafiksirovan*) on number 8 on purpose; it does not go over 8 at all, that's why people say that the company is lying to us, but what can we do?
>
> Conversation with Aida, a Djelinde resident

Tatiana, Aida's friend, who happened to be with us in the library, also shared her opinion:

> I firmly believe that the radiation meter is rigged; it is like a conspiracy against us. We are 'guinea pigs' here; even the doctors and scientists are visiting our village every two–three years to monitor us and examine how radiation is impacting our health. I was in Yakutsk (the capital city of Sakha) this summer, and many people were asking me if our village was planned to be relocated. There were so many rumours about relocations! When I talked to my friends here after, they said if the government and the company decide to relocate us, what can we do? We will simply move away.
>
> Conversation with Tatiana, a Djelinde resident

These statements confirm once again that rumours arise from within specific precarious contexts. However, these particular rumours about radioactivity and a 'rigged' radiation meter emphasise not only abstract uncertainty but also a physically threatening or potentially threatening situation, in which people feel a psychological need for a sense of security and safety. This threat of contamination seems to be quite tangible considering the above-mentioned details of the highly contentious extractive project in the Tomtor massif. Thus, rumours function not only to make sense of potential threats but also to psychologically manage them. The rumours about the Djelinde residents being used as 'guinea pigs' and the 'rigged' radiation meter were shared by residents many times, sometimes with a pinch of humour, but more often in serious and frustrated tones. I myself, baffled and intrigued by rumours about the meter, made a point of checking it every day throughout my stay in Djelinde. The number never dropped below or got above 8. I cannot say that this exercise reduced my own anxiety over radiation rumours, but I indeed grew more suspicious of both the meter and of the company's assurances regarding the lack of a contamination threat.

Interestingly, rumours of radiation engendered other relevant rumours, and many villagers shared rumours about potential forced relocations. The topic of forced relocations is not unfamiliar for Djelinde residents. I interviewed several elderly individuals in the village, who vividly remembered the 1950s forced relocations from the village of Sukhaany. These were part of the Soviet-era governmental project for agricultural and residential integration and centralisation (*ukrupnenie*). The majority of the Sukhaany population were relocated to the village of Khariyalaakh, but some were moved to Djelinde. The residual memories of those who had experienced *ukrupnenie* reinvigorated old fears and concerns among both the older community members and the youth of the village. Kirill was a local youth and a passionate cultural activist. When I asked him what he thought about the extractive plans and potential relocations. Kirill provided an overtly politicised answer:

> Those companies are literally squashing us; if they continue with their extractive activities, we will have nothing left, no fish, no nature, nothing. The companies have a lot of money and, if they work here, they ought to help the local community; we are Indigenous people and we have rights. However, if the Tomtor extractions start in 2025, I believe they will demand people […] leave the territory, and I do not even think the local people would want to stay here either because health is the most important thing. And the issue of extraction or non-extraction has been already decided by Moscow. Moscow is devouring everything.
>
> Conversation with Kirill, a Djelinde resident

Here, Kirill's statement exposes the murkiness of rumour margins, their discursive space that allows the coexistence of the spoken and the unspoken and the overt and the covert, and the creation of specific openings where local political and economic issues can be addressed. Undoubtedly, rumours about radioactive extraction sites and relocations do not provide resolution to local problems, concerns, and ambiguous situations; yet I argue that they represent dynamic responses to the social and political milieus within which they are collectively produced and reproduced as discursive constructions. Moreover, their retelling provided an opportunity to renegotiate communal fears and anxieties, as well as to challenge and reject hegemonic ideologies and practices. While sharing rumours with me, Djelinde's residents clearly understood that rumouring is not necessarily productive; Aida once explained to me, 'You hear the stories about some people getting skin sores and seeing a dead elk in the Tomtor site, but everything that people talk about seem[s] to be made-up stories and rumours; there is no one who could verify these stories'.

Yet this particular ambiguity of rumour origins and its elusive nature can have unintended consequences, such as creating discursive spaces for those rumoring to address socially and politically important, yet dangerous, issues. Moreover, re-encountering rumours was important, since anxieties over scheduled extractions and the potential industrial disturbance that would be caused by some sites on local territory was exacerbated by local knowledge of historical events that had taken place decades ago. Albina, a veterinarian with almost 30 years of professional experience, grew up herding with her parents; she often travelled in a professional capacity between the village and different herding locations. One day, Albina invited me for lunch; after, we got to talking about extractive activities, and she contended:

> They are planning to start extractions on the upper side of the river; during the Soviet time, we had an anthrax scare in that area. I was the only veterinarian at that time, and some herders told me that they saw multiple dead reindeer there. I went to check, and when I realised what it was, I ordered the herders to immediately relocate to a different, far away site. I called the administrative centre about the situation. The very next day we had a doctor arrive with the necessary shots for the herders and the rest of reindeer. If they get to that site and start extracting, I do not even know what can happen.
>
> Conversation with Albina, a Djelinde resident and veterinarian

Later, exploring the local newspaper archives, I did confirm that there was indeed such an incident in the history of the Olenyek district. Djelinde's residents (especially the older and more experienced herders and hunters) were acutely aware of the burial grounds of contaminated animal remains and abandoned herders' camps, which might still contain anthrax spores. Most of them had already shifted their herding routes, moving away from these dangerous sites. But recent extraction activities in proximity to both the herding sites and the potentially dangerously contaminated sites seemed to be re-producing anxieties and fears among the villagers.

6 Conclusion

Rumours and the narratives based on them can attest to different ways of knowing and different kinds of knowledge, shaping people's fears and their responses to those fears, representing the medium 'through which the unspeakable was spoken' (Stoler, 1992, 179). The 'spoken unspeakable' in the case of Djelinde mirrored community anxieties over projected extractive activities, which resulted in rumours about these activities' environmental impact and the transformation of local subsistence practices. Additionally, the potentiality of a radioactive threat from the Tomtor deposit site and the potentially damaging effects of such contamination on the environment engendered pervasive rumours about worsening health in the local population, and other factors over which community members had no control. The older community members, who had experienced forced relocations during the Soviet-era *ukrupnenie* programmes in the 1950s, also actively circulated rumours about government plans for new forced relocations should the extractive company decide to expand their activities closer to the village, or should there be a serious radiation threat or even a radioactive disaster in the area. Through this analysis of rumours in Djelinde, I contend that they opened up a specific productive space for alternative forms of communal expressions of anti-extractivism, and provided evidence based on which residents could understand and, most importantly, narrate history at a precarious and ambiguous time.

References

Agard-Jones, V. (2013) 'Bodies in the System', *Small Axe: a Caribbean Journal of Criticism*, 17(42), pp. 182–192, DOI:10.1215/07990537-2378991.

Bolten, C. (2014) '*Sobel* Rumors and Tribal Truths: Narrative and Politics in Sierra Leone, 1994', *Comparative Studies in Society and History*, 56(1), pp. 187–214, DOI: 10.1017/S0010417513000662.

DiFonzo, N, and P. Bordia (2007) 'Rumor, Gossip, and Urban Legends', *Diogenes*, 54(1), pp. 19–35, DOI:10.1177/0392192107073433.

Hicks, S. M. (2011) *Between Indigeneity and Nationality: the Politics of Culture and Nature in Russia's Diamond Province*, unpublished PhD Dissertation (Vancouver: University of British Columbia), https://open.library.ubc.ca/soa/cIRcle/collections/ubctheses/24/items/1.0072271 (accessed on 25 December 2020).

Karlsson, B. (2009) 'Nuclear Lives: Uranium Mining, Indigenous Peoples, and Development in India', *Economic and Political Weekly*, 44(34), pp. 43–49, DOI:10.2307/25663470.

Kirsch, S. (2002) 'Rumour and Other Narratives of Political Violence in West Papua', *Critique of Anthropology*, 22(1), pp. 53–79, DOI:10.1177/0308275X020220010301.

Li, F. (2015) *Unearthing Conflict: Corporate Mining, Activism, and Expertise in Peru* (Durham and London: Duke University Press).

Maj, E. (2012) 'Internationalisation with the Use of Arctic Indigeneity: the Case of the Republic of Sakha (Yakutia), Russia', *Polar Record*, 48(246), pp. 210–214, DOI:10.1017/S003224741100060X.

Masquelier, A. (2000) 'Of Headhunters and Cannibals: Migrancy, Labor, and Consumption in the Mawri Imagination', *Cultural Anthropology*, 15(1), pp. 84–126, DOI:10.1525/can.2000.15.1.84.

Perice, G. (1997) 'Rumors and Politics in Haiti', *Anthropological Quarterly*, 70(1), pp. 1–10, DOI: 10.2307/3317797.

Rosnow, R. L. (1988) 'Rumor as Communication: a Contextualist Approach', *Journal of Communication*, 38(1), pp. 12–28, DOI: 10.1111/j.1460-2466.1988.tb02033.x.

Samper, D. (2002) 'Cannibalizing Kids: Rumor and Resistance in Latin America', *Journal of Folklore Research*, 39(1), pp. 1–32.

Scheper-Hughes, N. (2000) 'The Global Traffic in Human Organs', *Current Anthropology*, 41(2), pp. 191–224, DOI: 10.1086/300123.

Scheper-Hughes, N. (1996) 'Theft of Life: the Globalization of Organ Stealing Rumours', *Anthropology Today*, 12(3), pp. 3–11, DOI: 10.2307/2783143.

Scott, J. (1990) *Domination and the Arts of Resistance: Hidden Transcripts* (New Haven: Yale University Press).

Shibutani, T. (1966) *Improvised News: a Sociological Study of Rumor* (Indianapolis: The Bobbs-Merrill Company).

Stoler, A. L. (1992) '"In Cold Blood": Hierarchies of Credibility and the Politics of Colonial Narratives', *Representations*, 37(Special Issue: Imperial Fantasies and Postcolonial Histories), pp. 151–189, DOI: 10.2307/2928658.

Taussig, M. (1980) *The Devil and Commodity Fetishism in South America* (Chapel Hill: The University of North Carolina Press).

Tichotsky, J. (2000) *Russia's Diamond Colony: the Republic of Sakha* (Amsterdam: Harwood Academic).

Trouillet, M.-R. (1988) *Peasants and Capital: Dominica in the World Economy* (Baltimore and London: The John Hopkins University Press).

White, L. (2000) *Speaking with Vampires: Rumor and History in Colonial Africa* (Berkeley, Los Angeles, and London: University of California Press).

White, L. (1997) 'The Traffic in Heads: Bodies, Borders and the Articulation of Regional Histories', *Journal of Southern African Studies,* 23(2), pp. 325–338, DOI: 10.1080/03057079708708540.

Index

www.ingramcontent.com/pod-product-compliance
Lightning Source LLC
Chambersburg PA
CBHW062308240926
51846CB00013B/654
* 9 7 8 9 0 0 4 5 3 8 8 4 9 *